RETHINKING
POLITICAL ISLAM

RETHINKING POLITICAL ISLAM

Edited by

SHADI HAMID
WILLIAM MCCANTS

OXFORD
UNIVERSITY PRESS

OXFORD
UNIVERSITY PRESS

Oxford University Press is a department of the University of Oxford. It furthers
the University's objective of excellence in research, scholarship, and education
by publishing worldwide. Oxford is a registered trade mark of Oxford University
Press in the UK and certain other countries.

Published in the United States of America by Oxford University Press
198 Madison Avenue, New York, NY 10016, United States of America.

© Oxford University Press 2017

CIP data is on file at the Library of Congress
ISBN 978-0-19-064919-7 (hbk)
ISBN 978-0-19-064920-3 (pbk)

1 3 5 7 9 8 6 4 2
Paperback printed by WebCom, Inc., Canada
Hardback printed by Bridgeport National Bindery, Inc., United States of America

CONTENTS

Engaging Islamists

Religion, Ideology, and Organization

ACKNOWLEDGMENTS

This book has been more than two years in the making. We had little idea of how it would all come out in the end, which is what made this such a fascinating learning experience for the both of us. There has long been a need for a deeper understanding of the groups that constitute the complex and sometimes contradictory world of political Islam. For better and worse, that need has grown only more urgent.

"Islamism," "radical Islam," Islam, and Muslims are all things that are under constant debate in Western capitals. The divisions over how to understand the role of Islam in politics have intensified. Islam—as a religion, as a political force, and as a perceived civilizational threat—will be at the center of an ongoing struggle of identity that draws in not just Muslim-majority countries, but also the United States and Europe.

We hope that this book can serve as a starting point for constructive discussion, covering twelve countries and addressing the question of how the rise of the Islamic State and the demise of the Arab Spring have forced a "rethinking" of political Islam—or not. We also hope that this volume can be more than that, taking readers inside a world that can often seem quite foreign and remote. We looked at these twelve countries side-by-side, in an attempt to make sense of the bigger picture. We discussed and debated with the diverse group of authors who contributed to this book, and we heard what Islamists themselves had to say about their own experiences.

This project began in January 2015, and we were fortunate enough to have so many willing participants who believed in and contributed to it. We are grateful to Martin Indyk, Bruce Jones, and Tamara Wittes for nurturing such a supportive research environment and helping make the Brookings Institution a center of scholarship on Islamism and Islam's role in politics more broadly. We also deeply appreciate the Henry Luce Foundation for their generous financial support of this project. This book simply wouldn't exist without them.

Finally, we want to thank our whip-smart contributors and the incredible Brookings team that provided research and logistical support over the course of the more than two years, including Anne Peckham, Elizabeth Pearce, Sumaya Almajdoub, Kristine Anderson, and Rashid Dar. We are indebted to our wonderful editor David McBride, who was incredibly patient and supportive every step of the way. Thanks are also due to Kathleen Weaver and the rest of the team at Oxford University Press for making the process as painless as possible.

CONTRIBUTORS

OVAMIR ANJUM is the Imam Khattab Endowed Chair of Islamic Studies in the Department of Philosophy and Religious Studies at the University of Toledo. His work focuses on the nexus of theology, ethics, politics, and law in classical and medieval Islam. His interests are united by a common theoretical focus on epistemology or views of intellect and reason in various domains of Islamic thought, including politics (*siyasa*), law (*fiqh*), theology (*kalam*), Islamic philosophy (*falsafa*), and spirituality (Sufism, mysticism, and asceticism). He brings his historical studies to bear on issues in contemporary Islamic thought and movements and is currently researching developments in Islamic political thought in the wake of the Arab uprisings of 2011. He obtained his PhD in Islamic Intellectual History in the Department of History, University of Wisconsin-Madison; his master's in social sciences from the University of Chicago; and his master's in computer science from the University of Wisconsin-Madison. He is the author of *Politics, Law and Community in Islamic Thought: The Taymiyyan Moment* (Cambridge University Press, 2012).

OMAR ASHOUR is a senior lecturer in Security Studies and Middle East Politics in the Institute of Arab and Islamic Studies, at the University of Exeter. He is an associate fellow at Chatham House in London and the author of *The De-Radicalization of Jihadists: Transforming Armed Islamist Movements*, the first book on transitions from armed to unarmed activism by several Islamist organizations in North Africa. Among his other publications is a Brookings study entitled "Collusion to Collision: Islamist-Military Relations in Egypt." Dr. Ashour specializes in asymmetric armed conflict, Islamist movements, insurgency and counterinsurgency, terrorism studies, and democratization (with a main focus on civil-military relations and security sector reform). He previously served as a senior consultant for the United Nations on security sector reform, counter-terrorism, and de-radicalization issues.

STEVEN BROOKE is an assistant professor of political science at the University of Louisville and an associate fellow at the Harvard Kennedy School's Middle East Initiative. His research interests include Islamist movements, authoritarianism and democratization, and spatial and experimental research methods. He received his PhD from the University of Texas at Austin in 2015.

AMR DARRAG served as Egypt's Minister of Planning and International Cooperation during Mohamed Morsi's presidency before the military coup in 2013. In 2014, he established and is currently Chairman of the Egyptian Institute for Political and Strategic Studies, a think tank based in Istanbul, Turkey. He was elected as Secretary General of the constituent assembly tasked with drafting the 2012 Egyptian Constitution. He is a founding member and was previously a member of the Executive Board of the Freedom and Justice Party (FJP). He served as chairman of the Foreign Relations Committee and chairman of the Development and Planning Committee of the FJP. Before that, he was elected Secretary General of the FJP in Giza Governorate, 2011. He was originally a professor of civil engineering at Cairo University and he received his PhD from Purdue University. He was elected as Vice-Chairman of Cairo University Staff Association, 1999–2008. He was also partner and top executive of several international and Egyptian engineering consultancy firms.

AMMAR FAYED is a Muslim Brotherhood youth activist and Istanbul-based researcher, focusing on Islamist movements, sociology of religion, and Middle East affairs. He served as special secretary to President Mohamed Morsi. He contributed to the book *The Salafi Phenomenon in the Arab World: Organizational Pluralism and Politics* (Al Jazeera Center for Studies). Fayed is a MA candidate in the Department of Political Science and International Relations at Istanbul Aydin University.

COURTNEY FREER is a research officer at the LSE Kuwait Programme. She holds a PhD in politics from Oxford University, where her thesis focused on revising rentier state theory by examining the sociopolitical role played by Muslim Brotherhood affiliates in Kuwait, Qatar, and the United Arab Emirates. She received a BA from Princeton University in Near East Studies and an MA in Middle Eastern Studies from the George Washington University's Elliott School of International Affairs. Courtney previously worked as a research assistant at the Brookings Doha Center and as a researcher at the U.S.-Saudi Arabian Business Council.

SHADI HAMID is a senior fellow in the Project on U.S. Relations with the Islamic World at the Brookings Institution and the author of *Islamic Exceptionalism: How the Struggle over Islam Is Reshaping the World* (St. Martin's Press). His previous book, *Temptations of Power: Islamists and Illiberal Democracy in a New Middle East* (Oxford University Press), was named a *Foreign Affairs* Best Book of 2014. Hamid served as director of research at the Brookings Doha Center until January 2014. Prior to joining Brookings, he was director of research at the Project on Middle East Democracy (POMED) and a Hewlett Fellow at Stanford University's Center on Democracy, Development, and the Rule of Law. Hamid is a contributing writer for *The Atlantic* and the vice chair of POMED's board of directors.

ANDREW LEBOVICH is a visiting fellow with the European Council on Foreign Relations focusing on North Africa and the Sahel. He is currently a doctoral student in African History at Columbia University in New York, where he studies religion, politics, and society in North Africa, the Sahara, and the Sahel. He previously worked for the Open Society Initiative in West Africa (OSIWA) as a Sahel consultant advising the organization on political, social, and security issues in West Africa and the Sahel, and for the New America Foundation. He has conducted field research in Mali, Niger, and Senegal, and has lived in France, Morocco, and Senegal. Andrew graduated magna cum laude from Dartmouth College with a BA in history in 2009. His writing has appeared in *Foreign Policy*, *The Atlantic*, and the *Combating Terrorism Center Sentinel*, among other outlets.

RAPHAËL LEFÈVRE is a research fellow at New College, Oxford University, where he specializes in Sunni Islamist movements in Lebanon and Syria. He is also a nonresident research fellow at the Beirut center of the Carnegie Endowment for International Peace, where he has published several reports on the political and security situation in the Middle East. He is also the author of a book on Syria entitled *Ashes of Hama: The Muslim Brotherhood in Syria* (2013), named a Best Book on the Middle East in 2013 by *Foreign Policy* magazine, as well as numerous book chapters and journal articles. He graduated with a PhD in politics and international relations from the University of Cambridge in 2016.

JOSEPH CHINYONG LIOW is dean and professor of comparative and international politics at the S. Rajaratnam School of International Studies, Nanyang Technological University, Singapore. He held the inaugural Lee Kuan Yew Chair in Southeast Asia Studies at the Brookings Institution, Washington, DC, where he was also a senior fellow in the Foreign Policy Program. He is the author of *Piety and Politics: Islamism in Contemporary Malaysia* (Oxford University Press, 2009) and *Religion and Nationalism in Southeast Asia* (Cambridge University Press, 2016).

PETER MANDAVILLE is a professor of international affairs in the Schar School of Policy and Government and co-director of the Ali Vural Ak Center for Global Islamic Studies, both at George Mason University. He is the author of several books, including *Islam and Politics* and *Transnational Muslim Politics: Reimagining the Umma*. He is a nonresident senior fellow at the Brookings Institution and a visiting senior fellow at the Pew Research Center. His government experience includes serving as a member of the U.S. State Department's Policy Planning Staff (2011–2012) and as a senior adviser in the Secretary of

State's Office of Religion and Global Affairs (2015–2016). His research has been supported by the Carnegie Corporation of New York, the John D. and Catherine T. MacArthur Foundation, and the Henry Luce Foundation, among others.

MONICA MARKS is a Rhodes Scholar and PhD candidate at Oxford University, specializing in comparative politics and Islamist movements. A doctoral researcher with the WAFAW program in Aix-en-Provence, France, and visiting fellow at the European Council on Foreign Relations, she began her studies of Arabic in Tunisia in 2007, and lived for four years in Tunisia following its revolution. She is currently based in Turkey, where she was a Fulbright Scholar in 2009–2010 and later a visiting professor at Istanbul's Bogazici University. Marks conducts research in Arabic, French, and Turkish.

NAEL AL-MASALHA is a longtime figure in the Jordanian Muslim Brotherhood and the director of the Al-Essra Hospital in Amman. He was previously a member of the Muslim Brotherhood's Executive Bureau.

TOBY MATTHIESEN is a senior research fellow in the international relations of the Middle East at St. Antony's College, University of Oxford. Matthiesen was previously a research fellow at Pembroke College, Cambridge, and at the London School of Economics and Political Science. He is the author of *Sectarian Gulf: Bahrain, Saudi Arabia, and the Arab Spring That Wasn't* (Stanford University Press, 2013) and *The Other Saudis: Shiism, Dissent and Sectarianism* (Cambridge University Press, 2015). His current research focuses on the Sunni-Shia divide and the legacies of the Cold War in the Middle East.

WILLIAM McCANTS is a senior fellow at the Brookings Institution, where he directs the Project on U.S. Relations with the Islamic World. He is also an adjunct faculty member at Johns Hopkins University and has held various government and think-tank positions related to Islam, the Middle East, and terrorism. From 2009 to 2011, McCants served as a U.S. State Department senior adviser for countering violent extremism. He has also held positions as program manager of the Minerva

Initiative for the Department of Defense; an analyst at the Institute for Defense Analyses, the Center for Naval Analyses, and SAIC; and a fellow at West Point's Combating Terrorism Center. He is the author of *The ISIS Apocalypse: The History, Strategy, and Doomsday Vision of the Islamic State* (St. Martin's Press) and *Founding Gods, Inventing Nations: Conquest and Culture Myths from Antiquity to Islam* (Princeton University Press).

MATTHEW NELSON is a reader in politics at SOAS (University of London). Before moving to SOAS, he taught at UC Santa Cruz, Bates College, and Yale University. He has held several residential fellowships—as the Wolfensohn Family Member at the Institute for Advanced Study in Princeton, as a fellow at the Woodrow Wilson International Center for Scholars in Washington, DC, and as a fellow at the Center for Interdisciplinary Research in Germany. Nelson has also served as an elected board member for the American Institute of Pakistan Studies, the South Asia Council of the Association for Asian Studies, and the Religion and Politics Section of the American Political Science Association. His research focuses on the politics of South Asia with a special emphasis on non-elite politics, Islam, and democracy. He completed his PhD in political science at Columbia University in 2002.

JACOB OLIDORT is currently Special Advisor on Middle East Policy and Country Director for Syria at the Office of the Secretary of Defense for Policy in the U.S. Department of Defense. From 2015–2016, he was a Soref Fellow at the Washington Institute for Near East Policy, where his work covered jihadism and Islamic political movements. He received his PhD in Near Eastern Studies from Princeton University, where his research focused on the intersection of Islamic law, theology and modern politics. His publications include "Inside the Caliphate's Classroom: Textbooks, Guidance Literature and Indoctrination Methods of the Islamic State" (Washington Institute, 2016) and "The Politics of 'Quietist' Salafism" (Brookings Institution, 2015). He regularly presents on jihadism to the U.S. government, including the Departments of State, Defense and Homeland Security, and his commentary has appeared in the *New York Times*, the *Washington Post*, and *Foreign Affairs*, among other outlets. A former Fulbright scholar (UAE), he taught at the

Elliott School of International Affairs at the George Washington University and is a term member in the Council on Foreign Relations.

SAYIDA OUNISSI is a member of the Tunisian Parliament (Ennahda Party) and serves as member of the Finance Committee. She has the distinction of being the youngest female to be appointed the head of an electoral list in Tunisia and has been recognized by international news media for her work to promote women's participation in Tunisian government. Largely educated in Europe, she has actively worked to promote wider recognition of the contribution of young Muslims and Arabs in European societies through a partnership with Euro-Med. Ounissi holds a master's degree from the Institute of Economic and Social Development Studies at the Sorbonne in Paris.

DAVID SIDDHARTHA PATEL is a senior research fellow at the Crown Center for Middle East Studies at Brandeis University, where he focuses on social order, religious authority, and identity in the contemporary Middle East. He conducted independent field research in post-Saddam Iraq on the role of mosques and clerical networks in generating order after state collapse, and recently completed a book tentatively titled *Order Out of Chaos: Islam, Information, and Social Order in Iraq.* Among his recent publications are briefs on "ISIS in Iraq: What We Get Wrong and Why 2015 is Not 2007 Redux" and "Repartitioning the Sykes-Picot Middle East? Debunking Three Myths." He has also conducted comparative research on the transnational spread of protests during the so-called Arab Spring and on changes in the support base of Islamist movements. Before joining the Crown Center, Patel was an assistant professor of political science at Cornell University. Patel received his BA from Duke University in economics and political science and his PhD from Stanford University in political science.

ASIF LUQMAN QAZI is a senior leader within Jamaat-e-Islami, one of Pakistan's most influential Islamist organizations. He is also the Executive Director of the Islamabad-based Center for Discussions and Solutions, which works to foster dialogue on issues of strategic importance to Pakistan. Born in Peshawar, Pakistan, Qazi received master's degrees in Economics from both International Islamic University Islamabad and Boston University. He also attended Baruch College in

New York City for further graduate study. After completing his studies, he returned to Pakistan to assist his father, the late Qazi Hussain Ahmad, who was head of Jamaat-e-Islami and a member of parliament. He remained Special Assistant to Ahmad for ten years. He has also served as Deputy Director for Foreign Affairs in Jamaat-e-Islami and has been elected to both the central and provincial shura (consultative councils) of the organization. He was previously lecturer in economics at International Islamic University Islamabad.

AVI MAX SPIEGEL is an associate professor of political science and international relations at the University of San Diego and the author of *Young Islam: The New Politics of Religion in Morocco and the Arab World* (Princeton University Press, 2015)—which was the winner of a *Washington Post* Abu Aardvark Middle East Book Award and the Religion and International Relations Book Award from the International Studies Association. Spiegel earned a doctorate from Oxford University, a master's degree from Harvard University, and a law degree from NYU. He has been a research fellow at the Brookings Institution, the Ali Pachachi Scholar of the Modern Middle East at Oxford University, a Frederick Sheldon Fellow at Harvard University, and a Fulbright Scholar and Peace Corps Volunteer in Morocco.

STACEY PHILBRICK YADAV is an associate professor of political science and chair of the International Relations and Middle East Studies programs at Hobart and William Smith Colleges in Geneva, New York. She is the author of *Islamists and the State: Legitimacy and Institutions in Yemen and Lebanon* (2013) and a number of articles on Islamist-leftist relations, women's partisan and post-partisan activism, and sectarian politics in Yemen. A regular contributor to *Middle East Report, Foreign Policy*, and the *Washington Post's* Monkey Cage, she also serves in executive board positions for the American Institute of Yemeni Studies and the Yemen Peace Project.

Introduction

Shadi Hamid and William McCants

AFTER DECADES SPECULATING ON what Islamists would do when they came to power, analysts, academics—and Islamists themselves—finally have an answer. And it is confusing. In the hinterland between Syria and Iraq, the Islamic State (popularly known by its old acronym ISIS) established a government by brute force, implementing an extreme interpretation of Islamic law. In Egypt, the Muslim Brotherhood presided over a controversial year in power, alienating most of the country's major political forces before being overthrown in a military coup in 2013.

The "twin shocks" of the Egyptian coup and the rise of the Islamic State have challenged conventional wisdom on political Islam, leading some academics and policymakers, as well as Islamists, to rethink basic assumptions about Islamist movements. The questions raised by the twin shocks were particularly pointed for mainstream Islamists,[1] who followed the rules of the electoral game but failed to see their agendas implemented as quickly or comprehensively as the Islamic State's. Was the lesson to push for more comprehensive change? Was it to make further compromises and concessions? Or was it to abandon electoral politics altogether?

Rethinking Political Islam is the first book of its kind to systematically assess the evolution of mainstream Islamist groups since the Arab uprisings, covering 12 different countries. In each of these cases, contributors considered how Muslim Brotherhood and Brotherhood-inspired movements have grappled with fundamental challenges: gradual versus revolutionary approaches to change, the use of tactical or situational violence, attitudes toward the nation-state, and how ideology and political variables interact. Unlike most other projects on political Islam, this book includes three of the most important country cases outside the Middle East and North Africa—Indonesia, Malaysia, and Pakistan—which, importantly, are also at least somewhat democratic, allowing readers to consider a greater diversity of Islamist experiences. It also includes an analysis of U.S. policy toward Islamist parties by a leading scholar of political Islam who served in a senior post within the Obama administration.

Over the course of two years, contributors read each other's drafts, exchanged ideas, and adapted their conclusions accordingly. The entire process unfolded online and invited commentary from other academics, lay readers, and members of the Islamist movements under study. The final chapters incorporate the fruits of these exchanges, which helped to tease out differences and similarities across the cases and clarify the authors' thinking about their individual countries. In this spirit of intellectual exchange and debate, we have included selected responses of Islamist activists and leaders, as they engaged with and responded to the various contributions. Readers will, for one of the first times in book form, have an opportunity to see experts on Islamism and Islamists themselves debating the future of political Islam.

WHY DO MAINSTREAM ISLAMISTS MATTER?

The Islamic State quickly became the most well-known Islamist organization in the world and the subject of near-constant media coverage. This is understandable, and for policymakers, the group did in fact demand urgent attention. But while groups like the Islamic State—because violence and terror are part of who they are—will always matter more from a counterterrorism perspective, the vast majority of Islamists are not violent nor do they advocate the wholesale change of government institutions. Moreover, as important as the Islamic State has become, it isn't—and doesn't claim to be—a mass movement. Its "vanguard" model is one where a relatively small group of ideologically committed individuals can have an outsized effect. We saw this in dramatic fashion during the Islamic State's capture of Mosul, Iraq's second-largest city, in June 2014. A first wave of around 1,000 fighters was able to overtake an Iraqi force of some 30,000 strong. At the same time, because the Islamic State seeks—and, from its perspective, only needs—the support of a tiny, committed core, its broader cultural, intellectual, and theological influence will naturally have its limitations.

Where states enjoy some degree of legitimacy, control all of their territory, and enjoy a monopoly over the use of force, the Islamic State can only gain limited ground. What tens (or hundreds) of millions of Arabs and Muslims think and do matters, and in many of these countries, they are affected more by mainstream Islamist movements—which ask for their votes, provide social services, and affect how ordinary Muslims understand their religion—than by groups like the Islamic State, which are opposed by the overwhelming majority of Muslims.

Even where Islamist parties appear to be severely weakened, as in Egypt, it would be a mistake to presume this outcome is permanent. In the previous decade, Islamist movements appeared not just weakened but also decimated in countries like Tunisia and Syria, but the openings of the Arab Spring returned them to prominence. Perhaps more important, the movements under consideration are, in some cases, going through unprecedented internal change and are rethinking what it means to be Islamist in an increasingly unstable, chaotic region.

WHAT DOES IT MEAN TO RETHINK POLITICAL ISLAM?

Islamists are not likely to become liberals; otherwise, what would be the point? Islamists are Islamists for a reason, after all, and being religiously oriented is one of the sources of their popular support. Some opponents of Islamists criticize them on the grounds that they haven't rethought the foundational premises of Islamism, but this seems to us like an unrealistic and even problematic standard. At the same time, it is important to not mistake tinkering around the margins and minor shifts in tactics as reflecting deeper ideological changes.

What we find in many cases is that Islamists are broaching controversial and difficult topics that are at the core of what it means to be an Islamist movement, including the relationship between party (*hizb*) and movement (*haraka*), internal organizational structures (the *tanzim*), the nature of the state, the use of violence, and the centrality of elections to the Islamist project.

This rethinking can be for both better and worse, depending on one's perspective. Islamists learning lessons doesn't necessarily mean learning the lessons that Western observers think they should learn. For example, Brotherhood youth in Egypt have moved in a more revolutionary direction, with some being open to what they term "defensive violence," which is at odds with their organization's decades-long commitment to peaceful activism. This constitutes rethinking, although it's probably not the kind that Western policymakers and observers may have had in mind.

A number of themes come up repeatedly throughout these chapters, which are based on extensive fieldwork in the countries in question. Among mainstream Islamist groups, there is a shared sense, despite the sheer diversity of cases, that the Arab uprisings and their aftermath have presented an unusually difficult set of challenges. There is little choice but to adapt in order to succeed or merely even survive. For the first time, Tunisia's Ennahda party has explicitly distanced itself from the "Islamist" label; Jordan's Muslim Brotherhood has splintered, with prominent leaders, including two former general guides, forming a competitor organization; the Muslim Brotherhood in Egypt has experienced the worst internal divisions of its 90-year history.

In the pre–Arab Spring era, there was only so much to think about. Among mainstream Islamists, a consensus had emerged that the way to succeed was fairly straightforward: bide your time, do your best to build social influence within regime constraints, make small but significant inroads in parliament, wait for a democratic opening, and then, when it came, fill the political vacuum. There was no need to spend too much time pondering questions of governance since the prospect of governance seemed so remote. The Arab uprisings first challenged this "model," then rendered it moot.

To use contributor Monica Marks's term, the *partification* of Islamist movements has been one of the most intriguing and important features of Islamist evolution since the 1990s. For decades, Western analysts and policymakers alike encouraged mainstream Islamists to embrace the democratic process, de-emphasize their religious origins, form "normal" political parties, and practice parliamentary politics. This was a natural fit for these groups, which weren't strong on theology but knew how to get out the vote, and get out the vote they did. This prioritization of elections—some within the various Islamist movements have called it an "obsession"—offered an easy out from difficult and potentially divisive debates around the nature and purpose of the nation-state. These were debates that became all the more relevant when Islamists in Egypt, Tunisia, Morocco, and Yemen all had opportunities to govern during and after the Arab Spring.

Having faced any number of setbacks, Islamist parties in each of the 12 countries have had to contend with basic questions of how change actually happens within constraining state structures and a regional and international environment in which major actors are suspicious of Islamists, particularly when they begin to approach the levers of state power. How Islamists react, naturally, has a lot to do with how the various revolutions, stalled revolutions, or non-revolutions evolved in each particular case. For example, were rulers toppled, therefore inviting a vacuum of leadership that well-organized Islamist groups could then fill? Did state structures collapse after revolution, thereby provoking outbreaks of violent conflict or civil war? Where rulers were not toppled, how did Islamist parties balance nominal loyalty to existing regimes with popular demands for political change?

Ruler Toppled but Not Followed by Armed Conflict

Our contributors agreed that the course of the revolutions since 2011 and the policies adopted by ruling regimes—old and new—constrained the choices made by mainstream Islamists. We can see this most plainly in Egypt, where the twin shocks narrowed the space in which the Brotherhood could contest the state's power legally without being labeled as ISIS-like by regime officials and supporters. As Steven Brooke documents, the state branded the group a terrorist organization to justify taking over the social services the Brotherhood once offered to millions of Egyptians. The Brotherhood's network of institutions had helped it generate goodwill prior to the revolution, which is why the government of strongman Abdel Fattah al-Sissi wanted to ensure that the movement could not rebuild its base of support. Forced underground and with the near entirety of its leadership in prison, exile, or hiding, the Brotherhood lost many of its ties to local communities and as "arms" or "wings" of the movement. The imperatives of seeking votes are often *not* the imperatives of a movement seeking widespread societal change and even social transformation. A preacher's extreme sermon might excite a small core but alienate the masses needed for electoral success. Conversely, a party leader's call for moderation to avoid alienating militaries or monarchies might depress turnout among more hardline or conservative supporters.

This dilemma was particularly acute after the Arab uprisings, when mainstream Islamists had to decide whether and how to contest elections. Some, like the Egyptian Brotherhood, maintained a blurry relationship between movement and party (with the latter ultimately dependent on the former), leading people to blame the movement for the party's misfortunes and vice versa. Ennahda is perhaps the most unique case, with party and movement being one and the same before transforming into a party and declaring a separation between "religious" and "political" activities. While such a move was generally welcomed by Western observers and the international community, it raised a new set of questions around what it meant to be an Islamist party that was no longer, in its own telling, "Islamist" but rather "Muslim democratic." Moreover, Islamist parties have been successful, in part, because they are not *just* parties; they represent or are tied to broader-based movements that can provide mobilizational capacity, organizational discipline, social service networks, funding for electoral campaigns, and a broader reach into less politicized sectors of society.

The tension between party and movement has been particularly evident among Brotherhood branches, which, over time, came to see elections as the primary mechanism for both social and political change, even when it came at the cost of traditional core concerns of preaching and social service provision. Indeed, if there is one finding that emerges clearly from the country comparisons, it is that Arab Brotherhood organizations view electoral victory as the definitive measure of success.

That was not always the case. Mainstream Islamists in the Middle East preferred in the past to focus on gradual social reform and religious education. Indeed, the founder of the Brotherhood, Hassan al-Banna, had a conception of gradualism that would proceed in a progressive fashion: starting at the individual and moving to the family, the community, and eventually the government. In practice, many Islamists find that adhering to this sequential gradualism becomes difficult when presented with the temptation of electoral success. As demonstrated by some of the Islamist responses in this volume, much of the post-coup reflection by Brotherhood members ponders the tension between hurrying back into electoral politics and taking a step back to rebuild their social base, with a focus on local communities.

HOW DO ISLAMISTS—AND THE INTERNATIONAL COMMUNITY—MEASURE ISLAMIST SUCCESS?

Avi Spiegel, an expert on Morocco's Islamists, elegantly poses the question of what it means for Islamists to "win":

> We love measuring and tracking "democracy," focusing on winners and losers, on horse races, victories, and defeats. We study these things, I suspect, because we are guided by the belief, perhaps even the zeal, that these outcomes matter—that the winners of elections actually win something. Yet, in authoritarian contexts—even post–Arab Spring contexts—does electoral success translate into success writ large? [4]

The bargain in Morocco has been clear enough. The PJD accepted the confines of a system in which the monarchy has veto power over all major decisions. In return, the PJD is allowed to legally exist, participate, and even enjoy a bit of power. In practice, this means that the PJD cannot, assuming it wanted to, significantly alter or transform the country's politics. Looking forward 5, 10, or 15 years, it is difficult to envision the PJD accomplishing much more than it already has.

Islamists in Pakistan, as Matthew Nelson writes, provide an intriguing counterpoint to the Moroccan "model." It is a counterpoint that few Moroccans—or Arab Islamists anywhere—seem very interested in. Jamaat e-Islami usually wins only a handful of parliamentary seats, yet, as Spiegel argues, it may very well be more influential than its Moroccan counterpart, in terms of "influencing judicial appointments, religious tradition, educational mores, and societal norms writ-large." There are other ways of winning besides, well, winning.

In Southeast Asia, similarly, Islamist parties, while gaining a significant share of the vote, have not been able to win outright on the national
level. They have, however, helped spread and normalize "Islamism"
throughout society, with even ostensibly secular parties embracing the
idea that Islam—and even explicit sharia ordinances—have an important role to play in public life. The lesson here may appear counterintuitive. The worse Islamists do in elections, the less of a threat they pose
to their non-Islamist competitors, who, in turn, seem to have less of a
problem appropriating Islamist-like positions for their own electoral
purposes.

Of course, the causal relationships become complicated: One of
the reasons that Islamists don't do as well in South and Southeast Asia
is because they're less distinctive, since these societies seem to have
coalesced around a relatively uncontroversial conservative "middle." As
Liow writes in his chapter, "The piecemeal implementation of sharia
by-laws across Indonesia has not elicited widespread opposition from
local populations." It's also likely no accident that Indonesia, Pakistan,
and to a lesser extent Malaysia are more democratic than their Arab
counterparts (with the exception of Tunisia). Democracy empowers
and encourages all parties, Islamist or otherwise, to seek the center,
wherever that may be.

Western policymakers, for their part, have long encouraged Islamist
groups to "normalize" themselves by accepting the rules of the game
(even if these were stacked against them), forming political parties, and
prioritizing electoral politics. They were not necessarily wrong to do so,
but the focus on elections limited the policies they prescribed and the
analytical frames they employed.

How the United States and Europe should respond to the rise of
Islamist parties (or even if they should treat Islamist parties as distinctive in the first place) has been a contentious question since at least the
early 1990s, when the Algerian military aborted the democratic process after an Islamist party won a decisive victory at the polls. Peter
Mandaville, one of the few academic experts on political Islam who has
also served in senior positions in the U.S. State Department, gives an
insider's account into the nuanced and sometimes contradictory attitudes toward Islamists during the Obama administration. He writes
that the U.S. government quickly came to terms with Islamist political

participation during the Arab Spring. After the Egyptian coup, however, American officials found it difficult to continue engaging mainstream Islamists without alienating key regional allies, particularly now that the anti-Brotherhood regional bloc had gained the upper hand.

Yet if one of the twin shocks complicated America's policy toward Islamist groups, the other—the rise of the Islamic State—may provide an opening. With Arab states seemingly unable to stem terrorist activity, religion-based electoral opposition is more easily framed as a non-violent alternative to violent extremists, thereby helping to delegitimize the appeal of the Islamic State and its ilk. In any case, Islamists will almost certainly return to prominence if and when there are political openings in various countries, and the United States will once again have to think more seriously about the very questions it has struggled to answer for nearly three decades.

When we embarked on the creation of this volume, our goal was to, at a minimum, challenge the conventional wisdom on political Islam and how to respond to, think about, and engage with movements that are often viewed with considerable skepticism if not outright suspicion and hostility. Our starting assumption is simple enough and hopefully uncontroversial: that we—whoever "we" are—do not have to like Islamists, but we do need to understand them, particularly in light of a rapidly changing social and political context in the Middle East and Asia.

Countries

I

Egypt

Steven Brooke

THE JULY 3, 2013, overthrow of elected president Mohamed Morsi set off a high-profile political battle between the Muslim Brotherhood and Egypt's new military regime. As part of this battle, the regime also began to engage in a lower-profile effort to disrupt and ultimately uproot the Brotherhood's vaunted network of nationwide social services.[1] This chapter chronicles the regime's campaign against the Brotherhood's social institutions, in particular schools and medical facilities, and considers what they mean for the future of the world's oldest and most influential Islamist movement.

Beyond its effect on the millions of Egyptians who relied on the Brotherhood's services to get by, the crackdown highlights the costs and viability of the Brotherhood's longstanding accommodationist and legalist approach to existing states. The group has historically situated its social service provision as complementary to the state and, ultimately, subservient to it. Yet the legal campaign against these institutions will potentially drive the Brotherhood to reorient its social service provision in a more decentralized and exclusivist direction. In other words, instead of providing social services broadly and above ground, the group may now be forced to prioritize members and affiliates that have been caught up in the crackdown. This can potentially complicate the Brotherhood's efforts to maintain connections to broader

Egyptian society in the short term and puts it in a weaker position when, if ever, the opportunity arises for the organization to rebuild the support it has lost.

The dramatic opening and closing of elections as sites of political contestation has also highlighted Islamist groups' dilemma of balancing between the political party, the *hizb*, and the social movement, the *haraka*. Particularly during periods of heightened authoritarianism, the Egyptian Brotherhood maintained a general separation between these realms, prompted by both the regime's legal constraints and the group's own reluctance to fully invest in politics while the regime held effective veto power.[2] But cracks in this wall appeared in 2011, as regime constraints evaporated and the incentives to attract Egyptians' support at the polls increased dramatically. Now, as the Brotherhood reassesses its missteps during a brief democratic interlude, key leaders have identified their inability to separate the group's social and political activities as a key mistake.

REGIME STRATEGY

A September 2013 court case established the legal basis for the regime to move against the Muslim Brotherhood's social service network. In that ruling (Judgment 2315 of 2013), the Cairo Court for Urgent Matters ruled that the Brotherhood was a terrorist organization. The court simultaneously established a committee to investigate and assess the possibilities for seizure of the Brotherhood's physical and financial assets.[3] At the end of December 2013, the committee completed its preliminary investigation of the Brotherhood's assets, and the lists of social service organizations allegedly linked to the Muslim Brotherhood soon leaked to the Egyptian press. The initial listing included 1,142 individual entities spread across each of Egypt's 27 governorates.[4] Among the institutions on the list were both organizations clearly linked to the Muslim Brotherhood and ostensibly independent organizations over which the committee judged the Brotherhood had extensive influence or control. Particularly notable were certain local branches of the sprawling Islamic organizations Al-Gam'iyya al-Shar'iyya and Ansar al-Sunna.[5] At around the same time as the list of community associations appeared, Egyptian newspapers published a list of 87 schools affiliated with the Muslim Brotherhood.[6] Both the community associations and schools were subject to an immediate asset freeze, further investigation, and potential confiscation of assets.

As of February 2017, the campaign against "Brotherhood-affiliated" community and charity associations was ongoing.[7] One indication of the scope of the campaign appeared in early 2016, when a report in the state-owned *al-Ahram* tallied the extent of the financial assets the government had confiscated. While independent confirmation is difficult, *al-Ahram* claimed that the investigative committee had seized 105 schools (with assets valued at approximately $32 million) and 43 hospitals (valued at $12.5 million). This was in addition to extensive assets recovered from businesses and personal bank accounts, as well as cash apparently seized during the course of the campaigns.[8]

The regime's effort against the Brotherhood is nested within a larger effort to recorporatize civil society and prevent the emergence of potentially independent centers of activism. For instance, in July of 2014, the regime floated plans to force all nongovernmental organizations (NGOs) operating in Egypt to dissolve and reregister with the Ministry of Social Solidarity within 45 days, although the deadline was later extended and the level of enforcement remains unclear.[9] As one NGO employee put it, "You register and you survive, but under very difficult conditions of work."[10] Since then the regime's attempts to control civil society have expanded dramatically, targeting individuals, their family members, and their financial assets, all in an attempt to eliminate spaces for its opponents to operate.[11] For the regime, the goal is to maintain a baseline level of social provisioning, yet forestall the possibility that potential opponents of the regime—Islamist or not—can leverage their activity into a political challenge.

It is unclear if the regime can have it both ways. President Anwar el-Sadat's embrace of free market reforms in the 1970s and the onset of Economic Reform and Structural Adjustment (ERSAP) in the 1990s have steadily degraded Egypt's social safety net. And for decades it has been nonstate providers, including Islamist groups, that have filled the gap for millions of Egyptians. For instance, in the years before the 2013 military coup, the Brotherhood's Islamic Medical Association (IMA) was serving approximately 2 million Egyptians annually.[12] One patient's complaint following the seizure of IMA facilities captured the frustration: "The government neither provides us with hospitals suitable for human beings, nor do they allow the hospitals that treat us well to continue operating!"[13] Suddenly shuttering this sprawling network risks provoking the very unrest that the regime intends to prevent.

On the other hand, allowing this network to continue in its current form poses apparently unacceptable risks to the regime. For decades, the Brotherhood's network of social services has deeply embedded itself in Egypt's cities and villages and earned the movement a reservoir of gratitude, if not outright support. So long as this network continues to exist, it will serve as a potential site of opposition against Egypt's new rulers, a place where Brotherhood activists can build support by leveraging their resources to help Egyptians cope with their everyday problems.

To balance their desire to repress the Brotherhood with the necessity of maintaining social stability, Egypt's rulers are appointing their own management teams—composed of government bureaucrats and security service figures—to oversee these institutions. In effect, they seek to minimize social disruption while forcing out those individuals most likely to be a bridge to the Muslim Brotherhood's organizational infrastructure, to the extent it still exists. Indeed, as security services forced out the management teams of hospital after hospital, regime officials continually stressed that the facilities would not close and that their quality would not suffer.[14] And as part of the attempt to blunt the effect of the closures, other state actors, including the various state-owned and affiliated funds (Misr al-Khayr, Jam'iyat Orman), have ramped up their efforts.[15] The military—Egypt's institution of last resort—has also become directly involved in social provision, distributing boxes of food and organizing medical caravans.[16]

The following sections detail how the regime has waged its campaign against the Brotherhood's social service network through an examination of the fates of two clusters of Brotherhood-affiliated institutions. The first examines one of the largest organizations that appeared on the list of community associations, the Muslim Brotherhood's IMA. The second examines the regime's efforts to control the Brotherhood's schools. Together, these two case studies not only illustrate the regime's attempt to uproot the Brotherhood's vaunted service network but also set the stage for the chapter's concluding discussion of the lessons a new generation of Islamist activists—and those that study them—might potentially take from the episode.

BROTHERHOOD MEDICAL NETWORKS

Prominent Muslim Brotherhood leader Ahmed al-Malt founded the IMA in 1977 to provide high-quality medical care at an affordable cost. The IMA is the largest and oldest of the Brotherhood's organized social service initiatives. On the eve of the military coup, the association operated 22 hospitals and seven specialized medical centers (four dialysis centers, an ophthalmology center, a fertility center, and a center for those with special needs). In addition, the organization was also active in the provision of mobile "medical caravans" that sent groups of doctors across the country.

Soon after the July 2013 coup, members of the security services visited each of the IMA's facilities to ensure that they were registered and that their paperwork was up to date. Additionally, the IMA was forced to cut ties with prominent members of the Muslim Brotherhood on its board, including Freedom and Justice Party parliamentarians Helmi Gazar and Gamal Heshmat. Other politically active Brotherhood personalities involved with the organization, such as Mohi al-Zeit, the director of the flagship Central Charity Hospital in Nasr City, and Medhat Asem, the chairman of the IMA, managed to flee the country. Others, such as Wael Talib, a key figure in the establishment of the IMA's facilities in Helwan, were arrested.[17]

In December 2013, the IMA appeared on the list of Brotherhood-linked community associations targeted for an asset freeze. Shortly thereafter, the IMA responded with a front-page ad in the state daily *al-Ahram* pleading with the regime to allow it to continue operations "on behalf of 2 million sick and tens of thousands of those who receive kidney dialysis on a continuing basis, and premature infants, and those unable to pay for their treatment, as well as those who visit the hospitals."[18] Outside of the dialysis centers, it wasn't initially clear how much the freeze actually affected the IMA's ability to function. In an interview conducted in the immediate aftermath of the decision, one IMA manager remained optimistic that the asset freeze would be lifted within days.[19] In an interview a few months later, the IMA's director of hospital management even claimed that three new hospitals were close to entering service.[20]

This optimism was misplaced. The regime clamped down suddenly in early 2015, formally assuming control of the IMA and seizing its assets.[21] The management teams of the individual hospitals were dissolved and reconstituted with pro-regime figures. Financial managers came under extra scrutiny because, according to the regime, some of the IMA's money was being used to "fund terrorism."[22] Putting a point on the change in orientation, the IMA's new chairman was the staunchly pro-regime cleric Ali Goma'a, the former Grand Mufti of Egypt.[23] Goma'a has been notorious for his anti-Brotherhood broadsides, including a post-coup sermon where, speaking about pro-Morsi protests, he urged members of the military and police to "shoot them in the heart. . . . We must cleanse our Egypt from these riffraff."[24] In the aftermath of the decision to nominate Goma'a, one patient at an IMA facility lamented that "the wolf now guards the sheep."[25]

THE MUSLIM BROTHERHOOD'S SCHOOLS

The Brotherhood's network of private schools serves as the second pillar of the group's broader social service network. As with the IMA (and community associations in general), the legal basis for state control over the Brotherhood's schools stems from the September 2013 court decision designating the Muslim Brotherhood a terrorist organization. Like the community associations, these schools were initially assigned to a type of receivership but allowed to continue operating under the control of a Ministry of Education committee. (In a further insult to the Brotherhood, this authority is called the "June 30th Schools Committee.")

The regime specifically complained that the Brotherhood had used its schools to incite violence against the military and police.[26] For example, one parent of a student described Arabic lessons where students were told the army and police were killing protestors. She elaborated:

> If the teachers were speaking about a historical episode of conflict between good guys and bad guys, the teachers would editorialize that the bad guys in the story were analogous to today's army and police.

The teachers would also inject politics into every discussion, and they would insist on describing the events of June 30th as a coup, rather than a revolution.[27]

The security services also directly intervened in the schools to arrest individuals they charged with recruiting for and organizing attacks on the regime.[28] For their part, those affiliated with the schools not only reject the charges but also point out the absurdity of the investigations. For instance, according to the director of the Hiraa' school network in Asyut, the regime introduced as evidence of the school's radical orientation a classroom cartoon of the Smurfs where one was apparently flashing the Rabaa (four fingers) sign, marking the August 14, 2013 Rabaa massacre of Muslim Brotherhood supporters.[29]

In contrast to the relatively smooth takeover of the IMA, the regime's efforts to bring the Brotherhood's schools to heel have proceeded much more haltingly.[30] One key bureaucratic hurdle is that all regime interaction with these facilities must run through the aforementioned June 30th Committee. The June 30th Committee guards its prerogatives fiercely— the courts have even indicted members of the Ministry of Education for dealing with the schools directly.[31] In other cases, the Ministry of Education's lack of an enforcement capacity has meant that the original boards of directors were able to essentially brush off the demands to dissolve and continue to operate as if nothing had changed.[32]

Another problematic issue (from the regime's point of view) is that the legal basis for seizing the Brotherhood's property—the September 2013 court decision—applies to corporate-owned assets only (for instance, the IMA). Yet many of those who own the schools are *individuals*, including prominent Muslim Brotherhood members such as Wafa Mashour, a Brotherhood candidate in the 2010 parliamentary elections and daughter of former General Guide Mohamed Mashour (d. 2002); longtime parliamentarian Mohsen Radi; and Khadija al-Shater, daughter of prominent Brotherhood leader Khairat al-Shater.

Despite their affiliations with the Muslim Brotherhood, a number of the schools' owners have challenged the regime's claim that it can seize their private property based on the September 2013 decision.[33] There have even been some successes—a number of schools immediately challenged the December 2013 finding that they were affiliated to the

Muslim Brotherhood, and three were reportedly released to their own-ers.[34] In late 2014, the owners of nine schools received a sympathetic hearing from lower court judges, who ruled that proceedings to seize their schools were not valid. In support of their opinion, the judges cited the Egyptian constitution's protection of private property from seizure except in extreme circumstances.[35]

This has led the Ministry of Justice and the security services to con-clude that the Ministry of Education is fundamentally incapable of bringing the schools to heel. For its part, the Ministry of Education claims that it lacks the enforcement capacity to fully implement the decision.[36] Summarizing the spat, *al-Masry al-Youm* (which has closely followed the case) pointed out:

> The Ministry of Education has failed to tighten control over the schools and implement the primary objective of the ruling on the seizure of the institutions: to "protect students' minds from extrem-ism." Instead, the Ministry of Education handled this as a mere for-mality, preferring instead to focus solely on managing the financial aspect of the schools' operation without paying attention to what is actually happening behind the scenes (literally "in closed sections").[37]

In January 2015, the government essentially rebooted its efforts to control the Brotherhood's schools. As a first step, it began to inject "new blood" into the process, appointing new boards of directors for all the schools.[38] Notably, the Ministry of Education emphasized that these new managers would all be precleared by the security services before assuming their duties, suggesting that earlier managers possessed sympathies with the Brotherhood (or at least antipathy toward the current regime).[39] Government officials also propagated new guidelines for the schools that included a ban on female students and teachers wearing the *niqab* (full-face veil) and can-celled requirements that students wear the *hijab* (headscarf).[40] According to Ministry of Education officials, the campaign is proceeding apace: In February 2015, the Minister of Education claimed that the Brotherhood's network of schools was "85 percent under control."[41]

The regime's attempts to trim the branches of the Brotherhood's education network received a boost from new antiterror legislation. In late February 2015, President Sissi signed into law a series of measures giving Egyptian authorities wide powers to designate, detain, and confiscate the assets of groups deemed a threat to public order. (Not coincidentally, the September 2013 case dubbed the Brotherhood a threat to public order.)[42] In effect, this establishes a firmer legal basis for seizing the Brotherhood's properties by closing the loophole many of the schools' owners used to challenge the designation—that there was no legal basis to seize their private property. The regime wasted little time in applying the law, designating 18 high-profile Muslim Brotherhood members and seizing their assets in March 2015.[43] With this new legislation in hand, in April 2015 *al-Masry al-Youm* reported that the Minister of Education was preparing to tighten controls over the schools to ensure that they remained free of Brotherhood influence.[44]

The new legal effort seems to have done its job. By the time the 2016 academic year began the schools had been completely restructured and were receiving students. Yet lingering suspicion of Brotherhood influence meant that the schools were still subject to drop-in inspections and government screening of teachers.[45]

FOLLOWING THE LAW WILL NOT SAVE YOU

A defining characteristic of mainstream Islamist groups in the Middle East has been their fundamental accommodation to the existence of current states. Mainstream Islamists participated in political systems, adopted national discourses, and largely subjugated their activism to regime laws. The Egyptian Muslim Brotherhood's historical conception of social service provision as something to be pursued openly and subjugated to the state—rather than subversive activity in competition to it—is a prime example of this accommodation.

From the organization's outset, the Brotherhood registered its social service organizations with the relevant government authorities, including the Ministry of Social Solidarity, the Ministry of Education, the Ministry of Awqaf (for mosque-based charities), and the Ministry of Health. At the organization's founding in 1928, Hassan al-Banna registered the Muslim Brotherhood with the British-controlled monarchy.[46] When the Ministry of Social Solidarity was established in 1939, all NGOs operating in Egypt were required to dissolve and reconstitute themselves by following the new guidelines, which the Muslim Brotherhood did.[47] In the post-Nasser period the organization likewise registered its social and civic activities with the government. The Brotherhood abided by these guidelines despite the fact that they gave the government tremendous power over the formation, operation, and even existence of their service networks.[48] In essence, for the Brotherhood, the benefits of free and legal operation outweighed the costs incurred by submitting to government regulation.

This is why the regime's crackdown on the Brotherhood's social service institutions took the group by surprise: they were betting on their history of legal operation to protect them. In an interview in January of 2014, shortly after the IMA appeared on the list of Brotherhood-affiliated community associations, an IMA manager emphasized the organization's cooperation with the Ministry of Social Solidarity and expressed optimism that the IMA would soon sort things out with the government. As he claimed, "We aren't the enemy of the state, we're part of it, despite the fact that we disagree with its policies."[49] Even after the regime takeover one year later, the IMA protested by pointing to its history of good relations with the ministry. "Not only has the Ministry of Social Solidarity not recorded a violation over the past year," the IMA's director of public relations argued, "but it has praised the IMA!"[50] Similarly, the Brotherhood argued that its network of schools adhered strictly to the Ministry of Education curriculum guidelines and that they operated in compliance with the law.

Unfortunately for the Brotherhood, not only did the legalist approach fail to protect its network of social services from the regime, it actually facilitated efforts to dismember them. As Quintan Wiktorowicz argues, authoritarian regimes proliferate laws and guidelines in civil society to render activism visible, and thus controllable.[51] When the regime decided to crack down on—or simply expropriate—the Brotherhood's service network, the group's legalist approach furnished the regime a ready-made "hit list" of properties, enterprises, and activists.

The specific character of Egypt's civil society laws also prevented the Brotherhood from using the court system to contest the regime's decisions. Specifically, Egypt's Law of Associations (Law 84/2002) includes a provision that gives the Ministry of Social Solidarity—and not an outside body such as Egypt's courts—extraordinary power to adjudicate any disputes that occur between an association and the ministry.[52] So the Ministry of Social Solidarity can dissolve an association, which can then only appeal the dissolution order *back to the ministry*. In effect, this means that third parties have no jurisdiction over dissolution cases unless the Ministry of Social Solidarity allows it. This is why the regime's campaign against the Brotherhood's community associations has proceeded so quickly: in late February of 2015 the Ministry dissolved 169 institutions from the list, and on March 1 they dissolved 112 more.[53] A further 99 were dissolved in mid-March.[54] Had the Brotherhood registered these social initiatives as businesses (as many of the schools were), it would have at least been able to contest the dissolution orders through the court system.

The Egyptian regime's unwillingness to tolerate a regulated and above-ground Islamist social service network potentially incentivizes the Brotherhood to shift activism underground, for instance, by providing services through informal social networks rather than institutions. But this would require the Brotherhood to change how the provision is operated, not least because it would bias the provision against non-members. Not only would this protect the existence of the network from infiltrators, it would serve as a type of extra benefit that only those in the Brotherhood could access.

A number of authors have examined the issue of social service provision through the lens of organizational economics, to help understand how movements encourage members to participate in potentially costly activities, such as demonstrations and violence.[55] In contexts where activism is risky, these authors argue, access to benefits such as social services must be contingent on participation in these activities or membership in the organization; otherwise, people will "free-ride" by accessing the benefits without paying the costs. So long as the Brotherhood–regime conflict continues, it incentivizes the Brotherhood to use social service provision to sustain such activism.[56]

Limiting services to protect the network from the government and incentivize high-risk activism would restrict the Brotherhood's ability to attract those outside its ideological orbit. In fact, one reason the

Brotherhood was able to make inroads with non-Islamists prior to 2011 was its broad and nonideological provision of social services. To the extent that the Brotherhood shifts the *way* it provides services to survive the current period of repression, it may find it difficult to use those same networks to rebuild its social support at some future point.

NAVIGATING THE MOVEMENT–PARTY DIVIDE

The problems surrounding the provision of social services following the crackdown have exacerbated longstanding tensions between the Brotherhood's broad goal of social transformation, to be achieved by the movement, and its narrow goal of political control, to be achieved by its party. Of course, the Brotherhood's social services have always been political—in the sense that they were designed to link the group's religious mission to the everyday problems facing citizens, and thus build a reservoir of sympathy and support. But for decades the Brotherhood took pains to keep this social mission at arm's length from the electoral one. Services were provided continuously and without the discrimination, ideological litmus tests, or checks on political allegiance that we might expect if they were operated by a typical political machine.

On the ground, balancing the imperatives of social activism and electoral mobilization was never easy, especially given the increasing prominence of electoral politics in the Middle East over the last twenty years. This shift, even in places where authoritarian regimes held tightly to political power, increased the pressure on Islamist groups to convert their social capital into electoral success. Eva Wegner, for instance, quotes a Moroccan Islamist who expresses frustration with how the two sides have blended together:

> In the past ten years we have invested too much in the party even though in our concept, our line of reasoning, this is only one part of our activities. We don't want to focus too much on the political aspects; us as a cultural, educational association, we prefer to concentrate on the educational and *da'wa* [missionary] issues.[57]

However, the dramatic rise in the importance of politics after 2011 supercharged incentives to put all the movement's assets in the narrow service

of electoral mobilization. Despite rhetoric about maintaining separation between the political and nonpolitical aspects of the Brotherhood's
identity, citizens on the ground found it harder and harder to determine
where one stopped and the other began.[58] This politicization reached
its apogee during the Muslim Brotherhood–Freedom and Justice Party's
massive program of social service outreach, "Together We Build Egypt,"
in the run-up to parliamentary elections in the summer of 2013 (the
coup ended preparations for these elections). For roughly six months the
Brotherhood used its social services to openly support the group's political ambitions, assembling medical caravans, beautification campaigns,
veterinary convoys, and other outreach efforts to help buttress the group's
sliding popularity.

The post-2013 period has prompted some Brotherhood leaders
to revisit the relationship between the party (*hizb*) and the social
movement (*haraka*). This springs from two realizations. First, they
believe that the post-2011 collapse of the wall between social services
and partisan activism sowed confusion in the minds of Egyptians
about the distinction between the movement and the political party.
Second, some Brotherhood leaders do not want the inevitable disappointments of politics—losing elections, pursuing failed policies,
compromising with ideological opponents, and so forth—to con-
taminate or cast doubt on the Brotherhood's longer-term mission
of societal transformation. According to Amr Darrag, Freedom
and Justice Party leader and cabinet minister in Mohamed Morsi's
government:

> It is clearly impossible for the group to compete politically against a
> large segment of the population but at the same time work alongside
> them socially. This is simply not achievable, and this is the largest
> mistake that took place. The Brotherhood bore the mistakes in [the
> party's] political tactics, despite the fact that the party benefited from
> the Brotherhood's support.[59]

Darrag's argument suggests that, at least among some in the organization, there is a growing awareness of the need to separate the two
halves of the movement, preventing the effects of political competition
from bleeding into the social activism and vice versa.[60] Gamal Hesmat,

longtime Brotherhood parliamentarian and board member of the IMA, suggests that this idea has broad support: "The whole group is determined to keep the competitive partisan side away from the educational and reform side and activities."[61]

It is not just the Egyptian Brotherhood that is (re-)assessing the exact shape of the relations between party and movement. The current conflict between the Brotherhood and the regime in Jordan and inside the Jordanian Brotherhood itself touches in some ways on the distinction between party and movement.[62] And Tunisia's Ennahda party has moved to separate its *da'wa* functions from its electoral activism. Prior to the party's annual congress in May 2016, an Ennahda spokesman said that there would be complete separation between the political party and religious activism: "We (Ennahda) will focus on the political sphere, and as for social activities, including cultural, charitable, preaching, and guidance, we will leave to the civil associations."[63] As Monica Marks summarized following the conference, this indeed happened:

> Many Ennahda leaders and supporters were initially skeptical of formalizing changes to the *hizb-haraka* (party-religious movement) relationship. Yet by spring 2016, most had come to support the revisions, which were carried by strong majorities of two thirds or greater in voting at this weekend's congress.[64]

However, it remains to be seen how Ennahda manages this separation on the ground and, in particular, whether it can be maintained amidst the fluctuations in popularity with which every political party must inevitably grapple.

CONCLUSION

Since the July 3, 2013 military coup, Egypt's new regime has dismembered the Muslim Brotherhood's nationwide network of social services. Just as this threatens the livelihoods of millions of Egyptians who rely on these services to meet their daily needs, the campaign has also been a tremendous blow to the Brotherhood, which has for decades emphasized the importance of social service provision to its overall mission.

The events of the past four years have essentially closed off the legal avenues for the Brotherhood to engage in social service provision.

The tumult of the past five years has also highlighted the need for Islamist organizations to resolve, or at least clarify, the differences between their twin identities as social movements and political parties. This tension has been long-standing, but the dramatic political changes in places like Egypt and Tunisia add urgency to the question. Leaders in the Egyptian Brotherhood have identified this in retrospect, isolating the group's failure to demarcate where the social movement stopped and political party began as a key mistake of the period. In Tunisia, however, Ennahda has sought to preempt any confusion, agreeing to statutorily separate partisan activity from religious and social work. The real test of the durability of this separation, in Egypt, in Tunisia, or elsewhere, will come when the incentives to use service provision for political gain are strongest.

2

Tunisia

Monica Marks

SINCE ITS JANUARY 2011 revolution, Tunisia has carved out a special status as the only genuine, albeit fragile, Arab democracy. Regional tumult, however, has repeatedly reverberated through the country. Egypt's July 2013 coup and the regional rise of violent Salafi-jihadism—embodied most powerfully by the Islamic State—sent shockwaves through Tunisia in 2012 and 2013, emboldening antidemocratic demands that threatened to destabilize its nascent democracy.[1] Neighboring Libya's descent into near statelessness and Gulf actors' willingness to bankroll reactionary projects in the region compounded these challenges.[2]

The Egyptian coup and rise of Salafi-jihadism posed especially thorny obstacles for Ennahda, the center-right Islamist party that led Tunisia's coalition government from October 2011 to January 2014. A Tunisian religious party originating from the Muslim Brotherhood (*Ikhwani*) school of Islamism, Ennahda had never held power before.[3] Instead, it was strictly banned for over 20 years under the regime of ex-president Zine el-Abidine Ben Ali, who attempted to label Ennahda a radically Islamist, even terrorist, actor in Tunisia's unfree press.[4] When Ennahda re-entered politics in early 2011, many Tunisians found its identity obscure and its democratic commitments suspect. As jihadist violence began spreading in Tunisia and the Muslim Brotherhood claimed victory in Egypt's elections, many

Tunisians predicted that Ennahda—a poorly understood Islamist actor with presumably transnational sympathies—would actively aid or at least tacitly abet the importation of Salafi-jihadism and comparatively conservative Egyptian-style Islamism to Tunisia.[5]

This chapter examines how regional developments, specifically the rise of the Islamic State and Egypt's coup, interacted with domestic political challenges to alter Ennahda's political behavior. I argue that the primary effect of those twin shocks was to narrow Ennahda's range of political maneuver, forcing it to adopt a more defensive, risk-averse posture. This was especially visible in Ennahda's handling of issues related to revolutionary justice, most notably an electoral lustration law that would have prohibited former members of Ben Ali's party from contesting Tunisia's 2014 elections. Although Ennahda had initially supported the law, domestic political pressure—amplified by jihadist-perpetrated assassinations and Egypt's summer 2013 coup—prompted its leadership to recant, ultimately blocking the law's passage.

The chapter concludes by positing that Ennahda itself isn't merely "rethinking Islamism." It is actively reformulating Tunisian Islamism, which it prefers to call "Tunisian Muslim democracy," as a highly localized, long-term project predicated on canny compromise, a malleable message of cultural conservatism, and the survival of a democratic—if not necessarily secular-liberal—political system.

A CONTEXT OF SUSPICION

Ennahda is a religiously rooted party with origins in the Brotherhood-inspired *sahwa*, or spiritual revivalism that swept the Middle East during the 1970s. The Islamic Tendency Movement (MTI), a precursor to Ennahda, formed in 1981. It brought together conservatively oriented Tunisians who were disillusioned by the secularly flavored authoritarianism of presidents Habib Bourguiba (1956–1987) and Zine el-Abidine Ben Ali (1987—2011).[6] The MTI's early adherents were generally first-generation university students with family roots in the country's interior and marginalized regions, who felt Islam offered guiding principles that could help reform society and politics.[7] In 1989, the group complied with a ban on religious references in party names and changed its name to Ennahda (The Renaissance). Nevertheless,

Ben Ali's government rejected its application for recognition as a political party, so Ennahda ran its candidates as independents in the 1989 elections.

Ennahda's desire to enter multiparty politics and its compliance with the regime's rules of the game did little to assuage the worries of Ben Ali, who sensed a political threat in Ennahda's strong support base and religiously rooted critiques of corruption, authoritarianism, and Western secularization. Like Bourguiba before him, Ben Ali sought to vilify Ennahda as extremist and even terrorist in nature. Reneging on early promises to initiate a democratic opening, or *changement*, in Tunisia, Ben Ali cancelled the 1989 elections after a stronger-than-expected showing from the Ennahda-affiliated independents, and instead used electoral lists to round up Ennahda members and their families.[8] Many *nahdawis* (Ennahda members) fled for exile, mostly to Western Europe. Thousands more remained in Tunisia, where many were jailed as political prisoners, along with leftists and other regime critics, during the 1990s and early 2000s.

The Ben Ali regime subjected Ennahda members and their families to numerous human rights abuses. These most commonly included blacklisting from employment and educational opportunities; obligation to register at police stations multiple times daily or weekly; and police harassment that sometimes involved sexual abuse, rape, and torture of both men and women.[9] Even Ennahda members in exile were routinely harassed, monitored, and denied important paperwork by employees of Tunisia's interior ministry, many of whom set up shop in the country's embassies abroad.

Following Tunisia's revolution, Ennahda's exiled leaders returned and its underground activists re-emerged. Yet the party faced a steep uphill climb. Given the extent of repression, Ben Ali's determination to equate Ennahda with terrorism, and the near complete absence of countervailing messages in Tunisian media, Ennahda re-entered Tunisian politics amid widespread suspicion that its democratic claims were not credible.

Early on, Ennahda fulfilled two pre-electoral promises: not supporting a presidential candidate in the October 2011 elections and entering into a cross-ideological coalition government with two secular parties.[10] These steps did little, however, to persuade many Tunisians that Ennahda—which claimed to be a democratic, Tunisian party—wasn't actually an illiberal, imported franchise of Egypt's Muslim Brotherhood. Suspicions ran especially high among secularly oriented Tunisians, many of whom feared Ennahda aimed to quite literally "re-orient" Tunisia away from Europe and its regionally progressive stances on women's rights toward the more conservative Arab east.

THE EGYPTIAN MUSLIM BROTHERHOOD: NOT A MODEL

Curious to learn how Ennahda itself might rule if it won the October 2011 elections, I conducted open-ended interviews with approximately 80 Ennahda leaders, grassroots activists, and party supporters over the summer of 2011. I asked 72 of them what kind of Islamist party, or Islamic governance model, Ennahda aspired to emulate. To my surprise at the time, not a single respondent volunteered the Egyptian Brotherhood as an inspiring example.

Instead, nahdawis at all levels tended to cast Ennahda as the enlightened cousin to the Egyptian Brotherhood's more recalcitrant older uncle. "We are related, yes, and we continue to be inspired by some of their ideas," said Ennahda leader Said Ferjani at the party's headquarters. "But we also have our own ideas ... and we have been moving forward for a long time. . . . We get our color [character] from Tunisia, which is often more open [than Egypt]."[11]

In fact, few nahdawis mentioned the Brotherhood at all unless explicitly prompted on whether it provided a model. "What about the Egyptian Muslim Brotherhood?" I pressed Yesmin Masmoudi, a 24-year-old who volunteered at Ennahda's youth wing in Sfax: "Ennahda took inspiration from Hassan al-Banna and other Brotherhood leaders over the years—can they be a model today?" She shook her head and smiled, waving a contradictory hand in the air. "Ask anyone in Ennahda. We are more advanced than the Brotherhood. We look to the Turkish model ... modern and Muslim at the same time."[12]

Interestingly, like Yesmin, the vast majority of nahdawis at all levels of the party offered Turkey's Justice and Development Party (AKP) as the most relevant model. They described AKP as embodying an enviable combination of piety, prosperity, and democratic credibility.[13] Ennahda president Rached Ghannouchi praised the Turkish model in August 2011, emphasizing the importance of pragmatic gradualism over maximalism: "AKP will gradually make Turkey a more Muslim country, through education, building the economy, and diversifying the media. That's our model—not law. Make people love Islam. Convince, don't coerce them."[14]

Party leaders, including Ghannouchi and other individuals who returned from exile, also frequently invoked Germany's Christian Democrats in summer 2011, saying that Ennahda likewise sees itself as a conservative democratic party with a religious reference that favors a liberal, open economy. Most Ennahda leaders at the time appeared less familiar with other regional Islamist parties like Morocco's Justice and Development Party (PJD) and characterized theocratic regimes in Iran and Saudi Arabia as hypocritical examples to avoid.

Whereas Ennahda leaders in 2011 saw Turkey's AKP and Germany's Christian Democrats as positive, relevant examples, they felt Egypt's Muslim Brotherhood could at times use *their* advice. "In Egypt the Brotherhood made the worst decision," said Osama Essaghir, an Ennahda Member of Parliament and member of the party's 150-member Shura Council.[15] "They decided to govern alone."

> One president, all alone with the powers. . . . That was very unwise. The day after [Brotherhood member Mohamed] Morsi won the [presidential] election, Sheikh Rached [Ghannouchi] flew to Egypt for one reason, just to tell Morsi one thing: do *not* govern alone.[16]

LONG-TERMISM

Leading voices in Ennahda expressed support for a long-term, minimalist approach well before Egypt's 2013 coup.[17] In June 2011, for example, Ghannouchi vowed that Ennahda would share power in a coalition government even if it won an outright majority in the October elections.[18] In making the case for strategic minimalism, Ennahda leaders frequently invoked the example of Algeria in 1990 and 1991, when the Islamic Salvation Front (FIS) won first municipal elections and then the first round of parliamentary elections. Their victory spooked Algeria's military regime, which aborted the elections and initiated a broad crackdown on Islamists—sparking a civil war that lasted over a decade and claimed as many as 200,000 lives.[19]

Ennahda leaders learned an important lesson from Algeria's experience, and from their own similar experience in 1989: namely, that prioritizing a politics of pragmatic gradualism—one that placed participation and long-term survival ahead of potentially fleeting short-term victories—represented the wisest path.[20] Unsurprisingly, given the Egyptian Brotherhood's comparatively maximalist approach, nahdawi frustrations with the Brotherhood frequently surfaced from late 2011 to mid-2013. "They are sacrificing a major opportunity to show that Islam and democracy are compatible," fumed one member of Ennahda's Executive Committee in December 2012. "This will hurt us if they keep on," the member said, acknowledging that Ennahda was often judged—unfairly, in their view—by the Brotherhood's actions.[21]

In what other Ennahda leaders later characterized as an effort to avert impending political disaster in Egypt, Ghannouchi delivered a speech in Cairo on June 4, 2013.[22] In the speech, Ghannouchi warned against "democracy of the majority," stressing that "a balance of power should be maintained." "Every society is diverse," he said, "and so we have to accept this diversity or face . . . conflict and chaos."[23]

One month later, on July 3, 2013, Mohamed Morsi was overthrown in a military coup that, though popular among many Egyptians at the time, heralded the utter reversal of Egypt's democratic transition. Nahdawis felt outraged by what they perceived as the antidemocratic overthrow of a justly elected president. Few in Ennahda's leadership, though, were truly surprised, having looked on with concern from Tunisia for months as Egypt's political situation deteriorated—partially, in their view, because of the Brotherhood's stubborn unilateralism.

In contrast to their relative equanimity after the coup, however, those same nahdawis were shocked by the subsequent massacre at Rabaa al-Adawiyya Square in Cairo, where approximately 1,000 people—most of them Brotherhood supporters—were killed a month later.[24] The United States and European Union responded tepidly to the coup and its bloody aftermath, reminding Ennahda leaders that—despite President Barack Obama's fleeting entreaty that America values "the dignity of the street vendor in Tunisia more than the raw power of the dictator"—the pre–Arab Spring paradigm, which prized authoritarian stability over democracy, still held sway in most Western capitals.[25] Regional support for Egypt's dictatorial new president, General Abdel Fattah al-Sissi, was even swifter, with Saudi Arabia and the United Arab Emirates bustling to bankroll his regime to the tune of billions of dollars.[26]

Such international support for Egypt's authoritarian reversal increased feelings of fear and isolation among nahdawis, who—despite firmly stressing that Ennahda was not a franchise of the Brotherhood— still felt a sense of ideological and historical kinship with it.[27] The coup in Egypt, its bloody aftermath, and the near complete absence of international condemnation against Sissi prompted Ennahda's leaders to take more seriously the possibility of democratic reversal in Tunisia. Many shuddered as they realized their country represented the sole democratic holdout in a region whose headwinds were blowing in a decidedly counterrevolutionary direction.

The coup and its aftermath also blunted Ennahda's increasingly critical approach to the Brotherhood. Nahdawis who had expressed strong reservations about the Brotherhood in interviews prior to the July 2013 coup seemed far more sympathetic and far less inclined to criticize afterward. This was especially true after the Rabaa massacre.[28] Some began wearing yellow Rabaa pins and stickers to demonstrate their solidarity with the victims. A huge number of nahdawis at every level of the party changed their Twitter and Facebook photos to the yellow Rabaa symbol. Many said Rabaa stood as a visceral reminder of the oppression they and their families experienced under Ben Ali. Counterrevolutionary reversal, which had previously struck some nahdawis as a distant possibility, suddenly seemed frightfully plausible.

THE RISE OF SALAFI-JIHADISM IN TUNISIA

Meanwhile, as the coup in Egypt was brewing, another regional shock— the sharp rise of violent Salafi-jihadism—was wreaking havoc at home in Tunisia.

The post-revolutionary rise of Salafi-jihadism in Tunisia—which pre-dated but ultimately intersected with the formation of the Islamic State—was a byproduct of both regional and local events. Tunisians had been heavily represented in prior waves of global jihad, including Afghanistan in the 1980s, Bosnia in the 1990s, and Iraq in the 2000s. Veterans of those prior jihads imprisoned in Tunisian jails under Ben

Ali used incarceration as a networking opportunity. Following their release in a general amnesty in spring 2011, some of those veteran jihadists, including the infamous firebrand Abu Iyadh, resumed recruiting. The laissez-faire landscape of post-revolutionary Tunisia, characterized by a temporary retraction of the security apparatus, also played a role. During that period, the stifling monolith of Ben Ali's regime—whose Interior Ministry strictly prohibited long beards, full-body veils (*niqabs*), and other forms of religious expression—receded to reveal a diverse population clamoring to be heard.

The young people who drove Tunisia's Salafi-jihadist surge tended to hail chiefly, but not entirely, from socioeconomically marginalized backgrounds.[29] Eager for meaning, rebellious, and imbued with a sense of revolutionary idealism, many viewed the Salafi-jihadist identity as exciting, countercultural, and hugely inspiring in its promise of a utopian ultra-Islamist future.[30] Salafi-jihadism in early post-revolutionary Tunisia was not a well-defined movement, but rather, as some scholars have recognized, a slippery "mouvance."[31] Some self-proclaimed Salafi-jihadists committed acts of violence, vandalizing Sufi shrines and attacking liquor stores. Others, however, claimed a forceful preaching campaign—not physical violence—was the proper way to interpret *jihad*, or holy struggle, in Tunisia.

While local and personal factors often drove interest in Salafism as a countercultural identity, one regional pull factor transformed it into something more transnational and more dangerous. Starting in mid-2011, the Syrian civil war, spurred by Bashar al-Assad's increasingly bloody crackdown, lured many young Tunisians to travel for violent jihad. Both male and female self-proclaimed Salafi-jihadists I spoke with in Tunisia between 2011 and early 2014 described the fight against Assad in rhapsodic terms as exciting and honorable—a chance at adventure, a shortcut to purpose, and an opportunity to liberate one's Muslim brothers and sisters from the yoke of brutality. The Syrian jihad began developing a "start-up" quality as the Islamic State rose to prominence in 2014, declaring itself a worldwide caliphate and gobbling up large swathes of territory.[32] Ultimately, more than 6,000 young Tunisians are estimated to have joined jihadist groups fighting in Iraq and Syria. Many of them joined the Islamic State.[33]

"OUR CHILDREN?" ENNAHDA'S EARLY APPROACH
TO SALAFI-JIHADISM

Many Tunisians, nahdawis included, were not entirely sure what to make of young Salafi-jihadists when they burst onto the scene in 2011. Ennahda was familiar with and had historical ties to "quietist" Salafism, or *salafiyya ʿilmiyya*.[34] But the newer trend of Salafi-jihadism—spearheaded by aggressive, sometimes violent young people who preached loudly and publically, frequently harassed women they regarded as inappropriately dressed, and sometimes attacked Sufi shrines—bewildered Ennahda.[35]

In 2011 and 2012, as Salafi-jihadists grew more visible—and disruptive—in Tunisia's public squares, Ennahda leaders missed vital opportunities to roundly condemn Salafi violence and instead tended to look on with a kind of puzzled pity. Most nahdawis initially regarded Salafi-jihadist youths as misguided victims of Ben Ali's religious oppression who needed socioeconomic and especially spiritual outreach.[36]

Ennahda members and leaders blamed Ben Ali for having undermined religious education in Tunisia to such an extent that young people—desperate for a sense of authenticity and meaning—turned to foreign Salafi-jihadist preachers online, often from Gulf states such as Saudi Arabia. Bourguiba, according to many nahdawis, had laid the groundwork for religious desiccation in Tunisia by sidelining the Zaytouna, Tunisia's historic center of religious learning, analogous to Egypt's al-Azhar. Yet it was Ben Ali, they insisted, who bore primary responsibility for the jihadist trend, because he took Bourguiba's approach much further, weakening the quality of Arabic language and religious education in public schools and vehemently suppressing nahdawi Islamists.

With no locally legitimate model of religiosity, nahdawis argued, an entire generation of young Tunisians were rendered vulnerable to Wahhabi-inspired literalism. Nahdawis characterized such literalism, which they said spread through online videos and publications created by preachers in the Gulf, as simplistic and inimical to Tunisia's tradition of Zaytouna-oriented reformism. The antidote, Ennahda argued, lay in reactivating locally legitimate sources of religious knowledge and scholarship. This meant reviving the Zaytouna as a seat of Islamic learning, improving the quality of religious education in schools, and engaging in religiously oriented civil society outreach to re-educate wayward young Salafis.

The other half of the solution, according to Ennahda, required promoting political inclusion for Salafis. Ennahda leaders hoped young Salafi-jihadists would be persuaded to support nonviolent political parties, such as a clutch of Salafi parties formed in 2011 and 2012. These included Hizb al-Asala (the Authenticity Party) and Jabhat al-Islah (the Reform Front), parties led by older men who advocated rigidly Islamist aims within the framework of multiparty democracy. Nahdawi leaders were great believers in the inclusion-moderation hypothesis—the idea, much studied by political scientists, that parties moderate as they participate in democratic systems. They believed that encouraging young Salafi-jihadists to participate politically, rather than excluding or oppressing them, would prompt them to integrate and moderate their positions.

Nahdawis' initial hesitation to adopt a securitized approach against Salafi-jihadists was heavily informed by their own experiences of oppression. Engagement, dialogue, Islamic education, and political inclusion, they felt, represented the best short-term options to contain and redirect jihadist anger, hopefully moving young Salafis toward milder, more realistic views.

This approach can be observed in a controversial leaked video, likely recorded in spring 2012, in which Rached Ghannouchi addressed a group of young Salafis. In the video, Ghannouchi entreats them to move slowly and consolidate gains lest—as in Algeria in 1991 and Tunisia in 1989—the speed of Islamist advancement spooks opponents. "We all went through the same and we suffered," Ghannouchi told them.

> Now you want to have a TV [station], radio [station], schools, and invite preachers. Why are you rushing things? . . . Do you think what we achieved cannot be taken away? This is what we thought when we were in Algeria in the nineties. . . . It turns out we misjudged the situation and went backwards.

But to the young Salafi-jihadists Ennahda's leaders were trying to mollify, the party's "*bishwaya bishwaya*" (slowly, slowly) approach seemed patronizing and paternalistic. "They constantly refer to us as their 'children' and try to tell us how we should behave," said Houda, a 24-year-old student, in August 2012. Houda identified as Salafi-jihadist and a member of Ansar al-Sharia in Tunisia (AST), the most prominent Salafi-jihadist group in Tunisia between the revolution and the rise of the Islamic State.[37]

> Be calm, our children. Go slowly, they say. But all their going slowly hasn't brought any results. They gave up sharia, they listen to the West.... I don't see what makes them so Islamic. They use lies to manipulate people just like any other party. Maybe they should be listening to us! We're going to make a change.[38]

Houda was one of 18 Salafi-jihadist youths, mostly women, whom I interviewed throughout 2012 and 2013, sometimes having meals with their families and staying over at their homes. Eleven of the eighteen had parents who identified with, but were not active in, Ennahda. Most of their families came from poorer urban or rural areas, and none of the nahdawi parents held university degrees.

Houda's mother and father, although not active in any Ennahda structures, supported the party and voted for it in the 2011 elections. Both expressed confusion with their daughter's choice to wear the niqab, or face veil, which she donned in February 2011, a month after the revolution. They discouraged her from participating in Ansar al-Sharia activities like *da'wa* (preaching) tents in which she and other young women would distribute conservative religious pamphlets to passersby. "I don't know why she does this," said Houda's mother to me in the kitchen while cleaning up after dinner one night. "The *hijab* (headscarf) is enough. She doesn't need to wear the niqab. I guess she's making a statement."[39]

These parents were not core Ennahda activists or leaders. Yet their experience as parents who identified with Ennahda's brand of center-right Islamism but felt deeply confused by their children's preference for radical Salafism paralleled Ennahda leaders' tendency to feel almost parental responsibility for the Salafi-jihadist youth they believed had gone astray. Nahdawi leaders' desire to calm down rather than crack down on Salafi-jihadist youth, their reluctance to employ harsh security measures against them, and their habit of referring to them as "children" who had lost their way all reflected a generational divide that sometimes manifested itself within families.

CRACKDOWN AND (RE)SECURITIZATION

Throughout 2012 and 2013, acts of Salafi-jihadist violence intensified. The September 2012 attack on the U.S. embassy and neighboring American school in Tunis was followed by two high-profile political assassinations in 2013. Each act of violence was planned and perpetrated by Salafi-jihadist groups, significantly increasing the political cost of maintaining a soft, inclusion-driven approach to Salafi-jihadism and the rise of Salafism more generally.[40] Meanwhile, more and more families were losing children to the jihad in Syria, with thousands of families affected. Fathers were filmed on national news programs journeying to Syria to find their sons; weeping mothers clasped pictures of their children, wondering whether they were still alive.

By Spring 2013, it had become clear to Ennahda leaders that their approach wasn't working. In April 2013, Ennahda declared Ansar al-Sharia a terror organization. In May 2013, the Ennahda-led coalition government faced off with Ansar al-Sharia in what was aptly termed a "public game of chicken" when the group tried to hold a large public conference in the city of Kairouan, located about three hours south of Tunis.[41] The government won. The conference organizers were denied a permit to hold the event. The conference date passed with less tumult than expected, despite some clashes between law enforcement and Ansar al-Sharia supporters in poor suburbs of Tunis where the Salafi-jihadist presence was especially strong.

For a large segment of the Tunisian public, though, as well as many scholars and analysts, Ennahda's response came too little too late. The party was roundly criticized for adopting a "slow and ambiguous" approach to Salafi-jihadism.[42] Its missteps were deftly exploited by Nidaa Tunis, an anti-Islamist party founded in mid-2012 driven by ex-officials from the Bourguiba and Ben Ali regimes as well as leftists and business elites. In Tunisia's fall 2014 elections, Nidaa Tunis cruised to parliamentary and presidential victories on promises to govern as capable *rijal al-dawla* (statesmen) who would restore the integrity and prestige of the state after years of nahdawi mismanagement—failures Nidaa ascribed not just to incompetence, but to what it claimed were Ennahda's covert links with violent extremism.

Since cracking down on Ansar al-Sharia, Ennahda has advocated a more securitized approach to Salafi-jihadism. Nahdawis I interviewed on the subject in 2013 and 2014 expressed discomfort with ongoing police brutality in Tunisia and the renewed spread of certain forms of Ben Ali–era police abuse. These have often targeted young people in poorer neighborhoods, particularly those sporting visible markers of Salafi conservatism like beards and niqabs. Though nahdawis privately criticized these trends, they have also stressed that the rise of Salafi-jihadism locally, embedded in the broader regional context of the Islamic State and transnational jihadist terrorism, has increased the political cost of voicing objection to troubling security measures. Hoping to be seen as a responsible team player, Ennahda adopted a more defensive, risk-averse posture on Salafism and security.

Following the Bardo museum attack of March 2015, which killed 22 and injured more than 50 people, for instance, Ennahda immediately released a statement voicing its support for a new antiterrorism draft bill that permitted extended incommunicado detention and weakened due process protection for terrorism suspects.[43] "If we say anything against this law, people will conclude that we support the Salafis ideologically," said one member of Ennahda's Shura Council. "Then we'll be back where we were in 2011. . . . That's too big a risk."[44] The law passed in July 2015 with unanimous nahdawi support.

THE BARDO CRISIS

Dissatisfaction with Tunisia's post-revolutionary government had been brewing since the Ennahda-led coalition assumed power in late 2011. Tunisians' everyday, lived realities—marked by high inflation, low wages, persistent unemployment, widespread corruption, and fear of insecurity—fell depressingly short of their revolutionary expectations. By mid-2013, unemployment rates remained stubbornly high, precious few visible infrastructure improvements had been made, and terrorism seemed to be rising. Such broad-based grievances played a major role in provoking opposition to the Ennahda-led coalition. Compounding these were suspicions that Ennahda's Islamist identity made it ideologically sympathetic to, if not actively supportive of, Salafi-jihadism.

Opposition figures in the leftist front, Jebha Chaabia, and Nidaa Tunis characterized Ennahda as an incompetent, retrograde group of outsiders whose attempt to import Brotherhood-style Islamism from the East had no place in indigenous Tunisian culture. Both groups sought to associate Ennahda with the failures of Egypt's Muslim Brotherhood and accused it of enabling jihadism in Tunisia. Jebha Chaabia, which lost one of its MPs, Chokri Belaid, to a jihadist-perpetrated assassination on February 6, 2013, held Ennahda directly responsible for his death.

Belaid's assassination triggered massive street protests in Tunis. Dissatisfaction with what many Tunisians saw as either Ennahda's incompetence, at best, or its Islamist-inspired indulgence of violent extremism, at worst, was widespread. Opposition parties, meanwhile, saw opportunity in the midst of tragedy as Belaid's assassination shook Ennahda's claims to popular legitimacy and support.

Ennahda's opponents felt further empowered by the success of Egypt's *Tamarrod* (Rebellion) movement in summer 2013. Tamarrod, which originally aimed to force Morsi to call early elections, ended up triggering the July 3, 2013 coup that toppled him from power. Secular critics of Ennahda formed a copycat Tunisian Tamarrod movement, flanked by support from the political parties Nidaa Tunis and Jebha Chaabia.

Leaders of these parties, including Nidaa Tunis founder and president Beji Caid Essebsi, had decried the Ennahda-led government as illegitimate since late 2012, when it became clear the National Constituent Assembly (NCA) would not fulfill its pre-election pledge of completing a new constitution and arranging parliamentary elections within a one-year timeline.[45] The coup against Morsi in Egypt, however, injected Ennahda's critics with a boost of confidence.

Essebsi dubbed the coup Egypt's "second revolution" and, along with other opponents of Ennahda, redoubled calls for Ennahda and its coalition partners to cede power to an unelected group of supposedly apolitical technocrats. They also called for the Constituent Assembly—the elected legislature drafting a new and hopefully democratically representative constitution—to be disbanded. Such a scenario would have enabled Nidaa Tunis and Jebha Chaabia to oust Ennahda and secure levers of governmental power through non-electoral means.

Despite the rise of a relatively small Tamarrod movement in Tunisia and the rhetorical support opposition leaders lent to a soft coup, efforts to topple Tunisia's governing coalition did not enjoy the backing of a large protest movement[46]—not, at least, until a second political assassination took place.

On July 25, 2013, jihadists assassinated Mohamed Brahmi. Like Chokri Belaid, Brahmi was an MP in Jebha Chaabia, which already held Ennahda responsible for Belaid's death. Brahmi's assassination tossed a lit match into a powder keg of political tension, transforming an already tense situation into a moment that threatened the entirety of the democratic transition.

Thousands of protesters streamed nightly into Bardo square, directly outside the Constituent Assembly, chanting for the government to resign. Ennahda balked, unwilling to cede its democratic mandate to a nebulous group of Nidaa-friendly technocrats who may or may not have derailed the transition. Nidaa Tunis, for its part, drew on rhetoric used in the anti-Morsi protests, claiming that, though unelected, their party possessed "*shar'iya al-shar'a*" (street legitimacy). Throughout August 2013, Ennahda and Nidaa Tunis rallied competing groups of protesters in the capital.[47] Though Ennahda claimed electoral legitimacy, the competition quickly became centered on questions of street legitimacy, with both actors vying to see which party could gather the largest number of people.

The Bardo standoff was ultimately resolved through a protracted National Dialogue process. A quartet of civil society actors, led by Tunisia's powerful trade union, the UGTT, later won a Nobel Peace Prize for its successful reconciliation efforts.[48] In January 2014, outgoing Ennahda prime minister Ali Laarayedh signed Tunisia's new constitution into law. Two days later he handed power to a technocratic caretaker government. The transition, though threatened, continued.

THE LUSTRATION ISSUE: TESTING ENNAHDA'S LONG-TERMISM

A critical component of resolving the Bardo crisis was Ennahda leaders' ultimate willingness not only to step down from power, but also to oppose passage of a controversial lustration law. This legislation, referred to as *qanun tahseen al-thawra* (law to immunize, or protect, the revolution) by its proponents and as *qanun al-iqsa* (exclusion law) by its opponents, would have prohibited ex-members of Ben Ali's disbanded party, the Constitutional Democratic Rally (RCD), from contesting Tunisia's 2014 elections.

Throughout the constitutional drafting process, Ennahda had—largely as a result of pressure placed upon it by civil society groups—compromised on a number of ideological issues. It walked back language describing men and women as "complementary," retracted an article that would have criminalized blasphemy, and abandoned efforts to include sharia as a source of legislation.[49] None of these classically Islamist sticking points, however, created as much discord within Ennahda itself as the debate over abandoning the electoral lustration law, which was immensely popular inside the party.

The Congress for the Republic (CPR), one of Enanhda's coalition partners and the most vocally pro–revolution party in the NCA, first proposed lustration legislation in spring 2012 to prohibit ex-members of the RCD from contesting elections for five years. Ennahda cast an internal vote of support for the law at its ninth party congress in July 2012. Over the following year, leading members of Ennahda generally described lustration as a natural and necessary step to protect the revolution.[50] They referenced other post-authoritarian countries that adopted such legislation, claiming lustration would protect Tunisia's nascent democracy from old regime actors.

By summer 2013, it appeared the NCA would likely adopt the lustration law. On June 28, 2013, parties in the NCA voted to move discussion of the legislation forward onto the floor for general debate. The law enjoyed broad cross-ideological support: the CPR and the majority of Ennahda parliamentarians, as well as many members of anti-Islamist leftist trends, strongly favored lustration.

As the summer drew to a close, however, some members of Ennahda's leadership came to view lustration as politically infeasible. The combined effects of the Egypt coup, Mohamed Brahmi's assassination, and the subsequent Bardo crisis severely constricted Ennahda's margin of strategic maneuver, raising the potential costs of pursuing lustration. Even at a time of relative stability, lustration legislation could have created a constituency for a coup. Passage of a lustration law would have disqualified Beji Caid Essebsi, founder of Nidaa Tunis and scion of Tunisia's anti-Islamist opposition—a man most Tunisians, even as early as 2013, believed would become the next president—from holding office.[51]

In such a volatile context, pursuit of lustration had become especially dangerous, something which Rached Ghannouchi realized. On August 25, 2013, he appeared on Nessma TV, a channel especially popular with Nidaa Tunis supporters, to reassure viewers that the lustration law would not be passed. Such reassurance would, he hoped, quell Nidaa's fears of electoral marginalization, possibly luring them to the bargaining table.[52] The following week, Ghannouchi met with Essebsi in Paris, raising speculation that a negotiated settlement to the impasse might be possible.

Ghannouchi's willingness to sacrifice lustration on the altar of a negotiated political settlement created immense tension within Ennahda. Ghannouchi superseded the will of the party's top governing body, the Shura Council, which had consistently expressed support for lustration. Many Shura Council members criticized Ghannouchi for both subverting strongly valued institutional procedure and sacrificing revolutionary principles.

Council members defied Ghannouchi's wishes by pushing again for the passage of lustration legislation, in conjunction with Ennahda's secular partners in the coalition government. In mid-December 2013, the NCA, with the support of most Ennahda MPs, attempted to attach a lustration provision to comprehensive transitional justice legislation. Realizing the continued popularity of lustration within Ennahda's legislative bloc, as well as its immense political risks, Ghannouchi went to the NCA to personally lobby Ennahda MPs to abandon lustration.

The December 2013 transitional justice law ultimately passed without a lustration provision. But the issue of lustration came up one last time on April 30, 2014. Despite Ghannouchi's months of lobbying, Article 167—which would have barred anyone who held a position of responsibility in the RCD from running in Tunisia's 2014 parliamentary elections—very nearly passed. Torn between political imperatives and revolutionary principles, many Ennahda MPs known for their strong attendance record punted by either abstaining or failing to attend the

Constituent Assembly on the day of voting. Ultimately, thirty-nine Ennahda MPs voted for the article, directly contravening Ghannouchi's leadership. Only five voted against. In the end, Article 167 failed to pass by just a single vote—that of an Ennahda MP who, at the last minute, switched his vote of support to one of abstention.

In his attempt to convince Ennahda MPs that lustration was best avoided, Ghannouchi used both political and religious arguments. Politically, Ghannouchi stressed that Tunisia was in a fragile period of transitional politics. In such a period, he argued, apparent gains could easily be reversed. Inclusive power-sharing, therefore, represented the best path to success—both for the self-interested survival of Ennahda and for the viability of Tunisia's transition as a whole. Religiously, Ghannouchi often invoked a parable involving the Prophet Mohamed to illustrate the wisdom of inclusion. "When the Prophet Mohamed stood victorious in Mecca," Ghannouchi said, "he told the infidels who did not believe in him, 'Adhabu, fa-antum al-tulaqa' (Go, you are set free)."

> He did not practice *iqsa* (exclusion) against them and did not pros-
> ecute them but instead included them in his army and they became
> leaders. And if it wasn't for that the Arabian Peninsula . . . would
> have fought civil war instead of spreading Islam all over the world.[53]

Many grassroots nahdawis, however, were reluctant to embrace such religiously rooted rationales. For many, the realpolitik facing Ennahda in the wake of the Egyptian coup was clear: offer political space to the old regime or risk an Islamist-excluding "second revolution" in Tunisia. "It makes me sick, but it is common sense," said Samia, a 46-year-old Ennahda supporter from Bizerte. "Before the coup in Egypt I would have said no—it is wrong to let these people back in, but now it is the only choice we have."[54]

The wife of one Ennahda member in the Mellasine neighborhood of Tunis jokingly said she respected Ghannouchi's attempt to find a religious explanation for abandoning lustration:

> He was for it, and now he is against it, and he's doing this [she flipped
> through a book laughingly] to find a reason why it is right. . . . It is

not right, and we [my husband and I] know that, but it is smart. . . .
So we will be smart.[55]

TRANSITION POLITICS

Many members of Ennahda strongly questioned both the wisdom and morality of abandoning lustration, which they considered an important protection as well as a proud statement of revolutionary principle. In the bitter months following the final vote against lustration, some nahdawis thought back to the Egypt coup and gleaned an exclusionary, rather than inclusive, lesson: that the Brotherhood's willingness to cooperate with *fulul* (old regime) actors, particularly the military, sowed the seeds of its downfall. Ennahda, they feared, might be repeating those mistakes. Such fears reached an apex in the fall and winter of 2014, when Nidaa Tunis proved victorious not only in the presidential election, which nahdawis had anticipated, but also in the parliamentary elections, which they had expected to win.

The active lobbying of Ghannouchi and other leaders helped quell these fears. Crucially, so too did Nidaa Tunis's willingness to include Ennahda in the governing coalitions it formed in 2015 and 2016. Ennahda became a crucial—if sometimes awkward—coalition partner for Nidaa Tunis, and continued integrating itself in Tunisian politics. Nahdawis' worst fears—namely that Nidaa would use its power to dismantle democracy and persecute Ennahda members and their families—had not come to pass.

Ghannouchi and other "long-termist" leaders deserve credit for creating the conditions that facilitated these outcomes. Ennahda leaders' ability to act if not rightly, then at least smartly, regarding lustration created an incentive structure more favorable to democratic transition. Allowing Essebsi and other former regime officials to run in elections heightened the appeal of staying in the democratic game for Nidaa Tunis and other leaders of the anti-Ennahda opposition.

RETHINKING ISLAMISM

Ennahda's compromise on lustration reflects the extent to which its leaders are recasting Islamism as an explicitly local, nationally bounded political project. Ennahda is wrapping itself more and more tightly in the Tunisian flag and embracing its Tunisian history. Building on the compromises pushed by Ghannouchi and other members of Ennahda's top brass, the party is on the path toward normalizing itself as a responsible political player in Tunisia. Accusations that Ennahda represents an imported franchise of the Egyptian Brotherhood, or a dangerous cancer that needs to be excised from the Tunisian body politic, still exist but are heard less frequently today than in the early days of Tunisia's transition.

The year 2016 was critical for the party. Ennahda leaders publically reiterated that the party's intellectual history and inspirations were rooted in figures from Tunisian history, ranging from the proto-feminist Tahar Haddad and anti-Islamist former president Habib Bourguiba—figures much vaunted by Nidaa Tunis and other secularly oriented Tunisians—to Bourguiba's arch-rival Salah Ben Youssef and the Tunisian religious scholar Sheikh Tahar Ben Achour. Ennahda also made the savvy move at its May 2016 congress of publicly disavowing the Islamist label, preferring to be known instead as a "Muslim democratic" party. It also took further steps toward "normalizing" the party by (a) facilitating broader membership of the party and (b) prohibiting members who preach in mosques from holding any local or national leadership roles. Such steps, combined with Ennahda's concerted efforts to Tunisify the party's identity and intellectual origins, offer fascinating windows into a moment of party normalization.[56]

Despite the tensions that dominated 2013 and the high levels of distrust between their two parties, Ghannouchi and Essebsi—often wryly referred to as the two sheikhs—were able to build a productive working relationship. Many Tunisians, however, have criticized this alliance as exclusionary and anti-revolutionary. High-level horse trading between Nidaa and Ennahda—driven in part by Ennahda's determination to secure its own survival and political integration—have, some say, sanctioned a form of backroom politics that puts the status quo ahead of much-needed reforms.

The crowning moment of nahdawi normalization, which highlighted the increasingly cozy relationship between Essebsi and Ghannouchi, came in May 2016 when Essebsi himself delivered the nationally broadcast keynote address at Ennahda's 10th congress. A stadium packed full of Ennahda members stood and cheered when Essebsi entered. They were relieved that, rather than throwing nahdawis back in prison, as many had feared, Essebsi was instead delivering the most powerful endorsement of Ennahda's legitimacy to date.[57]

For Ennahda, a movement long ostracized as pro-extremist and anti-Tunisian, the political dividends derived from such relationships is immensely valuable. Ennahda's core leaders have indeed put a premium on survival during the transition period. Though Ennahda leaders prefer not to use the word survivalism, they do acknowledge and defend having adopted a strategy of pragmatic minimalism during Tunisia's transition. Preserving Tunisia's transition and gradually building democratic institutions, they claim, take precedence over pursuing high-risk reforms that would engender direct confrontation with Tunisia's old regime elites. Ennahda strongly believes that such progress cannot happen if their party is locked out of Tunisian politics. Preserving Ennahda's seat at the table is—from the perspective of Ennahda's leaders—a critical precondition for preserving Tunisia's democratic transition itself. Conversely, Ennahda believes that its normalization in Tunisian politics will contribute toward the consolidation of the country's still fragile democratic transition.

SELLING SURVIVALISM

Local fallout from the twin shocks of Egypt's coup and the rise of Salafi-jihadism fueled the Bardo crisis of 2013—a pivotal moment that tested Ennahda's commitment to long-term pragmatism. Led by Ghannouchi, Ennahda's top brass arguably passed that test, pursuing an approach predicated on canny compromise and caution. Rather than hastily unpacking a box of ideological aims, Ennahda appraised its surroundings before moving forward, aware of the fragility inherent in "transition politics."

That approach, though, while shrewd, lacks the dynamism traditionally associated with principle-driven movements, be they revolutionary or religious in nature. Although card-carrying Ennahda members voted loyally for Ennahda in the 2014 elections, a series of compromises—especially on issues of revolutionary principle like lustration—impelled many to grow less active in the party's local and regional structures. Ennahda now faces the challenge of creatively packaging its brand of cautious conservatism to accomplish two goals: rallying its existing base and recruiting new party members. Recognizing this, Ennahda made proactive changes at its 10th congress to facilitate party membership and broaden its brand. Yet Ennahda's aversion to principled risk-taking may hamper its ability to craft an inspiring political message that energizes existing supporters and enables the party to expand beyond its historic base.

Ennahda's top leaders believe gaining electoral ground necessitates first gaining credibility as a Tunisian Islamist—or, as Ennahda has now officially labeled itself, a Muslim democratic party—one that places national stability and safeguarding the transition over specific matters of religious or revolutionary principle. This minimalist approach does not preclude the possibility of future ideological activism, but instead puts off issue-driven politics for a later date—ostensibly when Tunisia has weathered the storm of interim, transitional challenges and Ennahda's seat at the political table is assured.

Selling survivalism—be it the survival of one's own party or that of the transition itself—may prove trickier than selling old regime nostalgia, populist rejection of the existing system, or dreams of a rosier utopia. It remains to be seen how Ennahda will translate its approach to a fresh crop of potential party newcomers, and whether its base will stay loyal if normalization progresses enough that nahdawis no longer view voting Ennahda as an act of existential self-preservation.

3

Morocco

Avi Max Spiegel

AT THE 2006 ANNUAL conference of the youth wing of the main Islamist party in Morocco, the Justice and Development Party (PJD), the program was filled with sessions led by party leaders and activists on topics ranging from human rights to local governance, mobilization, and the Internet.[1] It also featured a session with representatives from Islamist parties across the Middle East and North Africa. When I asked a party leader why they had invited these guests from outside Morocco, he replied that it was important to "learn from them."

The admission was tinged with humility, with the implication that it was Morocco's Islamists who had the learning to do and that other older and more experienced Islamist parties could instruct them and show them the way.[2] In the following years, the party dispatched senior officials to Turkey to meet with the similarly named Justice and Development Party, the AKP. In the three years that followed, before the PJD dominated the elections in 2011 (and again in 2016) that propelled it to the prime ministership, its activists embarked on many such exploratory trips and conferences, including to Cairo to meet with the organization that had originally inspired its own founding, the Egyptian Muslim Brotherhood.[3]

As the Arab Spring spread across the Middle East, the northwest African country of Morocco barely seemed to register on the wider geopolitical map. Protests were smaller than in neighboring countries; its leader—King Mohamed VI—never faced the existential threats that other authoritarian rulers did. The king also appeared to stay in front of the protests, ushering in constitutional reforms that allowed him to retain the perceived mantle of reform. Even when Islamists appeared to take advantage of political openings across the region, events in Morocco barely registered in the Western consciousness. Attention seemed to focus on Islamist parties in Egypt and Tunisia—even though it was Morocco in 2011 which witnessed the first democratically-elected Sunni Islamist head of government in the Arab world.[4]

Has Morocco's moment finally arrived? As mainstream Islamist parties—those with roots in the Muslim Brotherhood model—appear to be on the wane throughout the Arab world, both of Morocco's Islamist movements are enduring. Indeed, it is not just the PJD that survived the Arab Spring. The country's largest Islamist movement, Al Adl Wal Ishan, or the Justice and Spirituality Movement (Al Adl)—a movement that boycotts elections and evades legality—has also navigated the revolutionary period and its aftermath with considerable agility.

In the wake of the 2013 Egyptian coup—the coup that spelled the end of the Muslim Brotherhood's dominance in Egyptian politics—I once again asked a PJD official about his relationships with Islamists across the region. When I reminded him of those earlier trips to study other parties, his response was telling, perhaps signaling that the power dynamics had slowly shifted. "Now," he said, with a new air of self-confidence, "people should study us."

This chapter heeds this call. Indeed, Morocco increasingly offers an important case study for understanding new and emerging paths of political Islam, or, in other words, how—and in what forms—Islamism and the political process can continue to interact. The Moroccan regime has often attempted, usually overambitiously, to hold itself out as a model for many things: for democracy, for reform, for so-called soft authoritarianism.[5] But today, perhaps, the country does offer something exceptional: a glimpse into sustaining forms of political Islam and of Islamist parties still holding onto relevance, if not (limited) power.[6]

This chapter seeks to explain the resilience (and relative success) of mainstream Islamism in Morocco and, in the process, help elucidate the forces shaping the next generation of political Islam. This resilience cannot simply be explained by the fact that Islamists in Morocco have come to understand Islam differently than their counterparts elsewhere (of course they did; all such actors exhibit unique, even idiosyncratic, religiopolitical worldviews). It is also not that they are luckier, more learned, more competent, or even somehow more ideologically committed to the political process than other Islamists.

Instead, I will argue here that their relative success can be explained by the confluence of three factors, or what I term "the three Cs": context, control, and competition. First, by "context," I mean the specific political and constitutional context in which Moroccan Islamists function. I am not referring here simply to the existence of a monarchical system—for not all monarchies are equal. Rather, I point to how the monarchy has exercised its authority: allowing Islamist political participation, but only within certain proscribed lines. Such lines often constrain Islamists' power and perhaps broader ideological pursuits but paradoxically also help ensure their survival and continued appeal.

Second, by "control," I focus here on the extent to which these groups exercise control over and within their internal organizations, specifically between the party (*hizb*) and its allied religious wing or movement (*haraka*). Largely unique among such movements in the region, Islamist groups in Morocco have mostly subsumed their affiliated religious units—not the other way around—to political imperatives and the authority of the party apparatus. Such an organizational relationship bears considerable strategic fruit, enabling the party to deploy the religious units at will and allowing the party to maintain and expand its base by offering a unique space to develop discipline among members, religiously oriented activism, and even internal opposition.

Third, and finally, by "competition," I am referring to the relationship of Al Adl and the PJD. The nature of this competition—specifically the way in which each continues to evolve in relation to the other and to cleverly seek relative market share—has allowed each to carve out unique appeal. Moreover, contrary to expectations, regional and domestic change—including the Arab Spring, the Egyptian coup, and the rise of the Islamic State—has not adversely affected these movements' trajectories. Both movements have, in fact, successfully navigated the tumult by expanding their appeal. They have done so by selling themselves as exceptional and unique—by promoting the idea that their approach, evidenced largely by their mere survival, is working.

ISLAMISTS IN GOVERNMENT

Islamists of the PJD spent close to three decades trying to form a political party, one that could finally participate in elections. After breaking from the country's first Islamist movement, the illegal Harakat al-Shabiba al-Islamiyya (Movement of Islamic Youth) in the 1970s, its early leaders experimented with various tactics: they altered their organizational configurations, merged with other parties, and even changed their name.[7] Yet, the ultimate obstacle to their participation— that is, the major stumbling block to the regime approving their multiple applications for party formation—was *not* that they represented a nascent political threat. (Indeed, during this time, the state allowed socialists, for example, to compete in elections, and even form the first ever "alternance" or opposition government.)[8]

When Islamists of the PJD finally formed their political party, they did so under the regulations set by the country's interior ministry and the king himself. They would be permitted to formally participate in elections, it turned out, only if they agreed not to challenge the religious foundations of the state—not to dispute the king's role as "Commander of the Faithful," or what the king termed "heresy." For an Islamist party with ideological roots in the Muslim Brotherhood, to cede religious legitimacy to the state would appear antithetical to its goals, or at the very least a difficult compromise to make.

Yet, the PJD's founders ultimately relented.[9] Senior leaders even went so far as to give up fundamental early goals—the creation of an Islamic state. They would cease to pursue such a state, one leading activist claimed, because the Moroccan state, under the leadership of the king, "was already one."[10] The PJD followed this path because even in those early years it was primarily motivated by its own survival. Party leaders needed to expand and maintain their base and compete with local Islamist competitors, particularly a growing Al Adl, by offering something no one else did: electoral participation. They also needed to take into account regional realities, namely civil war in nearby Algeria[11] as well as meet and pre-empt the looming threat of state repression.[12]

Whether these changes arose partly as a result of belief or tactics (or both), the party that emerged has capitalized on, and even internalized, these strategies. They have driven the way the PJD campaigns for office, how it mobilizes its base, how it devises its organizational and party structures, and ultimately, how it governs.

Consider the PJD's path to the prime ministership itself, an electoral success once deemed unimaginable by its members, the general population, and even the state. For the first elections in which they were allowed to participate in 1997, activists agreed to vote for another existing party.[13] In the elections of 2002, activists only contested a limited number of seats. In the local elections following the 2003 Casablanca bombings (often referred to as Morocco's 9/11), they agreed—once again at the behest of the monarchy—to limit the districts they would contest, hoping to avoid exacerbating tensions in the country.

When the party grappled with how to respond to electoral setbacks in the 2007 elections, it decided to accommodate rather than antagonize the state by electing as its leader Abdelilah Benkirane, who had a long-standing history of deference toward the monarchy. When the Arab Spring hit Morocco in 2011, the PJD opted, not surprisingly, to remain for the most part on the sidelines. Some party members voiced sympathetic notes about the protests, but in the main they worried that challenging the king would risk destabilizing the country and, more selfishly, disrupt their own long-awaited path to power.

Further, when PJD members contested elections in 2011, they agreed to give up their biggest mobilizing space—the mosque—and abide by earlier government rules that forbade parties from campaigning in places of worship. Indeed, they ran a campaign largely bereft of mentions of religion, instead focusing largely on opposing other parties and promising to renew the political process itself rather than opposing the state. The party stressed bread-and-butter issues, including job creation, unemployment, corruption, and minimum wage increases. In a typical campaign-related video, the head of PJD Youth, Khalid Bukkharri, implores voters to support the PJD because it can rid the political process of corruption.[14]

Once the PJD assumed office, it did so all the while under the king's auspices. Under rules set forth in the country's new constitution of 2011, the party that won the majority of votes would finally be guaranteed a right to the prime ministership. (Up until then, this was not assured. When the king had the power to choose whomever he wanted, such as after the 2002 elections, he looked past the election results and appointed a technocrat.) But while the new constitution paved the way for a PJD-led government, it also significantly regulated and constrained it. The king still maintained the power to veto appointments and to appoint, in the first place, the most critical ministries: the Ministries of Islamic Affairs and Defense, among others.

Benkirane's personable, even folksy, style has managed to transcend some of these structural constraints. His popularity is unprecedented in contemporary Morocco for a politician other than the king, whose own approval rating runs high compared to the abysmal ratings of other politicians. Benkirane addresses crowds in local dialects and appears to be personally unaffected by the spoils of power. For instance, his relatives told me how he still buys his furniture at used furniture open-air markets outside of Rabat. At one campaign event in 2015, Benkirane could not hold back his tears as he marveled at the thousands of people assembled to see him. The crowds gathered seemed to revel in Benkirane's display of emotion, drowning out his words with applause. His popularity is such that he reportedly now finally has a bodyguard.[15]

Benkirane has shown a willingness, also unique for Moroccan politicians, to speak out against the regime and even, at times, the king himself. Benkirane often rails, for example, about long-standing state interests and the entrenched economic and political forces that curtail his party's ability to rule, using metaphors such as "crocodiles" and "ghosts" to connote their omnipresence and hidden power.[16] Such statements clearly implicate the king himself, who controls the largest portions of the economy.

Some scholars have argued that such statements and Benkirane's popularity pose unprecedented challenges to the stability of the Moroccan regime, but such a view is misleading; in fact, the opposite is largely true.[17] Benkirane's antagonistic statements toward the ruling regime are exceptions, not the rule, and should be understood not as new challenges to the regime, but rather as well-timed strategic efforts to appeal to oppositional forces within the country, including anti-regime sentiment within his own party base and within competitor organizations like Al Adl. Indeed, Benkirane and his deputies have consistently fixated on party strategy and survival and on controlling party structures. Youth activists reported that Benkirane himself, as sitting prime minister, had a say in which candidates ran for head of the youth wing.[18]

Most of the time, Benkirane went out of his way to remind the public of the dominance of the king. In March 2015, he told party members that "Morocco has no future if we enter into conflict with our king."[19] The imagery of his speech was also significant: Benkirane spoke next to a framed photo of the king placed on a pedestal beside him. The king's picture was larger than Benkirane himself.[20]

Nowhere is the party's ability to survive more on display than in its evolving internal organization. The PJD arose from Tawhid wal Islah (Movement of Unity and Reform). But when the party was formed it had to decide whether to disband the "affiliated religion movement," to subsume it within the party, or to keep it alive as a separate entity. The party chose the third option, largely as a way to continue to be able to mobilize as many young people as possible. The movement continues to exist but remains largely devoted to supporting party mobilization, using explicitly religious messages to recruit supporters and rally the base. Its presence and activities, which largely consist of weekly Quranic study sessions for movement members, allow the party to attract young people interested more in religion than in politics while also enabling the party to assert control and discipline. The movement's organizational make-up, originally modeled loosely after the Muslim Brotherhood's *usra* or "family" model in which individuals were internally "promoted" based on how many new members they managed to recruit, has evolved into a sophisticated system more focused on the development of new party leaders. Activists frequently report that to be successful in the party, one must be active in the movement.[21]

Having a "separate" movement also gives the party plausible deniability over more controversial issues, allowing its newspaper (*Attajdid*) to write on topics that might appeal to diverse constituencies, including more conservative Islamists. The extent to which the movement has become part and parcel of the party machine was evident in the election of its new head in 2014. Both leading candidates had party roots: one was the party's former secretary general (and the country's former foreign minister) and the other was a former close government aide to the sitting prime minister and party secretary general, Benkirane.

PJD officials still evoke religion, but almost never in opposition to the state. In a debate over "freedom of conscience" in 2013, it changed its views to align with the monarchy, cementing its position that the king maintain the sole power to dictate religious authority. It also abided by a 2013 state edict that prohibited religious leaders, including imams, from running for office. Instead, for party officials, "Islam" itself often becomes a stand-in for public "morality" or "traditional values" and a means with which to reach its religiously conservative base. Since assuming office, such examples of strategic framing include (in) famous comments on women's place in the home, Islamic banking, Jennifer Lopez, or even portrayals of the Prophet Mohamed in Western movies.[22] Indeed, party leaders have taken to calling other political parties (particularly the monarchist Istiqlal Party) the "mafia," warning Moroccans of giving back control of the political process to secular and, therefore, unethical politicians.[23]

Regional and local competition compelled the PJD to double down on its strategies, particularly in the wake of the Egyptian military's coup and crackdown against the Muslim Brotherhood and its president Mohamed Morsi in 2013. The effects of Morsi's fall were felt not just in Egypt, where the Brotherhood, its affiliated political party, and even any allegedly "sympathetic" journalists, officials, protesters, or mere onlookers have at various points been arrested, jailed, beaten, and killed. The coup and its aftermath, including the fate of Tunisia's Ennahda party (discussed earlier in chapter 2), were viewed across the region as a challenge to the Islamist experiment in governance and as signifying the resurgence of pre–Arab Spring power structures.

The PJD in Morocco was not immune to these developments. After the coup in Egypt, newspapers in the country wondered whether the PJD face a similar fate. (One newspaper headline featured a picture of Benkirane with the headline: "Is he next?") The second-largest party in parliament, Istiqlal, seized on this political opening and announced its departure from the coalition government, with the aim of bringing down the PJD-led government. Istiqlal echoed the Egyptian military's rhetoric and condemned the Egyptian Brotherhood for "antidemocratic" behavior, blaming the group for its own demise.[24]

The PJD reacted to the Egyptian coup—its first existential challenge since assuming office—not by railing against the unchecked powers of authoritarian rule, but rather by seeking its aid. It responded not by defending the Muslim Brotherhood against the excesses of the Egyptian state or by reasserting its own Islamist identity, but rather by faulting the Brotherhood for mismanagement and poor performance. The PJD maintained that it was different from the Brotherhood and a better version of it—a kind of Islamism 2.0. It pointed out that it had done a better of job of working with other parties and of working side by side with existing state structures, rather than upsetting them. "They are not our Brothers," one leading party official told me after the coup.[25]

Even at the time of the coup, the PJD foreign minister's response was tepid, stopping short of condemnation and instead calling for "national unity" in Egypt; a top movement official, in contrast, was far more bellicose.[26] The message to party members was clear: statements from the movement are what we *really* think; statements from the party are what we *have* to say. But in the end, official policy was, as it continues to be, directed by the party.

When the PJD needed to find a new coalition partner to remain in power, it turned for help to its greatest benefactor: the monarchy. After the king responded favorably, Benkirane was clear in his gratitude, noting that his government would have fallen had it not been for the king, who renewed the grand bargain (for the time being): the PJD's survival would be assured if it supported the king.[27]

ISLAMISTS IN OPPOSITION

If the PJD's relationship with the state can be characterized by cooperation and even co-optation, Al Adl's appears, at least at first glance, to be one of confrontation and combativeness. Its roots lie squarely in the writings of its founder and late spiritual guide, Abdesslam Yassine. Yassine took steps to form what would become Al Adl in the 1970s, after leaving the largest Sufi movement in the country, the Tariqa Boutchichiya. Intent on building his own political movement and inspired by the writings of Sayyid Qutb, among others, Yassine began writing tome after tome (17 in total), each laced with grand plans for re-Islamizing society, for reconnecting Muslims everywhere, and for eventually replacing the Moroccan regime from the bottom up.[28]

The movement that came to be created in his footsteps, Al Adl, in many ways found its early inspiration not merely in a text of theological dissent, but in an act of defiance. In a public letter sent to King Hassan II in 1974, Yassine blamed the country's failings on its monarch, who had allegedly sold its fortunes to his rich cronies, to "Zionist" friends, and to special interests; Hassan II, Yassine argued, had put his own needs above that of the state. What was perhaps even more revolutionary was that Yassine addressed the king as his own peer, portraying himself as a scholar and leader equal to the Commander of the Faithful.[29] For this act, Yassine was sentenced to an insane asylum and to many subsequent years of house arrest.

In the interim, Yassine's incipient movement thrived in its leader's physical absence: leading protests against the state, mobilizing on university campuses, refusing to participate in elections, and publishing magazines and newsletters that showed more willingness than anyone else to brazenly criticize the state, even the king personally. The state responded by arresting top leaders and student activists and banning and confiscating their publications.

Thus, whereas the PJD embraced elections, Al Adl eschewed them. While the PJD sought legality at all costs, Al Adl appeared to thrive, even bask, in its own illegality. Yet, even though it has routinely been labeled "radical" or "immoderate" or "banned" or "illegal"—labels that suggest irrational or, at the least, irresponsibly contrarian behavior—Al Adl too played by, and continues to play by, the rules of the political game, which are rules laid down by the state. Throughout its existence and especially since the Arab Spring, the PJD's election, and the Egyptian coup, Al Adl's behavior has been strategic, reactive, and increasingly defined by its goals of survival and expansion.

When Mohamed VI took over the throne in 1999, Yassine wrote another letter, albeit tamer than the first. The king, hoping to appear more liberal than his father, responded by freeing Yassine from house arrest. The scholar was allowed to move, eventually relocating to the neighborhood of Souissi, the most expensive and elite neighborhood in the country, one inhabited by diplomats and foreign dignitaries. (As one Al Adl member noted, "Yassine is important. He should be surrounded by important people.")

Yassine's antigovernment stance allowed Al Adl to differentiate itself from the PJD because it attracted youth interested in standing up to the regime. Al Adl formed a quasi-political party in waiting in 1998, a year after the PJD formed, with the implicit aim of being better organized to compete with the PJD for supporters. During every subsequent election year—2003, 2007, 2011, and 2016—Al Adl undertook dramatic mobilization campaigns against the regime.

It was no surprise, then, that when anti-regime protests emerged during the Arab Spring, Al Adl soon assumed a leading role—for a time. Al Adl joined forces with a wide cross-section of Moroccans, including leftists, as part of the "February 20 Movement," named after an unusually large day of protests in 2011.[30] To listen to a debate between representatives of the PJD, Al Adl, and a leading socialist group in the country is to hear only two distinct schools of thought: an anti-regime stance embodied by Al Adl and the socialists and a pro-government stance embodied by the PJD.[31]

Yet, as the Arab Spring protests unfolded across the region, Al Adl suddenly decided to withdraw. What, then, drove the group, in December 2011, to leave the February 20 Movement, choosing to melt away into the political shadows once again?[32]

The decision, at first, seemed to make little strategic sense. This was a moment when opposition movements around the region were celebrating their biggest successes in history. Popular rhetoric Al Adl had embraced for decades was finally being adapted by the masses. Slogans only its supporters shouted for years about dissolving the monarchy, for example, were suddenly being chanted by protesters across the political spectrum, from left to right. This seemed, in many ways, like the obvious time for Al Adl to capitalize on these links and grow to new heights.

But instead, it chose the opposite path. Why? Once again, its behavior can only fully be understood when examined in relation to its main Islamist competitor. Al Adl in 2011 was moved by a fear of losing or alienating its base, just as it was since its founding. Members told me of other reasons for their departure from February 20: some logistical, some personal, some even emotional. Some bemoaned the lack of communication with leftists and their poor organizational skills. Some felt mistreated by their fellow protesters, even victims of prejudice. Some felt that leftists were antireligious and seemed to take umbrage at references to religion. According to one member of the February 20 Movement, Al Adl added little but prowess at protesting. "They could bring people to the streets, but that was it," she said.

Yet these challenges, not unlike many problems shared by new protest movements, were not insurmountable. Instead, the major factor in Al Adl leaving the February 20 Movement related to its main Islamist foe and the long-term fears over losing its own base. It is no coincidence that Al Adl returned to the shadows only weeks after the PJD's dramatic election victory. The ascent of the PJD to the prime ministership placed Al Adl in a difficult position. Benkirane was personally popular with many young Islamists. And Al Adl feared it could be seen as a "spoil sport," as getting in the way of the most momentous moment for Islamists in the region.

Recall that Benkirane was appointed prime minister during a wave of Islamist electoral victories in the region. In this context, Al Adl felt that it could not risk alienating its base by continuing to oppose the new, popularly elected government. Sometimes, as many explained it to me, one has to swallow a bitter pill, to make short-term concessions for the good of the long term. There was also an expectation in Al Adl that the PJD would ultimately stumble, because the monarchy would constrain its rule.[33]

As one member noted in the wake of the Egyptian coup, Al Adl "did what the Muslim Brotherhood should have done"—that is, took things slowly, waited, and watched events unfold. The Brotherhood should have recognized that the situation was fluid, that the Arab Spring was perhaps but a passing phase. Activists also gleaned from the Egyptian coup that Islamist groups should be wary of the power of Arab states—that regimes never disappear, pointing of course to the PJD's inability to enact real change in the face of the Moroccan regime's dominance. Indeed, leaving February 20 when it did allowed Al Adl to avoid some of the harshest state responses against February 20 members, including arrests, beatings, and house searches.[34]

Even though it ceased to formally cooperate with February 20, Al Adl still finds common ground, slowly, methodically, with leftists in ways that don't overtly threaten its own existence. Nowhere is this more on display than in Al Adl's organizational evolution. The group is often described by scholars and journalists as "banned yet tolerated"—which suggests that the group has been spared the fate of counterparts in Egypt that have faced brutal crackdowns. But such a formulation is incomplete. My research suggests that, just like the PJD, Al Adl is often permitted to engage in activities that challenge the regime on political grounds, but never those that might question the regime's religious foundations.[35] It regularly holds protests on anodyne issues such as economics, Palestinian rights, American foreign policy, corruption, or unemployment. Yet, once its activities extend too far into the public religious sphere—that is, outside its own private discussions of its own texts—crackdowns against it increase. By and large, Al Adl appears to realize this and abide by these limitations.

To facilitate its careful, cautious approach, the organization is now compartmentalized into two distinct wings or "circles": a religious circle (spawned at its formation in the early 1980s) and a political circle (created in 1998 at a meeting in Marrakesh, a year after the PJD began participating in politics). Just as is the case with the PJD's relationship with its affiliated religious movement, Al Adl's dual organizational front allows it to maximize its appeal to as many new recruits as possible. It can make room for many personalities and sensibilities within the movement: those, for example, who like Yassine's writings on Sufism and personal transcendence can find a niche, as can those for whom the group's antigovernment stances hold special sway. Members claim that the movement is undergoing organizational reform to better streamline its functions, but it is noteworthy that, as one activist explained, it is basing its reorganization on business models, not on other Islamist groups.

The group's political circle now appears to function with some degree of autonomy from its religious circle, increasingly resembling a political party in waiting. It holds internal elections for its guidance council and issues official statements on regional and international developments, such as congratulating the Turkish prime minister on his party's victory in local elections in March 2014.[36]

The Egyptian coup of 2013 did not change Al Adl's primary strategy; rather, it cemented it. The coup seemed to exemplify the risks of opposing an authoritarian regime too boldly. By exposing these dangers, it also reinforced Al Adl's strategy of slow, incremental, bottom-up political change. The group's leaders also used the coup to highlight their own criticisms of the Moroccan state and of the Arab state writ large, publicly faulting the power of repressive police forces and militaries. They even called upon international bodies to condemn the Egyptian military, as if to suggest that appropriate condemnation would never come from the Moroccan regime, a regime that the group considers capable of the same injustices as the one in Egypt.[37]

THE FUTURE OF THE "MOROCCAN MODEL" OF ISLAMISM

Political scientists have long written about the durability of authoritarian governments in the Middle East and about the strategies, techniques, and practices employed to buttress their rule.[38] The Moroccan case now compels us to consider the durability of emerging forms of political Islam: one that elevates a more modest, practical approach to political survival over any dramatic remaking of Islamist political thought. It is a model characterized by molding to state religious policy, deploying Islam selectively and strategically, resetting the power relationship between party and movement, and proactively navigating domestic and international competition.

The experiences of Morocco's Islamists also suggest that claims of political Islam's demise are overblown. Electoral Islamism is not dead but rather certain forms may no longer be viable. Islamists who work within the confines of the state, and even in subservience to its longstanding institutions, such as those in Morocco, Tunisia, and Jordan, appear to be faring better than those with more revolutionary tendencies. Yet, what sets Morocco's Islamists apart is not simply that they work within the confines of existing political structures, but rather the nature of the structures themselves. In other words, the particular structural contours of Moroccan state policy—specifically in relation to religious activism—have significantly shaped Islamist behavior and ultimately Islamist beliefs.

There is little doubt that extremist Islamist groups like the Islamic State have been emboldened by the Egyptian coup and by the larger perceived failures of the Islamist electoral experiment. But the experience of Islamists in Morocco suggests that mainstream Islamists could also benefit from such setbacks. In many ways, the Egyptian coup and the rise of the Islamic State have, counterintuitively, given Morocco's Islamists a new lease on life. This regional tumult has, first and foremost, altered expectations. As movements elsewhere continue to face challenges, succeeding might now simply mean surviving.

Previously dismissed as co-opted "puppets," Morocco's Islamists now appear more prescient than powerless. The coup in Egypt clearly showed that if a movement challenges the authoritarian state too much, it might suffer potentially existential consequences. Morocco's Islamists may have internalized this lesson from the neighboring civil war in Algeria two decades earlier. The PJD used to claim that it helped prevent Morocco from turning "into Algeria"; it now maintains that its actions protected Morocco from turning into Egypt, or worse Yemen or Libya.

The party remains intent on showing that it represents its own unique model, untainted by the mistakes of others. Such national pride can sometimes sound like a lack of self-reflection or perhaps even an Islamist anti-cosmopolitanism. "We are a Moroccan party" is a refrain heard often. Party leaders appear less interested in adopting new forms of political thought than in learning pragmatic lessons from their own context. Informing this, of course, is the not-so-subtle fear that importing new political ideas (or even appearing to import them) could seem threatening to the religious thinking of the regime.[39]

In the wake of the Islamic State's rise, Al Adl has also benefitted: its so-called radicalism simply does not appear as "radical" as it once did. Both

Al Adl's nonviolent activism and its commitment to working within the confines of the nation-state (even as it consistently finds fault with it) allow it to appear more mainstream than it ever did before. The group has seized this opportunity for wider appeal and access. Leaders meet with foreign embassy officials, travel more, and speak out more than they used to.

The ultimate question now is whether the approaches adopted by Morocco's Islamists are viable in the long term—whether, in short, their models of Islamist activism are sustainable. In the case of both the PJD and Al Adl, there is little to suggest the development of any long-term strategic goals beyond mere survival. If their predicament were represented by the metaphor of a race, it is still not clear what "winning" would look like. Yet, the effects of losing—of not being able to run in the race any longer—are far clearer. Indeed, grim examples abound from across the region. The effects of losing are acutely palpable: the inability to hold government jobs and the inability to maintain commitments and promises to its base for employment and security.

The PJD speaks little of far-reaching plans other than to continue fighting corruption within the existing system and to become the best political party it can be. Leaders of Al Adl continue to appeal for a "national pact," where they would bring together various oppositional movements, but it remains unclear what would transpire after such a pact was formed. Its leaders also talked, in the wake of the Arab Spring, of the desire for a "civil" state other than an "Islamic" one, but it nonetheless remains ambiguous what that state would actually look like.

Upon assuming office in 2011, one PJD leader was explicit about his party's aims: "Our goal," he said, "is survival." Three years later, the regional chessboard looked different; the Islamist electoral ascent was now on the wane. And that same leader bragged to a crowd of foreign government officials in 2014: "We're the one last Islamist party remaining in government in the region."[40] The implication was clear. Any long-term plans would be subsumed by short-term realities and structural constraints. Merely surviving was once again cause for celebration.

The forces motivating the monarchy to maintain the status quo are also compelling: as long as Islamists don't threaten the survival of the regime—and as long as those in the elected government, rather than the royal court, can act as shields or shock absorbers for unpopular government polices—there will be little motivation to crack down further. But what if the shield overwhelms the state, if the PJD leader, in other words, proves too popular? Another challenging scenario might include increased pressure from Morocco's Gulf allies to clamp down on Islamists. Yet, thus far, such allies appear quite content with Morocco's convenient blend of crackdown and co-optation.

An interaction between the PJD's then-leader, Benkirane, and Egyptian President Abdel Fattah al-Sissi exemplifies the dynamics between Moroccan Islamist parties, the government structure, and internal competition. Less than two years after Sisi deposed the Egyptian Brotherhood, Benkirane, as prime minister, was faced with the difficult and precarious position of meeting with him in the spring of 2015. For many PJD youth activists, the meeting was tantamount to hypocrisy: how could their leader shake hands with the man who so violently cracked down on Islamists in Egypt? Of course, at the time of the coup, the Moroccan king had congratulated Sissi, and Benkirane's foreign minister had even been dispatched to Sissi's inauguration. But for many in the rank and file, this face-to-face meeting was one step too far. Protests by young PJD members erupted in multiple cities across the country. A doctored photo of the meeting—in which Benkirane is pictured sitting on Sissi's lap—circulated on the Internet.[41]

Benkirane, for his part, sought to stem criticism by stating that he was meeting Sissi as an emissary for the country and the king—and not as a PJD member. His response was, no doubt, diplomatic, but it also evinced the deeper message that not only would he do whatever was asked of him by the king but also that he was able to sublimate his loyalty to the party to that of the state. The ability of the party base to protest, however, also offered up another lesson: that the presence of the *haraka* networks makes space for internal protest. How these tensions might play out under a less persuasive or popular party leader remains to be seen. Yet, even those within the PJD who are most critical of the accommodationist approach have relented or moved on, either to Al Adl or from politics in general. Even the historically most critical party leader, Mustapha Ramid, routinely abided by the king's edicts in his role as Minister of Justice in the Benkirane government.

In writing about the relative "success" of Islamists in Morocco, then, this chapter also calls for closer scrutiny of our very notions of Islamist "success." As Western social scientists, we seem particularly drawn to the study of elections. The data sets are available, and, indeed, we tend to reflexively study "them" the way we study "us." We love measuring and tracking "democracy," focusing on winners and losers, on horse races, victories, and defeats. We study these things, I suspect, because we are guided by the belief that these outcomes matter—that the winners of elections actually win something. Yet, in authoritarian contexts—even post–Arab Spring contexts—does electoral success translate into success writ large? What if long-standing regimes have stacked the deck—rigged the rules—to such an extent that electoral success might not mean what we think it does? In the Moroccan context, it becomes necessary to ask whether the PJD is really able to enact a far-reaching political agenda or effect widespread social change (or any kind of social change for that matter) in a context where the king still dominates the political sphere—particularly when it comes to religion.

In thinking critically about what "Islamist success" means, this chapter also suggests a closer look at non-electoral or extra-electoral Islamist activism. This is an especially important question in a post-coup moment where the Egyptian Brotherhood's experiment with electoral participation appears to have been nothing short of abject failure. Is it perhaps conceivable that parties and movements that do not participate in elections are actually having a more dramatic effect on society? Evidence in Pakistan, for example, suggests this, and certainly the activism of Al Adl in Morocco confirms this as well. Al Adl has become the largest Islamist group in Morocco *without* participating in elections. The PJD garners the headlines, the cabinet appointments, the fame, and the international attention, but perhaps Al Adl's activism is more durable. Perhaps the more influential model is the one we don't see every day. Thus, the Islamist "success stories" that emerge from the region might not be measured or marked by election results, but rather by the less concrete things: say, influencing judicial appointments, religious practices, educational mores, and social norms more broadly.

To participate or *not* to participate in the electoral process—that will be the question facing the region's Islamist parties and movements in the years to come. Regardless of the tactics and strategies such parties and movements opt for, the lessons of the Moroccan experience are unambiguous: abiding by the rules of the political process can help ensure some form of survival and increased, if still limited, influence. In the aftermath of the Arab Spring, the PJD's Benkirane analogized the ongoing protests in Morocco to a modest fire, one that heated rather than destroyed the political process. "The fire was sufficient to heat the bowl," he said. "Thank God, it was not enough to burn it." If it had destroyed it, then it would have also destroyed the main Islamist movements in the country—the PJD and Al Adl—who abide by and ultimately benefit from it. Increasingly, both movements endure by continuing not to "burn" existing political structures. Even if they do not outwardly defend the political status quo, the largest Islamist movements in Morocco continue to preserve and even bolster it. They do so because their survival depends on it.

4

Syria

Raphaël Lefèvre

THE SYRIAN CONFLICT HAS offered a unique opportunity for the Muslim Brotherhood to make its comeback on the political stage more than 30 years after President Hafez al-Assad forced them out of the country. The local Brotherhood branch, founded by Syrian clerics inspired by the ideas of Hassan al-Banna, entered parliament in the 1950s and 1960s before taking the helm of the Islamist opposition to the Baathist regime in the early 1980s and then seeking refuge abroad. In sociological parlance, the Syrian Muslim Brotherhood therefore transformed from an open *social movement* into a *social movement organization*, one characterized by a limited staff and membership base and driven by the "primary goal" of "organizational survival."[1] Its priorities, in other words, have more to do with survival and adapting to a volatile environment than with any specific political or ideological considerations.

On the one hand, the Syrian Muslim Brotherhood's development of an informal bureaucracy in exile has allowed it to train skilled politicians who have safeguarded the organization's core interests by navigating—with considerable pragmatism—Syria's troubled waters. On the other hand, however, the bureaucratization of the Brotherhood has also meant its "oligarchization"[2]—or the concentration of power within the hands of a few longtime Brotherhood figures. Not only has this dynamic raised the specter of factionalism and constrained the group's effectiveness on the ground but it has also alienated other Islamists who increasingly view the group as more interested in organizational preservation than in the actual implementation of its ideological agenda.

A PRAGMATIC LEADERSHIP

The Brotherhood's focus on survival and its development of a cadre of skilled politicians explain much of its success in becoming a driving force of exiled Syrian politics. The group has routinely been accused of directly "controlling" the opposition since the start of the conflict in 2011.[3] However, in actual fact, the Brotherhood has tended to exert its influence in indirect ways. For instance, when the Syrian National Council (SNC) was created in September 2011, Brotherhood officials neither tried to "Islamize" its political program nor claim leadership. Instead, they worked with other activists to build broad alliances. They backed opposition figures with backgrounds very distinct from their own to become heads of the SNC, such as Burhan Ghalioun, a secular Sunni activist; Abdelbasset Sieda, a Kurdish academic; and George Sabra, a Christian Marxist. In addition to forging these partnerships, the Muslim Brotherhood showcased its influence by acting as a bloc during SNC voting sessions—and this sometimes turned them into the opposition's kingmakers. Indeed, their internal cohesion and political organization stand in stark contrast to the fragmentation and shifting alliances that characterize the rest of the Syrian opposition to date.

Muslim Brotherhood politicians again demonstrated their political skill in December 2012 after the Obama administration pushed the SNC to integrate the National Coalition for Syrian Revolutionary and Opposition Forces, a new platform that was deemed more diverse and representative of the Syrian spectrum. The Brotherhood, at first reluctant to enter into a larger body in which their influence would be diluted, finally endorsed the move after nominating their strongman, Faruk Tayfur, as the new body's vice president. They also penetrated the National Coalition's decision-making circles through alliances with ideological fellow travelers, including the National Action Group for Syria, a grouping of ex-Brotherhood members from Aleppo; the Committee to Protect Civilians, a humanitarian and military platform active in Homs; and the League of the Syrian Ulema, a lobby group gathering religious scholars and headed by Mohamed Ali Sabouni, a figure close to the Brotherhood. Yet while this complex cocktail of mutual interests and Islamist sympathies, sometimes disguised, helped the Brotherhood secure political influence, it further alienated those who were already suspicious of its efforts to control the opposition. These criticisms reached their apex following the March 2013 election of Ghassan Hitto, an ally of Qatar seen by many as the "Brotherhood's man,"[4] as head of the Syrian opposition's "transitional government."[5]

The row over Hitto's election, his subsequent resignation, and the almost simultaneous nomination of Saudi-backed Ahmed al-Jarba as new head of the opposition also reflected the Brotherhood's entanglement in regional power struggles. The Brotherhood had initially supported the Qatari camp in the Syrian opposition in exchange for increased media exposure and political support. This, unsurprisingly, alienated Saudi Arabia. And when Riyadh ultimately seized the "Syrian file" from Doha in 2013, the new landscape naturally translated into a decrease in the Brotherhood's influence. This pushed some of its leaders to rethink their strategies. From then on, Faruk Tayfur did his utmost to fix the group's relationship with the kingdom—sparing little of his own political capital to court Riyadh and to support the Saudi agenda within the Coalition. His first steps in this direction were met with unease by other Brotherhood leaders.[6] Indeed, at precisely the same time, Saudi Arabia was encouraging the Egyptian army to crack down on the Egyptian Muslim Brotherhood. Yet Tayfur's realist approach eventually won over the rest of the organization. In January 2014, most of the Brotherhood members in the Coalition voted in favor of Ahmed al-Jarba when he ran for a second time as head of the opposition. "We all realized that we don't stand to gain anything from confronting Saudi Arabia," summed up a source in the leadership remarked to me.[7]

This pragmatism even enabled the Syrian Brotherhood to emerge unscathed from Saudi Arabia's March 2014 designation of the Muslim Brotherhood as a terrorist organization. "Saudi policymakers let us know that our organization would be spared from their decision to crack down on all Brotherhood branches in the region," one of the group's leaders explained with tangible relief. Thousands of known

Syrian Brothers now continue to safely work and live in the kingdom, where many took refuge after Hafez al-Assad's repression in the early 1980s. And in November 2014, when the Syrian Muslim Brotherhood designated as its new leader Mohamed Walid, a Syrian surgeon practicing in Jeddah, the Saudi authorities did not raise any objections.[8] In turn, Walid would have warm words for the kingdom. After his election, he thanked Saudi Arabia for "protecting" the Syrian Brothers in their exile and for "supporting" the Syrian revolution.[9] Perhaps more significantly, he called the kingdom a "strategic powerhouse for all Muslims in the world," supported its standoff against Iran, and gave his blessing early on to the Saudi military intervention in Yemen.[10]

A CENTRIST IDEOLOGY?

The accommodation with Saudi Arabia has also made long-standing political differences between the leaderships of the Brotherhood's Syrian and Egyptian branches much starker. This divergence is nothing new. But it emerged forcefully during the Arab Spring after high-ranking Syrian Brotherhood figures expressed bewilderment at the way their counterparts dealt with Egyptian politics and, in particular, with the opposition. A few months before the July 2013 coup, Zuheir Salem, a spokesman and chief ideologue for the Syrian Muslim Brotherhood, bluntly argued that it had been a "mistake" for the Egyptian Brotherhood to contest the presidential elections. "Egypt was a sinking boat and you cannot come and change it the way you are doing; I believe that we have to work within a coalition," he said, referring to the Egyptian Brotherhood's leadership.[11] The Syrian Muslim Brotherhood had also become increasingly critical of Mohamed Morsi and his handling of the conflict in Syria. In May 2013, an official Syrian Brotherhood publication used particularly harsh words to describe the Egyptian president's courting of Iran and Russia—two allies of Bashar al-Assad's regime. "It was painful for our people to hear President Mohamed Morsi's remarks in Moscow. . . . The Syrian people, including members of our [organization], are waiting for an explanation and wonder bitterly: where is President Morsi's attitude taking him?"[12] Even the Egyptian president's last-minute policy shift on Syria and his call for a worldwide "jihad" against the Assad regime were met with widespread skepticism. "The Syrian people know best what is needed for their future. Syrians don't need foreign fighters," asserted Ali al-Bayanouni, a top Syrian Brotherhood figure.[13] The Egyptian army's 2013 coup naturally pushed the Syrian Muslim Brotherhood's leadership to express solidarity with its Egyptian sister and to tone down its criticisms of Morsi, but unease between the two branches persisted.

Ideologically, the Syrian Brotherhood also sought to distance itself from its Egyptian counterpart. This desire was already visible a decade ago when the Syrian organization published a "National Honour Charter" and a "Political Project," whose content was reiterated in a "National Covenant" published in 2012. These documents stressed the need to respect the religious, cultural, and political diversity of the Syrian people while calling for the establishment of a parliamentary regime free from religious oversight. Practically, this meant that leaders of the Syrian Brotherhood were highly critical of the Egyptian branch's stipulation that neither a Coptic Christian nor a woman should be chosen as president of Egypt. They also rejected Egyptian calls for the establishment of an advisory council of clerics who would determine whether legal rulings conform to Islamic law. "We don't want to enter the realm of theocracy," summed up ideologue Zuheir Salem. To make its "centrist" (*wasatiya*) approach more concrete to the public, the Syrian Brotherhood spearheaded the creation of the Waad party in July 2013. This "national party with an Islamic framework" intended to demonstrate that Syrians can "work together" by gathering within a single grouping a number of Muslim Brothers, independent Islamists, and "national figures" including secular Sunnis and even some Christians and Alawites.[14] These moves helped place the leaders of the Syrian Brotherhood in the orbit of Turkish President Recep Tayyip Erdogan's AKP. Mostly based in Istanbul and with a field office in Gaziantep on the Syrian–Turkish border, Waad figures enjoy close ties to the Turkish government and they have often spoken of their admiration for the "Turkish miracle."

Officially, the birth of Waad was meant to separate the Brotherhood's religious and social activities, on the one hand, and its political activism on the other. Inside the new party, a decision-making process involving an equal number of Brotherhood members and nonmembers was specifically instituted to ensure a degree of independence from the parent movement. This initially contrasted with Egypt's Justice and Freedom Party, often seen as little more than an arm of the Egyptian Muslim Brotherhood. Enshrining a clearer distinction between a religious movement (*haraka*) and a party (*hizb*) had been a long-standing demand of a number of Syrian Muslim Brothers. "This new party is the product of the lobbying efforts undertaken by the most moderate Brotherhood members and some of the youth a decade ago," explained a high-ranking Waad figure. "It finally allows Muslim Brothers to work, free from organizational constraints, with whoever agrees with their vision of a post-Assad Syria—including secular Syrians and minorities." The rise of the new party also seemed to offer appealing career prospects to young Islamists frustrated by the older generation's monopoly on the Brotherhood's leadership. A figure close to the Brotherhood cynically observed that "the creation of Waad was a way to give positions to ambitious politicians frustrated by the lack of opportunities in the Brotherhood."

It remains to be seen whether Waad will retain its self-professed "political independence."[15] The party's independence was undermined by the November 2014 election of its own head, Mohammed Walid, as the new leader of the Syrian Muslim Brotherhood. Walid immediately resigned from his post, but suspicion now lingers that the party was always merely acting as the Brotherhood's political wing. "The whole idea behind the party was to show independence from the Brotherhood's leadership," an activist close to Waad bitterly complained. "Walid's election destroyed everything." The Syrian Brotherhood's new leader acknowledged as much when he stated in early 2015 that Waad had "not grown and developed as planned."[16] Indeed, to date, the Muslim Brothers still fund most of the party's activities, and they have yet to relinquish any of their seats to Waad members in the opposition Coalition. The debate is likely to intensify between advocates of a more radical separation between party and movement and those who argue that it is an ill-timed, costly, and mostly cosmetic initiative.

THE RISK OF FACTIONALISM

Tension between the Syrian Brotherhood's youth and the older generation largely pre-dates the debate over the Waad party. It dates back to the mid-1980s, when the group's efforts at establishing a "bureau-cracy in exile" to ensure organizational survival led to its "oligar-chization". Clique structures started to emerge and to compete with each other for internal power. Factionalism thus became a main feature of the Syrian Brotherhood. But additional cracks in the foundation appeared after the 2010 election of Riyadh al-Shuqfa as the group's leader. His election came to symbolize the vic-tory of a powerful bloc made up mainly of conservative figures from Hama and Idlib who belong to the older generation. Disappointment at the election results prompted a group of reform-minded Islamists from Aleppo in their 30s and early 40s to defect from the Brotherhood and to set up a parallel structure called the National Action Group for Syria.[17] "We were frustrated by the older generation's monopoly of power and we wanted to clearly separate politics from *da'wa* [religious activities] by having our own political platform," recounted a member of the splinter group. "Our vision was very much neo-Brotherhood." At first, the National Action Group gained traction by proposing political initiatives aimed at gathering the exiled opposition under one umbrella. It would become a founding member of the SNC, and its leader, Ahmed Ramadan, would rapidly emerge as one of the opposi-tion's most influential figures.

Yet a series of challenges surfaced that effectively stalled the rise of these ex-Muslim Brothers. Internally, many members grew frustrated with Ahmed Ramadan's central role in the group's decision-making process. "The National Action Group ended up making the same mis-take as the Brotherhood," resentfully argued one of its former mem-bers. "The platform became heavily centralized around very few key figures—and this felt like an insult in the face of those of us who also had ambitions." Figures close to the group also suggest that this cen-tralization of power eventually stymied debate and prevented the emer-gence of a clear politico-ideological vision capable of competing with the Brotherhood's. Externally, the tactical alliances forged between the National Action Group and the Syrian Brotherhood—initially meant to increase their mutual influence in the SNC and later in the Coalition—resulted in much confusion within the rest of the opposi-tion. "To me, whether they are Ikhwan [Brotherhood] or neo-Ikhwan is the same—they come from the same background and I oppose their agenda," summed up a left-wing member of the Syrian opposition. An official from the National Action Group agreed that it had "made mistakes" and that it would "take time" until the group developed an original political project and became a truly independent force.

Concurrent with the birth of the National Action Group, the Brotherhood took steps to prevent yet another generational split from its ranks. "Our youth have been very active at the level of the base—now we want to give them more opportunities to organize, launch initiatives, and reach leadership positions," explained a Muslim Brotherhood figure who belongs to the older generation. The crisis in Syria indeed seems to have fired up the youth, who, until then, were not particularly involved in the affairs of the exiled organization. After 2011, young Syrians affiliated with the Brotherhood flocked to Istanbul, where the group's headquarters is located, to take part in initiatives such as raising the Syrian revolution's profile on social media and setting up charities that provide aid to the refugees. Others are the driving force behind the publication of the group's weekly newspaper and, more generally, behind its public relations and outreach initiatives. Recent figures even suggest that as many as half of the Syrian Brotherhood's staff are junior members of the group.[18]

It is in this context that the new generation began playing a more important political role within the organization. The creation of the Syrian Muslim Brotherhood's youth office in 2012 provided the framework in which young members could organize as an internal lobby group and more effectively voice their grievances to the leadership. This, at least initially, seemed to yield results. The youth office obtained funds from the Brotherhood's leadership to organize a large conference in December 2012. The event gathered in Istanbul hundreds of youth who, because of exile, had until then been scattered throughout the world—it thus had an important socializing role. The conference also witnessed the rise of young and charismatic conservative politicians, a few of whom were subsequently asked to join the Brotherhood's top leadership.[19]

Yet the specter of further generational tensions still lingers over the Syrian Muslim Brotherhood. Politically, the youth contingent is dominated by idealist and revolutionary figures who don't see eye to eye with the older generation's attempt to seek an accommodation at all costs with Saudi Arabia and offer up any number of tactical concessions in the name of pragmatism. In January 2014, a statement by a "group of sons of the Muslim Brotherhood" criticized the leadership for tending to "ally with personalities and groups that seek a political settlement with the regime and that have strong ties to regional and international powers while it reduces its interaction with those revolutionary forces working to overthrow the regime using all means."[20] Organizationally, the youth are highly critical of the murky power struggle within the leadership that pits a bloc of Muslim Brothers from Hama and Idlib against those from Aleppo. In February 2014, younger members attempted to intro-duce greater transparency in the decision-making process, but their ini-tiative was thwarted by the Consultative Council (the *Majlis al-Shura*, which acts as the Brotherhood's internal parliament). As mentioned earlier, the election of 70-year-old Mohamed Walid as the head of the Syrian Brotherhood came as a bitter disappointment. In an attempt to heal the growing rift, the new leader nominated as his deputy Hussam Ghadban, then head of the Brotherhood's youth office.[21] But youth frustration still simmers. "We wanted to see a radical change in the group's leadership," recounted a young and self-described "revolution-ary" Muslim Brother. "What we got instead is cosmetic change and more of the same—the old generation is still very much in control of the Consultative Council and of the leadership."

THE DILEMMAS OF MILITARY WORK

In a further bid to appeal to the new generation, Mohamed Walid promised to "concentrate on the youth" and to allocate 75 percent of the Brotherhood's financial resources to activities inside Syria—which are overwhelmingly carried out by young Muslim Brotherhood members.[22] This is also part of the group's wider strategy to regain a foot-hold in the country after three decades abroad. "We may have influence in the exiled opposition but our organization cannot survive for long if it continues to be based outside of Syria," argued a member close to the leadership. Initially, this willingness to reconnect with Syrians and to contribute to the revolution on the ground led the Brotherhood to invest in humanitarian efforts. Its charity arm, Ataa Relief, has been one of the most active organizations in the refugee camps on the Syrian–Turkish border. The Brotherhood also opened an office in Aleppo and another in the countryside of Idlib. But in the context of the current conflict in Syria, part of the Brotherhood's strategy has also consisted of courting rebel groups and forming its own brigades—with mixed results.

These efforts only really took off in early 2012 when individuals belonging to the Muslim Brotherhood participated in the creation of the Committee to Protect Civilians (*Himayat al-Madaniyin*), a platform that distributes humanitarian aid around Homs and also provides rebel groups with "logistical support." A high-ranking Syrian Brotherhood figure recounted the strategy: "Given that the notion of armed struggle was still rather controversial in opposition circles, Brotherhood leaders temporarily decentralized decisions on this matter and left it up to members themselves to engage, or not engage, in that type of activity." Yet as the military struggle later came to dominate—and as some rebel brigades began to engage in looting and executions—rumors spread that the Brotherhood had grown frustrated and had formed its own rebel groups.[23] The move was formalized in December 2012 when the group's leadership announced the formation of the Shields of the Revolution Commission (*Hay'at Duro' al-Thawra*), a military platform gathering dozens of "centrist-minded" rebel brigades that "trust the Brotherhood."[24]

In theory, the Shields had the potential to be an influential actor on the Syrian rebel scene. Following its creation, it rapidly swallowed many smaller brigades. Its fighters became equipped with high-quality anti-tank weapons. And by clearly rejecting "all calls for *takfeer*, forced displacement, mass murder and sectarian and ethnic discrimination," the rebel platform portrayed itself as moderate in unambiguous terms—thus potentially attracting foreign backing.[25] Yet despite these advantages, the Shields failed to emerge as a significant force on the ground. While the Muslim Brotherhood's support initially attracted funding, it also accentuated the mistrust of other Islamist rebel groups—be they similarly centrist or more radical. Some viewed the Brotherhood as self-interested and still remembered the group's own history in the late 1970s when leaders called for "jihad" against the Assad regime and joined hands with other Islamist militias, only to retract from the alliance soon afterward and to escape Syria, leaving thousands of fighters behind. "We haven't yet managed to overcome the mistrust of the past," acknowledged a Brotherhood member tasked with handling relations with rebel groups in Syria. This effectively prevented the Shields from joining major rebel alliances such as the Islamic Front, the Syrian Revolutionaries Front, or the Army of Victory (*Jaysh al-Fatah*). In addition, the Brotherhood's lack of sophisticated understanding of military action led to confused decisions that weakened the Shields. For instance, an attempt to decentralize the platform's command-and-control structure to allow for local autonomy backfired. It took until October 2013 for Shields fighters from Idlib province to mount a coordinated attack with their counterparts in Hama on a regime checkpoint. The lack of tight hierarchy may also have led some brigades to "misbehave," in the words of a source inside the Shields.

These embarrassing failures eventually led the Muslim Brotherhood to reduce its support for the rebel platform. "The Shields have lost the support of many inside the Brotherhood," explained a figure in the leadership. "Some argue that we should not get involved in military activities since we are first and foremost an organization focused on *da'wa* and politics. Others are disappointed by the performance of the fighters on the ground. And most of us find that the whole enterprise cost too much money." The election of Mohamed Walid may have put the final nail in the coffin of the Shields. The new leader of the Syrian Muslim Brotherhood made it clear that he intends to essentially focus on "missionary and educational activities" inside Syria.[26] A source inside the Shields confirmed the Brotherhood's dwindling support: "Nowadays the group's leadership mainly provides us with media support as well as food and clothes—but we need money and weapons to continue training and operating in Syria." This growing tension has led a number of rebel groups to defect from the Shields over the past year. Most of the defectors have so far joined other mainstream Islamist rebel platforms close to the Brotherhood's ideology, including the Sham Legion (*Faylaq al-Sham*) and the Soldiers of Sham (*Ajnad al-Sham*).[27] This, however, could well change in the medium and long term. Indeed, extremist Islamist groups are on the rise precisely in the areas where the Shields have some presence. The al-Qaeda affiliate Jabhat al-Nusra, now rebranded as Jabhat Fath al-Sham, controls vast swathes of Idlib province, while the Islamic State, for long confined to its stronghold of Raqqa and to Eastern Syria, emerged as a powerful force in the countryside of Homs and Hama. Given the Brotherhood's decreased support for the Shields, some brigades could in the future be tempted to join these more radical alternatives—which, in addition to holding vast financial resources, also provide an increasingly appealing ideological model.

THE CHALLENGE OF EXTREMISM

The leaders of the Muslim Brotherhood were slow to grasp the ideological challenge stemming from the rise of extremist groups. At first they even refused to acknowledge their very presence on the ground. In April 2013, the Brotherhood's then-leader, Riyadh al-Shuqfa, insisted that "there is no extremism in Syria."[28] It would take the meteoric rise of the Islamic State for him to recognize their significance and to disassociate the Brotherhood from such radical groups. "We disagree with ISIS, first because of its extremist ideas, and second, because of its violent actions," he stated in September 2014 before advising Islamic State chief Abu Bakr al-Baghdadi to "refer to the Quran and the Sunna to understand Islam correctly and to improve his approach."[29] Yet even then he went to great lengths to argue that the Syrian people's inherent "moderation and tolerance" would make the Islamic State a temporary phenomenon that would quickly fade after the collapse of the Assad regime. His successor, Mohammed Walid, adopted a more forceful approach against Islamist extremists. Shortly after his election in November 2014, he criticized the Islamic State for "deviating from the Syrian revolution's track."[30] He also threatened the use of "self defense" against the Islamic State in the event Muslim Brothers came under attack inside Syria.[31]

But while the Brotherhood's leaders came to realize the security implications behind the rise of extremism, few seem to be aware of the dangers that the Islamic State's ideological orientation and achievements on the ground pose to the wider group. Frustrated by the Brotherhood's organizational rigidity and poor military performance, a small number of members may already have left the group in recent years to join more radical platforms such as Ahrar al-Sham, Jabhat al-Nusra, and perhaps the Islamic State too. There is a growing risk that the "Islamic" governance structures established by these organizations on the ground may become an increasingly appealing alternative to young Islamists alienated by the pragmatism and seeming political opportunism of the Brotherhood's leaders. "ISIS has succeeded where the Brotherhood has failed," summed up (with a hint of admiration) a former Muslim Brother who is now closer to radical Islamist groups in Syria. "It restored the Caliphate and took many Muslims back to religion." This vulnerability of some members to the ideology of radical groups seems to have its roots in the failure of the Brotherhood's educational program and curriculum (*tarbiya*).

Interestingly, the ideological moderation undergone by the Brotherhood throughout the 2000s was not free from internal controversy. The strongest resistance it faced came from the very clerics responsible for the group's educational program. This consequently meant that aspiring Muslim Brothers continued to be taught a variety of ideas and authors that naturally included Mustafa al-Sibai, the founder of the Syrian Brotherhood and a supporter of democracy, but also included radical figures such as Said Hawwa, who supported jihad against the Syrian regime in the 1970s and advocated the restoration of the caliphate.[32] "Those responsible for the educational program still teach the radical strands of Islamist thinking and, in the context of today's conflict in Syria, this has left a number of Muslim Brothers ideologically confused," explained a former member who himself went through the curricula. "The group's official discourse is one thing. But behind closed doors some clerics still call for the establishment of an Islamic state—without elaborating much further on what they actually mean by that."

The growing gap between the Brotherhood's official discourse and the kind of speech that some members are spreading at the grassroots level has become more evident since the U.S.-led air strikes on Islamic State strongholds in Syria and Iraq. The anti-Western tone of some Brotherhood clerics—something almost entirely absent from the official discourse of the leadership—reached new heights. A video featuring one such cleric was widely circulated on social media platforms affiliated with the Syrian Muslim Brotherhood. In it, he lambasted the United States in particularly harsh terms:

> There is a global alliance led by America, the world's leader in terrorism, whose crimes are more than to be counted and greater than

to be looked into. America has gathered its soldiers, troops, weapons, equipment and allies to allegedly destroy ISIS.... O Americans! O allies! Return home for we need you not! You are the cause of the plague and the reason for the ailment. You are the ones who have given these regimes power over us, shedding blood and destroying the crops and the stocks. O Americans! O allies! O Westerners! The Nation needs you not for it is a great time-honoured nation and you are those who installed all these oppressive regimes.[33]

In the video, the Syrian Brotherhood cleric also criticized the Islamic State for originating from "international intelligence agencies" and for declaring an "imaginary caliphate which all [religious] scholars have declared to be null and void." More appealing arguments may be needed to effectively counter the ideology spread by extremist groups. Mohamed Walid seemed to acknowledge as much in February 2015 when he stressed that "deep ideological differences exist between the Muslim Brotherhood and [the Islamic State]."[34] In a later intervention, he specified that "the imposition of sharia by force is a mistaken understanding of the texts and a mistaken understanding of Islam itself."[35] It will now be up to the group's clerics to embrace the "centrist" discourse of the Brotherhood's leaders—or risk losing parts of their base to more radical Islamist groups.

A NEW APPROACH TO THE BROTHERHOOD

The ways in which the Syrian Muslim Brotherhood has attempted to regain a foothold inside the country after decades of absence, and the type of challenges it has faced, illustrate the relevance of what is known as resource mobilization theory for the study of Islamic activism. Over the past decade, Brotherhood branches throughout the Middle East have mainly been analyzed as social movements. Researchers focused on the ways broad political structures affected grassroots support for the Brotherhood, and this approach may still be valid in relatively stable countries like Morocco or Tunisia. Yet in a regional political context marked by the return of state authoritarianism and an intensifying crackdown against Brotherhood branches, new theoretical lines of enquiry have emerged. One particularly interesting approach is to better understand the factors behind the Brotherhood's resilience despite all the challenges mentioned in this chapter.

What distinguishes Brotherhood branches from the countless other Islamist groups in the Middle East is the emphasis they place on the development of an informal "bureaucracy." And when they undergo repression and have to seek refuge abroad, their "bureaucracy" is one of the last tools they are left with. The case of the Syrian Muslim Brotherhood demonstrates the key role these internal structures can play in helping to raise a professional cadre of politicians, socialize the youth into party loyalty, and unite members with the ultimate purpose of preserving the organization under dire circumstances. It comes at a high cost, however, as the group may ultimately become more interested in "organizational maintenance" than in the actual pursuit of the political goals it was originally created for, something that may spur internal disagreement and dissent.

Resource mobilization theory, with the focus it puts on the need to study the internal and organizational nature of social movements, offers theoretical insights that are relevant beyond the case of the Syrian Brotherhood. It allows researchers to delve deeply into current internal debates within virtually all Brotherhood branches and to evaluate the importance of splinter groups emerging out of the organization on ideological, generational, or regional lines. This "neo-institutionalist approach" also encourages scholars to consider the changing nature of these groups' decision-making structures and internal struggles. Such avenues for research are crucial not only to better understand the groups themselves but also because, as this chapter shows, internal considerations, rather than ideological ones, often dictate key political decisions.

5

Yemen

Stacey Philbrick Yadav

FOR THE BETTER PART of 20 years, Yemen's political landscape was shaped substantially by the relationship between its largest Islamist party, the Yemeni Congregation for Reform (Islah), and the regime of former president Ali Abdullah Saleh. The 2011 uprising and ensuing transitional process and descent into war have altered the position of Islah by increasing the number of major players and reducing the significance of party politics at the center in relation to armed conflicts and populist pressure from the periphery.

The changing role of Yemen's Islah party offers important lessons not only for those interested in mapping Yemen's domestic politics but also for the study of Islamism more broadly. It speaks to the pressures that mainstream Islamist parties face in the revolutionary (and counter-revolutionary) climate of 2011 and its aftermath, balancing emerging opportunities for political power with extra-institutional challenges to party relevance on the ground. In Yemen, the most pressing issues have included the party's ambiguous position on wider populist mobilization, the murky relationship between the party's Salafi right flank and extremist organizations like al-Qaeda in the Arabian Peninsula (AQAP) and the Islamic State, and the impact of a fraught regional climate in which Muslim Brotherhood–allied parties face uncertainty and outright suppression.

Before the 2011 uprising and in the challenging years since, Islah has remained adaptive and dynamic, pursuing a strategy of self-preservation but not immune to miscalculation. In particular, this adaptability has come at some cost for centrist Muslim Brotherhood members within the party. While Islah has an ideological hard core of party leaders with clear Muslim Brotherhood ties, these figures have never been unconstrained in their ability to pursue their goals. Instead, they have needed to be ever mindful of a Salafi flank within the party that has regularly flirted with other centers of power, as well as a tribal faction with access to regime largesse. To add to this challenge, the party leadership has been over-reliant on external patrons and international organizations to maintain its political position in the context of a destructive, ongoing war.

To the extent that its leadership grounds its politics in the Egyptian Muslim Brotherhood's school of thought, it is fair to consider Islah a Brotherhood affiliate. Yet there are limits to this interpretation. On the one hand, Yemen's greater political openness in the 1990s and 2000s gave the Yemeni Brotherhood organizational opportunities that many others throughout the region, and certainly those in Egypt, lacked. On the other hand, the Brotherhood's necessary (and politically costly) relationships with other party factions mean that it has never been fully in command of Islah. This is an important reminder to approach Islamist organizations not as ideological monoliths, but as networks of actors situated in specific relationships, and to inquire as much into their allies and adversaries (both within and across organizations).

Taking this approach to Islah reveals the ways in which the Yemeni Muslim Brotherhood has adapted to survive decades of authoritarian encroachment—but also why it has struggled to navigate the tumultuous politics of a failed transition and civil war. Like other Brotherhood organizations in the region, Yemen's movement can be characterized as paradoxically "resilient and adaptable but also reactive and slow moving."[1] Ultimately, the Brotherhood's increasing difficulty in adapting is less about its Islamist ideology than it is about the declining relevance of formal institutions as the arbiter of political power in post-2011 Yemen. Islah poses the question, then, of what happens to mainstream, gradualist Islamists in moments of more radical change.

ISLAMISM BEFORE UNIFICATION

Because Yemen only came into being as a single unified state in 1990, "Yemeni Islamism" is not a single phenomenon but is grounded in complex histories and patterns of state–society relations. Intra-Yemeni regionalism remains a significant fault line today and is intimately interwoven with the story of Yemeni Islamism as well.[2]

Yemenis from the North and South were exposed to Muslim Brotherhood ideology through scholarly and political interactions with founder Hassan al-Banna and his followers in Cairo and Beirut in the 1940s, but the ideological lessons from these interactions tended to be of a generically republican and postcolonial nationalist variety.[3] Yemenis influenced by Banna criticized the legitimacy of the Zaydi Imamate in the North and British colonial rule in the South, but this critique was neither the sole purview of Islamists nor particularly sectarian in flavor, with Zaydi Shiite and Sunni intellectuals alike seeking guidance from their more organized and politicized Egyptian brethren. In part, this was a reflection of the doctrinal closeness between the Sunni traditions of the Shafi'i school and Zaydi Shiism, and the legacy of integration between members of the two communities.

Indeed, the political Left was, and for many years remained, the more significant target of Islamist mobilization. Following the establishment of a republican regime in the Northern Yemen Arab Republic (YAR), an organization led by students of the then more radical Brotherhood of the 1960s was promoted by the regime to counter real and perceived threats of leftist interference from the South.[4] This "Islamic Front" functioned as an auxiliary to the emerging state in the YAR, but given the weakness of representative institutions at the time, it functioned neither as a party nor a broad-based social movement.

In the 1980s, the leadership of North Yemen's Islamic Front was gradually incorporated into and empowered by the institutions of the the expanding bureaucracy of the YAR. Islamists carved out distinct ideological space under the wide tent of the ruling General People's Congress (GPC), even in the absence of formal partisan competition. President Ali Abdullah Saleh drew several future leaders of Islah into his governing apparatus, most notably Shaykh Abd al-Majid al-Zindani, a prominent Salafi figure, and Shaykh Abdullah bin Husayn al-Aḥmar, paramount sheikh of the Hashid tribal confederation, whose attraction to Islamism was largely driven by his social conservatism.[5] President Saleh also appointed the most prominent member of Yemen's Muslim Brotherhood, Yassin Abdul Aziz al-Qubati, to head the Ministry of Education.[6] A Brotherhood-affiliated newspaper was established in 1985, and when internal elections within the GPC were held in 1988, Brotherhood-affiliated Islamists won six out of the seven constituencies in which they competed.[7] As one scholar of the period remarked, "It was clear, even in the muddled conditions of no explicit parties or party platforms and of large numbers of candidates, that people wished for a change. In Sanaa the Islamists seemed like those who might promote such change."[8]

It was from this internal faction within the ruling party that the future leadership of Islah began to coalesce by the late 1980s. The unification of North and South Yemen in 1990 provided a major institutional incentive for Islah's formalization, even as the very concept of *hizbiyya* (multi-party politics) drove a wedge in Islamist ranks.[9] Senior Salafi figures rejected the notion of partisanship in favor of a more quietist *da'wa*, but Muslim Brotherhood members were keen to seize the political opportunities offered by new multiparty competition. In this, they followed reasonably closely the "template" of other Brotherhood organizations in the region, one characterized by "great responsiveness to the political context and legal environment in which they operate."[10]

Unlike other Brotherhood affiliates, Yemen's Brotherhood faction initially lacked the momentum to develop and unify into a strong social movement (*haraka*), prompting Brotherhood leaders to align with those Salafis who could countenance party building (like Zindani), as well as tribal figures, to build a broad tent of social conservatives. Several tribal and Salafi figures enjoyed popular support far greater than that of the Brotherhood leaders, who could command only a modest following in major cities and on university campuses in the early 1990s.[11] Many of the tribal figures were of Zaydi Shia background, and the Salafi and Brotherhood wings each had different visions of the relationship between state and society, making this a messy, uneasy grouping. But as the party's strong showing in the 1993 election would indicate, the three factions that jointly made up Islah could together pose a formidable threat to the Yemeni Left, while helping to further cement Northern dominance within Yemen's political elite.

THE UNITY REGIME AND ISLAH'S ADAPTIVE ISLAMISM

Governing in coalition with Saleh's GPC, the Muslim Brotherhood spent much of the 1990s under the Islah tent, building an organizational base on the national level by mobilizing on university campuses and via the networks of the Islah Charitable Society, one of only two genuinely national nongovernmental organizations with branches in every governorate. Like other Brotherhood affiliates in the region, the charitable society, while nominally independent, had overlapping membership with the political apparatus.

Alongside the Brotherhood faction's growing organizational capacity, the early decision of many Salafis to reject electoral politics effectively divided the country's Salafi movement and consequently strengthened the Brotherhood's position within the new Islah party, allowing Brothers to lay claim to influential leadership roles. While the biggest names in the party remained Shaykh Zindani and Shaykh Abdullah al-Aḥmar—with each representing important non-Brotherhood sources of mobilizational power—the Brotherhood designed and articulated party platforms, represented the party at partisan functions, and did the organizational heavy lifting involved in party building, moving quickly to establish branch offices, youth organizations, and campus affiliates in every governorate. Meanwhile, Salafis aligned with Islah engaged in heavily politicized *da'wa* through tertiary educational institutions and Zindani's Al-Imān University, relying on the party's relationship with the GPC to stave off leftist calls for curricular oversight.[12]

Islah's effort to build a national base should be understood not only as an expression of the Brotherhood's leadership but also in relation to North-South divides. The combined legislative impact of Islah and the GPC after 1993 gave "the North" a commanding majority in the parliament, fueling the Southern leadership's anxiety and ultimately contributing to the outbreak of civil war in 1994. While Salafi figures were the driving force behind the deployment of the armed Islamist auxiliaries that supported the North during the fighting, Muslim Brotherhood leaders lacked the capacity (and perhaps the will) to rein in targeted violence in the South.

Islah's transition from regime ally to adversary unfolded in fits and starts over the remaining years of the 1990s, facilitated by the obsolescence of the Yemeni Socialist Party after 1994. Islah participated in a governing coalition until after the 1997 parliamentary elections, when ministers began to resign in protest against the (predictable) encroachments of the Saleh regime. Still, criticism of the regime was not universal, with different views emanating from Islah's senior leadership. The shift toward opposition to Saleh was deepest and earliest among Brotherhood members, who began reaching out to non-Islamist parties without the support of senior tribal and Salafi figures. The result was deepening tensions within Islah. Both Zindani and Shaykh al-Ahmar endorsed President Saleh's 1999 move to amend the constitution and consolidate power under a directly-elected presidency, against vociferous opposition from disenchanted Muslim Brotherhood members.

By the early 2000s, the Brotherhood faction within Islah could count on the fruits of its institution building over the previous decade, as many campus activists entered the workforce and became increasingly influential within professional syndicates and other NGOs. This facilitated coordination with other parties, as both leftists and Islamists had pragmatic and effective leaders who hoped to limit Saleh's further consolidation of power. It was the combination of a changing global climate after the September 11th terror attacks and the assassination of socialist Jar Allah Umar in December 2002, however, that pushed Yemen's Muslim Brotherhood to stem both Saleh and the Salafi Right through the formation of a formal opposition alliance.

The six parties of the new Joint Meeting Parties (JMP) alliance (which included Islah, the Yemeni Socialist Party, Nasserists, Baathists, al-Haqq, and the Union of Popular Forces) naturally had considerable ideological differences and thus coalesced around issues of procedural reform, decentralization, and anticorruption.[13] Regime officials kept Islah busy, exploiting wedge issues among JMP members and between the Brotherhood and Salafi wings of the party. Brotherhood leaders within Islah shifted considerable attention away from building grassroots support outside of the capital toward sustaining their delicate alliances.

Not only were its ties to constituents eroded by this elite focus, but Islah's participation in the JMP also led to Salafi efforts to "discipline" Brotherhood members through campaigns of *takfir*, or excommunication, and even the establishment of a rival extrapartisan institution of Salafis bridging the gap between Islah and the ruling party. Brotherhood leaders, cognizant of the threat Salafi defection from Islah would pose to their own viability, were under considerable strain; while some pulled closer to the JMP, others refused to back opposition policies that they feared would further alienate Salafis. These internal conflicts contributed to the postponement of the 2009 parliamentary elections.[14]

The agreement to delay the elections may well have been a decisive one for the Brotherhood, as it further eroded the faction's credibility on the ground. Closing down formal institutional channels through which Yemen's increasingly educated and urban population could pursue its grievances against the Saleh regime, the postponement occurred alongside the growth of alternative channels of mobilization. Popular unrest arrived well ahead of the rescheduled elections, and neither the JMP nor Islah's Brotherhood leadership were well positioned to respond.

HOW ISLAH COMPARED TO OTHER BROTHERHOODS BEFORE 2011

Ideologically, the Brotherhood core of Islah can be characterized as republican and modernist in its outlook and priorities, advancing notions of citizenship that are nonsectarian, promoting some political equality for women, and most of all calling for accountable governance.[15] At the same time, non-Brotherhood pressures from within the party have meant that Islah as a whole has adopted positions and enacted policies that have been inconsistent with these principles. The establishment of the JMP exacerbated these internal divides. On the one hand, forming an alliance with leftists and other non-Islamists left the Brotherhood vulnerable to critique by Salafis of *takfir*. On the other hand, the formalization of the alliance gave Brotherhood members a network of allies and channels of support from outside the party with which to balance against internal demands and pressures.[16]

The tensions within Islah are reflected in how different factions have taken responsibility for the party's political and evangelical roles. The

Brotherhood exerted a strong grip on a complex set of intersecting institutions throughout the country, mobilizing students and women activists through dedicated youth and women's branches. The growing power of these groups was reflected in internal elections in the 2000s.[17] By contrast, the Salafi wing of the party played a larger role in the organization's *da'wa* efforts through "scientific institutes" that were not formally under the control of the party and are better understood as "aligned" with Islah. These institutions posed a particular challenge to the Brotherhood in the 2000s, as they advanced a less republican and more sectarian agenda and were seen as enabling, if not encouraging, violence. The Houthi–Salafi conflict thus became something that Brotherhood Islahis could not fully disavow, but which many found counterproductive to the JMP's reform agenda. In the transitional period after 2011, this tension came to a dramatic head as violence occurred between supporters of the Zaydi revivalist Houthi movement and rival militias aligned with Salafi factions of Islah.[18]

The centrifugal pressures that stem from the party's fragmentation mean that Islah's experience has differed from other Brotherhood organizations, which have maintained greater internal coherence and discipline. At its most polarized moment following the death of Sheikh al-Aḥmar in 2007 through the delay of the 2009 elections, it seemed possible that Islah might split into a Brotherhood wing tied to the JMP and a Salafi organization, with the latter potentially aligning with the regime. The 2011 uprising nonetheless showed that when the opportunity for a split presented itself, the party had some institutional stickiness. The Salafi faction could have very well defected in 2011 to the Rashad Union, a newly established Salafi party, but the benefits offered to Islah as a whole by the transitional process helped hold its disparate factions together, even as they did little to resolve its characteristic fragmentation. Indeed, this fragmentation may have been essential to Islah's adaptability, allowing the party to be many things to many people in a time of uncertainty.

ISLAH IN A CLIMATE OF REVOLUTIONARY CHANGE, 2011–2015

As with other countries that experienced populist uprisings in 2011, Yemen's Muslim Brotherhood was not the primary driver of mobilization but managed to secure a substantial share of power in the transitional process. As protest movements gathered strength in Tunisia and Egypt, Yemen's JMP responded with tepid, reform-oriented "pink protests" designed to signal its position as a loyal opposition with reformist, not revolutionary, demands.[19] This focus on reform was out of sync with the aspirations of many young activists. While Brotherhood leaders participated in protests, they took a backseat as youth activists in "Change Square" and other squares throughout the country organized for Saleh's ouster. This decline in the JMP's relevance (and, by extension, the Brotherhood's relevance) among protesters stood in stark contrast to international mediation efforts pursued simultaneously, which sought to work directly with organized opposition parties as representative of "the Yemeni people." Once it became clear that the Gulf Cooperation Council–backed transitional agreement would offer President Saleh and his associates legal immunity for crimes committed before and during the uprising, and that the transitional government would include many Saleh loyalists, protesters began to target the JMP itself, critical of an opposition that would agree to such concessions.[20]

With this shift in the protest movement came a shift in the Brotherhood's ties to its allies and adversaries. Whereas Brotherhood leaders initially sought to piggyback on youth enthusiasm, Salafi militias soon began to work to control protest spaces, in alliance with some tribal militias. Members of the Houthi movement, who had until this point participated alongside other protest groups against Saleh, also began to bring weapons to the protest squares, and the collaborative relationship that had developed among some Islahi and Houthi youth began to deteriorate.[21] While the violence of Islah and Houthi members pales in comparison to the warlike conditions that unfolded between tribal militias and factions of the fractured armed forces outside the capital, Islah–Houthi skirmishes nonetheless undermined the coherence of protest spaces and laid the foundation for substantial conflicts during the transitional period.

Islah generally, and the Brotherhood specifically, became the single greatest beneficiary of the transitional agreement after former president Saleh and his closest associates. The framework established by the Gulf Cooperation Council (GCC) and later adopted by the United Nations hinged on a power-sharing agreement between members of the JMP and the General People's Congress, the former ruling party. As the largest and best-organized member of the JMP, Islah played an important role in brokering the JMP's appointments, and was thus in a position to heavily shape the "opposition" half of the transitional government.[22] Given the divisions within Islah, this disproportionate reliance on the JMP also offered centrist Brotherhood members a lifeline at a moment of particular weakness.[23]

That said, unlike Egypt or Tunisia, Yemen is not a case in which the Muslim Brotherhood has governed as such. Instead, before the collapse of the transition period in early 2015, Islah's Brotherhood members worked to consolidate what hold they could over the institutions that, theoretically, would remake Yemen's political regime. The GCC transitional framework was focused at the top—it prioritized an uncontested presidential election over parliamentary elections or civil service reform, and it reallocated power primarily through cabinet and ministerial portfolios.[24] Because the "implementation mechanism" (as the formal United Nations endorsement of the GCC agreement is known) stipulated that the terms of the agreement "may not be challenged before the institutions of the state," any opposition to its terms took a necessarily populist form.[25] This could be seen in dramatic acts of opposition ranging from the "parallel revolution," a series of sit-ins and coordinated work stoppages throughout the public sector,[26] to the Life March, in which tens of thousands of Yemenis walked hundreds of kilometers on foot in protest against the immunity law required by the transitional agreement and endorsed by the transitional government.[27] In these and other cases, Islahi leaders, who had long campaigned for political accountability, faced an acute credibility challenge as signatories to and beneficiaries of an agreement that blocked accountability in multiple ways. Yemen's Muslim Brothers were thus in an ambivalent position.[28] On the one hand, leaders attempted to maintain ties to protesters and retain the mantle of opposition; on the other hand, as a part of the transitional government, they played a substantive role in suppressing new forms of dissent, including through the authorization of force against unarmed protesters opposing transitional terms.[29]

Even as its role of representative of "the opposition" was foundering in the streets, the GCC framework guaranteed Islah a substantial role in the National Dialogue Conference (NDC). Designed as the centerpiece of the transitional process, the NDC was intended to address thorny issues that fell outside of the relatively narrow scope of the transitional power-sharing agreement.[30] It included nine working groups, but Islah was particularly active—and polarizing—in two: the Sa'da committee (dealing with conflict in the historic Houthi homeland) and the Rights and Freedoms committee. It was in this context that Islah's internal fissures were most evident, with the party's delegates—responding to pressures from their right flank—pursuing more ideologically polarizing positions than the Brotherhood members represented in the transitional government. This pressure was intensified by the formation in June 2012 of a new Salafi party, the Rāshad Union, which had no role in the transitional government but was able to exert a rightward pull in NDC committee sessions by caucusing with Islah.

The substantive sticking points were ideological and related to familiar issues that many Islamist parties engage: the status of sharia in the country's legal system, the rights of women and non-Muslims, and issues of religious freedom. In the case of the Sa'da working group, the conflict between Islahis and Houthis in committee sessions paralleled the armed conflict that would escalate between militias aligned with both groups in 2013 and into 2014; their work was so stymied that the committee's final report was substantially delayed.[31] As armed conflict between rival militias intensified, Islahis and Salafi allies outside of the party sought to frame themselves as underdogs to mobilize anti-Houthi (and, in some quarters, anti-Zaydi) sentiment.[32] The end of the NDC raised the stakes for the Houthis, as they lost the only formal institutional voice they were afforded by the transitional framework and were thus returned to their position as political outsiders. It was in this context that they pushed to revisit the GCC framework in its entirety. Yemen soon found itself on the path to civil war.

ISLAH UNDER CONDITIONS OF WAR

The breakdown of the GCC transitional framework began well before Houthi militants arrived in Sanaa in September 2014, and is as much a story of the outsized empowerment of Islah (and the Brotherhood faction within Islah) by an unaccountable transitional framework as it is about the ambitions of the Houthi movement itself. This is particularly evident in the Houthis' explicit targeting of Islahis and Islah-affiliated institutions, as senior Brotherhood figures were detained, prevented from traveling, and harassed in other ways.[33] Brotherhood figures maintained an impressive commitment to nonviolence in the capital, but outside of Sanaa, they were neither able to exercise much influence over Salafi militias nor to offset the sectarian polarization that came from an increasingly aggressive campaign of violence by al-Qaeda. A conflict that was largely institutional became, over a series of months, almost intractably ideological.

The breakdown of the transitional process also reflected shifting fortunes for the Muslim Brotherhood on a regional level. Despite the threat of a republic on its borders, the GCC made space for Islah in the transitional framework for two main reasons. First, while the member parties of Yemen's JMP were universally undesirable in ideological terms (from the standpoint of most GCC countries), they were a preformed opposition that might be able to bring a speedy end to the conflict and promote reform over genuine revolution in the GCC's backyard. Owing to its long-standing role in Yemeni politics, Islah's leaders were also well known and at least some had political and financial ties to the Gulf kingdoms. Second, there was unquestionably less concern over Islahi Brotherhood members' republicanism than there might otherwise have been, given that the party's internal factionalism prevented much real Brotherhood autonomy and that the Brotherhood's grassroots base was so eroded by 2011. In other words, Islah was simply not a tremendous threat, relative to an electoral process in Egypt that Gulf actors could not as easily contain. That said, Yemen's Muslim Brotherhood was swept up in the broad Gulf campaign against the Brotherhood in 2014. Still, regional shifts—increased anxiety regarding Iran and polarizing sectarianism first among them—contributed to what Toby Matthiessen has called Islah's "rehabilitation" as a tactical ally in 2015, as major Islah figures sought refuge in (and called for war from) Saudi Arabia and elsewhere in the Gulf, and as the Saudis attempted to promote their war in Yemen with the support of their own domestic Islamist movement.[34]

Today, several senior Islahis remain in exile along with other members of the transitional regime. No longer an opposition in any meaningful sense, the party's Brotherhood leadership has committed to President Hadi's foundering government, in ways reminiscent of the party's old role as Saleh allies in the 1990s. The Muslim Brotherhood, lacking a strong social movement foundation for many years now, is heavily dependent on the legitimacy tenuously afforded it by international agreements and the actors who back them. While the Yemeni Brotherhood long disavowed violence as a political strategy in domestic politics, it now depends on an international coalition of armies that promises to restore their political position through force. While the Hadi government has been only fitfully committed to peace negotiations, a negotiated settlement is the likeliest way for the Brotherhood to emerge from the current military impasse with a modicum of institutional power. The fact of the government's equivocation in these negotiations seems to suggest that Islah (or at least its Brotherhood leadership) holds less sway than it did before the onset of the war.[35]

While it might be tempting to disregard Islah as "too different" to tell scholars much about Muslim Brotherhood politics owing to its internal fragmentation, it is also possible to read it as essential to the broader Brotherhood story. Islah reinforces what we know about the limits of politics without a strong grassroots movement, and of the risk of working primarily within existing institutions and state structures. It tells a cautionary tale of the vulnerabilities that come with alliances, with other Islamists and non-Islamists alike. And it shows how Brotherhood trajectories can be shaped by others' use of force, even when Brotherhood members themselves do not endorse violence as a political strategy. As an organization schooled in North Yemeni traditions of negotiation and accommodation, the Islah party has shown itself to be an adaptable organization capable of surviving Yemen's civil war.[36] Whether the same can be said for the fortunes of its Brotherhood leaders more specifically remains to be seen, but their political survival is likely to depend far more on forces outside of Yemen than those within.

6

Libya

Omar Ashour

ISLAMISTS AND THEIR ROLE in uprisings, democratic transitions, and political violence has been one of the most debated issues in the wake of the Arab spring's collapse. Libyan Islamists have been a critical part of an armed revolution that, with NATO's assistance, was able to topple the regime of longtime strongman Muammar Qaddafi. Several different Islamist currents in Libya have also been an integral part of the democratization process, including electoral competition, constitution drafting, and civil society activities. Libya's Islamists also became heavily engaged in the ongoing Libyan civil war. Islamists were not all on one side, however; the majority sided with the Tripoli government, and a small minority (mainly Salafis and former jihadist figures) sided with the Tobruk government. After the establishment of the United Nations–backed Government of National Accord (GNA) in December 2015, Islamist parties and factions were once again divided. Some, including the Libyan Muslim Brotherhood, accepted the GNA, while others attempted to undermine it or to condition their acceptance.

Before delving into the analysis, a few Libyan peculiarities need to be highlighted. First, the Libyan events of 2011 were the only political revolution of the Arab uprisings. As opposed to Tunisia, Egypt, Bahrain, Syria, and Yemen, revolutionary forces not only managed to topple the regime but also fundamentally altered the political system.

Tunisian, Egyptian, Bahraini, Syrian, and Yemeni pro-change forces did not have the capacity to do so, resulting in different trajectories of transition, stagnation, or deterioration. Political compromises between status quo forces and forces of change were the highlight in Tunisia. A bloody defeat for the supporters of the January 25, 2011 uprising was the main result in Egypt. Pro-democracy forces in Bahrain faced a similar fate. And a violent political stalemate between these forces, and within them, was the result in Syria and Yemen.

Between August 2011 and May 2014, Libya's pro-revolution forces had actually succeeded in substantially altering the status quo. They were able not only to take down the entire Qaddafi regime by force but also to institute unprecedented basic freedoms and free and fair elections for the first time in Libya's history. Libyan Islamists were at the core of the two processes. They significantly contributed to the fight against Qaddafi forces. Several Islamist groups, factions, and figures also participated in the electoral process, including post-jihadist ones, such as those from the defunct Libyan Islamic Fighting Group (LIFG). Islamists, with other Libyan conservative tribal forces, also tried to use their newfound institutional space to implement their understanding of sharia.

Since May 2014, when General Khalifa Haftar declared his second televised coup, Libyan politics has changed significantly. Before then, Islamists and their rivals were contesting politics on four fronts: a media front, an electoral and institutional front, a judicial front, and a military front. The latter was characterized by a "balance of terror" rather than full-fledged armed confrontation. Each political party or coalition was attempting to extend its influence over, and strengthen its alliance with, armed battalions of various affiliations. The May 2014 attempted coup turned that multidimensional conflict primarily into an armed one. The majority of Islamist forces, including the Libyan Muslim Brotherhood and ex-LIFG, were on the side of the Tripoli government, while a minority, mainly from the so-called Salafi-Madkhali trend and former jihadist figures, sided with the Tobruk government and General Hafter's forces. This was before a third government, the Government of National Accord (GNA) was established in December 2015, with international backing. The transformation of the conflict had major implications on Islamist behavior, especially in light of developments in nearby Egypt.

It is worth mentioning here that the Libyan branch of the Muslim Brotherhood is a significantly different organization from its Egyptian older sister, the main target of the July 3, 2013 military coup in Egypt. Two critical differences are worth highlighting. First, the Libyan Brotherhood had only a limited presence in the decades prior to the 2011 revolution. Since the late 1990s, the group was largely inactive on universities, provided no social services, and had virtually no mosques or public spaces to promote its views. Therefore, after the revolution, it had a limited base of support compared to the Egyptian Brotherhood and even Ennahda in Tunisia. Second, the Libyan revolution was primarily a popular armed one and the Brotherhood participated in it. So, as opposed to the Egyptian and the Tunisian Islamists, the Libyan Brotherhood's experience in collective armed action, within a multiactor coalition, was much more positive. That specific genre of armed action not only toppled a brutal dictatorship but also helped the Libyan branch to avoid the dismal fate of the mother organization in Egypt. These two key differences have had a major impact on the political behavior of the organization.

This chapter is divided into three parts. The first section provides an overview of the main Islamist forces in Libya, their backgrounds, and their role in the transition. The second analyzes the salient issues facing Libyan Islamists and how they affect their behaviors in Libya. These issues are the 2011 armed revolution, the 2012–2013 electoral process, the 2014 attempted coup and civil war that ensued afterward, and the rise of the Islamic State in Libya. The final section briefly concludes with implications for the study of Islamism.

LIBYAN ISLAMIST ACTORS: AN OVERVIEW

The Libyan Muslim Brotherhood

"The Muslim Brothers established this party. We are a national civil party with an Islamic reference.... We have Islamists and nationalists," said Al-Amin Belhaj, the head of the founding committee for the newly formed Justice and Construction Party.[1] With this March 3, 2012 announcement, Libya seemed set to follow the electoral path of Islamist success set in Egypt, Tunisia, and other Arab countries. After decades of fierce repression by the Qaddafi regime, the formation of a political party in Libya was a heady experience.

The Muslim Brotherhood's presence in Libya goes back to 1949. But their first clear organizational structure was established in 1968 and quickly froze in 1969 after the coup of Colonel Qaddafi.[2] The Brotherhood was never allowed to operate openly and suffered extreme repression. Indeed, when state television did broadcast something about the group, it was the bodies of its leaders hung from street lampposts in the mid-1980s. Qaddafi's media called them "deviant heretics" and "stray dogs." Fleeing repression, the Libyan Muslim Brotherhood was reborn in the United States, where members established the "Islamic Group—Libya" in 1980 and issued their magazine *The Muslim*. In 1982, many of the Brotherhood figures who were studying in the United States returned to Libya to re-establish the organization but ended up in prison or were executed.[3]

The Libyan Muslim Brotherhood made something of a comeback in 1999 and entered into a dialogue with the regime. Its rebirth was bolstered in 2005 and 2006 by Saif al-Islam Qaddafi's initiatives, which aimed to co-opt and neutralize opposition groups, particularly Islamist ones.[4] This led to doubts about the group's motivations during the 2011 revolution, charges Brotherhood leaders reject. "No, we did not plan the revolution and we weren't playing a double game with the regime," said Fawzi Abu Kitef, the head of the Revolutionary Brigades Coalition in Eastern Libya and the former deputy defense minister in the National Transitional Council (NTC), the body that led the revolution and then de facto governed Libya for a period of several months (March 2011 to August 2012) before the first elections.[5] Abu Kitef was a leading figure in the Brotherhood who spent more than 18 years in Qaddafi's jails, including the notorious Abu Selim prison.[6] Indeed, from the outset, the Brotherhood was supportive of the NTC, with some of its icons joining it, such as Abdullah Shamia, who was in charge of economic affairs in the NTC.

Libya's Muslim Brotherhood modeled its new party after Egypt's Freedom and Justice Party (FJP). The Libyan Brotherhood is much smaller than its Egyptian counterpart, however. In 2009, Soliman Abdul Qadir, the former general overseer of the Libyan Muslim Brotherhood, estimated the number of Brotherhood members in exile to be around 200 and inside Libya to be a few thousand, mainly concentrated in the professional and student sectors.[7] While those cadres would be critical for the movement and its party, they can hardly compare to the hundreds of thousands of the Egyptian Brotherhood.

During its first public conference in Benghazi in November 2011, the Libyan Muslim Brotherhood restructured the organization, elected a new leader, increased its consultative council membership from 11 to 30, and decided to form a political party. In their party elections, Mohamed Swan, the former head of the consultative council, narrowly defeated the former Brotherhood leader Soliman Abdul Qadir and two other candidates to become the leader of the new party, the Justice and Construction Party (JCP). "Participation in the party will be based on an individual, not group basis," said Bashir al-Kubty, the newly elected general overseer of the Libyan Brotherhood. He meant that the party would not be a political front.[8] "They want it to be like the FJP in Egypt, 80 percent Brotherhood and 20 percent others ... to be able to say that they are inclusive," said Gumaa al-Gumati, a former non-Islamist representative of the NTC in London.[9]

When Ali al-Sallabi, a Salafi-leaning Islamist figure once affiliated with the Brotherhood, proposed a National Rally Coalition to include the Muslim Brotherhood and other Islamists, Brotherhood leaders ultimately rejected the proposal. The group's objective in that phase of the transition was to ensure control over its political arm. It ostentatiously shunned alliances with post-jihadists (like those of the Libyan Islamic Fighting Group, which changed its name temporarily to the Libyan Islamic Movement for Change, or LIMC, before its members split into various factions) to avoid any international outcry. It also rejected initiatives proposed by ex-affiliates, like Sallabi, which they feared would send the wrong message to the rank-and-file.[10] Domestic and international legitimacy, expansion of audience, and internal discipline have been the determinants of the Libyan Brotherhood's behavior since the transition process began after Qaddafi's fall.

The ever evolving Libyan political scene posed several major challenges to Libya's Muslim Brotherhood, especially prior to the 2012 parliamentary elections. Unlike the Brotherhood in Egypt and Ennahda in Tunisia, Libyan Islamists had little history of interactions with the masses.

The Egyptian Brotherhood had a third life from the early 1970s, and over the next four decades it worked hard to build mass support in universities, professional syndicates, unions, and on the streets. Ennahda wasn't much different, although mass outreach efforts were frozen in 1990, after the Tunisian regime launched a brutal crackdown. Due to the complete lack of political opening over decades, the Libyan Brotherhood did not have any real opportunities to connect with ordinary Libyans. They also lacked any space to build organizational structures or institutions within Libya or to create a parallel network of clinics and social services.

Second, Libyan Islamists had to deal with persistent questions about their commitment to democratic values, women's rights, and pluralism. The attempt to be inclusive was clear at the Justice and Construction Party's first annual conference on March 2–3, 2012. Walid al-Sakran, nonmember of the Brotherhood, was a candidate for the party's leadership, and five women attempted to join the 45-member Consultative Council. Three were successful. But even if the leadership had been committed to pragmatism, the Brotherhood's more conservative base expect ideology to more directly influence behavior. The challenge for the leadership was to legitimate its pragmatic behavior, including coalitions with non-Islamists, to their followers. The experience of Islamists in exile in the West and their fluid circumstances both at home and abroad helped to ease the tension between political pragmatism and ideological commitments. This applies particularly to the Brotherhood and the LIMC, but not necessarily to local Salafis (who are more numerous than the members of both organizations but lack a structure and leadership).

Third, the constitution drafting process has posed thorny challenges. The reference to the sharia as the principal source of legislation in Article 1 of the August 2011 constitutional declaration raised eyebrows in the West and among Libya's liberals. Something similar happened when Mustafa Abdul Jalil, the chairman of the NTC, spoke about the superiority of sharia and the legitimacy of polygamy in the liberation speech of October 23, 2011. "We are an Islamic state," he said, pledging to get rid of regulations that failed to conform to Islamic law.

The Brotherhood, the LIMC, Salafis, and conservative figures perceived this as a victory. "The laws of Libya need to have an Islamic reference and that should be enshrined in the constitution," Bashir al-Kubty told me.[11] "The issue of the sharia is settled. It will be the supreme source of legislation.... There is no point in making this debatable or raising the Quran in Benghazi and Sabha," said Abdel Nasser Shamata, the head of the Crisis Management Unit in the NTC. His statement was a response to demonstrations of a few hundred in Benghazi and Sabha demanding the implementation of sharia in 2011 and 2012.[12]

The issue of sharia will remain a difficult, even intractable one as the country alternates between political transition and civil conflict. Libyan Islamists' relative electoral successes occurred in 2012 without a thorough update of their worldviews. This exacerbated political and ideological polarization, which became increasingly evident in the new Libya.

The Libyan Islamic Fighting Group

Established in 1990, the LIFG was modeled along the lines of the Egyptian al-Jihad organization: secretive, elitist, exclusively paramilitary, and aiming for decisive action to topple the regime.[13] However, Libyan authorities discovered the group, forcing it to declare its existence for the first time on October 18, 1995. A brutal crackdown followed and the LIFG led a three-year low-level insurgency based mainly in Eastern Libya. The group attempted to assassinate Colonel Qaddafi on three occasions in 1995 and 1996. By 1998, the Consultative Council of the LIFG decided to impose a three-year ceasefire in Libya, to be reviewed in 2001. But the events of 9/11 changed the group's calculations, as it put the leadership and organization in survival mode.

According to the LIFG leaders and members I interviewed in Tripoli, the dialogue with the Libyan regime started in 2005. In 2006, six members from the consultative council were involved in talks with the regime. By the end of 2010, the LIFG had published a book, *Corrective Studies in Understandings of Jihad, Enforcement of Morality, and Judgment of People*, in which it reviewed the ideas and fatwas advocating rebellion against rulers and casting individuals as apostates (*takfir*). In March 2010, Saif al-Islam, Qaddafi's son, heralded the release of LIFG commanders and praised their book in a public conference attended by Western diplomats, academics, and journalists.

Like the Muslim Brotherhood and its offshoots, the LIFG and the broader jihadist trend supported the February 2011 revolution, playing a significant role in the removal of Qaddafi's regime. This brought a wealth of paramilitary experience to Libyan revolutionaries. LIFG members and others were heavily involved in multiple armed conflicts, including in Afghanistan, Algeria, and Chechnya. But, in an effort to update its image, the LIFG first transformed itself into the Libyan Islamic Movement for Change (LIMC), and many of its figures were also members of the Tripoli Military Council. Two of its leading figures established the al-Watan (Homeland) Party and Tajammu' al-Umma al-Wasat (Centrist Umma Assembly) Party in November 2011 and April 2012, respectively.

The Salafi Trend

The existence of the Salafi trend in Libya goes back to the 1960s.[14] As in other countries, non-jihadist Salafism in Libya is divided into four subtrends: status quo or authoritarian Salafism, apolitical or scholarly Salafism, political-reformist Salafism, and armed Salafism. Despite being associated with Saudi theologians, status quo Salafism was able to grow under the Qaddafi regime, mainly due to its support of the legitimacy of authoritarian rulers, regardless of their behavior or "Islamic-ness," drawing on a major strain of Sunni political theology. Like some Egyptian Salafis, many of the sheikhs within this subtrend opposed the revolution. Between February and August 2011, some of them were used for pro-Qaddafi propaganda, issuing statements on television and radio to cast religious legitimacy on the regime and delegitimize the revolutionaries.[15]

After Qaddafi, the Salafi trend in Libya, despite its relatively large numbers, suffered from a lack of leadership and organizational discipline. Additionally, Salafi ideology, being more fluid than is often assumed, does not easily translate into specific political behavior. As a result, Libyan Salafis engaged in the electoral process, helped fuel political polarization, and participated in the armed conflict, but on rival sides.[16] One of the strands of armed Salafi-jihadism, however, was able to centralize its local structures and became a force to reckon with in Libya: the branch of the Islamic State in Libya, specifically its Cyrenaica and Tripolitania Provinces.

ISLAMISTS AND THE 2012 ELECTORAL LOSSES

"We certainly did not expect the results, but regardless ... our future is certainly better than our present and our past," said Sami al-Saadi, former ideologue of the LIFG and the founder of the aforementioned Umma al-Wasat Assembly, which came in third in Central Tripoli.[17] Saadi, once called "the Sheikh of the Arabs" by the Taliban's Mullah Omar and previously the author of the LIFG's antidemocracy manifesto, accepted the defeat of Islamists in Libya's first democratic elections.

Indeed, the results raised eyebrows, even for analysts who did not expect an Islamist landslide. In electoral district number one, where Derna lies (commonly referred to as an "Islamist stronghold"), the "liberal leaning" National Forces Coalition (NFC), a coalition of more than 60 parties and hundreds of civil society organizations, swept with 59,769 votes, while the Muslim Brotherhood's Justice and Construction Party only got 8,619. Umma al-Wasat Assembly came in third with 4,962 votes.

In the district of Abu Selim—where many Islamists were perceived as local heroes due to their sacrifices under brutal repression—the NFC still swept with 60,052 votes, defeating all six Islamist parties, which together received less than 15,000 votes. Overall, liberal-leaning parties won the most votes in 11 out of the 13 electoral districts, with the NFC winning 10 of those. Overall, the NFC claimed 39 seats, the JCP won 17 seats, coming in a distant second, while Umma al-Wasat secured only 2 seats.

Due to a somewhat confusing electoral law, those results only affected 80 out of the 200 seats of the General National Congress (GNC), whose mandate was to appoint a prime minister, a government, and a committee to craft the constitution. The rest of the 120 seats were reserved for individual candidates.

In some districts, though, Islamists weren't too far behind. Across Libya, they won second place in 10 out of the 13 districts, with the JCP winning 9 of those and the Salafi-leaning Originality Coalition winning 1. In Misrata, the JCP came in second, after the local Union for Homeland Party, but still managed to win almost three times the votes of the NFC, which came in fourth.

Islamists spearheading the opposition against Qaddafi were advised by Tunisian and Egyptian Islamists and used rhetoric full of religious symbolism in a conservative, Muslim-majority country. Not surprisingly for some, this was not enough. As discussed earlier, a key difference exists between the Egyptian Brotherhood and Ennahda in Tunisia, on the one hand, and the Islamists of Libya on the other: the history of institutionalism and interactions with the masses. In the four decades of Qaddafi's rule, Libya's Islamists were unable to build local support networks.

As a result of their organizational immaturity, Islamists were unable to unite under one coalition to compete with former prime minister Mahmoud Jibril's NFC. Instead, Islamist votes were divided between several parties. For example, the LIFG had to split votes between two large factions: the al-Watan Party, led by the LIFG's former commander, Abdul Hakim Belhaj, and Umma al-Wasat Assembly, led by the LIFG's former ideologue, Sami al-Saadi. Moreover, sometimes the Salafi-leaning Originality Coalition-affiliated parties competed against each other in the very same district, most notably district 11, where three of their parties came in 2nd, 7th, and 13th in Tajoura and Souk al-Jum'a. Additionally, Originality Coalition leaders failed to mobilize large sections of the Libyan Salafi community who boycotted the elections, mainly out of theological convictions that elections are religiously illegitimate.

Another reason for non-Islamist success is the "blood" factor. "I am not giving my family's votes to the Muslim Brotherhood. Two of my cousins died because of them," explained Mohamed Abdul Hakim, a voter from Benghazi.[18] Despite believing that Islam should be the source for legislation, he still voted non-Islamist. His cousins were killed in a confrontation in the 1990s, likely between the Martyrs Movement (a small jihadist group operating in his neighborhood at the time) and Qaddafi's forces. Nevertheless, many average Libyans, including Mohamed, do not distinguish between different Islamist organizations. For many, all Islamists are "Ikhwan" (Muslim Brotherhood). The "stain" of direct involvement in armed action, coupled with the fears of enforcing Taliban-like laws or an Algeria-like scenario of civil war, has harmed Islamists across the spectrum.

Islamist rhetoric during the election campaign also contributed to the poor showing at the polls. "It is offensive to tell me I have to vote for an Islamic party. What does that make me if I voted otherwise?! In Libya we are Muslims. . . . They can't take away my identity and claim it's only theirs," said Jamila Marzouki, an Islamic studies graduate who voted for the NFC, despite wanting Islam to be the ultimate reference for Libyan laws.[19]

There were other factors as well boosting the popularity of non-Islamists: The domestic and international legitimacy of Mahmoud Jibril, his tribal affiliation (the Warfalla tribe is about 1 million strong), and his leadership style, coupled with a hope-oriented campaign pitch (while also exaggerating the repercussions of an Islamist takeover and showing off Jibril's "piety"), all produced a convincing electoral success.

POLITICAL–MILITARY COALITIONS AND REGIONAL PATRONS

But if non-Islamists were able to claim victory in elections, Islamists and their allies in the General National Congress were able to form more effective coalitions and therefore control the majority of votes. This happened mainly by keeping these coalitions disciplined during voting. The NFC failed to do so, and the subsequent reduction of its bloc in the GNC led to further polarization and attempts to dissolve the GNC, most notably General Hafter's first and second coup attempts in February and May 2014.

Parliamentary elections were held on June 25, 2014, in the middle of Libya's descent into civil conflict. This time, all candidates ran as independents, with non-Islamist factions win the majority of seats. Election turnout was very low, however, at less than 18 percent, compared to 61.6 percent in 2012. The low turnout was mainly attributed to the escalation of armed confrontations following General Hafter's May coup, which rejected both the new elections and the GNC.

LIBYA'S ISLAMISTS AND REGIONAL DYNAMICS

The actions of regional players have not only exacerbated the polarization in Libya but also directly spoiled reconciliation efforts at critical junctures. The Sissi regime in Egypt is a prime example. As General

Abbas Kamel, chief aide of Abdel Fattah al-Sissi, said in a series of leaks published between November 2014 and March 2015: "This man is an opportunity, sir. He is speaking about the timing... They are planning something there [in Libya]. Yes, he is speaking about a form of secret cooperation ... unannounced to anyone... No one will hear or know about it... He will come to you."[20] "The man" was Ahmed Gaddaf al-Dam, Qaddafi's cousin and aide who was being pursued by Libyan authorities as well as by Interpol for alleged crimes against humanity. He had also been recently interviewed on a pro-regime Egyptian television channel to publicly declare his support for the Islamic State.[21]

The exact date of the leaked conversation is unknown, but it was almost certainly after Sissi's military coup on July 3, 2013 and before Hafter's first "television coup" on February 14, 2014. The leak revealed nothing particularly new but shed important light on the regional dimensions of the Libyan conflict. Sissi's military involvement in Libya became common knowledge in official and expert circles around November 2013. In August 2014, American officials exposed an Egyptian-Emirati secret airstrike in Tripoli—an unprecedented bombing raid by an Arab Gulf state on an Arab North African capital.[22] Further details were exposed of actions that clearly violated the arms embargo on Libya and UN Security Council resolution 1970. "We should not forget the favor of Egypt. Our ammo came from Egypt. 400 containers from there," said Saqr al-Joroushi, the commander of the "air forces" loyal to General Khalifa Haftar and the Torbuk government, while the cheering crowd chanted "Allahu Akbar."[23]

In February 2014, Egypt's air forces struck again, this time in Derna after Islamic State militants brutally slaughtered 21 Egyptian citizens in Sirte. After the strike, Sissi's regime sought United Nations approval for a military intervention in Libya, then for a naval blockade of the Tripoli government while lifting the embargo on the Tobruk side. All attempts were diplomatic failures.

"Sisi doesn't have credibility with, and he is in fact an opponent of, the moderate Islamists and they are already looking to use his bombings as a pretense to abandon the talks," a European diplomat noted in March 2015.[24] That may be an oversimplification on several levels.

While they are certainly part of it, the Tripoli government is not exactly run by "moderate Islamists" but by a multilayered coalition in which pro-revolution regionalists, such as Misratan revolutionary brigades and local council, are a very influential faction. The Tobruk government is not exactly "secular" either; It is a nonhomogeneous coalition of military factions, regionalist forces, pro-Qaddafi elements, and pro-revolution ones, with the military faction—led by Khalifa Haftar—having more clout. The latter believe in the "Sissi model" of takeover, including using Salafi figures to issue supportive fatwas for repressing rivals.

The Western-backed United Nations track offered an alternative route—with less bloody prospects and a potentially higher chance of defeating the Islamic State and like-minded organizations without empowering a ruthless dictator in the process. The immediate objective was to build and empower a Government of National Accord (GNA) led by Fayez al-Sarraj, alongside potentially unified and professional Libyan security and military forces. The GNA was established as a result of a fragile agreement whose final draft was signed by 19 leading politicians, from several sides, on December 17, 2015 (but also with a significant number of defectors, including the heads of the rival parliaments in Tripoli and Tobruk).

The strategy pursued by the Sissi regime has already produced a series of negative consequences within Egypt, and the results may yet prove even more damaging for Libya's already precarious situation, not to mention the rest of the region. The objective of Sissi's strategy is not about national reconciliation, social cohesion, or defeating violent extremism. It is more about eradicating political rivals, mainly the Muslim Brotherhood and other Islamist factions; empowering like-minded and loyal military figures; installing another repressive authoritarian regime on the borders of Egypt; and—where the other objectives intersect—defeating the Islamic State. But the tactics employed toward this last objective have been more likely to prolong the civil war in Libya and reduce any potential for reconciliation and democratization. And with these consequences, a stronger North African version of the Islamic State, or something like it, will remain a possibility, even after anti-Hafter military, pro-GNA forces were able to defeat the Islamic

State in Sirte in December 2016 and a coalition of Islamist and local jihadist militias defeated them in Derna in July 2015.

THE ISLAMIC STATE AND LIBYA'S ISLAMISTS

The very fact that the Islamic State was able to gain control of Sirte, Qaddafi's hometown, in February 2016 alarmed all sides of the Libyan civil war, particularly in the west (Tripoli and Misrata). The Islamist Libya Dawn,[25] a military force operating under Libya's chief of staff loyal to the Tripoli government, had deployed the 166th Battalion around Sirte in an attempt to take over the city center, the university, and other areas from Islamic State loyalists. In February 2015, the Libyan Muslim Brotherhood supported the takeover but did not officially declare any role in the fight. "ISIS forces there are estimated to be somewhere between 100 and 150 armed vehicles [pick-up trucks and four-by-four SUVs]," said Mohamed Abdullah, a General National Congress (Tripoli Parliament) member.[26] The ground troops of Libya Dawn, however, were not enough for a quick, decisive victory. But in May 2016, the GNA, using Tripoli's chief of staff and Libya Dawn forces, launched another attack on Islamic State strongholds in Sirte. This time, the attack was more successful due to international military, intelligence, and logistical support that included airstrikes by the United States.[27] By December 2016, the last Islamic State stronghold in Sirte's al-Jiza al-Bahariyya district, collapsed after intense fighting. It was a pyrrhic victory, however. Libya Dawn forces lost over 715 fighters and more than 3000 were injured in house-to-house urban battles.

The rise of the Islamic State posed a significant challenge, not only to the Muslim Brotherhood in Libya but also to Salafi factions, including the remnants of the LIFG and its offshoots. Young Libyan Islamist activists link the Brotherhood's failure in Egypt to the rise of the Islamic State in Syria and Iraq. In some Islamist circles, the radical narrative and propaganda of the "caliphate" and its three Libyan "provinces" (Cyrenaica, Tripoli, and Fezzan) are contrasted to the gradualist, boring, and unattractive approach of the Muslim Brotherhood and the failures of post-LIFG political parties and figures. This has implications for recruitment and radicalization. Derna is a good example of how Islamic State loyalists steadily advanced against other organizations, even as the latter had more resources and followers.

Libya's local jihadists in Derna publically declared their oath of allegiance to Abu Bakr al-Baghdadi, the leader of the Islamic State, on November 13, 2014.[28] The organization was able to recruit followers from multiple political factions. One of them was the local Ansar al-Sharia Derna. Another current of support came from the returnees of al-Battar (Amputating Sword) Brigade, a Libyan-dominated militia whose elements fought initially against the forces of Bashar al-Assad in Syria and then, after giving an oath of loyalty to the Islamic State, fought against multiple Syrian pro-revolution forces and the Iraqi army in Kirkuk.[29] But the main organization that constituted the local backbone of the Islamic State in Derna was the Consultative Council of Islamic Youth (CCIY). In terms of strength and membership, it ranked as the fourth militia in Derna in January 2014. CCIY officially declared its existence in May 2014, after a military parade in the streets of Derna. It steadily gained in recruitment, manpower, and firepower to control parts of the city center in October 2014, before giving the oath of loyalty to the Islamic State in November. The rise of CCIY/Islamic State in Derna coincided with the declaration of General Hafter's second coup attempt, the collapse of institutional political process in Libya, and the failure of the Muslim Brotherhood approach to political transitions, as demonstrated in neighboring Egypt.

The rise of the Islamic State in Libya did not stop in Derna. Overall, the manpower of the organization in Libya was estimated to be in the range of 2,000 to 3,000 in November 2015 by a United Nations report.[30] The estimate rose in February 2016 to become, more likely, in the range of 5,000 to 6,000 members.[31] From February 2015 to June 2016, the Islamic State was able to control and influence areas that extended from al-Hisha/Abu Qrin village about 100 miles west of Sirte to Bin Jawad town located 100 miles east of Sirte. The Islamic State was removed from Derna in July 2015 by a coalition of anti-ISIS armed Islamist and jihadist groups operating under the title of "Derna Mujahidin Consultative Council." The Islamic State also operated in three districts in Benghazi, mainly fighting against the forces of General Haftar. In other parts of Libya, including the western cities of Tripoli, Misrata, Sabratha, and Zuwara, the Islamic State operated in small cells, which lacked the capacity to control territory but were able to facilitate logistical support for the "provinces," as well as to strike when necessary, usually using urban terrorism tactics.

IMPLICATIONS FOR THE STUDY OF ISLAMISM

The Egyptian military coup of July 2013 has significantly affected the region in general and Libya in particular. The message sent by the coup to Libya, Syria, Yemen, and beyond is that of militarizing politics: only arms guarantee political rights, not the constitution, not democratic institutions, and certainly not votes. That message will have implications for Islamist political behavior, including both ideological and organizational consequences, affecting the study of Islamism for some time to come.

The Libyan Muslim Brotherhood has certainly taken a lesson from the Egyptian coup and the fate of Brotherhood leaders and members there. One lesson is the importance of having allies with "hard power" capabilities. Powerful regional militias, factions within armed institutions, and the arming of like-minded loyalists are all options that were partially pursued in Libya. Several Libyan Muslim Brotherhood figures understand that the two Islamist organizations that have stood the test of time and survived major onslaughts are Hamas and Hezbollah, mainly due to the relatively well-developed capacities of their armed wings, in a region where bullets consistently beat ballots. This should not be construed as a transformation toward jihadism. But it can engender a subcategory within an armed Islamist typology, mainly focused on a defensive "arms for survival" understanding of politics. The level of militancy can increase, however, depending on how repressive the political environment is, how radical the competitors are, and the responses of young audiences. The rise of the Islamic State in Libya, against all other Islamist actors, demonstrates some of the effects of the aforementioned factors.

The import of the inclusion-moderation hypothesis, which a number of other contributors to this volume have also discussed, has also been affected by post-uprising Islamist transformations. In Libya, there are two main relevant issues. The first is how political inclusion affects Islamist stances on constitutional liberalism. As seen in the General

National Congress, Islamist parliamentarians attempted to use their electoral heft to implement laws that contradict constitutional liberalism, including on minority rights and gender equality. The second consideration is that if inclusion proves to be permanently unsustainable in the region, which trajectory will unarmed Islamists ultimately take in an environment where moderation simply does not pay off?

7

Saudi Arabia

Toby Matthiesen

SAUDI ARABIA IS ONE of the most important Islamic countries, strategically located and with huge financial resources at its disposal. Given Saudi Arabia's crucial position as custodian of the two holy places of Islam, Mecca and Medina, as well as its increasingly proactive foreign policy, the question of what kind of foreign policy the country should have is important not only for Saudis but also Muslims more generally. Because debates about domestic politics are restricted in Saudi Arabia, debates about foreign policy have become arenas where conflicts between opposing social forces play out. These debates are of tremendous importance for the Middle East and beyond. Political Islam in Saudi Arabia thus has to be analyzed in the context of Saudi Arabia's regional policies.

In this chapter, I argue that apart from geopolitics, the dynamic relationship between the Saudi state and Saudi Islamists has been crucial in shaping the country's foreign policy, particularly since 2011. Islam has, of course, long played a role and been used as an ideological asset in Saudi foreign policy, especially since the time of King Faysal.[1] But other factors have tended to weigh more heavily on decision making in foreign policy.[2] Likewise, in the post-2011 period, Islam is mainly used to support foreign policy decisions that lay in the national interest of the kingdom as perceived by its rulers, for example, in Yemen and Syria, as well as in its opposition to Iran.

Since 2011, Saudi Islamist actors have had to respond to a rapidly changing regional environment and to power struggles in the Saudi ruling family that culminated in the coronation of King Salman and the appointment of his new administration in 2015. By and large, Islamist actors were appalled by the public Saudi backing of the 2013 Egyptian coup. The emergence of the Islamic State, on the other hand, was greeted with some sympathy, because the Islamic State could feed into anti-Iranian and anti-Shiite sentiment, which had been stirred up by Saudi and Gulf Cooperation Council (GCC) government rhetoric and media for years. In addition, the quick advances of the group contributed to its popularity in Saudi Arabia, as did the fact that thousands of Saudis and other GCC nationals joined it as fighters, commanders, and ideologues. But the flow of Saudi fighters and financing to Syria were publicly condemned and clamped down on by the government, especially after the declaration of the caliphate in mid-2014. Meanwhile, King Salman could build on his extensive contacts with various Islamist forces in the kingdom, which he had forged as governor of Riyadh since 1963. Indeed, he and his new administration seemed to be closer to Saudi Islamists, including supporters of the Muslim Brotherhood, than his predecessor King Abdullah had been.[3]

As a result, and probably because this fits into the Saudi narrative of the kingdom as the defender of Sunnis in the region, the war against the Houthis in Yemen that started in March 2015 was endorsed by Saudi Islamist forces from across the ideological spectrum. It was an opportunity for Islamist clerics and public figures to declare their support for the new king and the Saudi leadership, as well as Saudi regional policies, without losing face in front of their supporters.

A FRAGMENTED ISLAMIST FIELD

The question of what constitutes political Islam and "Islamists" in Saudi Arabia is rather difficult to answer. Unlike in most other Arab countries, Islamic scholars do wield considerable power in the political system and hold key positions as judges, ministers, and in the religious police. In other Arab states, Islamists have long confronted ostensibly secular, often Arab nationalist regimes. The Saudi case is more complicated, however.[4] In some areas, Saudi Arabia conforms to many Islamists' notions of what should be implemented in an ideal Islamic state, for example the public enforcement of morality, dress codes, the closure of shops during prayer times, gender separation, the collection of zakat, proselytizing at home and abroad, and the key role of sharia and ulama (clerics) in jurisprudence. So the "Islamist" field is extremely complex and hybrid, and many key Islamist figures are employed by the state. Others outside the formal state apparatus overlap with government-controlled institutions in many arenas, for example in mosques, charities, and the mass media.

Broadly speaking, one can classify the Islamist field as follows: First, there are the adherents of the official Wahhabi tradition. These are the clerics on the Council of the Committee of Senior Ulama and the ulama in the judiciary, the religious police, and parts of the education sector.[5] By and large, these clerics endorsed the kingdom's response to challenges at home and its role in the Arab counterrevolution since 2011. The Saudi grand mufti Abdulaziz al-Shaykh declared that protests were against Islam, forbidding them in other Arab countries (such as Egypt) and in Saudi Arabia. He then endorsed the 2013 coup in Egypt (even though the justifications of the coup depended heavily on the mass protests of June 30, 2013). The mufti also endorsed the crackdown on dissent and public protest inside Saudi Arabia, particularly against Shia citizens. He also denounced the Islamic State as un-Islamic and supported the Saudi-led intervention in Yemen.[6]

A second group, and an important one, is what one could loosely call the "Sahwa" or post-Sahwis—those who were involved in the movement termed the Islamic Awakening (al-Sahwa al-Islamiyya) that emerged in the 1980s and challenged the political dominance of the ruling family in the early 1990s. The Sahwa is an umbrella term for a group that was heavily influenced by Muslim Brotherhood networks in the kingdom and fused Brotherhood ideology with local Wahhabi tradition. It is worth remembering, however, that political parties are banned in Saudi Arabia, and all these networks operate clandestinely. They therefore have a less visible formal structure than elsewhere in the region.

These former Sahwis, who were, broadly speaking, associated with the Muslim Brotherhood trend, largely supported the revolutions in Tunisia and Egypt, as well as in Syria and Yemen, and welcomed the

Muslim Brotherhood coming to power in Egypt. They and their supporters visited Egypt, helped their brothers there, established media outlets, and invested in the country. Although these people have connections to individual Saudi princes and may be employed by the state bureaucracy, they were by and large critical of the Saudi handling of the Arab uprisings. Some of them, such as the popular cleric Salman al-Awda, signed a petition calling for political reforms in early 2011.[7] Indeed, in 2011 and 2012, there was some interaction between Sahwa Islamists, liberals, and political reformers of various persuasions. Together they unsuccessfully tried to push for democratic reforms in the country. One of the key groups behind this alliance was the Saudi Association for Civil and Political Rights (ACPRA), most of whose leaders have since been imprisoned for their activism.[8] Another issue that most activists and many Islamists in the kingdom agree on is the release of political prisoners.[9]

Salman al-Awda also published a book in which he praised public protests and the Arab uprisings.[10] He reaffirmed his position in an open letter to the government on March 15, 2013. In the letter he warned of a sociopolitical explosion if political prisoners were not released and reforms were not enacted immediately.[11]

So for most of the period from 2011 to 2014, Sahwa clerics disagreed with the Saudi government over the handling of regional challenges (with the partial exceptions of Syria, where both supported the opposition, even though there were disputes over which groups to support, and of Bahrain, where both supported the crackdown on the opposition).[12] But the emergence of the Islamic State and then the Houthi takeover of Yemen's capital in September 2014 posed severe challenges to Saudi Arabia and led to a realignment between these Sahwis and the Saudi regime, in particular after Salman took to the throne in early 2015.

The jihadists are another distinct strand of political Islam in Saudi Arabia.[13] Originally, Afghanistan and the Balkans were their main areas of operation, but they then moved their focus to Iraq after 2003, then Yemen, and, since 2011, Syria. In Syria, the foreign policies of the Saudi state and its support for the armed opposition in many ways overlapped with the short-term aims of the jihadists. But the successes of Islamic

State, the declaration of the caliphate, and the group's increasingly anti-Saudi rhetoric undermined this consensus.

While a number of terrorist attacks have occurred in Saudi Arabia since 2014, it is remarkable that throughout the period of 2011 to early 2014 there were no jihadist attacks in Saudi Arabia, even though Saudi leaders took such a forceful stance to support the *ancien régimes* in the region and undermine the democratic prospects of Islamists in Egypt and elsewhere. However, jihadist attacks increased since the summer of 2014, in particular attacks by Islamic State cells. They have targeted the Shia minority in the Eastern Province, an Isma'ili mosque in the southern city of Najran, as well as soldiers and security officials in other parts of the country.[14]

A last group within Saudi Islamism consists of Shia Islamists, concentrated in the Eastern Province. Profound changes have occurred among Shias since the beginning of the Arab uprisings. A protest movement emerged in 2011 and lasted, with interruptions, until late 2013. The movement was youth driven, but clerics and Islamist leaders were the figureheads of the movement.

SAUDI SUPPORT FOR THE EGYPTIAN COUP

Saudi Arabia has long given safe haven to Muslim Brotherhood supporters, in particular those fleeing Gamal Abdul Nasser's and Hafez al-Assad's crackdowns in the second half of the 20th century. They helped build many of the educational and religious institutions that were set up in Saudi Arabia during the oil boom of the 1970s when the country embraced political Islam as a counter-ideology against Arab nationalism and leftist ideologies.[15] In the early 1990s, the Sahwa movement started to criticize the ruling family over its alliance with the United States and the deployment of American troops on Saudi soil during and after the 1991 Gulf War. The Sahwa included many leaders and sympathizers of the local branch of the Muslim Brotherhood that came into being as a result of the migration of Brotherhood members to the kingdom. This episode was arguably one of the key turning points in the relationship between the House of Saud and the Muslim Brotherhood, and it largely explains the fears of Saudi leaders and their strong reaction to Brotherhood's rise during the Arab Spring.[16] This issue has been crucial in shaping Saudi foreign policy and the attitudes of Saudi and regional Islamists toward the Saudi regime.

Several Gulf states, above all Saudi Arabia and the United Arab Emirates, played an important role in the Egyptian coup of 2013.[17] Prince Bandar bin Sultan, the Saudi intelligence chief at the time, met with Egyptian military figures and urged Western countries to support a military takeover. The Egyptian Salafi Nour Party, which is said to have close ties to Saudi Arabia, endorsed the coup.[18] Some Salafis, on the other hand, particularly from the Sururi group in Saudi Arabia, criticized the government for supporting the coup.[19]

Supporters of the Muslim Brotherhood in the kingdom also voiced their frustration with the coup publicly and criticized the Nour Party for legitimizing the new regime.[20] On social media, the four-finger symbol came to epitomize the massacre of Muslim Brotherhood supporters in Rabaa al-Adawiya Square in August 2013. It was widely used by Saudis on Twitter and became a public way of expressing dissatisfaction with the Saudi government, albeit on a foreign policy issue. Most Sahwa clerics and other Saudi Islamist leaders denounced the Egyptian coup and, implicitly or explicitly, Saudi Arabia's role in it.[21]

Saudi Arabia, in turn, clamped down on these public forms of dissent, particularly any show of solidarity with the Muslim Brotherhood, which the government designated a terrorist organization in March 2014.[22] The government worried about Brotherhood sympathizers in the kingdom mobilizing political opposition to the regime as they had done in the 1990s. Using the four-finger symbol on Twitter was criminalized. The government also clamped down on a prominent publisher that had become a rallying point for Islamic critics of Saudi policies.[23]

There is also a strong military dimension to the Saudi alliance with Sissi's Egypt. Just days after Saudi-led forces launched airstrikes on Houthi targets in Yemen, a plan for a joint Arab military force was unveiled on March 26, 2015. The campaign highlighted the extent of the GCC's ambition to shape regional affairs and underscored the military support Egypt is supposed to provide in return for financial and political backing.[24] As I will discuss later, many Saudis think the alliance is useful, though the idea of propping up Egypt's finances indefinitely is less popular. However, most Saudi Islamists, in particular Sahwis and Salafi-jihadists, see the Sissi regime as illegitimate.

THE CHALLENGE OF THE ISLAMIC STATE

On Syria, there was a convergence of interests between the Saudi state and the Islamists, but both sides supported the Syrian uprising for different reasons. The aforementioned Salman al-Awda argued that the Saudi government used the Syrian conflict to position itself as a champion of revolutionary forces after having become the region's main counterrevolutionary force. He also stated that Saudi Arabia was, naturally, pursuing its strategic interests in the region, and this was reason enough to support the Syrian uprising.[25] But when jihadist groups started to harbor more regional ambitions rather than being solely confined to Syria (and Iraq), the alliance between the Saudi regime and Islamists over Syria became more problematic.

By early April 2015, the United Nations was estimating that 25,000 foreign fighters had gone to Syria to join Islamist militias. Many of those fighters later ended up in the Islamic State,[26] with several thousand believed to be Saudi nationals. It is difficult to discern the true extent of links between the Islamic State and Saudi Arabia, at the popular level. What is clear is that the Syrian rebellion initially had huge support among Saudis and was seen as a just uprising against a dictatorial regime. Saudis' support for the Syrian uprising also included a sectarian component, framed as a "Sunni" uprising against an "Alawite" and "sectarian" regime.

From relatively early on, funds and fighters flowed from Saudi Arabia and other Gulf states, notably Qatar and Kuwait, to Syria. Many of the Sahwa's clerics became strong supporters of the Syrian uprising and encouraged Saudis to send money to the rebels, and in some cases even encouraged Saudis to go and fight in Syria.[27]

The declaration of the caliphate by what was then still called the Islamic State in Iraq and Syria at the end of June 2014 altered perceptions in Saudi Arabia, however. It forced the Saudi government to reassess its support for the opposition in Syria especially since the Islamic State denounced the Saudi monarchy and vowed to expand into the kingdom. This was logical, given the large number of Saudis in the organization, and given that, once the caliphate was declared, conquering Mecca and Medina was bound to become one of the stated aims of the organization.[28] The Islamic State thus became increasingly active inside Saudi Arabia, carrying out several attacks.

On November 3, 2014, one day before Ashura, one of the holiest days in the Shia calendar, militants opened fire on a crowd leaving a Shia mourning house (*hussainiyya*) in the eastern oasis of al-Ahsa, killing several people. All organs of the state, including the official clergy, were quick to denounce the attack, and within a few days the security forces had hunted down the perpetrators while suffering casualties themselves.[29] But the attack, which was largely carried out by Saudis and for which the Islamic State claimed responsibility, raised questions about the extent of Islamic State support inside the kingdom, the capability of the security forces, and the state's willingness to protect its Shia minority. These concerns became even more pressing when, in May 2015, suicide bombers targeted Shia mosques in Qudaih outside Qatif and in Dammam. Both operations were claimed by the Islamic State's "Najd Province," which vowed to rid the Arabian Peninsula of the "rejectionists" (*rawafid*), a derogatory term to describe Shia Muslims.[30] Attacks continued throughout 2016.[31]

The sectarianism Saudi Arabia employs to contain its own Shia population and to rally support for its regional ambitions (especially its rivalry with Iran) has fueled the problem.[32] Saudi recruits for al-Qaeda and the Islamic State are often motivated by a desire to counter Shiism and Iranian influence in the region—strategic objectives that the Saudi media perpetuates ad infinitum.

Saudi Arabia initiated airstrikes against Islamic State targets in late 2014 but stopped after the start of the Yemen campaign in March 2015. Just two months into his reign, in a sharp reversal of established Saudi petro-dollar diplomacy, King Salman launched one of the biggest foreign policy adventures in Saudi Arabia's modern history—a military intervention in Yemen. Although the intervention was intended to crush the Houthi movement and reinstall the government of interim president Abd Rabbu Mansur Hadi, it also strengthened al-Qaeda in the Arabian Peninsula (AQAP), which profited from a power vacuum and anti-Houthi sentiment in South Yemen.

The Saudi branch of al-Qaeda had carried out a series of attacks in Saudi Arabia from 2003 to 2006. After its networks in the kingdom were dismantled, the remaining militants merged with the Yemeni branch to form AQAP in 2009 and used Yemen as their main base. They expanded their area of operations gradually.[33] Interestingly, unlike most other Saudi foreign policy initiatives since 2011, the Yemen campaign was strongly supported by the kingdom's Islamists. This may in part be because of affinities and links to Yemen's Muslim Brotherhood affiliate, the Islah party, which had suffered from the Houthi advance and was rehabilitated as a tactical ally of Saudi Arabia after the start of the Yemen intervention.

A DEADLY STORM OVER YEMEN

In the wake of the Saudi-led campaign against the Houthis, a remarkable discursive shift occurred among Islamists in Saudi Arabia with respect to the Saudi monarchy. The post-2011 regional policies of Saudi Arabia, in particular Saudi support for the Egyptian coup and its declaration of the Muslim Brotherhood as a terrorist organization, were viewed negatively by most Saudi Islamists, even those dependent on the Saudi state. Little criticism was voiced in public, although some key clerics and public figures did openly condemn the coup. The airstrikes against the Houthis, on the other hand, were almost unanimously supported, even by people who had previously been very critical of the ruling family and its handling of the Arab uprisings. The war symbolizes a new realignment of King Salman and his administration with Sunni Islamists.[34] Sectarianism seems to be one important factor in this regard. A striking example of this is Salman al-Awda, who strongly supported the Yemen intervention and even gave a religious justification for the killing of the Houthis. In a long interview on al-Jazeera, he reiterated the government narrative that Iran was taking over Arab lands and needed to be punished, which, in turn, made the Saudi-led intervention in Yemen legitimate. He also repeated a rather simplistic sectarian reading of the situation in Yemen and of Zaidism, the branch of Islam the Houthis subscribe to.[35] His website, *Islam Online*, also dedicated a special site to the military intervention.[36]

Mohamed al-Arifi, another prominent Saudi cleric with millions of followers on Twitter, also endorsed the campaign. He sent a message to the Yemenis fighting with the Houthis that they should abandon them in order not to be used by the "Safavid" state, a reference to the Persian Safavid Empire.[37]

Ayid al-Qarni, another prominent preacher, praised King Salman for his bravery and called the war a long-awaited chance for the "soldiers of God" to show the enemies of the kingdom their strength. He wrote a poem in support of the king with the title "Labbayk ya Salman" ("I am at your service, O Salman!"). His lyrics were turned into a song accompanied by a rather martial video that presented the war as a war against the "Majus" (Zoroastrians) that would eventually also lead to the death of Iranian supreme leader Ayatollah Ali Khamenei.[38] Meanwhile, Awad al-Qarni, one of the key clerics of the Sahwa movement, also generally supported the intervention, although not as vocally as others.[39] Saudi media, which is tightly controlled, unanimously supported the war.[40] There were thus hardly any publicly dissenting voices within Saudi Arabia, also in part because of draconian cybersecurity laws and fear of arrest.[41] Among the few Saudi voices critical of the war were those of dissidents abroad. Saad al-Faqih, a longtime dissident and Islamist activist based in London, broadly supported the intervention, saying he supported the defense of the Saudi borders and "national security." However, he was critical of the suffering that the Yemeni people had to endure as a result, and also criticized the way the army prosecuted the war. He in particular criticized Saudi Arabia for not reaching out earlier to the Yemeni Muslim Brotherhood and the Islah party, which in his view could have profoundly changed the situation.[42] For their part, the Shia Islamist opposition abroad more clearly and unequivocally denounced the Yemen war.[43]

THE SHIA ISLAMISTS

The kingdom's Shia population makes up about 10 to 15 percent of the population and is mainly located in the country's Eastern Province.

Since the 1970s, Islamist movements have become the most powerful political force among Shias, replacing the leftist and Arab nationalists that had been popular since the 1950s.[44] They led an uprising in 1979, which was repressed. Many of their leaders spent long years in exile, and tensions with the state remained high during the 1980s and early 1990s. An amnesty agreement in 1993 brought most exiles back and led to an alliance of the state with the Shirazi movement, the most prominent of the Shia Islamist movements. The Shirazi movement has by and large maintained its pro-government stance and did not openly call for protests as part of the Arab uprisings in 2011.

Still, most Saudi Shias supported the uprising in neighboring Bahrain and saw the Arab uprisings as an opportunity for change.[45] A splinter group of the Shirazi movement led by the cleric Nimr al-Nimr called for protests, and an uprising in Saudi Arabia's Eastern Province started in February 2011. It mainly involved peaceful protests but also occasionally armed clashes with security forces. A small militant faction remains active, particularly in the village of Awwamiyya. Nevertheless, the uprising was mostly crushed by the end of 2013, with hundreds of people imprisoned and more than 20 killed. Nimr al-Nimr was arrested and later executed.

A decentralized coalition of youth and opposition groups, the Coalition for Freedom and Justice occasionally calls for protests, although turnout is generally small. The coalition is broadly Islamist in outlook and advocates revolutionary change. Another trend of Shia Islamists is the pro-Iranian movement that is locally known as Khat al-Imam, referring to followers of the late Ayatollah Khomeini. Supporters of this strand formed a militant group, Hizbullah al-Hijaz, which existed in the late 1980s and the 1990s. Khat al-Imam broadly supported the protests since 2011 and demanded the release of Shias imprisoned for their alleged role in the 1996 Khobar Towers bombings and membership in Hizbullah al-Hijaz.[46] But Khat al-Imam did not take as confrontational a stance toward the government as Nimr al-Nimr's followers did. A figurehead of Khat al-Imam in Qatif, the cleric Abdulkarim al-Hubayl, eventually urged the youth to stop protesting and to refrain from using weapons against the security forces.[47]

Crucially, none of the key Sunni Islamist leaders spoke out in support of the protests in the Eastern Province, despite repeated efforts by Shia protesters to adopt inclusive and national slogans, for example, by calling for the release of Sunni political prisoners. In fact, the crackdown on the Shia protesters was another point of convergence between the government and Sunni Islamists, and was in part justified with sectarian arguments.

In the context of the Yemen war, the Coalition for Freedom and Justice called for a protest on Friday, April 3, 2015, to denounce the Saudi-led airstrikes on Yemen. The protest call was couched in anti-government language and denounced the airstrikes as an "aggression on Yemen," adopting the rhetoric of pro-Houthi and pro-Iranian media. Given the pro-war rhetoric in the country and efforts by the government to suppress dissenting voices, this was a clear provocation. Eventually, the protest was called off amid pressure from the government.[48] However, just a few days after the planned protest, security forces raided a house in Awwamiyya, looking for wanted men. This raised tensions, and intense gunfights erupted as the security forces came under fire by militants in the village. One security officer was killed, and several locals were wounded and arrested.

Under King Abdullah, anti-Shiism had become less prominent, in particular when "National Dialogue" sessions included prominent Shia figures. But a renewed public anti-Shiism was evident at least since the sectarian clashes in Medina in 2009 and the first anti-Houthi war of 2009–2010.[49] Increased tensions with Iran since 2011 and the Yemen intervention have led to a worsening of sectarian relations in Saudi Arabia, symbolized most strikingly by Islamic State attacks on Shia mosques.[50] A worsening of relations between Shias and the Saudi ruling family appears to be one of the outcomes of the rapprochement between King Salman and Sunni Islamists.

CONCLUSION

The period from 2011 to 2015 has seen profound political changes in the Middle East that have gone hand in hand with changes in Saudi foreign policy. Islamist actors in Saudi Arabia had to position

themselves vis-à-vis these fast-developing, unpredictable, and sometimes contradictory developments. The key events that defined
Islamist stances since 2013 were the Syrian uprising, the military coup
in Egypt, the emergence of the Islamic State and its declaration of
a caliphate, and the Saudi-led war against the Houthis in Yemen.
Generally, Saudi Islamists did not agree with the government's policies in Egypt and Tunisia, but they largely supported the crackdown
on the Shiite-led protests in the Eastern Province and Bahrain and the
war against the Houthis. In addition, the Saudi government and the
Islamists are equally hostile to Iran, which they see as being behind
many of Saudi Arabia's problems. Anti-Shia actions were therefore a
point of convergence between the government and Islamists, as much
as anti–Muslim Brotherhood policies and support for secular strong-
men were a point of contention.

There is considerable diversity of views among Saudi Islamists on
what lessons should be drawn from the Arab uprisings. One group
of younger Islamists and new Islamist intellectuals embraced democracy and elections and even argued that sharia should not be implemented immediately after a revolutionary situation but rather only
once voters choose to do so through democratic means. This was
a reflection of the Tunisian and Egyptian experiences. This group
includes people such as Salman al-Awda, Mohamed al-Ahmari, and
Mohamed al-Abd al-Karim. They reinvigorated the ideas of the
Sahwa, building on the political discourse of organizations such as
Association for Civil and Political Rights to advocate for democratic
change after 2011.[51]

While Islamists remain one of the key political forces in Saudi
Arabia, there is also a tendency among the younger generation to be
equally dissatisfied with the politics of Islamist movements as with the
old political order. Some have again become more interested in the
legacy of leftist and Arab nationalist movements in the region.

Others have been drawn to revolutionary violence as a result of the
failure of the Egyptian democratic experiment. The rise of the Islamic
State has given new impetus to those who accept violence as a political
tool, both abroad and at home. Saudi Islamists have supported a range
of violent actors abroad, but at home most have only called for political

reform and have refrained from challenging the ruling family directly. Indeed, King Salman has reached out to Islamists in an effort to unite Sunnis across the region and to strengthen Saudi Arabia's geopolitical influence. It is not the first time that the Saudi state and Saudi Islamists are joining forces to support what they see as "just wars." And the consequences may well be as long lasting—and unpredictable—as on previous occasions.

8

Kuwait

Courtney Freer

KUWAIT PRESENTS A UNIQUE microcosm featuring a variety of strands of political Islam. While undoubtedly a rentier state, reliant primarily on oil wealth and providing handsome disbursements to nationals, Kuwait also houses a vocal parliament where political blocs openly compete in elections. Among them are an active Muslim Brotherhood affiliate, four primary Salafi blocs, and two major Shiite political organizations. It is therefore something of an anomaly—far from the more authoritarian government systems that typify rentier states of the Gulf.

Despite featuring such a diverse range of Islamist blocs and experiencing some of the largest protests in the Gulf during the Arab Spring, Kuwait's political system has not changed dramatically. The chaos that erupted throughout the region brought back memories of the disarray of Iraqi occupation. Above all else, as Kuwaiti political scientist Sami al-Farraj put it, "Kuwait doesn't have the luxury to be unstable."[1] This overarching concern for stability has led Kuwait's ideologically driven Islamist parties to seek compromise and gradual reform over a strictly Islamist social agenda or radical political transformation— at least domestically. This desire for stability has become even more pronounced since the 2003 Iraq War and Arab Spring. In the face of regional instability following the uprisings of 2011 and the region-wide denigration of the Brotherhood after the failure of the Morsi government, the Kuwaiti Muslim Brotherhood and certain Salafi strands have focused on advancing political reforms more broadly rather than simply pushing a platform that was previously dominated by controversial proposals to Islamize society.

Following Islamists' short-lived political successes in Egypt and Tunisia, many feared that Kuwait's Muslim Brotherhood sought to "run the country."[2] In the face of the regional backlash against the Egyptian Brotherhood, the Kuwaiti government has maintained a delicate balance. Though it has been pressured to support moves against the Brotherhood taken by the Egyptian, Emirati, and Saudi governments (at least rhetorically), Kuwait has not restricted activity of its own Brotherhood affiliate, which continues its calls for political reform. Still, rumors abound about purges of Brotherhood members from government;[3] an Egyptian Brotherhood member was arrested in Kuwait in March 2014 after the Sissi government issued an international warrant for his arrest[4] and former Brotherhood parliamentarian Mubarak al-Duwailah was sentenced to two years in prison in April 2016.[5] Aside from these moves, however, the Brotherhood does not appear to be singled out by the Kuwaiti government as a political or security threat. The same could be said of the variety of Salafi political blocs in Kuwait, which have largely been allowed to continue promoting their platform.

THE MUSLIM BROTHERHOOD'S PLACE IN KUWAITI POLITICS

Notwithstanding its commitment to conservative social mores, the Kuwaiti Muslim Brotherhood's political bloc, the Islamic Constitutional Movement (ICM), today is, as one secular advisor to the Kuwaiti government put it, "politically more liberal than those who call themselves liberal."[6] In fact, the group's "leaders are frustrated because they feel that in a sense they have become more democratic than the political system in which they operate—and perhaps more than Kuwaiti society is ready for."[7] The ICM's agenda is shaped by local realities more than any desire to reach power. As one ICM member of parliament explained, "We are 100 percent loyal to [the ruling family]. We want reform, repair, not change."[8] In fact, the emir meets with members of the Brotherhood and attends their *dīwānīāt*, demonstrating that the Kuwaiti government, unlike others in the Gulf, "isn't in panic mode."[9] Though the government has never legally recognized the ICM,[10] its approach in dealing with the bloc, and with the Brotherhood in general, is far more accommodating than the repressive security-led approach seen elsewhere in the Gulf, primarily due to the organization's well-established place in the country's history.

One of the oldest Brotherhood branches in the Gulf, Kuwait's Muslim Brotherhood was formally founded a decade before the country's independence, in 1951. Beginning in the 1960s, members of the Kuwaiti Brotherhood's Jama'at Islah participated in parliamentary elections yet failed to make substantial gains until the 1970s with the decline of Arab nationalism. Throughout the 1960s and 1970s, the Kuwaiti Brotherhood benefited from government support through the nomination of its members to government positions, specifically in the education ministry, which housed a large number of supporters in curriculum development.[11]

Although Brotherhood members had contested seats in parliament since the 1960s, they did so as individuals, not as members of the organization.[12] In fact, some members of the Kuwaiti Brotherhood's older generation argued that the group's formal entry into electoral politics in the 1980s represented a deviation from the mission of *da'wa* and incremental progress toward the ideal Islamic state as explained by Hassan al-Banna.[13] Reservations also remained about the appropriateness of Islamists contesting elections in a non-Islamic political order and the movement's ability to act effectively in the political realm.[14]

The 1980s thus marked the first time Kuwait's Muslim Brotherhood appeared as a major political force, guided primarily by the goal of Islamizing Kuwaiti society by taking measures such as pushing gender segregation in education, restricting the availability of alcohol, and limiting nationality solely to Muslims.[15] Kuwait's activist Salafis also became politically organized during this period, and the influence of both Islamist currents was felt in new legislation.[16] With the dissolution of parliament in July 1986, the opposition coalesced around Brotherhood and Salafi Islamists, merchants, the growing intelligentsia, and former parliamentarians, all of whom called for the restoration of the legislature.[17]

The spread of revolutionary Islamist ideas in the 1980s also led to an internal split in the Kuwaiti Brotherhood. Two strands emerged: hardliners, who rejected participation in an un-Islamic government, and a more mainstream grouping, which considered the practice of political work a means of facilitating *da'wa*.[18] Former parliamentarian Abdallah al-Nafisi represented the rejectionist position. In 1987, Nafisi resigned from Jama'at Islah on grounds that the discipline of the political bloc was too tightly knit and not suited to the all-encompassing nature of Islam.[19] Although Nafisi had served as a member of parliament, he came to believe that reform was simply too slow and favored radical reforms instead.[20] His "comments contributed to the emergence of a new generation of the Muslim Brotherhood movement that began to clash with the methods of the traditional symbols of the movement in which they had been brought up in the seventies."[21] Nafisi considered a clash with the government to be inevitable, even proclaiming that "the greatest actual enemy to the Islamic movement is the regime."[22]

Prominent Brotherhood member Isma'il al-Shatti, on the other hand, advocated a more participatory stance. He referred to himself as a "gradualist reformer," who hoped to effect gradual change toward the Islamization of society through the political system.[23] Furthermore, he "explained that parliamentary work endowed the revivalists with societal credibility."[24] This internal division between these two strands led the Brotherhood to adopt inconsistent policies toward the regime, sometimes hoping to effect change through gaining ministerial positions and at other times joining the opposition to do so.

New circumstances under Iraqi occupation led the Muslim Brotherhood to focus increasingly on Kuwait's liberation rather than the social issues that the bloc had previously promoted.[25] The Brotherhood established a Committee of Social Solidarity inside the country, which aimed to increase living standards for Kuwaitis by disbursing treasury rations to markets of cooperative groups.[26] During the Iraqi occupation, the Brotherhood was instrumental in "supervising the provision of basic services to the citizens."[27]

In March 1991, following the liberation of Kuwait, the Brotherhood founded the ICM.[28] By creating a strictly political bloc while maintaining Islah as its social arm, the Brotherhood hoped to gain more influence in the rebuilding of postoccupation Kuwait. At this time, the strand within the Brotherhood favoring gradual change over a dramatic clash with the government gained primacy and became institutionalized through the ICM. Importantly, members of the Brotherhood did not consider the new emphasis on politics to be "a switch" from their past social work;[29] rather, it was seen as a maturation, which came about after Kuwaitis had effectively "run the country by themselves" under occupation.[30] Furthermore, since the movement had formally broken off relations with the international Brotherhood organization due to its refusal to support the liberation of Kuwait because of the involvement of Western troops, the Kuwaiti Brotherhood became more locally focused.

In the 1990s, ICM members focused on the gradual application of sharia rather than liberalizing Kuwait's politics.[31] Its primary strategy was to gain ministerial positions. But over time, the ICM sought to check government power rather than be an instrument of it. By pursuing fewer government positions, the ICM became more flexible.[31] The organization also learned to work more effectively with other movements toward common goals[32] and seemed willing to accept a middle ground, or an interim period in which sharia was not fully applied, to push other gains. For example, as Kuwaiti political scientist Sami Awadh notes, members of the Brotherhood are adaptable enough to accept an economic system with usury until a time when an Islamic system can replace it.[33] Such a willingness to effectively suspend ideological goals demonstrated the failure of Nafisi's faction of the Brotherhood that advocated for more immediate political and social change.

As the 2000s progressed, the ICM pushed for constitutional changes such as an elected prime minister, the institution of a single electoral district to reduce government gerrymandering, the legalization of political parties, and, eventually, the creation of a constitutional monarchy. It also continues to advocate wide-ranging social and economic aims, in keeping with traditional Brotherhood goals, such as "shap[ing] the

Kuwaiti citizen according to his unique Islamic identity and true Arab loyalty;" reforming the economic system "in line with the fair wealth distribution principles;" and making it "a more productive system in accordance with the Islamic principles of containment and integration."[34] By and large, however, the ICM's agenda highlights political reform efforts above issues of social policy, helping it to align with secular opposition parties.

Despite the fact that they share common goals, secular left-leaning political blocs and the ICM have often clashed over the issue of defending civil liberties. The ICM "supports liberalizing political reforms rather faithfully, but it draws the line when liberalization leads in a cultural direction."[35] For all its rhetoric about political freedom, the ICM has promoted measures that place limits on personal freedoms, such as the law on gender segregation in schools, rejection of female suffrage, restricting hours when women can work, and legislation punishing religiously offensive speech. As one Kuwaiti liberal put it, the perception is that "the Brotherhood used democracy to establish laws that are unconstitutional."[36] As a result, secular blocs often express their hesitance to ally with the Brotherhood. When asked about this, a former ICM parliamentarian remarked to me: "Of course we want Islam to be our social norm and the government to respect Islam."[37]

At the same time, because of the Brotherhood's emphasis on political reform, more conservative Islamists have criticized the ICM for promoting a strictly political rather than religious platform. This has provided an opening for Kuwait's more conservative, and traditionally less politically active, Salafi movement. The Brotherhood, not surprisingly, is considered both the more flexible and the less confrontational of the two Islamist currents. Indeed, the popular perception is that "you can speak reason with the Brotherhood. They're part of the system of elites, so they would never dream of overturning [the system]."[38] Although they ultimately desire to implement sharia, members of the Brotherhood take a slow, long-term approach to this goal, considering that "the Quran came in stages."[39] This more gradualist stance prevails today, as issues around government reform appear more urgent than ever. At times, such a position has threatened ties with Salafi blocs. When the two strands have been allied in parliament, ICM deputies have become "often saddled with responsibility for controversial stances [particularly regarding social policies], while the Brotherhood's inclination might be to take a more pliant or gradual approach."[40]

Despite the Brotherhood's relative popularity,[41] the most seats it has won in parliament was 6 out of 50 in 2006. The Brotherhood has never contested a plurality of seats, preferring to form coalitions with other blocs that grant it a degree of political cover.[42] By tempering their demands for Islamizing society, the ICM has come to hold a more powerful political position as a leading opposition bloc. Still, its more pragmatic approach has left greater space for the development of a more strict and maximalist Salafi current in Kuwait.

THE SALAFI MOVEMENT

The Salafi movement in Kuwait can be divided broadly between quietist and activist strands. The quietists are more powerful domestically, while the activists have more followers abroad.[43] Quietist Salafis tend to be less politicized, preferring to focus on "peaceful proselytization and daily religious practices."[44] Activists, on the other hand, favor "broader political involvement."[45] In Kuwait, however, this distinction is somewhat blurred, as members of both the quietist and activist strands contest seats in parliament.

Kuwait's Salafi movement became organized in the mid-1960s among quietists, "when a small group of youth adhering to the Salafi Da'wa came together and drew up a basic instructional program, aiming at awakening Kuwaiti society."[46] Like the Brotherhood, Kuwait's Salafis focused initially on apolitical issues, namely education and charity.[47] From the beginning, the Salafi movement considered itself distinct from existing Islamist organizations. As Salafi religious authority Shaykh Abdullah al-Sabt explained, "We know that these groups had closed themselves through narrow partisanship. . . . That was one of the reasons which led us to reject these groups and establish for ourselves a real Salafi Da'wa."[48]

By the end of the 1970s, the Salafis had found a following in Kuwaiti society, in particular among merchant families.[49] By the 1980s, the Salafi trend also gained a foothold in labor organizations and student unions, achieving an "unprecedented level of organizational development."[50]

Kuwait's Salafis developed a more coherent organizational structure under the banner of the Society for the Revival of the Islamic Heritage (RIHS) in 1981, guided by the ideology of Egyptian cleric Shaykh Abd al-Rahman Abd al-Khaliq.[51] While the RIHS's founding documents cite charitable purposes, it became an umbrella organization for Salafis in Kuwait and their primary institutional outlet for political participation.[52] The RIHS also benefited from state support as well as funding from the Saudi religious establishment. Notably, Abd al-Khaliq was "one of the first Salafis who extensively wrote books and articles about politics and intended to reform Salafi jurisprudence about politics and participation in social protest and using new media."[53] In fact, Saudi clerics went so far as to issue a fatwa condoning the Salafis' political activity,[54] which Abd al-Khaliq announced on the eve of the 1981 polls.[55] Kuwait's 1981 election marked the first time anywhere in the world that Salafis participated in parliamentary elections, with the RIHS winning two seats.[56]

With the dissolution of parliament in July 1986, members of the RIHS, like the ICM, became more independent of the government, though they had never held as many posts as the ICM. RIHS followers began "serious participation with the other political powers to put pressure on the political decision-makers to return parliamentary life to the country."[57] Salafi members of parliament, along with the ICM, joined the Constitutional Movement, which included a variety of ideological currents and urged reform and restoration of parliament.[58]

During Iraq's invasion and subsequent occupation of Kuwait, many Kuwaiti Salafis fled the state for Saudi Arabia, where they became involved with Saudi Salafi networks.[60] Activist Salafis in Saudi Arabia were appalled by the Saudi government's decision to allow the U.S. military into the kingdom and responded with a burgeoning protest movement, Islamic Awakening, or Sahwa, which demanded wide-ranging political reforms[61] and appealed to Kuwaitis residing in Saudi Arabia during the Iraqi occupation.[62] Meanwhile, other Kuwaiti Salafis sided with the quietist strand, represented by the Saudi ulama, who did not oppose Kuwaiti liberation at the hands of Western militaries, as had been decided upon by their legitimate, and unquestionable, rulers.[63] The RIHS became divided along quietist and activist lines following the Iraqi occupation, with the quietists overtaking the RIHS under Shaykh Abdullah al-Sabt's direction.[64] Despite claims to the contrary, the RIHS has since maintained close ties with the Saudi religious establishment and is sometimes criticized for being "a puppet of Riyadh" or "even cooperating with Saudi intelligence."[65]

The Islamic Salafi Association (ISA), established in 1991 and linked to the quietist RIHS, is focused on social morality yet uses political means to enforce it, making it something of a hybrid between activist and quietist. Indeed, the ISA's parliamentary agenda is concerned primarily with Islamizing laws, instituting sharia as the sole source of legislation, and banning "vices" such as music concerts and alcohol.[66]

The ISA competes for followers from the same pool of urbanized elites (or *hadhar*) as the ICM, yet it touts itself as less politicized than the Brotherhood. Members even criticize other political figures who they consider to have insulted the emir, who, as an Islamically legitimate ruler, they believe to be above criticism.[67] More extreme quietists of the Madkhali school, however, consider the RIHS to violate the principles of Salafism by having an organizational structure and participating in elections.[68] "For them, participating in politics and creating formal organizations lead to the corruption of one's belief, making people loyal to the organizations and their leaders instead of to God."[69]

In 1996, the Salafi Movement broke off from the ISA, uniting people primarily on the basis of their dislike of quietist Salafis, whom they regard as tools of an American–Saudi conspiracy to silence political demands in the Gulf.[70]

The Umma Party (Hizb al-Umma), meanwhile, is the only political bloc that calls itself a party (political parties are formally banned). It emerged in 2005 largely from members of the tribal *badu* population inspired by sharia scholar Hakim al-Mutairi.[71] Although al-Mutairi had hoped to convert the Salafi Movement into a political party, he clashed with his deputy Shaykh Hamad al-Ali, who insisted on maintaining the group's loose structure.[72] Mutairi thus left the movement to found the Umma Party.[73] Significantly, the party was the first political bloc to unambiguously call for popular sovereignty, with parliament determining the makeup of government, including the prime minister and other cabinet appointments.[74] It is thus disliked by conservative

Salafis, who believe Mutairi is guilty of "blurring the distinction between salafi and Muslim Brother thought and for compromising the strict adherence to the text by allowing too large a role for reason in its interpretation."[75]

Since the Arab Spring, as illustrated by the proliferation of new Salafi organizations in Kuwait, the activist strand has become increasingly influential. Still, the quietists have generally been better represented in government, with the RIHS dominant and many of its members enjoying positions in the Ministry of Religious Endowments. Nonetheless, none of the activist Salafi movements has managed to break through in terms of parliamentary representation, due in part to their similarities with the already represented Muslim Brotherhood.[76]

Activists have tended to have only 1 member in the parliament, Walid al-Tabtaba'i, while the more quiescent ISA has tended to have 8 to 10 members. The relative electoral weakness of the activists is probably due to the fact that the Muslim Brotherhood's Islamic Constitutional Movement, which traditionally has had strong parliamentary representation, provides an appropriate platform for many who are attracted to activist Salafism. Unlike the Brotherhood in other countries, most of the cadres of the ICM are influenced by Salafism, and their discourse is similar to that of Salafi activists.[77]

Still, Kuwait remains a meeting place for activist Salafis and was seen, at least before the Arab Spring, as the only Middle Eastern country where Salafis could freely express their ideas. In fact, Shaykh Abd al-Khaliq claims that the idea that "Egyptian Salafis should participate in politics emerged during the meetings and workshops that these Salafis had attended in his house and mosque."[78]

The freedom granted to Salafi groups in Kuwait has extended to their charitable activities outside the country, with serious consequences in recent years. Several Salafi charities have funded some of Syria's most powerful militant organizations, and Kuwait has become, in the words of U.S. Treasury Undersecretary David Cohen, "the epicenter of fundraising for terrorist groups in Syria."[79] Kuwait criminalized the financing of terrorist organizations only in 2013, thereby allowing Salafi charities, of both the activist and quietist strand,[80] a relatively free hand to finance extremist groups. The government has been hesitant to restrict such support for extremist groups largely due to the popularity of the cause. "According to one of the prime minister's advisers, the government would risk pushing the country into instability if it imposed any constraints on the bank transfers and other means of sending money to Syria."[81] By supporting the Syrian opposition, then, Kuwaiti Salafis have managed to gain a degree of popular support at home, while not threatening their position in domestic politics by stoking violence at home.[82]

Inside Kuwait, Salafis' participation in parliamentary life has "diminished the ideological gap between the Muslim Brotherhood and Salafis that existed in an earlier period."[83] In fact, their primary difference more recently has been the ICM's willingness to form parliamentary coalitions with Shiite deputies, something Salafis refuse.[84] The Brotherhood, as the more politically pragmatic organization, has traditionally been willing to ally with any bloc that would advance its reform agenda, regardless of sect.

DEVELOPMENT OF KUWAITI ISLAMISM TODAY

Throughout the 2000s, Kuwait's Muslim Brotherhood and activist Salafis came to resemble one another more closely, banding together with other opposition movements to advocate for broad-ranging political reform. The 2006 debate over reformulating electoral districts brought both blocs into the opposition in arguably the most vocal, public manner since the suspension of parliament in 1986. They cooperated with leftist groups that supported dividing Kuwait into 5 rather than 25 electoral districts. Such redistricting, they believed, would change the nature of elections: "In the opinion of reformers, this matter would transform elections from occasions to buy votes and to launch campaigns to a race on the basis of program and ideology."[85]

Not all Salafis supported the move, however, with many members from tribal districts opposed, as they feared the new law could diminish their political power.[86] As the most organized political bloc, the ICM played a leading role in the "We Want Five" movement,[87] whose supporters organized large demonstrations throughout May 2006. In the midst of political upheaval, the emir was forced to dissolve parliament and call for new elections in June; the new, largely Islamist and oppo-sition parliament proceeded to pass new electoral legislation, a major coup for the newly united opposition.

The secular-Islamist opposition also joined efforts to root out graft, which came to a head with their demands to formally question Prime Minister Shaykh Nasir al-Sabah on charges of corruption. In November 2008, three independent Salafi members of parliament initi-ated a request to interpellate Prime Minister Shaykh Nasir on charges of, among other things "failing to perform his constitutional duties and achieving the wishes of the people."[88] Then-Salafi Movement par-liamentarian Walid al-Tabtaba'i justified the request not according to religious reasoning, but rather democratic constitutional governance.[89] Shaykh Nasir was finally grilled, behind closed doors, in December 2009 over his handling of the financial crisis and possible misuse of state funds, marking the first time a premier had been interpellated. Still, the government had only agreed to allow this questioning after new elections had produced a sympathetic parliament.[90] Predictably, Shaykh Nasir was not removed from office, as the vote of no confidence failed to muster the required votes.

Such public displays of government manipulation united opposition movements further. Beginning in 2009, Walid al-Tabtaba'i sided with opposition, including members of the ICM, in calling for enhanced parliamentary power and the right of the people to directly elect their government.[91] Tabtaba'i went so far as to proclaim in September 2012 that "we the people have decided that Jabir al-Mubarak will be the last prime minister from the House of al-Sabah."[92] Similarly, ISA deputy Khalid Sultan came out in support of "an 'elected government,' i.e., forcing the emir to choose his prime minister based on the parliamen-tary majority."[93]

By the late 2000s, as opposition to government policies grew, mem-bers of the Brotherhood and activist Salafis kept up the pressure, using Twitter to voice criticisms and participating in protests.[94] The February 2012 election, spurred by the government's resignation and dissolution of parliament amid mass protests, produced a landslide for the oppo-sition, with Islamist, tribal, and liberal candidates winning 34 of 50 parliamentary seats.[95] The Brotherhood won all four seats it contested, while Salafis from across the spectrum won a total of 10 seats, making them the most represented Islamist trend in parliament.[96] In a desire to prioritize political reform, the opposition agreed to *not* focus on amending the constitution to declare sharia the primary source of legislation.

The new parliament was voided, however, four months later, when the constitutional court (composed of the emir's appointees) declared the dissolution of the previous parliament unconstitutional.[97] The court therefore reinstated the pro-regime 2009 National Assembly. The secular-Islamist opposition coalition protested the reimposition of the 2009 parliament, which ultimately never met because its reinstitution was so controversial. Several political blocs (including liberal groups along with the ICM and ISA), youth associations, and labor unions formed the National Front for the Protection of the Constitution in September 2012, which also consisted of the majority bloc of some 34 opposition parliamentarians elected in February 2012. In October 2012, warning of "chaotic sedition that could jeopardize our country [and] undermine our national unity, " the emir had the cabinet change voting rules ahead of the December 1 elections.[98] In addition, the emir "issued a decree to change the electoral process, abolishing the country's complicated system that allowed each voter multiple votes.[99]

The opposition, to which the ICM and most Salafi groups belong, boycotted the December 2012 polls, leading to a low 39 percent turnout rate (compared to 60 percent in February) and returning a pro-government National Assembly.[100] Sunni Islamist representation was the most drastically affected, decreasing from 23 MPs to 4.[101] Considering the inability of parliament to advance the Brotherhood's agenda, the ICM did not view the boycott as diminishing its political capital more broadly.

In June 2013, weeks before the military coup that overthrew the Muslim Brotherhood–dominated government in Egypt, the Constitutional Court dissolved parliament for the second time in one year, but left the same electoral law in place. Many opposition groups, including the ICM, several tribal leaders, Salafi figures, and liberal groupings, again boycotted the polls. When asked about the logic behind the ICM's two boycotts, one former ICM member of parliament explained that they were meant to expose the government as the source of political grid-lock.[102] He stated: "The more we stay away, the more we show it's the government that cannot perform."[103]

KUWAIT'S SUNNI ISLAMIST MOVEMENTS IN THE POST-COUP ERA

National malaise persisted in the immediate aftermath of the Arab Spring, with left-leaning opposition leader Musallam al-Barrak urging a return to protests until new elections were called under new electoral laws.[104] The ICM and ISA support Barrak's ultimate goal of a constitutional monarchy, appearing to privilege such restructuring over social reforms. In early 2013, the ICM signed a 23-page document drafted by Musallam al-Barrak, Brotherhood figure Jama'an al-Harbash, and Tariq al-Mutairi of the liberal Civil Democratic Movement.[105] Political trends ranging from secular left-ists to Salafis, as well as the largely Brotherhood-dominated Student Union, have signed the document, which "proposes a full parliamen-tary system, with a stronger legislature, independent judiciary and revised criminal code."[106]

Significantly, as part of the opposition coalition, the ICM and activ-ist Salafis dropped their once-central demand of amending Article 2 of the constitution to specify sharia as *the* primary source of legislation.[107] Both groups have seemed increasingly willing to work alongside other opposition movements to ensure progress on political reform.

Due to their continued cooperation in the face of government restrictions, the authorities have detained Islamists and leftists alike for criticizing other Gulf states. The leader of the Umma Party, Hakim al-Mutairi, was detained in March 2016 for insulting Saudi Arabia, while Tariq al-Mutairi of the liberal Civil Democratic Movement was also detained due to Saudi complaints about some of his statements on Twitter.[108]

Neither the Brotherhood nor the Salafi trend, however, is being considered "a security threat," as both continue to operate openly.[109] While the Brotherhood is maligned elsewhere in the region, in Kuwait it is "regarded more as a political nuisance than a security threat."[110] The April 2016 sentencing of former ICM parliamentarian Mubarak al-Duwailah may point to a more targeted crackdown on Islamists in the future, informed by the Emirati example. Duwailah was sentenced to two years in prison[111] on charges of insulting and endangering ties with an ally and insulting leaders of an allied state after remarks he made about Abu Dhabi Crown Prince Mohammed bin Zayed al-Nahyan being "against Sunni Islam."[112]

Having experienced growing government restrictions and seen even worse elsewhere in the region, Islamists and secular opposition movements appear to be banding together and are considered more dangerous to the government as a result. As noted by Shadi Hamid, "The shared experience of repression ... encourages opposition groups to focus on what they have in common. After all, they have a shared enemy—the regime. So they agree to prioritize the fight for basic freedoms and democracy. Ideological divisions are put to the side."[113] Mubarak al-Duwailah explicitly called for the overcoming of traditional differences in a January 2016 statement shortly after his arrest, signaling a very public effort to overcome longstanding ideological divides.[114]

Opposition unity was tested when early elections were called in November 2016. Most of the opposition competed, aside from some secular blocs and the ISA, the Salafi Movement, and the Umma Party. The ICM won all 4 seats it contested, while Salafis, mostly independents, gained another 4 seats. Islamist representation extends beyond these 8 seats, however, since other independents sympathetic to the ICM and Salafi groups were also elected. Overall, the new parliament has a very different profile than its predecessor, with only 20 of the 50 incumbents re-elected and with the broad-based opposition winning almost half of the seats (24 of 50). With their relatively strong position in parliament, Islamists in Kuwait will likely continue to promote the anti-corruption and pro-reform agendas on which they ran, in conjunction with other blocs when helpful. In fact, the first joint opposition meeting was held less than a week after the polls, following the announcement that Shaykh Jaber al-Mubarak al-Sabah would be reappointed as prime minister.

Kuwait's Muslim Brotherhood and Salafi movements thus remain leading political actors inside Kuwait—in part due to the fact that there is little organized liberal competition. As the liberal activist Ahmad al-Baghdadi put it, "Kuwait has liberals, but there is no liberalism. There is a big difference between the two. You will find liberal individuals, but liberalism as a concept in society remains weak."[115] In such an environment, Islamists are poised to remain ideologically and politically appealing to the Kuwaiti population. Certainly, in the Kuwaiti context, "religious affiliation is stronger than the liberal one because it is ideology-based and uses religion, the heritage of the people."[116] The allure of such movements exists despite the fact that they have never earned a plurality of seats in parliament and even in the face of the political defeat of Islamist parties elsewhere in the region, namely Egypt.[117]

In the postcoup environment, Kuwait's Islamists are working more closely with other opposition groups, a move that provides them political cover and helps them to avoid the mistakes of Egypt's Islamists, who were accused of failing to work with other parties. During this period, Salafis have also increasingly acted like Brotherhood movements, privileging political reform over traditional goals of Islamizing society. As Nathan Brown writes: "The more salafis involve themselves in semi authoritarian politics, the more they respond like Brotherhood-type movements."[118] Kuwait's Salafi blocs have historically been more persistent than the Brotherhood in pushing socially conservative legislation, with members of parliament proposing in 2012, for example, a decency law "to ban flirtatious behavior and 'indecent attire' in public, which would include swimsuits on beaches."[119]

Islamists have had to adopt a degree of flexibility in their social positions to maintain relevance in the most politically liberal state of the Gulf, however. For example, as early as 2005, when women were granted the right to vote and run for parliament, which the ISA opposed, ISA member of parliament Ali al-Omair stated that although "my religion does not permit women to serve in the assembly, if a lady is elected into parliament, we have to deal with her. We can't isolate ourselves in parliament."[122]

As discussed earlier, the Kuwaiti Muslim Brotherhood is considered to be more influenced by activist Salafism than branches elsewhere.[123] Kuwait's Brotherhood has maintained its commitment to Islamic social values, at least in rhetoric, as have Salafis in parliament. Where they differ is primarily in their willingness to cooperate with outside groups: the Kuwaiti Brotherhood is willing to work with Shiite coalitions in parliament and has traditionally held a more measured view of the

United States and the West more generally after Kuwait's liberation from Iraqi occupation at the hands of an American-led coalition.

Although the domestic influence of Kuwait's Islamists in the past was felt primarily through legislation concerning social and educational reform,[123] today the country's Islamists are more willing to advance broader political goals, even if this requires them to form coalitions with secular blocs and even if it provokes further government crackdown. Though much of this is likely a tactical change to give such actors greater license to pursue their social policies in the future, the experience of working with non-Islamists to liberalize Kuwait's politics may have lasting effects on the ways Islamists think about the state and the protection of individual liberties, as it has in Tunisia and Morocco.

9

Jordan

David Siddhartha Patel

ANALYSTS OFTEN DESCRIBE THE historical relationship between Jordan's Hashemite monarchy and the local branch of the Muslim Brotherhood as "symbiotic" and, compared to elsewhere in the Arab world, relatively non-confrontational.[1] The Jordanian Muslim Brotherhood has never been driven underground; its leaders were never systematically jailed. Its organizations survived the banning of political parties under martial law in 1957, after which the movement operated openly as a registered charitable society and, in 1992, formed a political party. The Brotherhood was allowed, even encouraged, to expand throughout the kingdom when it offered an alternative to pan-Arab and leftist movements that the monarchy considered a greater threat than political Islam. In return, the Brotherhood never challenged the legitimacy of the Hashemite regime, including during the 1970–1971 Jordanian Civil War and after the controversial Israel-Jordan Peace Treaty of 1994. The consistency of this relationship distinguishes the Jordanian Brotherhood from its sister movements elsewhere, where periods of regime persecution and suppression impacted Islamists' organization, leadership, strategy, and "habits of thought and behavior."[2] The "twin shocks" of the fall of Mohamed Morsi in Egypt and the rise of the Islamic State in neighboring Iraq and Syria have not fundamentally changed this relationship.

The Jordanian Muslim Brotherhood has a broad conception of reform and seeks to gradually "reestablish the Islamic way of life" in the kingdom.[3] It enthusiastically participated in elections when parliamentary life in Jordan resumed in 1989. Since the 1993 elections, the relationship between the regime and the Brotherhood can be characterized by a repeated strategic interaction. In the months leading up to each election, (1) the Brotherhood publicly calls for specific changes to the electoral system, such as the number of votes each voter can cast, apportionment, and redistricting, and (2) the regime then announces incremental changes to the system, after which (3) the Brotherhood decides if it should participate in or boycott the imminent election. The interaction is guided by the Brotherhood and the government's belief that a boycott delegitimizes, to some extent, the election and resulting parliament in the eyes of the Jordanian public or the international community or both.

Before the start of the Arab Spring, this strategic interaction had been repeated four times: prior to the 1997, 2003, 2007, and 2010 parliamentary elections.[4] Despite the election of Mohamed Morsi in Egypt in June 2012 and his overthrow in July 2013, the Jordanian Muslim Brotherhood and the regime continued this pattern of interaction prior to Jordan's parliamentary elections in January 2013 and September 2016. In other words, the Arab uprisings, including the coming to power and fall of Islamist parties in Tunisia and Egypt and the rise of the Islamic State, did not alter the *nature* of the strategic dynamic between the Hashemite monarchy and the Jordanian Brotherhood. Regional events only affected the parameters of the interaction, such as the specific electoral reforms the Brotherhood demanded and perhaps shifting its "reservation point"—the minimum set of reforms under which the group would participate. But the fates of sister movements and the emergence of the Islamic State did not fundamentally alter the gradualist goals of the Brotherhood in Jordan or upend its relationship with the regime. The Muslim Brotherhood demanded electoral reforms, the palace announced incremental reforms, and the Muslim Brotherhood then decided whether or not to boycott.

The remainder of this chapter is divided into three parts. Part one elaborates on the argument made previously, focusing on what the Jordanian Brotherhood did and did not do to advance its agenda when

Islamists' fortunes rose elsewhere—during the Arab Spring. Part two briefly discusses cleavages among Jordanian Islamists, including the relationship between Salafis and the Muslim Brotherhood and what I argue is the more important but often overlooked cleavage: the ongoing and growing divide between Jordanian Islamists of Palestinian origin and Transjordanian Islamists. The split in the movement caused by the Zamzam Initiative (discussed later) and the rise of an alternative Jordanian Muslim Brotherhood group is merely the latest in a series of defections by Transjordanian Islamists. The regime's "deregistration" of the Muslim Brotherhood can be understood as an attempt to pressure the organization to commit to participate in parliamentary elections in 2016 (which it did). Part three concludes with a royal comment on the relationship between the Jordanian Brotherhood and the Hashemite regime.

THE JORDANIAN MUSLIM BROTHERHOOD, FROM SPRING TO WINTER

After protests spread to Yemen, Bahrain, Libya, and beyond, many analysts, both in the region and elsewhere, thought that Jordan was the most vulnerable regime still standing. This belief was reinforced by the rise of nascent protest movements among tribal, youth, and locally based *hirak* groups in Transjordanian-majority areas, such as Dhiban and Karak, which are often characterized as part of the heartland of support for the Hashemite monarchy. But when the Muslim Brotherhood joined protests in Amman and urban centers, its demands did not escalate to call for the overthrow of the regime, and coordination with new protest groups remained limited.[5]

The most that can be said about changes to the Jordanian Brotherhood's demands after the start of the Arab uprisings is that it became more overt in demanding constitutional changes to constrain the monarchy's institutional prerogatives. For example, the Brotherhood called for removing the powers of the king to dissolve parliament, select the prime minister without input from parliament, and appoint the Upper House.[6] At the time, Brotherhood leaders claimed that this emphasis on constitutional reform marked a real shift.

The Brotherhood's shift to emphasizing constitutional reforms alongside electoral ones, however, is overstated for three reasons. First, the Brotherhood had long talked about such reforms. Its reform initiative of 2005 lists as its number one priority "to carry out urgently-needed political and structural reform to activate the section of the constitution that proclaims that the ruling system is a constitutional monarchy with a representative government, and to ensure that parliament assumes a position in keeping with this."[7] Its post–Arab Spring statements largely elaborate this established point. Second, the Brotherhood's most vocal statements about constitutional reform came after the king established a Royal Committee for Constitutional Review in April 2011[8] and as he issued a series of four "discussion" papers on reform issues.[9] The phrase *malakiyya dusturiyya* (constitutional monarchy) was already in the air before Muslim Brotherhood leaders started using it; the "red" line had faded to pink. Finally, the Jordanian Brotherhood basically was asking for the same reforms that the Moroccan king had already proposed for himself. In the range of demands that it could have made, the Jordanian Brotherhood selected a set that would not overly antagonize the monarchy and, perhaps, still save face for the group within the wider circle of Muslim Brotherhood organizations. It did not call for the regime to be overthrown, and it did not challenge the basic legitimacy of the Hashemites.

Some observers noted that the Muslim Brotherhood organized almost weekly protests in downtown Amman and reported this as evidence of the Arab uprisings spreading to Jordan. These protests had been recurring, though, since the early to mid-2000s in the exact same place and manner. After Friday prayers at the Grand Husseini Mosque in downtown Amman, the Brotherhood would organize, often with smaller leftist allies, a procession to a square at Ras al-Ein. A single Brotherhood truck distributes flags and banners at the beginning of these marches and collects them at the end, serving as an amplification system and stage during the event. All such protests are highly choreographed, controlled by the Brotherhood, and approved by the security forces. Jillian Schwedler has written about the nontransgressive nature of these protests, both before and during the Arab uprisings.[10] The Jordanian Muslim Brotherhood was not protesting in ways it had not done before. Its tactics did not shift. It did not permit members to test the boundaries of what the security services would tolerate.

All participants understood what game they were playing, and neither side tried to change the game. The Brotherhood demanded "real" constitutional reforms to the electoral system to make it more representative of the demographics and will of the Jordanian people. The 41 amendments proposed by the Royal Committee were approved, including additional protections to personal rights and the creation of a constitutional court to monitor legislation. The regime also tinkered, once again, with the electoral system. In April 2012, the regime unveiled a new draft electoral law that met some longstanding demands of the Islamic movement (e.g., abandoning the controversial single nontransferable vote [SNTV] "one-person, one-vote system") but also introduced a mixed system where seats would be allocated to both districts and a national list proportional representation system.[11] Almost immediately after the election of Morsi in Egypt, the Jordanian Muslim Brotherhood announced it would boycott the upcoming Jordanian elections if the draft electoral law was not further amended. In particular, the Brotherhood demanded that a greater percentage of seats be allocated for party candidates, and, although the increase it demanded was greater than what it had asked for in the past, the range (30 to 50 percent) remained in line with their gradualist approach.

Morsi's rise to power in Egypt appears to have influenced the Jordanian Brotherhood to demand greater reforms, but not maximalist ones. It did not lead them to demand changes that would open a path to win a majority of seats in parliament. The regime largely ignored the movement's most important demands and implemented other reforms, such as the establishment of an independent election commission that would blunt international observers' criticisms.[12] The election was held in January 2013, but without the participation of the Jordanian Brotherhood after the group decided to boycott.

Although the Arab uprisings did not alter the *nature* of the interaction, they appear to have increased the minimum set of concessions that the Brotherhood expected in order to participate. However, the precise mechanism of impact is unclear; most accounts simply say that the Jordanian Brotherhood was "inspired" or "encouraged" by events elsewhere. Maybe they expected future diplomatic, organizational, or financial support from an empowered Muslim Brotherhood in Egypt, which would decrease the "cost" of rejecting the king's proposals. Maybe Islamist victories elsewhere led them to believe that they had more support among the Jordanian public than they had previously, or maybe they were trying to use the illusion of widespread latent support to get a better deal.

Two final and interesting conjectures have to do with inter–Muslim Brotherhood "competition." Perhaps the Jordanian Brotherhood feared participating and not getting as much electoral support as Islamist parties had received in Tunisia and Egypt. Moreover, the Jordanian interaction described previously paralleled but (perhaps not unintentionally) trailed by a few months a somewhat similar process in Morocco. In March 2011, the Moroccan king announced a plan for comprehensive constitutional reform, pledged to reduce his powers, and appointed an ad hoc constitutional committee. The Jordanian king appointed his committee in April 2011. The Moroccan king announced the details of the new draft constitution in June, and voters overwhelmingly approved it in a referendum on July 1 (98.5 percent approved with 73 percent turnout). Henceforth, Moroccan kings would be obligated to appoint the prime minister from the party that won the most seats in parliament and the prime minister would be the head of government with the (theoretical) power to dissolve parliament. The Jordanian committee issued its much less far-reaching reform plan in August: the king would retain the ability to appoint the prime minister, although would do so in consultation with parliament. Morocco's Justice and Development Party (PJD), the country's largest Islamist party, participated in the parliamentary election on November 25 and won a plurality with 107 of 395 seats; their leader was appointed prime minister four days later, as called for by the new constitution.

In contrast, the Jordanian Brotherhood immediately rejected its country's amendments as not going far enough. One possible explanation is that it felt less constrained. Unlike the Jordanian Brotherhood, the PJD, as discussed in Avi Spiegel's chapter, faces a strong domestic competitor in Al Adl Wal Ihsan, which basks in nonparticipation and illegality. The Brotherhood in Jordan does not have a serious Islamist rival with which it must contend. Yet, why would the Jordanian government put the Brotherhood in such a situation if it knew that the group would reject its proposed reforms?

INTRA-ISLAMIST CLEAVAGES

This section is divided into two parts. The first briefly discusses relations between the Muslim Brotherhood and Salafis in Jordan; the second discusses cleavages within the Muslim Brotherhood. A large body of literature argues that authoritarian governments often seek to divide opposition, often along ideological lines.[13] I suggest that communal differences better capture divisions among Jordanian Islamists than ideological ones.

Salafis

The vast majority of "Salafis" in Jordan are political quietists, and many have effectively been co-opted by the regime.[14] Many prominent Jordanian Salafis, such as Ali bin Hasan al-Halabi and Salim al-Hilali, studied under the prominent Salafi scholar Mohamed Nasir al-Din al-Albani, and Albani's anti-jihadist and relatively pro-monarchical orientation remains influential.[15] Many non-jihadist Salafis have been incorporated into state institutions (especially the Ministry of Religious Endowments) or are allowed to preach independently and conduct outreach. There have been few significant moves by Salafis in Jordan to organize to participate in elections, although some scholars who run as independents are Salafis and some members of the Muslim Brotherhood have clear Salafi leanings, such as Mohamed Abu Faris.[16] Several prominent Salafi scholars have published books criticizing the Jordanian Muslim Brotherhood, but their impact on the Brotherhood has not received serious attention by scholars. Jordanian Salafis spend much of their intellectual energy defending Albani's ideas from criticism by other Salafi scholars.

Meanwhile, there are several currents of Salafi-jihadism in Jordan. One Salafi-jihadist current looks to influential ideologue Abu Mohamed al-Maqdisi, who is critical of any Muslims who take jobs in the Jordanian government. A number of small Salafi-jihadist organizations exist or have existed in Jordan, but many were discredited or dismantled by security services after the 2005 terrorist attack on hotels in Amman.[17]

So far, the rise of the Islamic State appears to have had little effect on the Jordanian Muslim Brotherhood. Analysts' estimates vary widely, but several thousand Jordanians have gone to fight in Syria since the beginning of the uprising there, many to fight with al-Qaeda affiliate Jabhat al-Nusra (now known as Jabhat Fath al-Sham after publicly distancing itself from al-Qaeda).[18] Information is limited, but these jihadists seem to be disproportionately Transjordanians (as opposed to Palestinian Jordanians) and more likely to be from Salafi circles than those of the Brotherhood. An unknown number of Jordanians—estimates vary from a few hundred up to 3000—have joined the Islamic State as either fighters or to work in their court system and bureaucracy, but the group appears to have made few inroads into Jordanian territory. In May 2014, a group in Ma'an offered an oath of loyalty to the Islamic State in a YouTube video as the "Ma'an Martyrs' Brigade," but nothing has been heard from them since. The February 2015 release of the video showing the gruesome killing of Jordanian Air Force pilot Muath al-Kasasbeh quieted criticisms of the Jordanian role in the anti-ISIS coalition and, at least temporarily, turned public opinion dramatically against the Islamic State.

Intra-Brotherhood Divisions

Journalists and academics studying the Jordanian Muslim Brotherhood generally focus on ideological coalitions within the movement and track the successes and failures in internal elections of purported "hawks," "doves," "centrists," and "Hamasists."[19] Shura Council and executive positions are often analyzed to assess which of these "currents" or coalitions within the movement is ascendant at any moment.

In contrast, my research suggests that electoral contestation transformed Islamic politics in Jordan into a form of ethnic politics.[20] Over time, the Jordanian Muslim Brotherhood came to rely more and more on the votes of Palestinian-Jordanian Islamists and lost the support of Transjordanian Islamists. In the 1989 elections, the Brotherhood had found electoral support among both native Transjordanians and Jordanians of Palestinian origin. Sixteen of their 22 deputies (73 percent) elected in 1989 were from districts with a Transjordanian majority. In subsequent elections, however, the movement's candidates won fewer seats in Transjordanian majority districts but continued to win at the same rate in Palestinian-Jordanian majority districts. Consequently, the Brotherhood's political arm, the Islamic Action Front, increasingly came to represent one "ethnic" group—Palestinian Jordanians. In the 2003 elections, only five of its 17 parliamentarians (29 percent) came from Transjordanian majority districts. Brotherhood support has vanished from the southern Transjordanian heartland, where the movement won only a single seat in the 2003 and 2007 elections.

Why did this occur? I argue that the ethnic transformation of the Jordanian Brotherhood was an unintended by-product of electoral rule changes in 1993 and gerrymandering in 2001. Changes in voting rules had different effects in different districts; they interacted with differences across communal groups to dramatically reduce the electoral prospects of Brotherhood candidates in Transjordanian districts but not in Palestinian-Jordanian majority districts. Redistricting in 2001 deepened Islamists' disadvantages in Transjordanian areas by effectively creating two electoral systems in Jordan: mostly single-member districts in Transjordanian majority areas (equivalent to a first-past-the-post system) and multimember districts in Palestinian-Jordanian majority areas (equivalent to an SNTV system). Since Transjordanians rely more on government jobs and services than Palestinian Jordanians do, survey data show that they are more likely to want an elected representative who has *wasta*, or connections. The Brotherhood's willingness to boycott elections and its confrontational interactions with the regime make its parliamentarians poor interlocutors with government bureaucracies.

The difference between so-called "hawks" and "doves" has more to do with disagreements on how accommodationist the Islamic movement should be towards the Jordanian government than it does with ideological differences. Jordan's peace treaty with Israel and controversy over individual Brotherhood members' connections with Hamas contribute to ethnic tensions within the movement. But electoral boycotts and poor relations with the regime affect members from Transjordanian-majority areas more than those from Palestinian-majority areas because of differential demand for state services and jobs across those two communities. This relates to *hizb-haraka* (party-movement) relations to the extent that the Muslim Brotherhood's relationship with the regime affects the group's political party, the Islamic Action Front (IAF).

In short, what is usually described as an ideological divide is better understood as an "ethnic" or communal one. Islamism is not declining among Transjordanians; they are simply not looking toward the Muslim Brotherhood to represent them any longer. Defectors from the Brotherhood leadership since 1989 have disproportionally been Transjordanians. Of the 33 Muslim Brotherhood deputies from 1989 or 1993 or both, I identified 10 who subsequently resigned or were expelled from the Brotherhood for going against nomination decisions, boycotts, or the bloc's position on votes of confidence. Eight of these 10 are Transjordanian, and most represented Transjordanian majority areas such as Karak, Tafileh, and Madaba. At least 5 were prominent leaders within the Brotherhood and held executive positions in internal organs. Similarly, members of the Shura Councils and executive bureaus of the Muslim Brotherhood and IAF who have left since 1989 are disproportionately Transjordanians. Transjordanian defectors from the Brotherhood formed the Islamic Center Party (ICP) in July 2001 with other aspiring politicians from outside the Islamic movement. The core of the ICP is overwhelmingly Transjordanian, and its leaders are mostly from Salt; several are from the same family.

Developments in the past few years have exacerbated this ethnic cleavage within the movement. The decision to boycott the 2013 parliamentary elections—the second boycott in a row—triggered what some observers have described as the most important challenge the Jordanian Brotherhood has ever faced. As during previous boycotts, several members left the organization and ran as independents. But a larger split took shape when a group of mostly Transjordanian "doves" met in Amman's Zamzam Hotel in October 2013. With government officials in attendance, they called for a greater focus on domestic (i.e., "Jordanian") issues and for developing a reform program based on the broad principles of Islamic civilization.[21] This is not a new "post–Arab Spring" divide; rumors of such a split have surfaced regularly since the doves lost internal elections in 2008. In February 2014, the Shura Council of the Muslim Brotherhood expelled 10 members associated with this Zamzam Initiative, including a former general-overseer of the organization, ostensibly for violating the organization's bylaws. These members are mostly Transjordanian,[22] and Zamzam leaders say that only 15 percent of the 600 politicians involved in the group are Brotherhood members.[23] In its origins and composition, the Zamzam Initiative resembles, in many ways, the earlier ICP "split."

In March 2015, the Jordanian government approved an application from defectors from the Brotherhood, including some of those affiliated with the Zamzam Initiative, to form a licensed Jordanian charity under the banner of the "Muslim Brotherhood Society." The original Muslim Brotherhood was licensed in Jordan in 1945–1946 as a "charity" and as an "Islamic society" in 1953, but specifically as a branch of the mother Muslim Brotherhood in Egypt. It remains unclear if the Jordanian government sees the bureaucratic decision in March 2015 as the licensing of a new charity or the adjustment of the status of the old organization, but the regime exploited this opportunity to pressure the Muslim Brotherhood. In effect, there currently are two Muslim Brotherhoods in Jordan: the older, established, and larger faction, which remains nominally connected to movements elsewhere, and the new "Jordanian" Muslim Brotherhood, which appears committed to greater collaboration with regime initiatives. On several occasions, the government has stated that the old Muslim Brotherhood is illegal or unregistered or both. In March 2016, the government banned the organization from holding internal elections, and the following month police closed the main Muslim Brotherhood office in Abdali in Amman, as well as offices in several other cities.

A number of analysts describe these actions as a "major crackdown" on the Jordanian Brotherhood; some equate it to an existential crisis for the organization. This analysis presented in this chapter suggests a different interpretation. Following the Brotherhood's boycott of two consecutive parliamentary elections, the regime used bureaucratic and regulatory tools to essentially coerce the Muslim Brotherhood to participate in the subsequent elections which took place in September 2016. Brotherhood activists were not rounded up and detained. Although their headquarters was closed, police merely sealed the doors with tape. The organizational network of the Brotherhood was not dismantled. The king wanted the Brotherhood to participate in (and therefore help legitimize) elections and not boycott a third consecutive vote. Internal divisions within the Jordanian Brotherhood and the fall of Islamist allies elsewhere provided an opportunity for the regime to weaken the relative bargaining power of the Brotherhood heading into yet another iteration of the pre-election strategic game described earlier in the chapter. The regime's gambit succeeded. In June 2016, the IAF announced that it would participate in elections slated for September. A day later, the unrecognized Muslim Brotherhood, denied the ability to hold internal elections for a new leadership, appointed an "interim committee" to replace its executive committee and lead the organization during this period.[24] A relative moderate, Abdul Hamid Thuneibat, was selected to lead this committee. The unrecognized Muslim Brotherhood and its allies participated in the 2016 election as the "National Coalition for Reform" and won 15 seats, including 10 held by IAF members. None were in the south. The recognized and Transjordanian-dominated "Muslim Brotherhood Society" and the Zamzam group won 5 seats.

If the organizations do not reconcile, it is too early to say what long-term impact this "split" in the Jordanian Muslim Brotherhood will have, but it is important to note that it is not a new divide. The Muslim Brotherhood survived the breaking away of the Islamic Center Party a decade earlier and the occasional defection of leaders; it likely will similarly survive this most recent loss of several dozen activists and prominent members. The regime might use the court system and bureaucratic licensing to aid the breakaway faction, but it is unclear if the mostly Transjordanian Islamists leaving or being expelled from the Muslim Brotherhood will be able to take any of the organization's networks and charities with them. In July 2015, the Department of Land and Survey reportedly transferred ownership of several properties to the new and licensed Muslim Brotherhood,[25] but there are no indications that the networks, charitable societies, and institutions of the movement have shifted their allegiance or would cooperate with such a change. The parallel Islamic sector will most likely remain loyal to the older Muslim Brotherhood organization. But, if permanent, this split further divides Jordanian Islamists along "ethnic" lines; it makes the Muslim Brotherhood ever more dependent on Jordanians of Palestinian origin and could make them even more likely to boycott elections in the future. In the short-term, however, the regime succeeded in inducing the Brotherhood to participate in elections and not boycott a third, perhaps decisive, consecutive time.

CONCLUSION

King Abdullah was remarkably candid during conversations in early 2013 with Jeffrey Goldberg of *The Atlantic* and expressed his dislike and mistrust of the Jordanian Muslim Brotherhood, whom he referred to as a "Masonic cult" and "wolves in sheep's clothing."[26] Leaders of the Brotherhood met with the king two months after the Arab uprisings began, but the two sides present vastly different accounts of what transpired during the meeting. Brotherhood officials claim that they were invited to join the government and implicitly offered their choice of ministries. The king's account is worth quoting at length:

> They were the first people I saw in the Arab Spring. They were the loudest voice, so I brought them in, and they said, "Our loyalty is to the Hashemites, and we stood with you in the '40s and '50s and '70s," and I said, "That is the biggest load of crap I have ever heard." And they were like, "Aaaargh"—they were shocked. . . . "My father told me that you guys watched the way things were going, and when you saw that my father was winning, you went with him." I said, "This is complete and utter bullshit, and if we're going to sit here and bullshit each other, then we might as well have a cup of tea and then say goodbye. . . . If you want to have a serious conversation here's where we start."

The king proceeded to outline areas of common interest and then said, "I think you're part of the Jordanian system, and I think you should be part of the process. . . . I think we all leave this meeting feeling really good, but—I'll be honest with you—there's 10 percent distrust from me, and 10 percent distrust from you, I'm sure. But we have good vibes here."

King Abdullah continued by saying that, after the meeting, Brotherhood leaders went to Cairo to meet with the Egyptian Brotherhood's General Guide and, after seeing what the Brotherhood had achieved there, decided not to participate in the national dialogue committee.[27]

My analysis suggests that both the king and the (old) Muslim Brotherhood understand precisely the game they are playing, and that both sides prefer continuing to play it rather than interact in a different, presumably more confrontational, way. The regime has resisted pressure from its allies—Saudi Arabia, Egypt, and the United Arab Emirates—to crack down significantly on the Brotherhood.[28] The one thing everyone in Jordan seems to agree on is that no one knows what will happen in the absence of the Hashemites, and with instability in Syria and the Muslim Brotherhood on the run in Egypt, both the king and the Brotherhood share an interest in keeping their established game going. The regime's bureaucratic support for the Zamzam Initiative and recognition of the new Muslim Brotherhood Society will be limited; it was a tactic to coerce the 70-year-old organization to rejoin the electoral process. As much as the king and regime would prefer a more conciliatory and participatory Muslim Brotherhood, they recognize that further dividing the Islamic movement between mostly Palestinian-Jordanian "hawks" and mostly Transjordanian "doves" risks politicizing the country's most salient cleavage and could give rise to new social movements and political actors claiming an Islamic identity, including radical ones.

10

Pakistan

Matthew Nelson

THIS CHAPTER EXAMINES THE fragmented terrain of Islamist politics in South Asia—both mainstream and militant—with a focus on Pakistan. I examine two political parties, namely, the Jamiat-e-Ulama-e-Islam (JUI), led by Sunni Deobandi ulama (clerics), and the Jamaat-e-Islami (JI), led by lay Muslim professionals, as well as militants broadly affiliated with these two groups.[1]

The chapter has three parts. The first focuses on the meager electoral fortunes of the JUI and the JI—fortunes that peaked at 11 percent of the popular vote in 2002 before falling back to a postcolonial average of around 5 percent. The second focuses on various forms of nonparty religious outreach. The third describes some of the ideologically affiliated militants operating in Afghanistan and Pakistan's Tribal Areas. (In this context, I touch on evolving links between militants in South Asia and militant formations based in the Middle East—especially al-Qaeda and the Islamic State.)

For many of the actors discussed here, the terms of political success are not defined by success at the polls. Instead, they are defined within a competitive push to "Islamize" prevailing social norms and practices. This ideological objective is pursued via electoral politics, peaceful nonparty activism, and militancy—a complex *mix* of methods not seen in most of the groups featured elsewhere in this book.

HISTORICAL BACKGROUND: ELECTIONS

Before the formation of Pakistan in August 1947, the views of those who established the JI and the precursor of the JUI—India's Jamiat-e-Ulama-e-Hind (JUH)—differed from those of Muslim Brotherhood founder Hassan al-Banna. Suspicious of modern Arab or South Asian Muslim "nationalism" and its explicit *territorial* constraints, they insisted that new forms of religious and political solidarity should be grounded not in the cultivation of new "nations," but rather in a more pious *ummah* (global Muslim community).[2] Above all, they opposed efforts by Mohammad Ali Jinnah and his broadly "secular" Muslim League to create a Muslim-majority state known as Pakistan. They saw Jinnah's push for Pakistan as a nationalist ploy to divide South Asian Muslims: Indian Muslims on the one hand; Pakistani Muslims on the other.

Shortly after the founding of Pakistan, however, both the JI and those who departed from the JUH to establish a pro-Pakistan configuration of the same group known as the JUI sought to rehabilitate their "nationalist" credentials. Within Pakistan's protracted constitutional debates, both parties claimed that the Muslim-majority state envisioned by Jinnah would require careful oversight to avoid the introduction of any law that might be considered repugnant to the terms of Islam. At the same time, however, each disagreed about which group should be charged with this supervisory task: whereas the JI stressed the leadership of a revolutionary vanguard led by lay Muslim professionals like JI founder Abul Ala Maududi, the JUI favored the leadership of religious scholars trained in Deobandi madrasas.

Each group lobbied Pakistan's Constituent Assembly to promote what they saw as an "Islamic" constitution; however, the formal legal impact of their views was largely thwarted by Pakistan's bureaucratic, military, political, and judicial elite.[3] Initially, drawing attention to its energetic student wing (the Islami Jamiat-e-Tuleba, or IJT, which Hassan al-Banna's son-in-law Said Ramadan helped to establish in Karachi after 1947), the Jamaat-e-Islami stressed the cultivation of its own leadership cadre within Pakistan's university-educated bureaucratic and professional elite.[4] But, over time, realizing that any effort to shape the formal legal architecture of Pakistan would require a far more substantial presence within Pakistan's elected National Assembly, the JI also branched out to contest local elections, beginning with provincial elections in the Punjab during the spring of 1951.[5]

Even as the JI entered Pakistan's electoral arena, however, the JUI opted to keep its distance throughout the 1940s, 1950s, and 1960s. In fact, it was not until the campaign preceding Pakistan's first national election in 1970 that JUI-affiliated ulama entered the electoral process to contest what they saw as a pattern of religious-cum-political central-ization under the JI's founder, Abul Ala Maududi. Mainstream elec-toral politics, however, did not draw existing forms of Islamist activism together.[6] Instead, it emerged *alongside* persistent divisions between "lay" (JI) and "clerical" (JUI) elites.[7] Even within the JI, the decision to field candidates in Karachi's municipal elections (1958) prompted an internal split—above all, a split between electoral pragmatists and religious ideologues that led some ideologues (e.g., Amin Ahsan Islahi) to resign.

Throughout this Cold War period, anticommunist pressure also shifted the terrain of Pakistani student politics away from left-wing groups like the National Students Federation (NSF) in favor of right-wing student groups like the JI-affiliated IJT.[8] In fact, a string of cam-pus-based victories for the IJT produced a powerful *combination* of "mainstream" and "militant" student politics, with mainstream student unions controlled by the IJT providing institutional cover for a band of campus-based vice-and-virtue vigilantes commonly known as the Thunder Squad.[9] Off campus, however, the electoral performance of religious parties like the JI and the JUI remained extremely weak, partly owing to an expanding program of political repression orchestrated by Pakistan's first military dictator, General Ayub Khan (1958–1969).[10]

The marginalization of parties like the JI and the JUI was particu-larly apparent during the elections of 1970 when, having contested more than 150 seats, the JI won just 4. The JUI fared somewhat bet-ter, winning 7 National Assembly seats (out of 105 contested) and 9 provincial seats. In fact, the JUI helped to form provincial gov-ernments in Balochistan and Pakistan's Northwest Frontier Province (NWFP), with JUI leader Mufti Mahmud emerging as NWFP's chief minister.[11]

Both the JI and the JUI operated at some distance from Pakistan's military and civilian elite during the 1950s and 1960s. But during the 1970s, this pattern began to shift, particularly after the partition of Pakistan in 1971 and the formation of Bangladesh—an event that prompted Pakistan's new prime minister, Zulfiqar Ali Bhutto, to reart-iculate a "religious" sense of Muslim nationalism as a bulwark against the divisive terms of "provincialism."[12]

Maududi resigned as leader of the Jamaat-e-Islami in 1972. But dur-ing the next 15 years, his successor Mian Tufail Mohammad went on to develop much closer ties with those at the center of power—above all, the military dictator who ousted Prime Minister Bhutto in 1977, General Zia-ul-Haq. Domestically, Mian Tufail supported Zia's bid to "Islamize" Pakistan's public school curricula (as well as its crimi-nal laws) even as he criticized Zia for his failure to hold elections. Internationally, Mian Tufail also praised Zia's involvement in the anti-Soviet politics of Afghanistan, paying special attention to mujahideen formations with ideological inclinations close to the JI, such as Hizb-e-Islami.[13] Mainstream electoral pressures and transnational mili-tancy, in other words, were not incompatible during the Zia years. On the contrary, long-awaited National Assembly elections in 1985—conducted on a nonparty basis—brought these two elements closer together.[14]

After the Soviet withdrawal from Kabul in 1989, Afghanistan's burgeoning civil war saw the focus of Pakistani military and politi-cal patronage shift away from those tied to the ideological perspective of the JI (e.g., Hizb-e-Islami) in favor of guerilla commanders with close ties to the Taliban and, thus, to various Deobandi madrasas. This shift did not eliminate the JI; it merely pulled the prevailing balance of forces away from JI-affiliated mujahideen in favor of those with closer ties to the institutional orbit of the JUI.

Within Pakistan, religious militancy typically unfolds in ways that remain at least one step removed from any direct association with the JI or the JUI. More often, this militancy is associated with ideologically affiliated "partners" like Hizb-e-Islami or the Taliban.[15] This pattern of loose affiliation poses certain challenges for analysts, leading many to assume close ties in the absence of explicit evidence proving otherwise. For parties like the JI and the JUI, however, this analytical dilemma ("guilty until proven innocent") has not been completely unhelpful. In fact, sweeping generalizations tend to highlight broad patterns of ideological overlap while at the same time shielding both the JI and the JUI from the culpabilities that might follow from direct institutional ties. Within Pakistan, right-of-center politics has never been limited to mainstream religious parties or militants; instead it has been dominated by military dictators like Zia-ul-Haq and, more recently, mainstream politicians like Mohammad Nawaz Sharif of the Pakistan Muslim League. In fact, within this right-of-center space combining mainstream parties, militant factions, and military leaders, Pakistan's "religious" parties are often reduced to a purely supporting role. Ratcheting public discourse to the right, they remain ideologically influential notwithstanding their cautious relationship with violence and their persistent failure at the polls.

In 1987, Mian Tufail's successor as leader of the JI, Qazi Hussain Ahmad, launched a concerted effort to shift his party's base beyond its original "vanguardist" orientation. He sought to create a mass party focused on broader concerns—including a more overt anti-imperialist and anti-Western agenda.[16] Together with the grassroots institutional focus of the JUI, this mass-based orientation allowed the JI and certain elements of the JUI to combine forces as part of a ruling right-of-center coalition led by Nawaz Sharif after 1988. Known as the Islami Jamhoori Ittehad (Islamic Democratic Alliance), this coalition was formed with assistance from Pakistan's Inter-Services Intelligence Directorate, the ISI, to counter the early resurgence of left-wing populists like Benazir Bhutto. On a more general level, however, it grew out of the earlier dictatorship of General Zia—a dictatorship that incorporated both the JI and key elements of the JUI (especially the JUI-S faction led by Sami-ul-Haq) as well as Mohammad Nawaz Sharif, who served under Zia as chief minister of the Punjab between 1985 and Zia's death in 1988.

As the war in Afghanistan receded from the headlines, those affiliated with the JI and the JUI-S did not hesitate to join the Islamic Democratic Alliance (IJI).[17] In fact each saw this electoral alliance as an important vehicle for recapturing some of the patronage opportunities previously enjoyed under Zia. During the elections that followed Zia's death in 1988, however, this new coalition did not simply march into power. Instead its results were mixed. On a national level, it was defeated by Benazir Bhutto, who won 93 seats as compared to the IJI's 54 (of which 8 were affiliated with the JI).[18] On a provincial level, it won in the Punjab, allowing Nawaz Sharif to remain in office as Punjab's provincial chief minister.

Benazir Bhutto's government was short-lived, however. In 1991, it was dissolved by Pakistan's president on charges of corruption and mismanagement, ushering in a new round of elections. And, this time, the performance of the IJI improved. In fact, the IJI won both in Islamabad (securing 106 National Assembly seats, with 8 attached to the JI) and, once again, in the Provincial Assembly of Lahore.[19]

Like Benazir Bhutto's government, this IJI government (led by Nawaz Sharif) was short-lived. Once again, Pakistan's president stepped in to dismiss it just two years later in 1993, allowing Benazir Bhutto to return to power in subsequent elections that reduced the strength of the JI to just 3 parliamentary seats.[20] Clearly, the JI was not on a winning trajectory. In fact, when Bhutto was dismissed for a *second* time, in 1997, the JI announced its intention to boycott the next round of elections, describing Pakistani polls as "corrupt."

The IJI, having been dissolved following the dismissal of Nawaz Sharif in 1993, was not revived. But, in the ensuing 1997 elections, Nawaz Sharif won by a landslide. In fact, he returned to power with a whopping single-party majority of 63 percent in Islamabad and 88 percent in Lahore.[21] Still, his government did not last long. After just two years (1997–1999), Sharif was deposed in a military coup—a coup led by General Pervez Musharraf that, somewhat ironically, revived the dwindling fortunes of Pakistan's Islamist parties.

Building on the "anti-imperialist" rhetoric previously cultivated by the JUI and, somewhat later, by the JI, Pakistan's religious parties stepped forward to capitalize on the sense of public anger that had emerged after America's invasion of Afghanistan in October 2001.[22] In fact, when Musharraf announced a new round of elections during the fall of 2002, the JI and the JUI charged into the limelight, leading a new religious alliance known as the Muttahida Majlis-e-Amal (MMA), or United Council of Action, to secure their best-ever result of 45 parliamentary seats.[23]

These 45 seats allowed the MMA to play a key part in Musharraf's ruling coalition while, at the same time, forming yet another provincial government in the Northwest Frontier Province (NWFP) bordering Afghanistan. In effect, the JI and JUI re-emerged after years of electoral obscurity to rejoin that rare breed of religious parties: the breed that has actually governed.

Within the NWFP, the MMA introduced a controversial Hisba Act to monitor public "morality." However, its spirited vice-and-virtue brigades did not last long; the act was quickly struck down by the Pakistan Supreme Court as an arbitrary form of Sunni parallel justice providing inadequate protections for sectarian diversity while ignoring established forms of due process. The MMA also introduced a federal bill seeking to punish unrepentant male apostates with execution. However, this bill failed to emerge from its standing committee; in fact, even today, Pakistan has no statute governing the terms of apostasy. In effect, the MMA's "Islamization" agenda stalled. And as it did, the MMA began to follow in the footsteps of so many ideological parties before it: diluting its ideological agenda, it sought to construct a populist program of provincial economic reform.[24]

When General Musharraf's political fortunes began to fade after nationwide demonstrations protesting his ouster of Supreme Court Chief Justice Iftikhar Chaudhry, the electoral fortunes of the MMA began to suffer as well. During the 2008 elections, for instance, the NWFP's MMA government was badly defeated and, with the JI deciding (once again) to boycott the polls, the national MMA was reduced from its peak of 45 parliamentary seats to 7—although, even then, the JUI faction led by Fazlur Rahman (JUI-F) managed to secure a place in the new federal coalition led by Benazir Bhutto's widower, Asif Ali Zardari.

Finally, during the 2013 general elections, both the JI and the JUI returned to figures more in keeping with their average performance since 1970. With a combined total of just 5 percent of the vote, the historically "populist" JUI-F won 15 National Assembly seats (all concentrated in the NWFP, which was renamed Khyber Pakhtunkhwa in 2010), while the more consistently "ideological" JI was limited to just 4.

In 2013, younger religious voters seemed to be drawn away from religious parties like the JI and the JUI in favor of a previously obscure right-of-center party known as the Pakistan Tehreek-e-Insaaf (PTI, i.e., the Party of Justice) led by former cricket champion Imran Khan.[25] (In 2013, Khan's PTI emerged as the second-largest party in all of Pakistan's major cities. In fact, the PTI went on to form the provincial government of Khyber Pakhtunkhwa in coalition with the JI.)

Despite the *rhetorical* appeal of religion, then, the evidence clearly suggests that voters in Pakistan are not actually drawn to parties that limit their agenda to a narrow interpretation of sharia. Even when the JI and the JUI found themselves in a position to shape government policy—as they did as leading members of the MMA coalition in the Northwest Frontier Province after 2002—voters were put off by the extent to which their "religious" policies failed to address (or directly challenged) their core *material* concerns.[26]

For 65 years, religious parties have struggled to win national elections in Pakistan. Their persistent record of marginalization, however, cannot be traced to any one historical factor: when not been harassed by military dictators (Ayub Khan, 1960s), they have cozied up to them (General Zia, 1980s; General Musharraf, 2000s). And yet, having done so, they have persistently found themselves punished as authoritarian "collaborators" whenever Pakistan has reverted to civilian elections. Indeed, even when these parties have not opted to boycott elections, their religious identity has been offset by right-of-center parties like the Pakistan Muslim League (PML) and, in recent years, the PTI—parties that exploit similar forms of religious rhetoric in ways that dilute the distinctive "Islamist" appeal of Islamist parties.

BEYOND ELECTIONS: OUTREACH

As noted above, repeated electoral failures have drawn Pakistan's "religious" voters away from explicitly religious parties like the JI and the JUI in favor of alternative right-of-center parties like the PML and the PTI. Recalling the basic distinction between *hizb* (party) and *haraka* (movement), however, these same failures have also led some to pull away from electoral politics altogether—this time, in the direction of

Muslim *da'wa* (religious outreach) with a focus on education, social welfare, and private religious reform.

When it comes to social welfare, "Jamaati" groups like Al-Khidmat and "Deobandi" groups like the humanitarian Al-Khair Trust figure prominently. These groups have become increasingly well known for their contributions to medical care and large-scale relief in the wake of natural disasters, such as the Kashmir earthquake in 2005 and catastrophic flooding throughout Pakistan in 2011–2012.[27] At the same time, however, both groups have also been accused of channeling funding to like-minded militants in Kashmir, such as Hizb-ul-Mujahideen and Jaish-e-Mohammad articulating, respectively, "Jamaati" and "Deobandi" views.

The rapidly expanding space occupied by social welfare organizations like Al-Khidmat and Al-Khair Trust, however, pales in comparison to that occupied by religious activists involved in the field of education—an enormous and dynamic enterprise stretching all the way from Jamaati and Deobandi madrasas to a growing mix of fee-based private schools. These schools peddle their own brand of doctrinal education along with the public sector curriculum underpinning the government's annual exams.[28]

Within the realm of Muslim *da'wa*, however, competing Jamaati and Deobandi activists also move beyond the sphere of social welfare and education to build on the evangelizing outreach of (1) media-savvy personalities like Israr Ahmed and Javed Ahmed Ghamidi (both of whom joined, but later abandoned, the Jama'at-e-Islami) and (2) peripatetic lay Muslim missionaries like the globe-trotting Tablighi Jama'at (which grew out of, but then rejected, key features of the madrasa-based Deobandi tradition still embraced by parties like the JUI).[29]

Israr Ahmed followed early JI defectors like Amin Ahsan Islahi in criticizing the JI's embrace of electoral politics. But, having left the JI, Ahmed went on to form two evangelizing organizations of his own—namely, Tanzim-e-Islami (the Islamic Association) and Tehreek-e-Khilafat (the Caliphate Movement)—to promote the re-creation of a global caliphate in a region often described as the region of "Khorasan" (roughly encompassing eastern Iran, Afghanistan, northern Pakistan, and Central Asia).[30] Ahmed was a key media personality during the late 1970s and 1980s, mostly at the urging of General Zia. In fact, his daily television appearances were quite influential; his role in radicalizing public religious and political discourse has often been described as "enormous."[31] Few were surprised when, during the 1990s, he emerged as a supporter of the Taliban and their expanding political role in Afghanistan.

The media platform of Javed Ahmad Ghamidi is even better known than that of Israr Ahmed, particularly given the boost Ghamidi received after 1999 from General Pervez Musharraf. Unlike Israr Ahmed, however, Ghamidi has not stressed the revival of a global caliphate. Nor has he supported the Taliban in Afghanistan. Instead, recalling the work of his mentor, JI defector Amin Ahsan Islahi, Ghamidi has articulated a more thoroughly individualized approach to contemporary religious reform—in many ways, an intellectual approach combining text-based analysis with a commitment to ongoing religious "self-polishing."[32]

Whereas Ahmed stresses the pursuit of state power, then, Ghamidi stresses personal piety—two very different elements of the "Islamist" program first articulated by JI founder Abul Ala Maududi. Having said this, however, both Ahmed and Ghamidi target the same demographic that Maududi targeted as leader of the JI, namely, Pakistan's professional middle classes. This is important, because, within the realm of Muslim *da'wa*, Pakistan's "Deobandi" Tablighi Jama'at is very different, engaging a much wider social base. Often described as the largest religious reform movement in the world, Tablighis are known for their door-to-door evangelism, calling ostensibly "lapsed" Muslims, not to Deobandi madrasas (like the JUI), but rather to Deobandi mosques.

Within Pakistan, it is impossible to rank the relative importance of party-based politics and Muslim *da'wa*. Nor is it possible to tease out a simple relationship in which one anticipates or produces the other. Each proceeds in tandem. The social welfare and humanitarian work of JI affiliates like Al-Khidmat, for instance, has not enhanced the electoral fortunes of Jamaat-e-Islami itself. Nor has the rise of Deobandi movements like the Tablighi Jama'at advanced the electoral performance of the JUI. Apparently, ideological *affiliations* do not drive *affiliates* to the polls.

TRANSNATIONAL POLITICS: MILITANCY

Moving away from the relationship between grassroots activism and Muslim voting, "inclusion-moderation" theories consider the relationship between Muslim voting and militancy, stipulating that electoral success is likely to *reduce* the appeal of extremism and violence.[33] Unfortunately, the reach of such theories has been limited in Pakistan. Indeed, whatever electoral success Deobandi parties like JUI have enjoyed—particularly in provinces like the Northwest Frontier Province (now Khyber Pakhtunkhwa)—that success has largely failed to reduce the level of militancy associated with Deobandi Taliban groups in neighboring areas like FATA (Pakistan's Federally Administered Tribal Areas).

What we see in Pakistan is actually a complex pattern in which the link between religious parties and Muslim militancy, including the link between mainstream parties like the JI or the JUI and militants with "Jamaati" or "Deobandi" affinities, is closely bound up with the work of the Pakistan Army—an army with a habit of projecting its authority beyond its traditional base in West Pakistan (and, especially, the Punjab) via (1) militants broadly associated with the JI (Al Badr in East Pakistan during the 1970s; Hizb-e-Islami in Afghanistan during the 1980s; Hizb-ul-Mujahideen in Kashmir after 1989) and (2) militants associated with the same network of Deobandi madrasas tied to the JUI (Jaish-e-Mohammad and Harkat-ul-Mujahideen in Kashmir; the Afghan Taliban; and so on). Indeed, religious militants in Pakistan maintain a complex *mix* of ties: "ideological" ties with mainstream parties and "operational" ties with parts of the Pakistan Army.

Even as one begins to appreciate this complex mix of ties, however, it is also important to stress that the Pakistan Army has not merely *collaborated*, but also *clashed*, with JI- and JUI-linked militants. In particular, it has clashed with militants tied to formations like the (Deobandi) Tehreek-e-Taliban Pakistan (TTP)—the so-called "Pakistani Taliban."

Typically, the JI and the JUI work *with* the Pakistan Army to distinguish between what are known as the "good" and the "bad" branches of militant formations like the Taliban. The Afghan Taliban, focused on seizing power *outside* of Pakistan (i.e., in Afghanistan), are regarded as the "good" Taliban, whereas the Pakistani Taliban are seen as the "bad" Taliban because they attack the existing social order, including the Pakistan Army, inside Pakistan itself. On several occasions, however, religious parties like the Jamaat-e-Islami have struggled to define their relationship with these two different branches, with JI leader Munawar

Hasan balancing his support for the Pakistan Army with a countervailing pattern of support for the TTP (which attacked the Pakistan Army for its role in supporting America's "global war on terror" after 2001). In fact, when TTP leader Hakimullah Mehsud, based in Pakistan's Tribal Areas, was killed by a U.S. drone strike, Hasan lauded Hakimullah's "anti-American" credentials and described him as a Muslim "martyr."

For many years, both branches of the Taliban swore allegiance to the same Emir-ul-Momineen or "Leader of the Faithful," Mullah Omar (known for sheltering Osama bin Laden during the 1990s even as he maintained close ties with the Pakistan Army). Mullah Omar was not seen for several years, however, and, when his death was finally revealed in 2015 two years after the fact, some insisted that his eldest son Mohammad Yaqoob should succeed him. This view, however, was not widely held, and for nearly a year, the Afghan Taliban were torn apart by infighting. Some Afghan Taliban commanders considered forming an alliance with the newly created Islamic State. But, eventually, most chose to accept the authority of a new emir named Mullah Akhter Mansour.[34]

The Pakistan Army sought to encourage talks between Mullah Mansour and the Afghan government in Kabul.[35] But the Afghan government saw Mansour as "irreconcilable" and, in April 2016, Mansour was killed inside Pakistan by a U.S. drone, leading to yet another succession crisis and the emergence of a less charismatic Taliban leader known as Maulvi Haibatullah Akhundzada.

In many ways, the Pakistan Army has tended to see the Afghan Taliban as a key resource in a much larger push to offset the emergence of any close relationship between the Afghan government and the government of Pakistan's archrival, India. But even as the army has sought to promote a role for the Afghan Taliban in Afghanistan—by transforming Afghan Taliban "militants," if you will, into a "mainstream" political party like the JUI—the army has *simultaneously* sought to contain the disorder surrounding renegade Taliban fighters inside Pakistan itself. It has done so first with a series of negotiated but fragile ceasefires in Pakistan's tribal areas and, then, turning to the very center of Islamabad, with an attack on a well-armed mosque known as the Lal Masjid (Red Mosque) during the summer of 2007. (The political implications of this step could be seen in the fact that

JI leader Munawar Hasan and JUI-S leader Sami-ul-Haq supported a fatwa seeking to invalidate the funeral prayers offered for any soldier killed in the attack.)

The immediate effect of this attack on Islamabad's Lal Masjid did not lay in the pacification of renegade Taliban militants; instead, it prompted those fighters to *consolidate* their efforts in a new militant formation known as the "Pakistani" Taliban (a.k.a. the Tehreek-e-Taliban Pakistan, or TTP).[36] Initially, the TTP was led by Baitullah Mehsud from South Waziristan. But, when Baitullah was killed by a U.S. drone, his role was taken up by another member of the same tribe, namely, Hakimullah Mehsud.[37] Hakimullah was also killed by a U.S. drone. The leadership of the TTP then shifted to a figure named Fazlullah—famous for his role in the attack on Nobel Peace Prize winner Malala Yousafzai.

The selection of Fazlullah in 2013 was controversial for at least two reasons: first, because unlike Baitullah and Hakimullah before him, Fazlullah was not a Mehsud tribesman; and, second, because for the first time Fazlullah's primary base of support was not in FATA but in a "provincial" tribal area known as Swat.[38] Like the fragmentation within the Afghan Taliban that followed the death of Mullah Omar, Hakimullah's death ushered in a period of intense unraveling, including a series of defections in which some TTP commanders threatened to shift their allegiance to the Islamic State.

Islamic State leader Abu Bakr al-Baghdadi had declared himself "caliph" in June 2014, effectively usurping the role of "commander of the faithful" that al-Qaeda and the Taliban had long associated with Mullah Omar. Shortly thereafter, al-Qaeda leader Ayman al-Zawahiri responded with the formation of a new al-Qaeda franchise in South Asia known as al-Qaeda in the Indian Subcontinent (AQIS).[39] Since then, Islamic State leaders managed to exploit various moments of instability within both the Afghan and the Pakistani Taliban. As noted above, for instance, many of those who opposed the leadership of Mohammad Yaqoob (Afghan Taliban) and Fazlullah (Pakistan Taliban) considered joining forces with the Islamic State. Dissident TTP commander Hafiz Said Khan, similarly, pledged allegiance to Baghdadi as the leader of a new Islamic State "province" known as Khorasan, even as—somewhat confusingly—another TTP commander by the name of Omar Khalid Khorasani formed a splinter group known as the Jama'at-ul-Ahrar initially suspected of enduring ties to al-Qaeda.[40]

It is, perhaps, somewhat ironic that within Pakistan those with the closest ties to the Islamic State have *not* been "Salafi" groups like Jama'at-ud-Dawa or Lashkar-e-Taiba. (These groups remain far more closely tied to the Army.) Instead, the liveliest support has come from fragments of the "Deobandi" tradition. Indeed, there may be a further irony—namely, that within Pakistan "Deobandis" appear to occupy both ends of the mainstream–militant spectrum simultaneously: whereas Deobandi supporters of the JUI have enjoyed more electoral success than any other religious party in Pakistan, Deobandi supporters of the TTP have emerged as the most ferocious opponents of the state.

Clearly, when it comes to broad ideological formations like Deoband, analytical conventions regarding the relationship between "mainstream" and "militant" are often turned on their head. Not only has the influence of enormous Deobandi movements like the Tablighi Jama'at failed to ensure any consistent measure of success for Deobandi parties like the JUI, but whatever electoral success the JUI has enjoyed—not only at a provincial level in Khyber Pakhtunkhwa but also at a federal level in Islamabad (where JUI leaders have held cabinet positions in several different coalition governments)—this electoral success has failed to deter rampant forms of Deobandi militancy (both in conjunction with the army and against it). Evidently, when it comes to Islamist politics in Pakistan, "mainstream" and "militant" politics are not at all incompatible.

CONCLUSION

Just a few months before he expressed his appreciation for the militancy of TTP leader Hakimullah Mehsud, former JI leader Munawar Hasan exchanged visits with Egypt's Muslim Brotherhood–affiliated president, Mohamed Morsi—first in Cairo (June 2012) and then in Islamabad (March 2013). Hasan later hosted a rally in Islamabad to protest Morsi's ouster by General Abdel Fattah al-Sissi—a rally attended by the former vice chairman of Imran Khan's PTI, Shah Mahmood Qureshi.

In this context, internal JI party elections in March 2014 were significant. Not only did they mark the first time a sitting JI leader (Munawar

Hasan) sought re-election only to be replaced after just one term in office, but they also provided the JI's new leader Siraj-ul-Haq with an opportunity to distance himself from Munawar's comments supporting the TTP, thus restoring his relationship with the army. Perhaps the JI sought to cultivate closer ties with the Pakistan Army after seeing Egypt's President Morsi ousted in June 2013. Perhaps Siraj-ul-Haq merely sought to consolidate his ties with "pro-army" parties like Imran Khan's PTI.[41] Either way, the JI seemed to feel that, moving forward, some effort to sustain its relationship with the army was important.

In Pakistan, Jamaati and Deobandi conglomerations broadly affiliated with the JI and the JUI are rarely forced to choose between "mainstream" and "militant" politics. On the contrary, their engagements run the gamut from elections to extremism simultaneously. Neither group is defined by either form of engagement. Even beyond elections and extremism, their affiliates are deeply involved in education, televangelism, humanitarianism, civil society activism, and more. It is, in fact, this wider *mix* of engagements that underpins their enduring influence. This is the mix of engagements that sustains their influence notwithstanding a persistent pattern of failure at the polls.

11

Southeast Asia

Joseph Chinyong Liow

ALTHOUGH THE ARAB SPRING prompted discussions of Islamism, political participation, and democracy across the Muslim world, mainstream Islamists in Southeast Asia were *not* greatly influenced by the uprisings and their aftermath. They were not looking for models of democratic change, having already much earlier opened the door to democracy (in the late 1990s during the Asian financial crisis). Islamists in Southeast Asia also have nebulous ties with their counterparts in the Middle East despite the potential for stronger links to be forged. Still, it is useful to compare the trajectory of Indonesian and Malaysian Islamists with their fellow travelers further west if only to provide some indication of how Arab Islamists might fare given similar political circumstances.

This chapter will advance five arguments, some of which may appear at cross-purposes with each other. First, although Islamist parties in Indonesia and Malaysia have gained electoral support in recent years, that does not necessarily correlate with greater support for Islamism. Second, Islamists in Southeast Asia have by and large eschewed revolutionary approaches to political change. With the minor exception of militant groups who have sought to create Islamic states in Indonesia and Malaysia, Islamists who seek to implement sharia have remained committed to the political process. Third, in both Indonesia and Malaysia, structural conditions have enhanced the prospects of Islamists achieving their sociopolitical goals. In Malaysia, the incumbent government led by the Malay nationalist party, UMNO (United Malays National Organization), has facilitated the gradual introduction of Islamic strictures in government, while post-Suharto Indonesia has decentralized lawmaking, allowing regional and local governments the latitude to introduce various kinds of sharia laws. Fourth, Southeast Asian Islamists have not been dogmatic about their ideology. This has as much to do with expediency and opportunism as it has with Islamic traditions in Southeast Asia, which are historically more accommodating of pluralism. Fifth, transnational links are stronger between Islamist civil society organizations outside the realm of mainstream politics than they are between Islamist political parties themselves.

THE ROOTS OF POLITICAL ISLAM IN INDONESIA AND MALAYSIA

Since independence in 1945, Islam has enjoyed an important—if often ambiguous—place in Indonesian politics. This became immediately evident after independence, when a vociferous debate surfaced among claimants to the fledgling colonial state over the place of sharia in the new constitution. The most contentious issue was whether a seven-word clause—"with the obligation for adherents of Islam to practice Islamic law"—should be included in the preamble of the constitution. Commonly known as the Jakarta Charter, the debate was resolved in favor of secular nationalists who feared that the embryonic state would unravel if Islam were given too prominent a place given the concerns of large non-Muslim communities in Eastern Indonesia.

Through most of their time in office, presidents Sukarno (1959–1965) and Suharto (1966–1998) essentially marginalized political Islam—represented during the early years of independence by the Masyumi party—although the expression of religious piety in civil society was permitted by the state to bolster its legitimacy in the eyes of more pious Muslims. Paradoxically, it was during this period in the political "wilderness" that the seeds for new patterns of Islamic thinking and activism were sown, and which eventually bore fruit. Primarily rooted in student movements through the 1970s and 1980s, "civil" Islam would emerge to play a crucial role in mobilizing Islamist forces in the post-Suharto era.[1]

The watershed for Islamism in Indonesia came in 1997 when a financial crisis catalyzed a widespread reform movement that eventually led to the overthrow of Suharto's New Order regime. This reform movement, known in popular local parlance as *Reformasi*, saw the emergence of hitherto low-key opposition figures into the public arena to agitate for Suharto's resignation. Among these were a host of Islamist activists, including those of Masyumi lineage. With the introduction of free elections in 1999, Islamist parties such as Partai Keadilan Sejahtera (PKS, or Justice and Prosperity Party), Partai Bulan Bintang (Crescent and Star Party), and Partai Persatuan Pembangunan (United Development Party) competed at the polls in 1999, 2004, 2009, and 2014 on an Islamist platform that included introduction of sharia laws and a greater role for Islam in society and state affairs.[2] Nevertheless, these parties saw mixed fortunes. Except for the notable performance of the Muslim Brotherhood-inspired PKS, the newest among the Islamist parties, Islamists failed to make any significant headway at the national level.[3]

Unlike Ennahda in Tunisia or the Egyptian Muslim Brotherhood during the Arab Spring, Indonesian Islamists never came to power on their own; at best, they were minority members of ruling coalitions. One reason is that in post-Suharto Indonesia, the Islamist agenda, rather than being concentrated in one or two parties, became dispersed across a spectrum of Islamic and Islamist parties because of the fragmented nature of Islamic authority and the institutional weaknesses of the parties themselves, leading to a dilution of the Islamist (indeed, the Muslim) vote, as well as the broadening of the Islamist agenda.[4]

This broad canvas of Islamist parties is absent in Malaysia. In Malaysia, the standard bearer of Islamism has primarily been the Pan-Malayan Islamic Party (PAS), although more recently the ruling and ostensibly secular UMNO has pursued policies that are easily construed as "Islamist" as well (e.g., policing and regulation of non-Muslim activity in defense of Islam and supporting PAS initiatives to implement sharia by-laws). As a political party, PAS was ironically born within UMNO itself, when members of the Religious Bureau of UMNO questioned the commitment of the party's leadership to Islam and Muslim interests, and broke away in 1951.

Regardless of the party's overtly religious character and motivations, its religious track record in Malaysian politics is checkered. Through the 1950s and 1960s, it pursued a religio-socialist agenda inspired by Sukarno. After the May 1969 race riots, PAS moved further right along the ideological spectrum and transformed into a Malay nationalist party that contested UMNO's claim to leadership of the Malay community against the backdrop of heightened communitarian consciousness. By 1982, PAS moved to implement ulama (Muslim religious scholars) rule in the party leadership through the formation of a Consultative Council (Majlis Shura), made up of clerics who would oversee all party policies and set it on course for a stronger and more explicitly Islamist agenda.

The early 1980s witnessed a flurry of consequential events in the Muslim world that informed this reorientation not only in PAS but also, as it turned out, in UMNO. This included the Afghan mujahideen struggle; the Iranian revolution; the introduction of Islamic government in Pakistan; the rise of Islamist movements and parties in Egypt, Tunisia, and Turkey; and the general heightened Islamic consciousness of the Malay-Muslim population as appeals to Islam as "the solution" gained greater currency across the country.

In response to the shifting mood in Malaysia, the UMNO-led government of Mahathir Mohamad sought to seize the initiative by harnessing Islam to justify its developmental policies. It did so by orchestrating an Islamization process, which expanded the size and scope of the religious bureaucracy at the state and federal level, created Islamic banking institutions, and established an Islamic university. At the time, the policy stood in marked contrast to developments elsewhere in the Muslim world where regimes experiencing similar pressures from Islamist opposition forces, such as Egypt and Turkey, chose to discredit, rather than leverage, the Islamist agenda.

ARE PEOPLE WHO VOTE FOR ISLAMIST PARTIES ISLAMISTS?

The Bali bombing of October 2002, barely a year after the September 11 attacks in the United States, saw the world bestow on Southeast Asia the epithet of the "Second Front" in the global war on terror.[5] While most analysts recognize that terrorist and militant groups are not representative of the Muslim population of Southeast Asia, there is consternation in some policymaking circles over the "conservative Islamic high tide"[6] that seems to be sweeping the region. The flowering of Islamic organizations and the growing influence of Islamist movements and parties, particularly in Malaysia and Indonesia, are often pointed to as evidence. In the 1999 and 2008 Malaysian elections, PAS slowly increased its popularity and number of seats in parliament, albeit as part of an opposition alliance that included a major non-Muslim partner. The 2004 Indonesian elections saw the PKS winning 7.3 percent of the total votes and 45 seats in parliament, a number significant enough to make it a junior partner in President Bambang Yudhoyono's first coalition government. This was the first instance of Islamists in the executive branch since Masyumi's experiment in the mid-1950s.[7] Beyond tangible indicators such as electoral results, commentators also detect a general "Islamic resurgence" from the increased Islamic "consciousness" in the daily life of Muslims of the region, manifested primarily in the adoption of Muslim dress, mosque attendance, and the proliferation of Islamic symbols.[8]

One might be tempted to link the rise of this Islamic consciousness with the success of Islamist parties at the polls. But there are a number of sociopolitical and economic reasons apart from simply religious motivations that have led people in Southeast Asia to vote for Islamist parties. For instance, PAS has managed to secure support from non-Muslims, while both PAS and the PKS have opened membership to non-Muslims.[9] Indeed, participation in the political process has encouraged a number of religiously-oriented parties to shape a broader and more inclusive political agenda, one that moves away from demands for the strict implementation of Islamic codes. In fact, Islamist parties and movements have in many cases contributed to the development of the democratic ethos by welcoming political liberalization and participating in the electoral process.[10]

It would be instructive here (especially for policymakers) to note the difference between spirituality or pietism as a personal conviction and its public expression as a form of religiosity. Whereas the former is largely related to the realm of personal convictions and the fulfilment of individual religious duties, the latter can have important social and political implications. In the social realm, it can manifest itself in the call for greater adherence to Islamic norms and codes. In Indonesia, for instance, some scholars have noted an inverse correlation between religious piety and support for Islamism in the form of either Islamist parties or stricter Islamic legislation.[11]

Several reasons account for this in Indonesia. First, some of the parties at the forefront of the drive to implement sharia have not been Islamist parties, but secular parties such as Golkar, the largest political party in Indonesia. Second, voters assessed Islamist parties not solely according to their religious credentials, but also according to how well they were able to "deliver the goods" in terms of sound policy proposals and the personal appeal of their candidates. Given the proliferation of political parties in the post-Suharto era—including Islamist ones—the electorate sought other ways to differentiate between parties, beyond abstract ideological platforms. Third, Islamist parties themselves avoided excessive focus on Islam in their campaigns. As Greg Fealy noted of the 2014 elections: "None of the four Islamic parties that passed the 3.5 percent parliamentary threshold campaigned using Islamic concepts or doctrines. Rather, their appeals to their core constituencies emphasized the practical benefits that they had or would deliver to their supporters."[12] All this points to the dilution of the Muslim vote and broadening of the Islamic agenda in Indonesian society since the fall of Suharto's New Order and the advent of democracy.

Having said that, we should also recognize that there are diverse voices in Southeast Asia that want a greater role for Islam in the political realm. Some want to implement sharia for Muslims (with non-Muslims exempt); others want to make Islam the official ideology of the state. Such groups and individuals also advocate the use of myriad methods to achieve their aims, ranging from participation in the political process to the waging of armed struggle, although the latter has remained relatively rare.

IDEOLOGICAL MALLEABILITY: ISLAMIC LEGISLATION AND THE ISLAMIC STATE

Not unlike many of the other Islamist movements discussed in this volume, a key characteristic of the standard bearers of political Islam in Southeast Asia such as the PKS in Indonesia and PAS in Malaysia has been their apparent readiness to compromise on their ideological commitments to enhance their appeal. A close look at their positions on Islamic legislation, one of the keystone issues on any Islamist agenda, illustrates this point.

Assessments of the PKS's performance in Indonesia's 2004 general elections mostly attributed the party's surge in popularity to its campaign platform of "clean and caring government." By casting its language in reformist and egalitarian rather than creedal terms, the PKS managed to distinguish itself from a slate of parties widely perceived as elitist and tainted by corruption. Notable during the election campaign was its restraint over the issue of implementation of sharia and formation of an Islamic state, which served to broaden its appeal among a religious but still largely pluralistic Muslim electorate.

Cognizant of the political costs associated with the explicitly Islamist appeals of its 1999 campaign when party leaders assessed that their performance was adversely affected by an overtly Islamist agenda, PKS leaders sought to contextualize, if not outright skirt, questions around the place of sharia on their agenda without necessarily disavowing it. True to form as an ideological offspring of the Brotherhood, PKS leaders have consistently maintained that their political agenda is anchored on issues of social welfare, anticorruption, and good governance, all of which are informed by sharia.[13] As PKS leader Tiffatul Sembiring put it: "People often simplify sharia as cutting off hands and stoning. Sharia is very broad, covering all aspects of life and having a universal nature. In our understanding, a government creating public welfare performs *amar ma'ruf* (doing what is correct) in the sense of sharia, and one eradicating corruption carries out *nahi mungkar* (rejecting what is wrong) as obliged by sharia."[14] To allay fears, the party leadership declared that they would not press the implementation of sharia before educating the population on its merits.[15] Rather, its implementation would be a natural outcome of the gradual, bottom-up Islamization of society through education and good governance.

At first glance, this calibrated perspective on sharia marked a shift from the PKS's disposition during its earlier forays into mainstream politics. When its predecessors first participated in elections in the late 1990s, they were involved in heated debates over whether to revive and implement the Jakarta Charter in the national legislature, which would have obliged the Indonesian government to endorse the introduction of sharia laws to govern the life of Indonesian Muslims.[16] Though the PKS eventually distanced itself from other Islamist parties that championed the Jakarta Charter resolution, it continued to advocate for society to be more explicitly organized around Islamic principles. Its approach was typified by its support for the Medina Charter, based on the practice of the Prophet Mohamed during the early Medinan period of Islamic history when Muslims lived in harmony with tribes that were permitted to retain their own customs and religious rites.[17]

When both charters were subsequently defeated, many Islamists recalibrated their strategy, pressing for the introduction of as many elements of Islamic legislation as possible at the regional level short of calling for the full implementation of sharia and an Islamic state. The front-line battle for enactment of Islamic law was thus moved out of the national assembly to provincial and district legislatures. In so doing, supporters of greater Islamic legislation—including those in the PKS—took advantage of the post-Suharto era of decentralization in which local legislative bodies were granted expanded powers and influence, including the right to formulate laws and regulate local affairs.[18]

Since 2004, Islamic by-laws have been implemented in a number of provinces, including West Java, West Sumatra, South Kalimantan, South Sulawesi, and Aceh.[19] Significantly, mirroring to some extent what happened in Malaysia, these by-laws were initiated not by Islamist parties but by Golkar, the secular party that previously had been Suharto's vehicle to power. While some had predicted that the appeal of sharia would eventually wane in Indonesia, evidence appears to point to the contrary. In Aceh, Islamic laws implemented since 2001 has resulted in several public canings, including an episode where a widow was caned after she was accused of adultery by a group of men who broke into a house and found her with a married man, but not before the men had gang-raped her and beaten up her companion.[20] Significantly, the piecemeal implementation of sharia by-laws across Indonesia has not elicited widespread opposition from local populations. In point of fact, according to some surveys, there are indications that Indonesians have generally supported the introduction of more, not less, sharia-type legislation. One example is the 2013 Pew survey of

Muslim attitudes, where up to 70 percent of Indonesians interviewed desire sharia to be the legal code of the country.[21]

The elusive responses of the PKS to queries about its position on sharia, which have been tactically predicated on ambiguity, cannot, however, be read as a discernible ideological shift in the party. This has been stressed clearly by scholars who observed that

> Formally, PKS declares its support for the current format of the Indonesian state: that is, a unitary republic based on the religiously neutral ideology of *Pancasila*.[22] But the party's doctrinal documents make clear that it regards comprehensive Islamization of the state and implementation of sharia law as a longer term goal.[23]

Moreover, amid the cut and thrust of local election campaigning, PKS leaders have been known to support sharia implementation, or at least make statements to that effect.[24] Similarly, party leaders have spoken out strongly in support of an Anti-Pornography Bill devised not only to regulate the circulation of pornographic material but also to police social activities deemed offensive by conservative Muslims. Underlying this is the PKS's belief—drilled into its cadre through its *tarbiyah* (religious education) programs—that the implementation of sharia, while a necessary expression of personal and communal piety, must nevertheless be a gradual process flowing from a religiously conscious society, and not something that can be implemented by edict or executive decree.

In Malaysia, Islamist movements such as PAS, the Angkatan Belia Islam Malaysia (Muslim Youth Movement of Malaysia) or ABIM, and newer movements like Hizb ut-Tahrir Malaysia and Ikatan Muslimin Malaysia (Malaysian Muslim Network, ISMA) have all pushed for the implementation of sharia laws, in particular highly controversial Islamic criminal laws. It is important to note that a large segment of the incumbent UMNO party has also been either sympathetic to this push or, in some cases, actively involved in agitating for implementation of sharia.

Since 1994, most Malaysian states have adopted the Sharia Criminal Offenses enactment. These enactments were designed to regulate the private life of Muslims such that they "measure up" to the exacting moral demands of sharia as interpreted by the growing and increasingly proactive state Islamic bureaucracies.[25] Moral police set up by these state religious bureaucracies routinely raid night clubs, parks, and hotels in an effort to curb un-Islamic practices such as alcohol consumption and *khalwat*, the consorting of unrelated men and women.

Until the mid-2000s, the hallmark of PAS's struggle has been the quest for the application of sharia, with particular emphasis on the enforcement of *hudud, qisas*, and *ta'zir* punishments.[26] As early as 1993, PAS had already submitted a hudud bill for discussion in the Kelantan state assembly that it controlled shortly after winning the 1990 state election. The bill included a section legislating against hudud offenses such as wine drinking, apostasy, unlawful sexual intercourse (*zina*), robbery, and accusing someone of zina without evidence.[27] Prepared by a committee comprising PAS ulama, the state Mufti, and other ulama in Kelantan state's Islamic Religion and Malay Council, the bill proved highly controversial. Among the criticisms were how the bill was prejudiced against women and introduced draconian and inhumane punishments.[28] In response to the blowback, PAS ulama began to campaign fervently for the implementation of the laws by issuing various publications and organizing public forums and seminars to discuss the issue.[29] Although the bill was eventually passed in the Kelantan Parliament, it was not ratified by the Malaysian federal government and thus could not be implemented. In Terengganu, a similar bill was enacted in 2002 during the short period when PAS controlled the state assembly. Once again, the laws were not gazetted due to opposition from the central government. Ironically, despite rejecting the hudud bills of PAS, the Malaysian government found itself harried to move closer to the agenda of PAS when officials within the state religious bureaucracy, many of whom were either members of the UMNO party or supporters of it, started putting pressure the government to introduce such laws.

Many government officials and UMNO leaders argued that it was the responsibility of the government in an Islamic state to strive toward the implementation of sharia.[30] Indeed, the quid pro quo that led Malaysian ulama to support Mahathir Mohamad's Islamic State declaration (when the former prime minister controversially declared publicly that Malaysia was already an "Islamic state" without detailing how that was so) and Prime Minister Abdullah Badawi's Islam Hadhari pronouncement (designed to spotlight the "moderate" aspects of Malaysian Islam) was that the government would eventually institutionalize sharia legislation, including hudud.[31] Nakhaie Ahmad, the then chief of Yayasan Dakwah Islam Malaysia (Islamic Dakwah Association of Malaysia) and a former PAS leader, posited that hudud must be implemented and mentioned that various provisions needed to be prepared to make this possible. For instance, a detailed study of the legal system, sharia courts, and supporting enactments needed to be undertaken before hudud could be implemented. He also criticized UMNO leaders for condemning the hudud laws as obsolete and not suited to contemporary society.[32] In short, the demand for implementing Islamic law is winning support from a wide spectrum of Malaysian Muslim society (including elements within or linked to the ruling party) and is not merely an agenda confined to opposition Islamists, as may be the case in some other Middle Eastern contexts.

In a sign that both the Malaysian government and Islamist opposition were beginning to converge on the hudud issue, Annuar Musa, chief of UMNO-Kelantan and chief justice of the Kelantan's sharia court, declared in January 2014 that the state was prepared to consider applying hudud laws. In response, PAS leadership in Kelantan formed a technical committee to study the implementation of sharia ordinances.[33] UMNO's gambit in Kelantan paid off on two counts: it shored up the party's religious credentials and its appeal as an Islamic party, while applying immense pressure on the opposition Pakatan Rakyat or People's Alliance, whose component parties have harbored residual suspicion of PAS's Islamist agenda despite entering into a coalition with them. Indeed, although some of PAS's allies took the position that the implementation of hudud may be tolerable in Muslim-majority regions so long as non-Muslims stand outside its jurisdiction, others have been less forthcoming. In point of fact, even if such a delineation is possible in theory, in practice it would be difficult to implement especially when a crime, for example zina, involves Muslims and non-Muslims.[34] On March 19, 2015, the Kelantan state assembly passed the Sharia Criminal Code II Bill 1993 (amended 2015) with the support of 12 UMNO assemblymen, and PAS President Abdul Hadi Awang submitted a private member's bill (bills introduced in the Westminster parliamentary system by members who do not hold cabinet positions) in parliament to discuss amendments to the Sharia Court Act of 1965, which would pave the way for the implementation of hudud in Kelantan.

Unlike the PKS in Indonesia, there have been significant differences of opinion within PAS over the urgency of the Islamic state agenda, as well as the manner in which to pursue it—with the contours of two broad camps forming. The ulama, who have led the party since 1982, have generally championed the top-down formation of an Islamic state in Malaysia. This is evident in the party's attempts to implement Islamic law where it has held power, such as in the states of Kelantan (since 1990) and Terengganu (1998–2004), as discussed earlier. While these attempts faced legal and structural impediments due to Malaysia's federal constitution, Islamic laws have been drawn up for these states with a view to eventual implementation.[35] Moreover, the ulama leadership has argued that the electoral swing to opposition parties is indicative of greater sympathy for Islamic governance. The Ulama Council declared to that effect: "The Malaysian people today have high hopes for PAS toward the advancement of the country. Moreover, many among them hope to see an Islamic state and welfare state come into being that would guarantee peace and prosperity to all Malaysians."[36]

On the other hand, reformist technocrats and activists who mostly flocked to the party during the height of the Malaysian reform movement in the late 1990s have argued that, rather than forcing the implementation of sharia by way of political pronouncements and executive decree, the formation of an Islamic state and introduction of sharia should be the "natural outcome" of a gradual, bottom-up Islamization of Muslim society in Malaysia.[37] These reformists stood at the forefront of PAS's entry into the opposition coalition known as the People's Alliance, rationalizing the move as an outcome of *ijtihad* (independent reasoning) and *tajdid* (intellectual renewal) toward the Quranic imperative of al-Wasatiyah (the middle path).[38]

However, while reformists saw this as part of wider "post-Islamist" trends that also encapsulated developments in the Middle East in 2011, conservatives were less sanguine. Relations between the two factions came to a head during internal elections of June 2015, when conservatives swept into all major leadership positions in the party and its youth wings. This prompted intense discussions within the reformist faction about whether to split from PAS and create a new Islamist party to continue the struggle as part of the opposition coalition, or to remain within the party but under conservative leadership. As for the conservatives, their victory in party elections was quickly followed by the severing of ties with secular opposition allies in the Democratic Action Party on grounds that the latter's criticism of its sharia law agenda was tantamount to interference in internal party matters and a contravention of the alliance agreement.

Differences between conservatives and reformists over the means, however, have had little impact on the ends. Indeed, even reformist technocrats have been compelled under the weight of public scrutiny and political pressure to concede that creating an Islamic state and implementing Islamic legislation remains the party's ultimate goal, albeit a long-term one. Rather, it is over the question of the prioritization of the Islamic state goal vis-à-vis other more immediate political objectives that one finds a greater degree of ambiguity. This is evident from PAS's track record in national elections, where the party's popularity has appeared to decline whenever it pushes an overt Islamic agenda.[39]

Nevertheless, this does not imply that the electorate is any less keen on Islamic strictures. After all, there is, as this chapter has argued, little that differentiates between PAS and UMNO today insofar as an Islamic agenda is concerned. Rather, as with the case of Indonesia, where there is more than one Islamist party or program to choose from, Muslim electorates tend to look at other aspects of political platforms as well. In Malaysia, this includes issues of local and national governance and economic policy that are pursued *alongside* the implementation of sharia. For PAS, there is the further dimension of non-Muslim support, which it actively seeks out. Unlike Indonesia, the demographics in Malaysia are such that any Islamist party with pretensions of coming to power must secure a measure of non-Muslim support. UMNO has done so via its non-Muslim partners in the National Front coalition. PAS's challenge at any given moment is to fine-tune the tactical utility of promoting an Islamic state—which endears the party to the conservative Malay-Muslim heartland—without compromising its fledgling popularity among non-Muslims, who, while openly opposed to discriminatory policies of the ruling party, are nevertheless afraid of the prospect of further implementation of Islamic legislation, in particular the Islamic penal code.

SOUTHEAST ASIA AND TRANSNATIONAL ISLAMISM

Muslim activists and Islamists in Southeast Asia have always been well aware that they are part of a wider network of believers. They have sought with varying degrees of success to build on these linkages to strengthen their own mobilization at home. Much of this has involved attempts on the part of Islamic organizations and parties to coordinate efforts with coreligionists abroad to advocate for Muslim causes.

Within the region, student groups such as Himpunan Mahasiswa Islam (Indonesia), ABIM (Malaysia), and the National University of Singapore's Muslim Society of Singapore often come together to facilitate informal networks of Islamic groups. An annual meeting of the three groups is held on a rotational basis. These meetings are meant to strengthen the ties between the three groups and enhance their proselytizing among Muslims in the broader region. Some earlier leaders of this network, such as Anwar Ibrahim, Ghani Shamsuddin, and Nurcholish Majid, would go on to play major roles in their respective countries. Members of PAS Youth and ABIM were also known to have visited Indonesian Islamist leaders such as Mohamed Natsir, the former Indonesian prime minister who led the Islamist Masyumi party in the early to mid-1950s.[40] It was during one of these meetings that Natsir advised future deputy prime minister-cum-opposition leader Anwar Ibrahim to join PAS, but Ibrahim eventually joined UMNO.[41]

At the international level, Islamist parties and groups from Southeast Asia frequently attempt to coordinate their efforts to address Muslim causes.[42] In 1988, PAS organized a major gathering of Islamist organizations entitled the "International Gathering for the Solidarity of Muslims," which was attended by representatives of Islamist groups from Pakistan, Egypt, Indonesia, Philippines, Iran, Afghanistan, Saudi Arabia, and Sudan.[43] With the outbreak of the 1990 Gulf War, a group of Islamist parties including Pakistan's Jamaat-e-Islami, the Muslim Brotherhood, and PAS, and led by Turkish Islamist leader and future prime minister Necmettin Erbakan, traveled to Europe and the United States to lobby for a resolution to the conflict. Of note was what came out of these efforts—the creation of the International Gathering of Islamic Groups with a secretariat in Istanbul.[44] PAS and the PKS have been important members of this body. Throughout the 1990s, it tackled issues affecting Muslims such as the conflict in Bosnia, Kashmir, and Chechnya and generally articulated anti-Western and anti-American positions.

Since the fall of the Suharto regime in Indonesia and after the September 11 attacks and the ensuing war on terror, a second phase of Islamic resurgence took shape in Southeast Asia. Unlike the first wave where Muslim voters became more religiously attentive, the second wave further politicized Muslim religiosity and brought to the fore debates over the imposition of stricter Islamic laws and the need for an Islamic state. At a global level, Muslims in Indonesia and Malaysia are forging a greater sense of solidarity with their religious counterparts in other parts of the world and becoming more attuned and responsive to Islamic conflicts worldwide.

The September 11 attacks and their aftermath presented a difficult dilemma for Islamist parties in Southeast Asia. Officially, both PAS and the PKS issued measured condemnations of the terrorist attacks.[45] Subsequent American actions in Afghanistan and Iraq were, however, met with vocal condemnation. The situation was further complicated by the discovery that the terrorist organization Jemaah Islamiyah was comprised of some individuals who were sympathizers of these parties. While certain PAS leaders urged their members to fight alongside the Taliban,[46] the former leader of the PKS, Hidayat Nur Wahid, was more cautious and refrained from openly advocating support.

Southeast Asian governments capitalized on the global fear of Islamists to demonize Islamist opposition parties.[47] In the case of PAS, the immediate effect was its poor electoral performance in the 2004 elections where it lost the support of non-Muslim Malaysians. In time, however, Muslim voters grew increasingly disturbed by what they saw as the disproportionate retaliation of the United States against the Muslim world, with many coming to view the war against terror as a war against Islam.[48] This anti-Americanism and anti-Westernism continues to linger, spurred by the perceived double standards as exemplified in global reactions to the Charlie Hebdo affair, when Western

leaders rallied in support of the principle of freedom of speech, a principle which many Southeast Asian Muslims saw being used to deni-
grate their religion. Muslims in Southeast Asia increasingly came to see
themselves as members of an international community of grievance.
Islamists channeled this sense of frustration toward galvanizing support for Muslim causes and against Western hegemony. Needless to
say, this has been a significant factor in sustaining a steady stream of
support for Islamist parties and civil society groups.

The level of cooperation and coordination between Islamist groups
within the region and beyond in "defense of Islam" are further evident in two instances. In the wake of the American invasion of Iraq,
a number of Islamist parties convened in London to discuss potential
responses. This meeting included the Muslim Brotherhood (branches
from Egypt, Jordan, and Iraq), Jamaat-e-Islami (from Pakistan and
Bangladesh), Turkish Islamists as well as PAS and the PKS.[49] The participants agreed to organize a worldwide peaceful protest to take place
in March 2003. Each of the parties further agreed to pressure their
respective governments to boycott American and British products
and to organize humanitarian aid for the people of Iraq. Both PAS
and the PKS organized demonstrations in Malaysia and Indonesia,
respectively.

The second case in point is the Islamist reaction to the Israeli war
against Hizbollah in 2006. Islamist parties and groups in Southeast
Asia quickly moved to coordinate their efforts to provide assistance to
Hizbollah. On August 12, 2006, PAS organized the Southeast Asian
Islamic Organizations Roundtable Conference for Palestine and
Lebanon. Representatives of Islamist parties the world over, includ-
ing Pakistan, Bangladesh, and Sri Lanka, and Islamist groups from
Cambodia, Brunei, India, Indonesia, Thailand, Myanmar, and Malaysia
were in attendance.[50] Even the Iranian government sent a senior cleric,
Ayatollah Ali Tashkiri. Hamas sent its leaders Khaled Meshal and
Khaleel Al Hayea as representatives.

In his opening speech, the moderator of the event Dato' Yeop Adlan
Rose, former Malaysian deputy high commissioner to Singapore and a
member of PAS, condemned the atrocities committed by the Israelis.
He went on to blame the United States, the United Kingdom, and
other Western powers for their support of the Israeli state.[51] He then

went on to criticize the Organization of the Islamic Conference (OIC), describing it as impotent, and called for the mobilization of the Muslim *ummah* through a different global platform. All the subsequent speakers reiterated this call for a new platform for Muslims.[52] In so doing, the Islamist groups in attendance were essentially presenting themselves, through their newly established body, as an alternative to the OIC.

The second wave of Islamic revival also saw the emergence of new Islamist players. One such group is Hizb ut-Tahrir (HT), which defines itself as an international political party seeking to implement sharia and re-establish the Islamic caliphate. HT has chapters in over 40 countries including Malaysia and Indonesia. The movement first found a foothold in Southeast Asia in the late 1980s, but it was not until early 2000 that the movement emerged openly in Indonesia and Malaysia. HT's attraction for many Southeast Asian Muslims lies in its overtly anti-Western ideology. Unlike many of the Islamist parties that accept elements of Western society such as democracy and capitalism, HT rejects these ideas as un-Islamic. What is further evident from close consideration of Islamist participation in transnational networks is the existence of something of an implicit hierarchy among Islamist movements worldwide. Islamists in Malaysia and, to a lesser extent, Indonesia continue to genuflect in the direction of Egypt's Muslim Brotherhood, at least for inspiration. Conversely, attempts by Indonesian Muslim political leaders to reach out to the Egyptian Brotherhood to share their experience of democratization after military rule were met with polite disinterest.

THE CHALLENGE OF THE ISLAMIC STATE

Authorities in Indonesia have confirmed that more than 150 Indonesians have traveled to Syria and Iraq, while their Malaysian counterparts have suggested that up to 70 Malaysians have gone to fight. It is likely that in both cases, the actual numbers are significantly higher. The Singapore government has also revealed that several of its nationals have made their way there, while the Philippines has expressed concern that the Islamic State could also recruit from among the Bangsamoro populations in their southern islands, although there is currently no evidence of Filipino or Thai Muslims being involved. Indonesian and Malaysian nationals have already been involved in martyrdom operations in Syria.

When the Islamic State declared the formation of the caliphate on the first day of Ramadan in June 2014, it was widely reported in Indonesia and, in some small segments of the Muslim population, celebrated through pledges of allegiance.[53] In Malaysia, members of Muslim political parties and civil society groups celebrated the martyrdom of a Malaysian who died in Syria fighting alongside the Islamic State.[54]

Noticeably, the Islamic State appears to have gained some, albeit limited currency in certain quarters of Southeast Asia's large Muslim demographic. This support derives from several factors. At an abstract theological level, the Islamic State's Southeast Asian sympathizers are cognizant of the fact that its struggle resonates with several hadith concerning Bilad al-Sham (Greater Syria) that prophesied the creation of a Khilafah Minhajul Nebuwah—an ideal caliphate many Muslims believe will emerge near the end of times following the fall of dictators in the Arabian Peninsula, as well as an eschatological struggle between the Imam Mahdi, or messiah, who would be supported by forces raising black banners, as well as the Dajjal, or antichrist. This millenarian perspective has been making its rounds in discussions and local publications on the Syrian conflict in both Indonesia and Malaysia.[55]

A second aspect of the group's appeal is sectarian. The challenge of the Islamic State is seen in some quarters as an extension of the Sunni–Shiite schism; to wit, the struggle against Bashar-al Assad's Alawite regime is considered legitimate not just in Islamist circles, but more broadly. Much in the same way, Islamic State militancy in Iraq is seen as a consequence of Sunni grievance against the Shiite-led government of former prime minister Nouri al-Maliki. These narratives have to be understood in the context of tense Shiite–Sunni relations in Southeast Asia: Shiite Islam is banned in Malaysia and not widely accepted in Indonesia.[56] Finally, many Southeast Asian Muslims have been motivated by the sheer magnitude of the humanitarian crisis in Syria to lend support, principally in terms of financial contributions to Islamic charities purporting to be assisting Syrian victims of the conflict, although a small number have also joined medical missions.

While the Islamic State has been embraced by several radical groups, it has been rejected and virulently condemned by others. Jemaah Islamiyah, the notorious terrorist organization responsible for several suicide bombings in Indonesia over the last decade and a half, has accused the Islamic

State of *takfir* (Muslims accusing coreligionists of being non-Muslim) and dismissed them as *kharawij* (heretics). Others, such as the conservative Majlis Mujahidin Indonesia (Indonesian Mujahidin Council), have cast doubt over the Islamic State's religious credibility, proclaiming that it is an organization and not a caliphate, and hence has no legitimate claim to the loyalty of Muslims. Furthermore, it pointed out that the process of appointing Abu Bakr al-Baghdadi as caliph violated Islamic law as it did not take place before a religious Shura Council that represents the global Islamic community.

THE ARAB SPRING

The Arab uprisings were closely followed by Islamist parties in Southeast Asia. Not without reason, it was in Indonesia that the protests of the Arab Spring, especially in Egypt (and including the subsequent coup), were predicted to resonate. Both Egypt and Indonesia have large Muslim majorities and share similar strategic positions in their respective regions as major powers; both had historically been ruled by authoritarian military regimes; and both had a growing Muslim middle class, although it is debatable whether the size of Egypt's middle class was anywhere near what was created by the economic growth in Indonesia under Suharto's New Order regime, corruption and nepotism notwithstanding. Both Indonesia and Egypt were also home to significant Islamist undercurrents. In Egypt, the Muslim Brotherhood managed to successfully penetrate society on such a scale that it could emerge as the most viable party after the collapse of the Mubarak regime. In Indonesia, Muslim activism was circumscribed during the Suharto rule, but never eliminated. Indeed, it was the *tarbiyah* (Islamic education) networks that sustained an Islamist discourse, which in turn would generate the cadre-ization of the PKS, catapulting it into national prominence.

Given Indonesia's democratization following the collapse of Suharto's regime in 1997—which ushered in a tempestuous few years of social upheaval—it should be no surprise that the ouster of the Mubarak regime and the Arab uprisings were widely embraced by Indonesia. During this period, there was much talk about how Indonesia's own democratization experience could serve as a "model" for the reform processes underway in the Middle East. In hindsight, however, it appears few Arab activists actually took these discussions seriously, especially given the tendency, discussed earlier, for Arab Islamists to disregard developments taking place elsewhere.[57]

To be fair, Egyptian Islamists faced a different dilemma after the fall of Mubarak than Indonesian Islamists faced after Suharto's fall. The Brotherhood was strong enough to capture the presidency and legislature if it wished (and it did). In Indonesia, no Islamist party could do so. Indeed, such was the discrepancy that Indonesian Islamist parties themselves such as the PKS looked to the success of Islamists in Egypt and elsewhere as a source of inspiration to energize their own struggle.[58]

In Malaysia, the Arab Spring quickly played into the hands of an opposition that was engaged in major—and increasingly tense—competition with the UMNO-led incumbents. Under the leadership of Anwar Ibrahim, who had since his student activism days culti-vated close personal relations with Muslim Brotherhood members, the Malaysian opposition coalition led by Ibrahim's Keadilan party (which included PAS) quickly called for a "Malaysian Spring," draw-ing comparisons between the ruling government in Malaysia and the overthrown regimes in Egypt, Tunisia, and Libya. Demonstrations were staged to express solidarity with their counterparts in the Arab world, but these quickly shifted gear to become platforms for attacks on the Malaysian regime. Opportunism aside, there was also an ele-ment of coreligious affinity and cross-fertilization, particularly among PAS members, as well as members of the UMNO-affiliated ulama, who had always held the likes of Rached Ghannouchi (cofounder of Ennahda in Tunisia) and the Brotherhood-linked cleric Yusuf al-Qaradawi in high regard.[59]

If the Arab Spring failed to deepen relations between Islamist par-ties in the Middle East and Indonesia (and Malaysia), the military coup in Egypt did prompt widespread condemnation in Southeast Asia. Specifically, the coup was portrayed by conservatives in various Islamist parties as a conspiracy between the United States and Israel to remove the democratically elected Islamist leadership. In Malaysia, PAS strongly opposed the anti-Morsi coup, organizing large demonstrations and using its publication, *Harakah*, to condemn the military's actions.[60]

The late Mursyidul 'Am (spiritual guide) of PAS, Nik Aziz Nik Mat, even lashed out at the Saudi regime for endorsing the Egyptian military's killing of civilians after the coup, opining that "the truth belongs to God alone, not to the East and not to the West. Although the custodian of the two holy places has been honored with this duty (to rule over Makkah and Medina), it does not necessarily mean they hold the key to the truth."[61]

PAS reformists criticized the coup as a blatant contravention of democratic principles and the will of the Egyptian people, the majority of whom voted in Morsi. Notably, this view was also shared by the Malaysian leadership, with Prime Minister Najib Razak openly criticizing the coup. Meanwhile, in Indonesia, the Egyptian military was widely disparaged for overthrowing Morsi. Given Indonesia's own historical experience with military regimes and political upheaval, it was no surprise that criticism came not just from the Islamists, but from across the political spectrum.[62] As in Malaysia, several street protests and demonstrations were organized by Indonesian civil society groups against the coup, though nothing substantive or lasting materialized.[63]

CONCLUSION

Despite PAS's relatively strong showing in recent Malaysian elections (especially in 1999 and 2008 but to a lesser extent in 2013) and the general expectation that the PKS will improve its electoral standing in future Indonesian elections, the likelihood of any Islamist party coming to power in the region remains small. As the chapter stressed at the outset, an increase in Islamic consciousness among the Muslim population in Southeast Asia does not necessarily translate into political gains for Islamist parties on the national level. A good case in point here is the Tablighi Jamaat. The Tablighi Jamaat, which is the largest Islamic movement in the world in terms of sheer numbers, has played an important role in catalyzing a revival of personal piety and adherence to individual Islamic religious obligations in Southeast Asia. It has, however, remained strictly apolitical, asserting the need to concentrate on personal and individual reform. Adherence to the Tablighi Jamaat's conservative beliefs in the social sphere is thus not necessarily indicative of any political position or voting pattern.

There are, however, as noted earlier, parties and movements in Southeast Asia that remain strongly committed to developing an Islamic state. When analyzing the potential impact of these groups on the future of Southeast Asia, it is important to remember that despite similarities in rhetoric and objectives, no two Islamisms are alike. Islamic and Islamist parties and movements have employed myriad methods ranging from democratic participation to militancy. Islamist parties and the methods they employ are constantly shaped by the sociopolitical contexts within which they operate, requiring analysts to be ever attentive to local and regional particularities. For now, though, Southeast Asian Islamists are for the most part in favor of gradual and incremental advancement of their goals through active participation in political processes and the continued building of transnational networks. While they cannot claim outright electoral victories nationally, they can point to real tangible success in contributing to the "Islamization" of society and even state bureaucracies, something that cannot necessarily be said of many of their Arab counterparts.

Engaging Islamists

12

Islamism and U.S. Foreign Policy

Peter Mandaville

ON THE FACE OF it, the Arab uprisings of 2011 appeared to pose numerous challenges to U.S. policy in the Middle East. First and foremost
among these was the demise of several regimes—particularly Egypt,
Yemen, and Tunisia—whose leaders had been firmly aligned with
America's strategic priorities in the region. And when it became clear
that the primary beneficiaries of the region's new political realities
would be various Islamist parties and movements, Washington found
itself faced with another dilemma. Conventional wisdom suggested
that the United States had a deeply entrenched discomfort with such
groups. Some observers saw the United States as ideologically averse
to Islamism, whereas others traced this attitude to lingering fears in
Washington that even mainstream Islamists—those who have chosen
to participate in the democratic process—harbored agendas that ultimately ran counter to U.S. security interests. In some cases, the United
States had been complicit in or, at the very least, had turned a blind eye
to efforts by its client regimes in the region to suppress and criminal-
ize Islamists. Thus, when these groups initially came to dominate the
transitional politics of the Arab world in 2011, Washington seemed to
face something of a predicament.

Several years on from these momentous events, the situation seems
to have reversed itself. Across the region, Islamist parties have been
toppled from power (Egypt), put on a political back foot (Tunisia), or

turned into deeply polarizing forces within society (Libya). How has U.S. policy dealt with the phenomenal rise and equally dramatic fall of mainstream Islamist actors from 2011 on? Is it possible to identify a shift in U.S. policy toward these groups? Given recent developments, how is Washington likely to approach the question of Islamist engagement going forward?

THE MYTH OF "ONE MAN, ONE VOTE, ONE TIME"

To properly answer these questions, it is important to first have a general sense of how political Islam has figured in U.S. foreign policy over the last few decades. While we know from declassified State Department cables that the Egyptian Muslim Brotherhood was on the radar of the U.S. government during the 1950s and 1960s, American foreign policy granted no particular significance to these groups other than to wonder whether their religious nature might make them useful partners in checking the spread of socialism in the Third World.[1]

Political Islam did not become a discrete issue within U.S. foreign policy until the 1979 Islamic Revolution in Iran. For many years, that event shaped American understandings of Islamism even though the revolutionary ideology behind it was not in line with the orientation of most other Islamists and, indeed, was highly atypical even within Shiite history and tradition. Meanwhile, during the 1980s the United States aligned itself with the Afghan mujahideen in their struggle against Soviet invasion because they were viewed through the lens of Cold War politics. This led the United States to see the mujahideen primarily as a counterweight to Soviet expansionism, and to pay little attention to the political and security vacuum created by the eventual Soviet withdrawal from Afghanistan—the very crucible that eventually gave rise to al-Qaeda.

However, the event that set the tone for U.S. policy toward mainstream Islamist movements and parties (of the Muslim Brotherhood ilk) was undoubtedly the Algerian elections of 1991. When it became clear that the Islamic Salvation Front (FIS) was poised to win the two-thirds parliamentary majority required to change the country's constitution, the Algerian military intervened to annul the elections. The ensuing political conflict plunged Algeria into civil war for the better part of a decade. In a speech on U.S. policy toward the Middle East delivered in the spring of 1992, senior U.S. diplomat Edward Djerejian indicated that it was prudent of the Algerian army to have prevented the FIS from coming to power because Islamists reaching power through the ballot box would have been a case of "one man, one vote, one time." In other words, Islamists would make instrumental use of democracy to capture the state, only to subsequently dismantle the democratic system to ensure they could not be removed from power. Ever since, the fear of a "one man, one vote, one time" scenario has supposedly been the dictum governing U.S. policy toward Islamists.[2] At its core has been the belief—or at least the strong suspicion—that the Islamist embrace of democratic ideals is likely a tactical shift in the service of a longer term totalitarian vision.

THE REGIONAL ROOTS OF ISLAMIST POLICY

Islamist movements, for their part, were evolving rapidly with the times. By the mid-1990s, there were clear signs that these groups could no longer be understood by reference to the original vision of Islamist "founding fathers"—such as the Egyptian Hassan al-Banna or Pakistan's Abul Ala Mawdudi—who had been active in the first half of the 20th century. In 1996, for example, a group of young leaders within the Egyptian Muslim Brotherhood split from the movement and attempted to establish a separate political party, Hizb al-Wasat (Party of the Center). They complained about the Brotherhood's conservative and intransigent leadership and its inability to update its vision and agenda.

In addition to these clear generational and ideological differences within Islamist groups, the trend toward Islamist participation in democracy continued unabated. By the mid-2000s, Islamist parties had become fixtures in the mainstream politics of Morocco, Egypt, Palestine, Lebanon, Jordan, Yemen, and Kuwait. In Turkey in 2002, the Justice and Development Party (AKP), whose roots lay in Turkey's Islamist movement, won a landslide victory and has now been in power for more than fourteen years.

During this same period, however, U.S. policy toward Islamists remained very cautious. In 1995, Washington announced that it was ceasing all contact with the Muslim Brotherhood in Egypt. In the years following 9/11, some of the more influential voices shaping views of political Islam in the United States were those—such as Israel and Egypt—that wished to advance an understanding of Islamism consistent with their domestic interests. By 2003, most Islamist parties in the Arab world had decided to boycott the United States in a gesture of protest at the American invasion of Iraq. In 2006, the U.S. rejection of Hamas' victory in the Palestinian legislative elections seemed to confirm in the eyes of many the idea that the United States was simply unwilling to do business with Islamists.

This interpretation of U.S. attitudes toward Islamism is far too simplistic. Looked at from a different vantage point—and augmented with additional information—those things that seem to suggest an ideological aversion to Islamism on the part of the United States can be seen in a different light.[3]

Take Washington's apparent decision in the 1990s to cut off ties with the Egyptian Muslim Brotherhood. Speaking in 2005, the U.S. Secretary of State Condoleezza Rice asserted that "we have not engaged with the Muslim Brotherhood . . . and we won't," justifying this position by reference to the group's legal status in Egypt. Of course, the U.S. government frequently engages all over the world with groups deemed illegal by local governments and, in fact, low level outreach to the Muslim Brotherhood continued even as Rice made this seemingly categorical declaration. All of this suggests that the decision to stop talking to the Brotherhood a decade earlier had been the direct result of a request from the Egyptian government rather than a deliberative policy shift initiated in Washington. During that period, the Mubarak regime had been looking for every opportunity to tarnish the reputation of a movement it saw as a political threat by linking the Brotherhood in the eyes of the public with terrorism (a preview, in other words, of the policies of President Abdel Fattah al-Sissi). It hoped that an announcement from Washington that the Brotherhood had been removed from its list of local interlocutors would enhance this effect. In her announcement, Condoleezza Rice justified the policy shift as a response to a favor requested by a close and trusted ally of the United States. In other words, the U.S. decision to cut off contact with the Brotherhood tells us more about U.S.–Egypt bilateral relations than it does about how the U.S. viewed Islamist groups.[4]

Similarly, the uproar in Washington about the 2006 Hamas victory is best understood as a function of U.S. concerns about Israel's security and the fact that a group officially designated as a terrorist group was poised to take over the Palestinian Authority (PA)—thereby making it all but impossible under U.S. law for economic assistance to flow to the Palestinian territories.

There are also other clues suggesting that U.S. policy toward Islamists was more complicated than might first appear. For example, in a number of countries around the world—including Indonesia and Yemen—Islamist parties participated in democracy training programs funded by the United States Agency for International Development (USAID) and the National Endowment for Democracy (NED) throughout the late 1990s and 2000s. It is difficult to reach the conclusion that the United States feared the rise of Islamists if U.S. government agencies and American taxpayer dollars were actually helping these groups to compete politically. Furthermore, over the course of the 2000s, it had become routine for U.S. government officials to meet with representatives of Islamist parties from the Middle East on the sideline of events and conferences organized by prominent think tanks in Washington, DC, such as the Carnegie Endowment for International Peace, the Project on Middle East Democracy (POMED), and the Center for the Study of Islam and Democracy (CSID).

REVISITING ISLAMIST ENGAGEMENT

There were signs quite early in the Obama administration that the United States recognized the need to re-evaluate its stance on Islamist groups. By late 2009, an informal working group on Islamism within the State Department was looking at the issue and systematically cataloging U.S. diplomatic engagements with Islamists abroad. The latter exercise revealed that American diplomats serving in countries where Islamists were active actually had fairly regular contact with representatives of these groups. There were of course a few notable exceptions, such as Egypt, where blanket proscriptions against Islamist engagement were in effect. But these were the exceptions rather than the rule.

In fact, there was no such thing as an overarching U.S. policy position on Islamists. While custom dictated that these groups were generally not received in Washington, DC (if and when they could even obtain visas to come to the United States) and while the United States exhibited a clear preference for working with non-Islamist segments of civil society, it was not uncommon for diplomats serving in the political section of U.S. embassies in the Middle East to meet from time to time with Islamists. (Engagement with groups such as Hamas and Hezbollah, officially designated by the U.S. government as terrorist organizations, was—and is—regarded as a wholly separate matter.) In net terms, the "limited contact" policy followed by the United States during this period meant that Washington was not equipped to fully understand, or try to shape, a segment of Arab political opinion and activism that was clearly on the rise.

So by the time the Arab uprisings toppled regimes in Tunisia, Egypt, and Libya in 2011, the United States had already been giving some thought to the need for a new approach to Islamists, based in part on a realization that these groups were now thoroughly part of the political mainstream in many countries. In 2010, the U.S. National Security Council began work on a Presidential Study Directive focused on the question of what a push for genuine political reform in the Middle East would look like—including the normalization of Islamists as political actors. The immediate challenge after the revolutions of 2011 was therefore not one of figuring out how to countenance the basic idea of increased engagement with Islamists—Obama administration officials had already come around on that issue a couple of years prior to the uprisings—but rather the question of how, in practice, to implement a new engagement policy and to identify an appropriate set of issues around which to build a new outreach strategy.

The very particular geography of Arab transition made things tough in this regard. In Egypt, the United States had had very little in the way of meaningful contact with the Muslim Brotherhood for more than 15 years. In Tunisia, Ennahda had been so heavily suppressed by the Ben Ali regime that U.S. diplomats in that country never had any opportunity to get to know them. The same went for Libya, where Muammar Qaddafi had all but eliminated the Brotherhood as a force in society. In sum, the United States suddenly found itself needing to engage with Islamists in precisely the countries where it was least equipped to do so.

The most straightforward way to characterize U.S. policy on Islamists after the Arab uprisings is to say that Washington decided *not* to have a specific and separate Islamist policy. There was a recognition within the administration that the motivation and agenda of Islamists varied considerably from country to country and that it was impossible—and unhelpful—to treat all such movements and parties in the same fashion. Having a policy toward Islam*ism*, understood as a broad ideological tradition, seemed unwise since U.S. policy is generally calibrated in terms of American interests in specific countries. In much the same way that the United States does not have a policy toward parties of the center right, or green parties, it made little sense to have a specific policy toward Islamism writ large.

As is clear from speeches given by Secretary of State Hillary Clinton and Obama himself in the weeks and months following the Arab uprisings, the United States sought to make clear that it wished to treat Islamists as nothing more than one among many new political actors shaping the future of Arab politics. It signaled areas of ongoing concern, however, by clarifying that it was willing to work with all groups that renounce violence and support the full and equal rights of all citizens, including women and minorities. Privately, the United States also placed great emphasis on the expectation that the Muslim Brotherhood would maintain its peace agreement with Israel as a precondition for ongoing diplomatic cooperation.

When it came to the practicalities of engaging Islamists in 2011, some cases were easier than others. Within a couple months of Ben Ali's ouster in Tunisia, for example, senior Ennahda leaders were visiting Washington and securing relatively high-level meetings at the State Department. In Egypt, however, the magnitude of the sensitivities around the Muslim Brotherhood made things far more difficult. One of the more complicated challenges here was actually a function of American domestic politics. Many members of the U.S. Congress perceived the Egyptian Muslim Brotherhood as not dissimilar to Hamas. Several prominent legislators raised questions about the administration's intentions vis-à-vis the Brotherhood, with a few arguing that U.S. economic assistance to Egypt should be curtailed if Islamists came to power. In addition to managing these home-front challenges, American diplomats also had to race to keep up with a rapidly evolving political situation in Egypt. As a firm reminder that engagement is in fact a two-way process, the Muslim Brotherhood was initially rather wary of meeting with—or officially acknowledging any meetings with—the U.S. government for fear of appearing too hasty and willing to do business with a country it had criticized harshly for decades. Once it was confident of its political dominance in Egypt toward the end of 2011, however, the Brotherhood was only too happy to play up Washington's apparent embrace.

NORMALIZING ISLAMISTS

Arguably, the real test of U.S. policy toward the Egyptian Muslim Brotherhood did not come until Mohamed Morsi assumed the presidency in the summer of 2012. Up until that point, with the Supreme Council of the Armed Forces (SCAF) still running the country, Washington felt confident that its long-standing and trusted ally, the Egyptian military, would serve as an ultimate guarantor of stability regardless of whether Islamists were winning elections. Once the SCAF was relieved of power in August 2012, however, Washington braced itself for the worst. And it was alarmed by some early signs: Morsi's first international trip would include China and Iran, raising fears in Washington that the Brotherhood planned to reorient Egypt's geostrategic alignment away from the West.

The United States found itself pleasantly surprised, therefore, when Morsi went on to offer a quite strident critique of Tehran's role in exacerbating Syrian violence. Then, in the autumn of 2012, when violence flared up in the Gaza Strip, Morsi played an instrumental role in brokering Washington's much-hoped-for ceasefire. This willingness to help advance U.S. agendas in the region, coupled with the fact that the Egyptian government maintained most other key aspects of security cooperation with the United States, apparently convinced the White House that the Muslim Brotherhood could be relied upon as a partner. Indeed, it seems that the United States more or less reverted quite quickly to a variant of its Egypt policy of the previous several decades: work with and support whoever is in power in Cairo so long as U.S. strategic interests are protected. A corollary of this policy, of course, is the idea that Washington is expected to refrain from harsh criticism of what happens in the Egyptian domestic realm. And indeed, the United States said and did relatively little about the various democracy and human rights abuses that occurred under both the SCAF and Morsi—not to mention during the tenure of current president Abdel Fattah al-Sissi.

As Egyptian politics grew increasingly fraught and unstable in late 2012 and 2013, Washington, DC, along with several other European governments, made various efforts to convince President Morsi to make concessions to the opposition to stave off growing popular discontent. Apparently confident that he had the situation under control and the security apparatus under his thumb, Morsi refused to alter course. When Defense Minister Abdel Fattah al-Sissi announced in July 2013 that he had assumed control of the government—with Morsi under arrest—the United States expressed measured concern but stopped short of labeling the events a coup to avoid jeopardizing ongoing military aid and security cooperation.

U.S. POLICY TOWARDS ISLAMISM AFTER THE 2013 COUP

After the military coup of 2013 in Egypt, Washington faced a conundrum. If it supported Sissi's toppling of the country's legitimately elected president, it would appear to be going back on its strong commitment in 2011 to take the cause of democracy seriously in the Arab world. When Egypt's security forces killed approximately 1,000 people protesting the coup outside Cairo's Rabaa al-Adawiya mosque in August 2013, we saw the violent tip of a longer spear designed to systematically eradicate the Muslim Brotherhood as a political actor and to recategorize the group's identity and activities under the mantle of "terrorism." Preoccupied by concerns with regional stability—sectarian civil war in Syria, increased violence in Libya and the Sinai, failing governance in Iraq, ongoing concerns about Iran's nuclear ambitions—Washington largely acquiesced in this campaign against the Brotherhood.

The question of the Muslim Brotherhood soon turned into the pivot point of a regional geopolitical divide, with countries supportive of Islamists (namely Turkey and Qatar) squaring off against a coalition of nations (Egypt, Saudi Arabia, the United Arab Emirates) dedicated to suppressing the Muslim Brotherhood. The rise of the Islamic State complicated Washington's calculus vis-à-vis the Brotherhood. The

United States has been loath to do anything that might offend those countries—Saudi Arabia, the United Arab Emirates, and Egypt—on whom it relies for countering the Islamic State and other extremist groups.

What this means in practical terms is that since the summer of 2013, U.S. engagement with the Muslim Brotherhood has been all but impossible—certainly within Egypt itself. Several key Brotherhood leaders managed to leave Egypt before the height of the crackdown and to take up exile in countries such as Turkey, Qatar, the United Kingdom, Malaysia, and Sudan. Multiple and seemingly competing Muslim Brotherhood "external offices" have been established outside Egypt, with senior figures from different factions within the Brotherhood— such as former Minister of Planning and International Cooperation Amr Darrag and Deputy General Guide Ibrahim al-Munir—seeking to establish credentials and a power base among movement members still residing in Egypt.

The Brotherhood also represents the dominant political force within the diasporic Egyptian Revolutionary Council (ERC), established in the wake of the 2013 coup. ERC members, who represent multiple political and ideological orientations, began shuttling between Western capitals to lobby against the new Sissi regime and, at least initially, to demand the reinstatement of the Morsi presidency. While there were doubts as to whether the ERC had any meaningful influence or support in Egypt, some of its leaders obtained meetings in cities such as Brussels and Washington, DC—often invoking the ire of local Egyptian diplomats and prompting angry recriminations from Cairo. In one particularly notorious incident from early 2015, a Muslim Brotherhood member of the ERC visiting Washington, DC, took a picture of himself making the four-fingered hand gesture that indicated solidarity with the victims of the Rabaa killings in a government meeting room in front of the State Department insignia. This photo was widely disseminated on social media and generated a strong backlash from the Egyptian government, which accused the United States of engaging with a terrorist group.

By the later part of 2015, there were indications that the ERC and other exiled Brotherhood figures had softened their demands and taken a more pragmatic measure of their circumstances. At the same time, however, internal politics within the Brotherhood were heating up, with multiple figures representing various factions claiming to speak on behalf of the movement. Such fragmentation made the U.S. policy calculus even more complex, since it was no longer clear whom the United States should meet with even if it were willing and able to engage with the Brotherhood.

Discussion of the Muslim Brotherhood in certain Western capitals since 2013 has taken on a broader significance. In 2014, the UK government announced that it would be undertaking a review of the Brotherhood with a specific focus on the question of whether the movement could be linked to terrorism. This announcement immediately stirred controversy, not least of all because it was widely rumored that London had been strongly encouraged to undertake the review by governments in the Gulf with major UK arms procurement contracts pending—especially the United Arab Emirates and Saudi Arabia. The UK Muslim Brotherhood review dragged on into 2015. On multiple occasions it seemed that the British government was on the verge of publicly releasing some of its findings, only for such disclosures to be deferred amid ongoing diplomatic and domestic sensitivities. Perhaps as a sign of frustration with apparent UK prevarication, the Emirati government in late 2014 issued a new list of terrorist groups that contained the names of multiple UK- and U.S.-based organizations, such as Islamic Relief Worldwide, the Council on American-Islamic Relations, and the Cordoba Foundation, widely viewed as mainstream—prompting the United States to indicate that it did not concur with the Emirati assessments.

Finally, in late 2015, the British government released a summary of the key findings from its review. It stopped short of designating the Brotherhood a terrorist organization, although it did find evidence that figures in some of the Brotherhood's transnational networks had likely been involved in fundraising and other forms of material support to groups such as Hamas. Separately, in early 2016, the UK Parliament initiated a formal inquiry regarding the status of the Brotherhood in British foreign policy, based in part on concerns about the motivations and approaches surrounding the government's previous Muslim Brotherhood review.

Since 2014, the U.S. government, at least prior to the election of Donald Trump, said little about the Muslim Brotherhood except to indicate, when asked, that it does not view the group as a terrorist organization—despite repeated entreaties from Cairo to designate the Brotherhood as such. After the State Department photograph incident referenced earlier, the U.S. government stopped meeting with representatives of the ERC or the Muslim Brotherhood in Washington, DC. In what appeared to be a convergence between the political right and Egyptian government lobbying, several members of the U.S. Congress in late 2015 introduced legislation in both houses designed to force the State Department to issue a finding on whether the Brotherhood merited designation as a Foreign Terrorist Organization (FTO). While the legislation was approved in committee on a party line vote, it did not come up for a full vote before the congressional session expired. After Donald Trump's victory in the 2016 U.S. presidential election, some of his advisors began to suggest that designation of the Brotherhood would be a priority for the new administration. In January 2017 the previous legislation was reintroduced in congress, while the White House appeared to be considering moving forward with its own executive action on the issue.

NONVIOLENT ISLAMISM IN THE CONTEXT OF ISLAMIC STATE

Since 2014, the Muslim Brotherhood along with various democracy and human rights advocates have—with good reason—been urging the United States to raise concerns with the Egyptian authorities regarding the judicial process and the treatment of Brotherhood detainees. While there are signs that Cairo has been responsive to lobbying on very specific and isolated cases, there has been no broader shift in tack as a result of this pressure.

There is, however, another vantage point from which to view the question of nonviolent political Islam in the present regional context—and one that would perhaps allow discussion of the Muslim Brotherhood to proceed under a different heading. This requires backing out from the domestic context of Egypt or any other single country, such as Jordan, where governments have restricted the activities of nonviolent Islamists, and to examine the question in its broader regional context. With the rise of the Islamic State since 2014 and the adoption by certain governments of a narrative in which Islamism of any kind is tantamount to terrorism, religiously inspired political activism has lacked any meaningful channel of expression. This state of affairs has, in effect, handed to the Islamic State and al-Qaeda a monopoly on Islamist politics. Young

people in Egypt and elsewhere who understand their political commitments in Islamic terms are faced with a stark binary choice: silence or
militancy.

In the short to medium term, then, it may be possible to open up a
new kind of conversation about nonviolent Islamists with key regional
governments by framing it as part of a broader discussion of regional
security and the effort to defeat the Islamic State. It is unlikely that
the Egyptian authorities would welcome the Muslim Brotherhood back
into the political fold anytime soon, but that is not necessarily required.
If encouraged to open up a little more political space—a message probably most effectively delivered by the likes of Riyadh or Abu Dhabi—
the Egyptian government may shift or at least render more complex the
decision calculus of frustrated and disenfranchised citizens starting to
consider the extremist option.

LOOKING AHEAD

As with so many aspects of its Middle East policy today, the United
States finds itself mired in contradictions when it comes to political
Islam. On the one hand, engagement with the Muslim Brotherhood in
Egypt seems utterly out of the question, while on the other, Washington
enjoys fairly normal relations with similar Islamist groups and parties
in countries such as Tunisia, Morocco, and Kuwait. Viewed in another
way, this apparent schizophrenia is actually evidence of a certain level
of policy consistency: the idea that the United States approaches its
engagement with such groups based on its country-specific interests
and prevailing political circumstances. Seen in this light, it is not at
all strange that the United States should be comfortable doing business with Islamists in countries where they are a normalized part of the
political landscape and where doing so does not jeopardize U.S. interests.

While the political setbacks suffered by Islamists in 2013 and 2014
may provide the United States with a temporary reprieve from the challenge of dealing with mainstream Islamists in the hard case of Egypt,
this is clearly an issue that Washington will ultimately have to confront. The Egyptian security apparatus cannot eradicate the Muslim
Brotherhood as a force in society, and it is likely that at some point the
government in Cairo will have to renegotiate the return of Islamists to

public life (as they did in the 1970s). Even after the coup of 2013, opinion polls conducted by the Pew Research Center seem to suggest that the Muslim Brotherhood is still viewed favorably by a significant portion of the Egyptian public.[5] Although it is clear that many Islamists have yet to embrace a full conception of political pluralism, they are hardly distinctive in that regard when one looks at other countries in the region that enjoy strong support from the United States.

Two apparent trends seem likely to make this an even more pointed and challenging question in the years ahead. First, the ongoing fragmentation and factionalization within the Egyptian Brotherhood holds some real risk of seeing some elements adopt a more directly confrontational and potentially even violent orientation. At the same time, Islamists elsewhere in the region—such as in Tunisia and Jordan—seem to be going in the other direction as they increasingly accommodate themselves to formally secular political systems or circumstances in which their political agency is severely circumscribed. In 2016, Ennahda member of parliament Saida Ounissi (in an earlier version of her chapter in this volume[6]) and then Ennahda leader Rached Ghannouchi went so far as to question whether the label "Islamist" was even an appropriate way to describe the platform and agenda of parties such as their own. Amr Darrag of the Egyptian Muslim Brotherhood has also sought to initiate a debate within the organization about the appropriate relationship between religious and partisan activities, arguing that these two realms should be separate and that Brotherhood members should be free to start, join, or vote for multiple political parties.

While it is clear that the ongoing struggle in the region to define the meaning and nature of Islamism—or to transcend the standard model of political Islam altogether—will continue to complicate U.S. policy calculations in the years ahead, the crux of the matter still comes down to certain fundamental questions that Washington has already begun to broach. In a speech given by then Secretary of State Hillary Clinton in 2011, the United States openly recognized that it would be impossible to have enduring stability and security in the Arab world in the absence of democracy. Of course, it remains to be seen whether this kind of thinking has any place in the foreign policy discourse of Donald Trump, with early signs suggesting otherwise. Ultimately, U.S.

policy toward Islamism must be a function of a broader strategic insight regarding the necessary democratic foundations of regional security. The coming of genuine democracy to the Middle East will necessarily involve the participation of Islamists. The United States does not have to support their policies or values, but it does, for the sake of long-term stability, need to pay careful attention to the quality of the political processes that bring them to—and remove them from—power.

13

Politics or Piety? Why the Muslim Brotherhood Engages in Social Service Provision

Amr Darrag, Freedom and Justice Party Leader, in Conversation with Steven Brooke

AMR DARRAG

Steven Brooke, in chapter 1, provides an informative and well-researched overview of the current Egyptian regime crackdown on social service and educational organizations perceived as affiliated with, or in a position to raise the profile of, the Muslim Brotherhood. His examination seems intended to explore three distinct questions: first, whether the social movement (*haraka*) or the political party (*hizb*) is to be privileged by the Brotherhood in the future; second, whether the appeal of the Brotherhood's approach will diminish in favor of the Salafist-jihadist model; and a third, albeit related, question of whether the crackdown on the movement's social service networks will increase the potential for violence.

I concur with the factual elements of Brooke's account and I agree with him that this lens provides a unique and much-needed framework through which to consider these important questions. Yes, the closure of space for social services—when coupled with the closure of so many other avenues of life in Egypt—could possibly lead to extremism on the part of some. Yes, I too hear many murmurs among younger Egyptians about the appeal of a confrontational, radical approach, and again, yes, we need to think more seriously about the relationship between a revivalist religious and social movement that is the Brotherhood and the question of political participation in a nonrepressive, truly representative political environment.

And whereas I do not disagree with the specific representations in the chapter, I disagree with some of the overall framing. In effect, Brooke conveys the sense that individuals choose an ideological stance and a course of action largely because of extrinsic, rather than intrinsic, factors. In other words, the author seems to argue that how individuals behave in the face of regime repression stems more from the avenues the regime leaves open rather than their own assessment of right and wrong. Furthermore, the author appears to posit that the primary motive for the Brotherhood's provision of social and educational services is also extrinsic. Brooke does acknowledge that "services were provided continuously and without the discrimination, ideological litmus tests, or checks on political allegiance that we might expect to see if they were operated by a typical political machine." Elsewhere, though, he makes a fairly large logical leap to suggest that this is because "the Brotherhood overwhelmingly viewed social services as would a *political party*, in the sense that they were a way to reach out to and mobilize voters."[1] The author also cites the Brotherhood's long history of registering its social service and educational institutions with various governmental bodies as support for the contention that the Brotherhood deliberately operated within regime rules.

Service, Belonging, and Polity

This narrative represents one of the most important areas of contention between members of Islamic movements and those who study them, and if readers are to understand Islamic movements, they must bear the following in mind. The Brotherhood is fundamentally an Islamic social movement, not just a political one, and it teaches its members to view the value of service, first and foremost, through a religious lens.

Service builds character. Service is a form of charity that is obligatory on those who can provide it and is diminished by reward, praise, or other forms of recognition. Finally, and this is an aspect central to founder Hassan al-Banna's message and is a defining feature of the contemporary Muslim Brotherhood: Service to compatriots is an act of building *our* country and serving *our* people. Service reinforces the notion that these unrepresentative, corrupt, authoritarian, nepotistic regimes are but a transient, unnatural imposition on the fabric of society rather than having any permanence.

Furthermore, Islamic movements like the Brotherhood are interested in preserving structures like the nation-state. Some Salafi and many jihadist groups (not my preferred terminology) do not share this perspective. They do not see the people of their countries as *their* people. They are quick to engage in the ultimate act of delegitimization (*takfir*). They do not see current nation-states as *their* countries and hence it's easy for them to decide to dismantle what is already there and set up what they envision as parallel countries. They decry and belittle the Brotherhood's recognition of the nation-state, and they claim to seek what they believe to be the only legitimate form of community in Islam—a transnational caliphate. The Muslim Brotherhood and others hold the view that Islam respects and encourages ever-widening circles of allegiance, attachment, and belonging. The smallest of those units is the family, toward which one has clear obligations, and the largest of those is humanity as a whole, passing through smaller units such as neighborhoods, clans, and tribes if applicable, then communities and nations, and then the transnational.

The fundamental basis for this progressive unity is not religious or ideological, but rather geographic. Support for this position exists throughout the trajectory of Muslim theology, history, and political thought, starting with the personal and societal emphasis on obligations to neighbors (irrespective of their faith). These obligations are then expanded through the Constitution of Medina (establishing mutually beneficial relations between Prophet Mohamed—peace be upon him—and the original inhabitants of Medina), and then we see contemporary articulations of citizenship, which are quite compatible with the Constitution of Medina (e.g. from religious thinkers like Ennahda's Rached Ghannouchi,[2] Essam Teleema of al-Azhar, and others).[3]

The caliphate in Banna's conception can exist because cohesion exists across far smaller units not independent of, or irrelevant to, it. Banna's articulation of his understanding of the caliphate was very brief. He posits that the caliphate is the articulation of broad-based unity and affirms that the Muslim Brotherhood seeks to re-establish a caliphate. But he also asserts that there are many prerequisite steps before a caliphate can begin to be a realistic notion, such as cultural, economic, and social integration, as well as the evolution of treaties that define and enshrine mutual cooperation leading to an entity resembling a Muslim league of nations (the model of the European Union is probably closest to this concept). Throughout its history, the Muslim Brotherhood has supported the progressive unity mentioned earlier and avenues for greater cooperation among all nations, according to principles of mutual respect.

There is, of course, much hand-wringing over the idea of the caliphate from some Western politicians and writers who cast it as a byword for everything that is to be feared about Islam and Muslims. Some concerns are credible and require further examination, for example religious freedoms and equality, while some other concerns are merely an extension of viewing Muslims as an exotic "other." We should ask why "states" desiring a "more perfect union" or European countries working toward "an ever greater union" are seen as both natural and laudable, but Muslim nations working toward the same are viewed with suspicion, requiring endless justification.

Service, Utility, and Violence

The inability of many analysts to understand a spiritual, faith-based motivation for the choices Islamists make, individually and collectively, represents a barrier to understanding the nature of "political Islam." The narrative of service provision as a pathway to power cannot explain the resilience of social service provision over decades of repression and restriction. From 1977, when the Islamic Medical Association was founded, to the eve of the January 25, 2011 revolution, there was never a point in Egypt where it was even remotely conceivable that Islamists would gain a sliver of political power, let alone a fair measure of it. Furthermore, in the context of the authoritarian nature of Egypt's governments, any such "gains" were always at the mercy of arbitrary repression by the regime. The regime was willing to, and did, impede service delivery by the Muslim Brotherhood throughout the 1980s, 1990s, and 2000s, and at no point during this period was a path to political liberalization becoming clearer as a result of the Brotherhood's engagement with society.

The passage of time perhaps obscures the fact that the regime was intent on crippling the Brotherhood through any number of measures. Brotherhood members were subjected to military trials, youth members were routinely apprehended, torture regularly employed, and all means of public participation progressively closed through the so-called *siyasat tagfeef al-manabe* (roughly translated as the policy of drying out resources and avenues of activity). A key difference between the Mubarak and Sissi regimes is that the former feared international opprobrium while the latter believes, and for very good reason, that the international community, specifically the United States, will acquiese to, or even support, massive repression. Yet under President Anwar al-Sadat and then Mubarak, service provision continued, expanded, and became entrenched. I fully realize that many analysts and readers have difficulty abandoning utility-based interpretations in favor of intrinsic, faith-based motivations, and this is a barrier that should be explicitly acknowledged. And it is because of this—because many of our actions are not the most expedient or the most utilitarian, but rather are principled and faith-based—that the movement continues to have adherents. And it is also precisely for this reason that violent, radical approaches will continue to have limited appeal among Brotherhood members and supporters. (In other words, it is very unlikely that those faithfully committed to serving their societies, irrespective of differences in faith or political trends, could turn to destroying those same societies through engaging in violence or terrorism.)

To be a bit more thorough, let me further contextualize utility-based interpretations of the Muslim Brotherhood's behavior. There is no doubt that Muslims are obligated to think, to reflect, and to employ the best means to bringing about their desired ends. Accordingly, individual and group actions are not irrational or detached from considerations like the likelihood of success. However, it is the framework for understanding "rational" choices that seems to be misunderstood. For the Muslim Brotherhood, the primary drivers are moral and religious. The ends are multilayered. Service delivery in the form of food aid, accessible education, or healthcare serves multiple objectives: It helps people in need; it brings with it a spiritual return for the individuals involved in providing assistance; and it improves society. If the result of Brotherhood-led service provision is that the regime is pushed to engage in further service delivery and improves its responsiveness to people's needs, then this is a success. If such improvements are sustained and institutionalized, this is a further success, and so on. If service provision fails to improve our popularity, this does not lead to a "reassessment" of the utility of service provision as a primary, core mission of the Muslim Brotherhood.

The Brotherhood's reach in the mid-1940s in terms of social service provision and popularity was impressive. The repression that followed in the 1950s and 1960s occurred with a fair measure of popular support for the regime of Gamal Abdul Nasser. A completely utilitarian approach would have led to the conclusion that service provision is an unreliable means of securing popular support. The Brotherhood did *not* reach that conclusion, and this was deliberate. Indeed, other groups came to precisely that conclusion starting in the 1950s and continuing to the present day. The chasm between the Muslim Brotherhood and these other groups is the Brotherhood's privileging of faith over utility while not discounting the latter, where other groups, such as the Islamic State, privilege utility over morality and faith while occasionally discounting the latter in the name of the former.

Hence, while Steven Brooke's analysis is excellent and insightful and does add an important dimension to the conversation, it does not truly reflect the mind of Islamists such as myself and others I know. Yes, service is a form of outreach and a way for people to know the movement. But no, being shut out of the space of service provision does not, in and of itself, lead people to strike a path to violence or to question fundamental tenets of their mission and identity. There will be exceptions, of course, but the norm will not be that. The fact that some individuals will feel that there is no avenue before them other than violence is a reflection on the failure of repressive regimes and the international reaction to them, rather than a reflection on the success or lack thereof of our own philosophy. So, while the use of violence is an important phenomenon to study and reflect on, and while it may incur a very high cost to society, what needs to be examined—and what is more relevant to understanding violence—is why the international community supports and normalizes repressive, authoritarian regimes when the evident result is the radicalization of their citizens.

But beyond this question of violence from within the ranks of Islamists, a more concerning outcome of the regime's appropriation of social and educational services is the one outlined by the author in his conclusions: As this nepotistic, corrupt regime that has little concern for individuals' welfare destroys the last remaining means of helping Egyptians preserve a measure of dignity, the prospect for widespread social action becomes more real. For example, labor disruptions have intensified since the military coup.[4] The full effect on the poor of the abrupt cessation of subsidies in the context of financial corruption and the lack of a social safety net has not yet been felt (and a major destabilizing effect is yet to be seen following recent agreements with the International Monetary Fund, coupled with unprecedented inflation and the complete failure of the military regime to achieve any successes in the economy). In short, the factors that can often lead to widespread disruption and protest are increasing rather than decreasing.

Moving Forward

The aforementioned emphasis on the centrality of service to the worldview of Islamists is not an attempt to absolve the Muslim Brotherhood from errors over the past five years. It is important in this context to highlight the fact that the Brotherhood is currently conducting an extensive review of its practices, particularly over the last six years since the January 25 revolution. This review extends to long-term strategy and the overall conceptualization of the nature of the struggle between civilians and military rule. One of the key elements under review is the relationship between the Brotherhood, as a religious and social movement, and the Freedom and Justice Party (FJP)—or any other future Islamist political parties for that matter.[5] Since the establishment of the FJP, the intention was to establish a clear line of separation between the two entities. In reality, that separation may not have been completed as intended.

As some have pointed out, the FJP leveraged the goodwill that the Brotherhood had established and drew on the movement's social credit to gain legitimacy with voters. In retrospect, I believe that this was a mistake, caused more by the unusual circumstances that Egypt faced, rather than as a result of a deliberate strategy. Prior to 2011, few Egyptians anticipated that the day would come when their fellow citizens would finally take to the street to bring Mubarak down. The leveraging of the Muslim Brotherhood's goodwill occurred because it was the Brotherhood, not the FJP, that was party to the events of January and February 2011, simply because the latter did not exist then. To Egyptians, it was the Muslim Brotherhood, and not the FJP, that made sacrifices for Egypt. And so, perhaps as a reflexive reaction to the question "why should voters trust your stewardship of the economy, the government, and so on," the FJP leveraged the Brotherhood's goodwill and popularity. I say this not to justify the overlap, but rather in the course of trying to critically examine the practices of the past.

Conversely, the Brotherhood was unable to completely let go of the FJP, although the relationship evolved considerably over time. I can say that the majority opinion within the Brotherhood today is to totally disengage the movement from any partisan competitive work when the space for political and social activity is restored. We believe there is a need for a truly independent political party (or parties) with strong grounding in an Islamic worldview that seeks to translate that worldview into a living reality. That party will have to elaborate its own platforms and positions; it will develop its own talents and cadres; and it will be free to assume a principled but pragmatic approach to politics. There is also a need for some Islamists to engage in new political parties together with non-Islamists, where more inclusive platforms are established; to develop programs that would mobilize wider spectra of Egyptians from different backgrounds to address the chronic problems facing Egypt, particularly during any transitional period after the end of the era of military rule. We also believe that there is an ongoing need for an effort aimed at broad-based religious, societal reform. If the Islamic movement as a whole is successful in understanding and implementing both religious and political efforts separately, then there would be no pressing need to connect social work to any political agenda.

One final point: We now understand the actions of the current regime in a somewhat different light from a simple regime versus opposition binary, with the Brotherhood represented in the latter. We believe that the battle currently taking place in Egypt is one of a militarized, centralized authoritarian vision of Egypt, borne of the legacy of Mohamed Ali (d. 1805), which conceptualized Egypt essentially as a garrison to serve the army. The military establishment, as it is configured today, continues to prioritize the interests of the military over the interests of the nation and its citizens. There is a sardonic reflection, common among many Egyptians, on this relationship between the army and the nation, to the effect that while other countries have armies that serve them, our army has a country that serves it. As long as this relationship persists, the Egyptian citizen will always be alienated from the so-called Egyptian state, at least as it is articulated by army-aligned nationalist politicians and "thinkers." And so today we are thinking about how to rebuild Egypt in a way that incorporates effective local governance and the empowerment of civil society with better national decision making. This transition will undoubtedly be challenging since Egyptians have a long-standing tradition of centralized authority. Nevertheless, this tradition has been under considerable stress for the past 50 years due to the ineffectiveness of the state, largely due to rampant corruption and poor administration. A closer examination of mechanisms for conflict resolution and the structure of the informal and microeconomy—and, importantly, an emphasis on decentralization and local authority—may yield valuable lessons for reconfiguring Egyptian governance.

STEVEN BROOKE RESPONDS

In his response to my chapter for *Rethinking Political Islam*, Freedom and Justice Party leader Amr Darrag raises a number of noteworthy issues. I will have to think more deeply about these points, but at the moment it might be useful to elaborate on two things in particular: first, what I see as the precise connection between the Brotherhood's social service provision and its political support, and second, the dynamics of societal radicalization and violence in today's Middle East.

As Darrag rightly notes, social service provision serves as a way for members to express their own intrinsic commitment to their religion and movement, to serve others, and to provide a practical example of Islam's relevance to daily life. In my own research, those involved in the Brotherhood's social services speak passionately about their personal and religious commitment to their work. But social service provision also has a more instrumental side: building, over time, a mass of popular support for the organization's ideas and goals, which can then be transformed—gradually—into broader social and political change.

As a researcher, I am particularly interested in going beyond intuitive but vague statements about how social services won the Brotherhood supporters and identifying more precisely the mechanisms behind this process, particularly during the authoritarian rule of Hosni Mubarak. One common answer is that the Brotherhood—like political parties everywhere—used its social services as a type of clientelism. But Darrag is right that this type of thinking was anathema to those involved in the effort, and the evidence strongly supports his contention. And as I wrote in my original working paper, there was no evidence of the discrimination, ideological litmus tests, or linkage of services to voting behavior that we might expect to find were these operations focused baldly on winning elections.[6] Of the millions of Egyptians who interacted with and benefited from the Brotherhood's services, some would go on to become supporters of the group, and some would even vote for the Brotherhood's candidates because of it. But others would use the services while remaining staunch Brotherhood opponents.

This leads to a somewhat paradoxical conclusion: if the Brotherhood were using their social services simply to buy electoral support—as their critics frequently charged—then they would have become indistinguishable from the myriad other parties in Egypt that do precisely this. Historically, I would argue that the Brotherhood's social services were effective at generating social and political support precisely because they were depoliticized, regular, and not linked to the electoral calendar. The group provided high-quality and compassionate care and, in effect, let the work speak for itself. But we need to distinguish, at least to some extent, between the organization's social service provision pre- and post-2011.

In light of this, Darrag's critique of some of the Brotherhood's behavior in the post-Mubarak period, that "the FJP leveraged the goodwill that the Brotherhood had established and drew on the movement's social credit to acquire legitimacy with voters," is a key insight. I think that allowing this overlap to occur—which, as Darrag notes, was as much a product of particular circumstances as a considered strategy—reduced, at least in the popular imagination, the Brotherhood's social service activism to a simple electoral logic. And I think this misstep actually underscores the success of the Brotherhood's prior depoliticized, society-focused approach as opposed to an electoral, state-focused one. I find it interesting that both Darrag and Brotherhood youth activist Ammar Fayed's contributions to this volume discuss a growing consensus that, in the future, the Brotherhood must erect a firewall between the political and social sides of the organization. It will be fascinating to watch this debate play out theoretically and practically across the Middle East over the next few years.

One of the benefits of *Rethinking Political Islam* is to identify how, as the organizers of the project put it, "the subsequent 'twin shocks' of the coup in Egypt and the emergence of the Islamic State are forcing a rethinking of some of the basic assumptions of, and about, Islamist movements."[7] A key question—if not *the* key question—is how these events should prompt us to reconsider the relationship between Islamist groups and violence. As Marc Lynch has written, many of the conclusions we had reached about Islamists and violence prior to the Arab Spring rest on factors and mechanisms that have since changed dramatically:

> The Brotherhood as examined and studied in this literature over the past several decades no longer really exists. The core characteristics that defined the Brotherhood's internal organization and strategic environment, and which guided political science research about it, no longer operate.[8]

I have no special insight into the current—let alone the future—trajectory of the Brotherhood in regards to violence. I am skeptical that the Brotherhood will up and abandon the gradualist approach that made it so successful for so long, but I cannot rule it out. State repression under Gamal Abdul Nasser radicalized and ultimately fractured the

Brotherhood, and the efforts of Egypt's new military rulers against the Brotherhood are at least equal to Nasser's predations. But even after the Rabaa massacre, which Human Rights Watch called "killings . . . on a scale unprecedented in Egypt," the Muslim Brotherhood largely defied expectations of violent radicalization and, as the political sociologist Neil Ketchley argues, "successfully consolidated their organization to wage a national campaign of non-violent protest."[9, 10]

But I also think a more productive avenue of inquiry in light of recent, and rapid, developments in the region is to ask: "How attractive is the Brotherhood as a model for organized religious activism?" Before the Arab uprisings, and during the flurry of electoral competition that briefly followed, the Brotherhood dominated the news, and the headlines often spoke of their political successes. But today I am unsure what being a member of the Brotherhood in Egypt might offer a young Muslim. One cannot get involved in politics, protest, or even organize in civil society without incurring significant risks to life and limb. In these conditions, many will simply become apolitical. Others may find violence—what Brotherhood youth activist Ammar Fayed calls the "dominant political language" of the region today—a more attractive outlet.

More generally, Darrag's essay helpfully reminds us that many of the processes we discuss—such as engaging in service provision, the relationship between social and political change, or sorting out gradual versus revolutionary activism—occur among individuals with strong beliefs about what is right and wrong. So while seeking to account for the movements, regimes, and international alliances that are currently reshaping the Middle East, we should not lose sight of individuals' personal and often deeply felt commitments. This is why, as our research techniques evolve to provide deeper understandings of political Islam, we should always be ready to sit down and seriously listen to what Islamists themselves have to say.

14

Ennahda from Within: Islamists or "Muslim Democrats"?

Sayida Ounissi, Ennahda Member of the Tunisian Parliament,
in Conversation with Monica Marks

SAYIDA OUNISSI

Editor's Note: A version of this chapter was originally published on the website of the Brookings Institution in March 2016, before Ennahda leader Rached Ghannouchi's May announcement separating partisan activities from religious outreach and rebranding the party as "Muslim democratic."

As an Ennahda member of parliament in Tunisia, I've always been interested in how we're portrayed both by the academics who study us and by the media. I've often felt a strong discrepancy between what we would read about ourselves, as an Islamist party, and who and what we actually are.

In this piece, I would like to address some of the issues raised by Monica Marks, Avi Spiegel, and Steven Brooke in their contributions to *Rethinking Political Islam*. First is the very identity of Ennahda and why it is important to further discuss the supposed Muslim Brotherhood paternity of our movement. Second, I focus on what the failure of the "legalist" approach means for the next generation of Egypt's Muslim Brotherhood and its consequences for the rest of the Arab world. This also offers an occasion to reinterpret the real impact of the Egyptian coup of July 3, 2013 on the Tunisian transition. Third, the last section rethinks how we label a party like Ennahda and asks whether "Muslim democrat" might be a more accurate description of the party's orientation, rather than the traditional designation of "Islamist."

Ennahda: The Tunisian Muslim Brotherhood or Bourguiba's Illegitimate Child?

I think it is time to recognize that the traditional approach that links all contemporary Islamic value-based parties to the Muslim Brotherhood as a sort of "parent company" has reached its limits, especially in light of recent decisions taken by these parties. The founding context of Ennahda is more complex than a tentative importation of Hassan al-Banna's ideology into Tunisia by Rached Ghannouchi. The very nationally grounded trajectory of the founders of the Islamic Tendency Movement (which later became Ennahda) says a lot about the characteristics of the Tunisian Islamic movement.

Much can be gleaned in this regard by examining the intellectual and religious origins of Tunisia's Islamic movement. For instance, the two main founders of Ennahda, Abdelfattah Mourou and Rached Ghannouchi, were both graduates of Zaytouna University, the first Islamic university in the Arab world. Founded in 737, it gained a reputation for being responsive to the changing needs of society. Understanding this is significant, as Abdelfattah Mourou's spiritual father is Sheikh Hmed Ben Miled, a Zaytounite, rather than someone like Sayyid Qutb, as many may erroneously assume. Ben Miled played a key role in Tunisia's national liberation movement. He was heavily engaged in the struggle for the modern Tunisian state and a supporter of the state institutions that formed its bedrock. There is a famous picture of Miled with a group of scholars from Zaytouna in front of the parliamentary building taking part in legislative consultations during President Habib Bourguiba's regime.

In the movement's early years, Ennahda's religious circles were oriented toward Sheikh Tahar Ben Achour's teaching and legal judgements. A president of Zaytouna University and adherent of the Maliki school of jurisprudence, Ben Achour was one of the modern fathers of a more rationalist approach toward Quranic exegesis (*tafsir*) that emphasized the importance of *maqasid al-sharia,* in other words the objectives or ends, rather than the means, of Islamic law. An arch-enemy of the traditionalists, he was pushed out of the university in 1960.

Many Ennahda leaders, such as Rached Ghannouchi himself, also participated in the rehabilitation of the controversial scholar Tahar Haddad against traditionalist pushback to his ideas. Haddad wrote against the more conservative scholarly wings of Zaytouna in his book *Women in Sharia and Society.* He also held politically progressive positions on trade unions and social welfare. These are just some of the figures who shaped a distinctly Tunisian progressive and rationalist approach toward sacred texts, providing fertile ground for Habib Bourguiba to proceed with the modernization of state law, especially with regards to social and personal statutes.

My aim here is not to deny the influence of thinkers whose ideas traveled beyond their borders, such as those of Hassan al-Banna, or of the supranational fora where Islamist parties gather, debate, and exchange ideas, but rather to note that the impact of such factors is not as decisive as one might think. That said, they were certainly important at the intellectual level, and the plethora of Egyptian Muslim Brotherhood publications were the main philosophical "food for thought" of the Tunisian movement, which subsequently reinterpreted that literature in the context of its own unique, local ideological environment.

It is my belief that the "Grand Soir" of Islamist movements is more a post hoc construct rather than a real (and realizable) objective of political actors who have, in reality, showed much more pragmatism than originally prophesized. One could even go so far as to say that Ennahda's founding generation were the illegitimate children of Bourguiba, insofar as they subscribed to the idea of a struggle for national independence, the necessity of a social renaissance, and the importance of modern governance tools.

As Monica Marks notes in her chapter, Ennahda members consider themselves different from the Muslim Brotherhood at both the ideological and political level. Despite this, after the 2011 revolution, there is still the tendency among a range of analysts to consider Ennahda as simply the Tunisian branch of the Muslim Brotherhood. This has led to a misinterpretation of the path the party has taken since 2011. Furthermore, in Ennahda's case, being able to experiment with more than four years of actual political governance has had more impact on its identity and political discourse than decades of underground activity.

The approach and objective of integrating within the state is to secure the presence of the party not only as a legal, "normal" entity but also as a legitimate political force able to both develop public policies and implement them. To change things from outside of the system has been an illusion that most political parties, Islamist or otherwise, no longer believe in. The process of ownership is long and necessary. As for Ennahda, this process began in 2011 with the party's legalization and its first experience in leading a coalition government with two secular parties.

Many Islamist parties (like in the case of Morocco's Justice and Development Party, or PJD) are setting up a range of new activities and strategies, demonstrating the sort of long-term vision these organizations want to develop, far from the unpredictable counter-reactions of a system in transition.

During Brookings' U.S.-Islamic World Forum in Doha in June 2015, we had the opportunity to discuss and debate with other young Islamist activists from across the Middle East (Egypt, Morocco, Turkey, Saudi Arabia, Kuwait, Jordan), whether in power or in the opposition.[1] It brought out the local nuances of positions and proposals in each country. Even if we aren't always looking for examples to follow from outside our own national contexts, other models can be instructive as counterexamples and signposts to avoid pitfalls. But some of these experiences can also inspire. For example, Ennahda, the Turkish Justice and Development Party (AKP), and the Moroccan PJD have accumulated significant experience in successful state-driven economic development.

I always find myself surprised when analysts express surprise at the pragmatism of these parties. There seems to be an implicit expectation that these groups will behave like secretive and archaic religious brotherhoods, even when the entire expressed purpose of these groups is to govern and to participate in the shaping of public policy. For example, Ennahda's *tazkiya* process (whereby party members "vouch" for prospective applicants) has been more or less transformed into a simple nonbinding recommendation. Many other "management"-type strategies are being modernized as the separation process between the party (*hizb*) and the movement (*haraka*) progresses.

It is time to look deeper at the professionalization of political parties in the Middle East, especially those in transitional countries like Tunisia. Within Ennahda, we consider the debates about the identity of the state and the relationship between religion and politics (including the place of sharia in the hierarchy of norms) to have been

resolved during the constitutional process of 2011–2014. The resulting constitution, one that Tunisians are quite proud of, is a text that
is unlikely to be significantly amended anytime soon, especially after
four years of charged and thorough debate around the document's
provisions. In fact, political parties which were still campaigning on
these potentially divisive topics during the 2014 parliamentary elections were roundly defeated. Even Hamma Hammami, the candidate from the far left party, the Popular Front, found it necessary to
reassure voters that he was Muslim and that he loved the Prophet
Mohamed during a television interview without even having been
asked about it. Interestingly, Nidaa Tunis—a party defined by its
anti-Islamism—relied heavily on religious rhetoric during the parliamentary and presidential campaigns despite its "secular" label. I
remember one of its young members, after an appearance in a debate
with us on France 24, telling me that French journalists should stop
calling them *laique* (supporting the separation of religion from politics) because they are not and do not want to be seen as such by
Tunisians.[2]

The maturity of parties like Ennahda is also apparent through the
sorts of subjects they raise in public debate. It is no longer a matter
of the relationship between Islam and state anymore, or traditionally
"Islamic" issues, but rather a commitment to finding solutions to
corruption, economic development, social issues, and human rights.

The Failure of the "Legalist" Approach and the Consequences of the Egyptian Coup

The failure of the legalist approach of Egypt's Muslim Brotherhood
has had a significant impact on the way a young generation of Arabs,
regardless of their political preferences, see institutions and political systems. For the Islamists among them, it seemed that despite their efforts
to understand and play by the rules, they would never be accepted.
Decisive results at the ballot box could be contested. Elections were not
a genuine means to access power. Moreover, the brutality of military
repression is heightening feelings of defiance among Islamists toward
the state and its institutions. More than a military coup, the events in
Egypt represent a major missed opportunity to reconcile a whole generation with the state.

The risk of violent reaction from the younger generation cannot be dismissed, though it is worth noting that, since the coup, the pro-Brotherhood student organizations that are still demonstrating against military oppression have been careful not to fall into the trap of using violence. That said, there is a correlation between the military coup and subsequent crackdown and the rise of the Islamic State and other extremist groups in Egypt. Violence begets violence, and this infernal cycle is nourished by dictatorship, whether based on military power, secular ideology, or Islamic rhetoric. We shouldn't be surprised by the loss of credibility of much-vaunted "universal values," which weren't strong enough to protect democratic transitions, human rights, and individual liberties in much of the Arab world. This failure has led to a loss of faith in democracy as the way to manage a society or as a good system for power sharing.

We usually read that the Egyptian coup essentially induced Ennahda's decision to step down and accept the handing over of power to a technocratic government whose main mission was to organize legislative and presidential elections within a year's time. This has often been interpreted as a surrender on Ennahda's part, with the ouster of the Muslim Brotherhood in Egypt as a kind of turning point in Ennahda's thinking. I think this view doesn't quite capture the full picture and tends to forget a number of important things.

Initially, the start of the Tunisian political crisis in the summer of 2013 wasn't triggered by the coup in Egypt but rather by the assassination of Mohamed Brahmi, a prominent leftist politician. This reignited the country's previous crisis of February 2013, following the assassination of the politician Chokri Belaid. Though the Egyptian coup may have accelerated the process and reinforced the demands of the secular opposition, the confrontation inside Tunisia preceded the removal of Mohamed Morsi from power.

But, more generally, we need to go back to the very start of the democratic transition in 2011 to better grasp how events unfolded. Consider, for example, the attitude of Ennahda since the October 2011 elections, after which the party decided to share power with two very ideologically different parties, the secular-liberal Congress for the Republic (CPR) and the socialist Ettakatol. I consider this a continuation of a process that started in 2005 with the 18 October

Collectif, when various parties from the opposition to President Zine al-Abidine Ben Ali decided to launch an inclusive dialogue process to reach consensus on fundamental issues.

The conclusions of these discussions were published in a book, which summarized areas of agreement on core concerns, such as the civil character of the state, the nature of the regime, the importance of civil liberties, and women's rights.[3] In other words, sharing power and prioritizing dialogue over exclusivism was part of Ennahda's philosophy well before the Egyptian coup and even the uprisings of 2011.

Since the start of the democratic transition, it was not unusual to hear Rached Ghannouchi speaking about the importance of making the process as inclusive as possible, regardless of the political weight of the various parties. This, he argued, was the best way to secure the transition. A desire to minimize political resistance to democratization by inviting the maximum number of political actors to participate reflects a clear commitment on the part of Ennahda leaders. The polarizing nature of the lustration debate in 2013—over whether or not to bar old regime figures from electoral participation, which Monica Marks discusses at length—led us to further conclude that exclusion couldn't be the solution if we wanted to sustain the health and stability of the transitional process. The Libyan and the Iraqi experiences of lustration played an important role as counterexamples, helping to convince Ennahda parliamentarians to vote against the proposed electoral exclusion law to avoid a similar scenario. Given all of this, it shouldn't be surprising to see Ennahda calling for unity and inclusion. As the head of a list of candidates in the parliamentary elections, I campaigned on national unity, defending the proposal for a national coalition government. To be sure, it required considerable time and effort to explain to voters the necessity of bringing in as many political forces as possible to support vital economic and social reforms. It is not necessarily easy to campaign for the benefits of a complex and unusual political balance.

These positions were taken in consultation with Ennahda's Shura Council after an intense internal debate. The negative trajectory of the Libyan revolution, the deteriorating situation in Iraq, and the internecine conflict in Syria ended up convincing the majority of Tunisians that lustration isn't always a solution to political crises.

Another thing to keep in mind is that the major threat at the time was the dissolution of the Constituent Assembly and the exclusion of Ennahda from the constitutional debate. Irrespective of anything else, this could have derailed the entire democratic process. Ennahda, however, managed to secure the constitutional process by ensuring that the constitution was finalized under the Ennahda-led government of Ali Laarayedh before handing over power to a temporary technocratic government. This, quite simply, was a success from our perspective. The Egyptian scenario played the role of an a posteriori counterexample in formulating Ennahda's decisions.

The Meaning of Being a Muslim Democratic Party in the 21st Century

When Rached Ghannouchi first used the term "Muslim democratic," it was an effort to help the media understand the pitfalls of instantly and unanimously labeling diverse political actors as "Islamists," despite their differences. Highlighting the parallel with Christian Democratic parties in Europe, like Germany's Christian Democratic Union, seemed to be the easiest way to signify Ennahda as a political party bringing together both democratic principles and religious values.

Many, both inside and outside of Ennahda, were initially surprised by this new label and began to wonder what changes, if any, it implied at the political level. The fact is we can no longer use a term so charged with negative connotations when describing what we consider to be one of the most positive phenomena taking place in the Muslim world today. For the vast majority of Muslims, the Islamic State and its ilk are those who misinterpret and abuse Islam and use religion as a marketing tool for unspeakable, inhumane acts and for a brutal war for territory with no end. We believe we have a critical role to play in countering the Islamic State. The Islamic scholars Ennahda members consider as references are serious and legitimate sources of religious interpretation when it comes to positions on violence, barbarity, the modern state, civil liberties, and the objectives (*maqasid*) of sharia.

It would be a waste of time and energy for us to take up the task of constantly distancing ourselves from a violent and dangerous ideology that is precisely the sort of model we are fighting against. No one, for instance, would seriously link the French socialist president François Hollande with Georges Cipriani, the historic leader of the terrorist group Action Directe, despite both of them hailing from political groups that claim inspiration from the same ideology. We, unfortunately, are not afforded the same treatment and must therefore make our differences from the Islamic State and other extremists clear to all.

In a nutshell, "Muslim democrat" is the most accurate term to describe what Ennahda has been trying to accomplish since the beginning: reconciling Islam and democracy in the Arab world.

MONICA MARKS'S RESPONSE

Ennahda Member of Parliament Sayida Ounissi contributed a rich reflection to this volume. Her remarks presaged key decisions taken at Ennahda's 10th Congress, held May 20–23, 2016. Here, I'll engage briefly with just two of the fascinating themes Ounissi raised— Ennahda's integration as a Tunisian national actor and relabeling as "Muslim democrats"—and connect those themes directly to Ennahda's recent congress.

Ounissi first confronts accusations, common among secularly oriented Tunisians who have opposed Ennahda on ideological grounds, that Ennahda was birthed in the *Mashriq* (Arab East) and lacks proper Tunisian bona fides. Instead of representing the local branch of a shady international Muslim Brotherhood cabal, though, Ounissi argues that Ennahda has pursued a "very nationally grounded trajectory" since its inception, guided by leading figures in Tunisia's reformist and Zaytounian schools of thought.

Ounissi's emphasis on the "Tunisianness" of Ennahda's intellectual history formed an essential subtheme at Ennahda's 10th Congress. In his opening address on May 20, party president Rached Ghannouchi claimed that Ennahda's support for unity and national reconciliation is not a *safqa taht al-tawila* (under-the-table deal) but anchored in Ennahda's view of Tunisian history:

> Ennahda is a force for unity and togetherness, not for separation and division. So we see Khaireddine al-Tunsi, Ahmed Bey, Moncef Bey,

the late *za'im* [leader] Habib Bourguiba, Farhat Hachad, Abdelazziz Thaalbi, Salah Ben Youssef, Sheikh Mohamed Tahar Ben Achour, and Tahar Haddad, God's mercy be upon them and others, as symbols of our beloved nation.[4]

Ghannouchi asserted—before a crowd of 13,000 *nahdawis* (Ennahda members) and on national television—an inclusive re-remembering of Tunisian history, one that embraced both former president Habib Bourguiba (president from 1957 to 1987) and his archrival Salah Ben Youssef, politicians whose struggle for control of the anticolonial movement foreshadowed important class-based and cultural rifts between Tunisia's interior and coast.

Despite the pride of place Bourguiba holds in Tunisia's collective memory, some Tunisians—particularly those from interior, more religious, and more Arabophone backgrounds—resent the favoritism he showed Tunisia's *sahel* (northern coastal) regions and steps he took to weaken Tunisia's traditional religious institutions. Ennahda supporters have historically been among such critics of Bourguiba, not least because of the hostility with which Bourguiba approached Ennahda and its leaders throughout much of the 1980s.[5]

In his 2014 campaign for president, Beji Caid Essebsi played both on nostalgia for Bourguiba and historical tensions between Bourguiba and Ennahda. Promising to restore *haybat al-dawla* (state prestige) by re-empowering Tunisia's traditional political class, Essebsi ran as a present-day incarnation of Bourguiba—impersonating even his dress and speech patterns. This fueled Ennahda supporters' fears that Essebsi represented a continuation of Tunisia's autocratic past and intended to crack down on conservative Tunisians' freedom of expression and association.

Yet, despite such antipathies, Ennahda's 10th Congress asserted, at least at the rhetorical and elite political levels, a historical reconciliation with Bourguibism. In perhaps the most quotable part of her reflection, Ounissi previewed this reconciliation, arguing one could call Ennahda's founding generation the "illegitimate children of Bourguiba" insofar as they supported "national independence, the necessity of a social renaissance, and modern governance tools."

Recasting Ennahda as Bourguiba's long-lost, prodigal child helps the party rationalize post hoc its alliance with Nidaa Tunis and with Beji Caid Essebsi, Bourguiba's great admirer. Perhaps more important, though, forging a shared understanding of Tunisian history— one in which Ennahda is understood to have been molded by some of the same forces of Tunisian reformism that influenced prominent anti-Islamist actors—forms a critical plank of Ennahda's longer-term effort to legitimize itself as a normal Tunisian political actor. Against depictions popularized under former dictator Zine el-Abidine Ben Ali (1987–2011) that painted Ennahda as a retrograde group of Wahhabi-inspired criminals, the party is slowly but surely hitting back, wrapping itself in the flag of Tunisian reformist intellectual history.

But, as Ounissi implies, this redoubled effort at Tunisifying Ennahda, or uncovering its pre-existing but long ignored Tunisianness, isn't merely tactical. It's part of a broader nationalization of Ennahda's thinking— and in the thinking of *Ikhwani* (Muslim Brotherhood–oriented) parties across the region replacing larger international goals with an increasing focus on limited, national goals. Though Ennahda still sees itself as connected (albeit in a cousin-like way) to Morocco's PJD, Egypt's Brotherhood, and Turkey's AKP, it has come to see itself foremost as an essentially Tunisian actor, focused on the nationally limited goal of bringing pragmatic, Islam-inspired good governance to the Tunisian polity. Idealistic transnational aims—crafting an *ummah* beyond the Tunisian citizenry—have become the province not of Ennahda, but of Salafist groups.

Ounissi acknowledges it wasn't always this way. The Egyptian Muslim Brotherhood's writings used to make up Ennahda's "main philosophical food for thought." Yet, even then, Ounissi stresses that Ennahda members read and "reinterpreted that literature in the context of [their] own unique, local ideological environment." That's true. It's also true that essential pieces of the Brotherhood canon—for instance, the works of Brotherhood founder Hassan al-Banna and firebrand thinker Sayyid Qutb—simply aren't as widely read or as resonant with nahdawis as they used to be.

Many nahdawis instead cite the work of an Algerian scholar Malek Bennabi as having a greater impact on Ennahda's thinking than Qutb's, especially since the 1990s. Bennabi's influence has come up many times in my interviews with Ennahda leaders and base-level supporters, and shows through in works written by Rached Ghannouchi in the 1990s. The scholars Francesco Cavatorta and Fabio Merone highlight the influence of Bennabi and the Tunisian-North African roots of Ennahda's intellectual heritage at some length in an article published in 2015. They note that as Ennahda outgrew the Qutb-inspired Ikhwani strand of thought "a process of rediscovery of more local sources of ideological commitment to Islamism was initiated."[6]

That process, Cavatorta and Merone argue, has enabled Ennahda to view Tunisian modernity and reformism as originating not with secular symbols like Habib Bourguiba but from a deeper, shared history of Islamic reformist thinkers. Locating reformism on Tunisian soil allows the party to position itself as a natural product of Tunisia's ecosystem rather than a wave washed in from the Wahhabi Gulf.

Moreover, locating flexibility and reformism within the Islamic tradition has allowed Ennahda to understand itself not just as a Tunisian actor but as an authentically Islamist party, even as it has made compromises that contravene traditional expectations of what an Islamist party is and does (i.e., create an Islamic state and implement sharia).

Cavatorta and Merone correctly argue that Ennahda has, from its point of view, "been able to fulfill the Islamic project by subscribing to a political system that enshrines liberty and justice"—principles it sees as fulfilling the ultimate objectives of sharia.[7] This squares with internal conversations and justifications Ennahda developed while making religious compromises—on sharia, blasphemy, and more—throughout the 2012–2014 constitutional drafting process. For instance, Ennahda came to accept the idea that sharia should not be mentioned in Tunisia's new constitution because that constitution upheld freedom, justice, and human dignity—higher principles and objectives of sharia that superseded the importance of mentioning the word itself.[8]

Ennahda's ability to rethink the meaning of Islamism was shaped not only by tactical concerns but also by a long process of internal reflection and dialogue that began well before Tunisia's revolution, and was—as Ounissi notes—presaged in cross-ideological opposition talks that saw Ennahda forge key agreements with secular parties during the 2000s.[9]

On a related note, Ennahda's recent relabeling as "Muslim democrats" reflects less a transformational rupture in how the party views itself than frustration with outsiders not understanding its supposedly true democratic nature. We can understand Ennahda's relabeling as also connected to this process of Tunisification. Through its rebranding, Ennahda hopes to be identified not as outsider Ikhwani Islamists but as a national Muslim democratic party sprung from the Tunisian soil—the same reformist soil that produced Abdelaziz Thaalbi, Habib Bourguiba, Tahar Hadad, and other guiding lights of Tunisia's self-proclaimed modernists.

Interestingly, it should also be noted that those modernists—chief among them, leaders of Nidaa Tunis—prefer *not* to be called *almaniyeen* (secularists) for a very similar reason. The word "secular" in Tunisia often transmits negative connotations—marking one a product of European or even colonially imported ideas. Nidaa Tunis, aspiring to position itself as a powerful, locally accepted actor on the Tunisian scene, hence identified as "a modern party for a Muslim people," using the word "modernists" as a more palatable euphemism for "secularists." One could argue that Ennahda is taking a similar approach to the word "Islamist," swapping it for a more palatable label that avoids outsider connotations and aligns it instead with the Tunisian center, a center that both Ennahda and Nidaa Tunis understand to be Muslim, modern, and democratic—though each of these are malleable, quite vague terms that mean different things to different Tunisians (and hence possess the power to politically organize and inspire).

As Ounissi's reflection indicates, adopting the term "Muslim democrat" indicates less a shift in how nahdawis see themselves—for they have seen themselves as Muslim democrats for some time now—than an effort to help media and outside actors understand the party on its own terms. Referencing common conflation of the term "Islamism" with the Islamic State, she says: "It would be a waste of time and energy for us to take up the task of constantly distancing ourselves from a violent and dangerous ideology that is precisely the sort of model we are fighting against." At the end of the day, Ouinissi says, the term "Muslim democrats" more usefully communicates the positive connotations of what she claims Ennahda has been "trying to accomplish since the beginning"—namely, "reconciling Islam and democracy in the Arab world." As I have discussed elsewhere, overblown statements regarding Ennahda's 10th Congress—indicating that Ennahda completely severed the relationship between religion and politics, or that the phrase "Muslim democrat" represents an about-face in how the party already conceived itself—are exactly that: overblown.[10] A variety of rationales rooted in Ennahda's history—in conjunction with a long process of debate between and among Ennahda's base and leadership—helped the party support the congress's changes. In general, nahdawis see these changes not as self-contradictory or as a tactical form of *taqiyya* (religiously sanctioned lying), but as consonant with the party's history and overall approach to Islamism—or, as it would like its critics to see it, Muslim democracy.[11]

In closing, the "Tunisianness" or "Tunisification" of Ennahda's trajectory should be of great interest to scholars. How did the influence of both traditional and reformist Zaytouna thinkers, including Tahar Ben Achour, shape Ennahda's early *halaqat* (religious discussion circles) and philosophical orientation? Which nahdawis first sought to rehabilitate more controversial reformist thinkers like famed Tunisian women's rights advocate Tahar Hadad, when, and why? How exactly did Ennahda come to acquire the reputation—shared among many of its secularly oriented domestic critics—of being a non-Tunisian movement oriented towards the Muslim Brotherhood or, even more radically, to the rigidity of Gulf Wahhabism, and how much of that reputation was fairly earned? How do we reconcile such critiques with the reality that Ennahda boasts the broadest and deepest core constituency of any political party in Tunisia? Each of these questions would make the topic of an excellent thesis, and they represent precisely the sorts of questions that historians interested in Tunisian Islamism, or in what we might call the "nationalization" of Islamist movements more broadly, should be asking.

Ennahda's 10th Congress and Ounissi's contribution to this project, which presaged it, offer fascinating windows into a moment of party normalization and nationalization—snapshots that importantly illuminate, too, the ways Islamist movements, and confessional or ostracized movements more broadly, seek to build legitimacy and cultivate trust in transitioning democracies.

15

Is the Crackdown on the Muslim Brotherhood Pushing the Group Toward Violence?

Ammar Fayed, Muslim Brotherhood

Editor's Note: Ammar Fayed is a Muslim Brotherhood youth activist and Istanbul-based researcher. This is translated from the original Arabic.

The military coup of July 2013 forced the Muslim Brotherhood to retreat to a climate of secrecy after the group had spent just a year working openly and in power. The authorities soon designated it as a terrorist organization and banned around 1,200 of the civil institutions affiliated with the group or its members, to say nothing of the thousands killed and imprisoned. The Brotherhood was left with no other option but to protest in a climate characterized by exclusion and McCarthyism.

This chapter discusses the effect of this unprecedented security campaign on the group's ideology and its internal decision-making processes. This is an important topic to explore especially after the arrest of the group's most influential leaders and the prevailing state of uncertainty in the region. Violence, whether from the state or from armed militias, has become the dominant political language in the nations that experienced Arab revolutions, with the possible exception of Tunisia (which itself has not been spared from growing terrorist threats). Even so, I argue here that the likelihood of the Muslim Brotherhood resorting to violence in Egypt is less than what many observers believe. Much of this has to do with the current structure of the organization and the model of thought

244

and culture that has governed it for decades. This, however, is not inconsistent with the increased possibilities that a not-insignificant segment of
members and supporters will resort to responding to the state's violence
with violence, whether on an individual, decentralized level or by joining more violent groups such as Sinai Province or Al-Murabiteen, or
even by joining the ongoing wars in Syria and Iraq.

THE SOCIAL AND THE POLITICAL: RETURNING TO THE FIRST FOUNDING

Since its formation, the Muslim Brotherhood has primarily been a
social movement, whose program depends on effecting social change
as a foundation and a condition for political change. Therefore, Hassan
al-Banna was concerned with first changing and reforming the social
order before changing the political order, as changing the latter was
contingent upon reforming the former. As a result, attention was primarily directed to the *ummah* rather than "the authority."[1]

This is one of the fundamental issues that confronts any researcher
or historian writing about the Muslim Brotherhood. Certainly, Hassan
al-Banna sought large-scale political change and was not satisfied with
religious preaching and fighting against moral deviations within society. However, political reform, from his point of view, was not possible
without changing the conditions of society itself, as he considered the
political system (the ruling authority) a natural result of the state of
society. Therefore, when he founded the Muslim Brotherhood in 1928,
his focus was solely on societal conditions and completely avoided any
political participation. The first internal by-laws of the Brotherhood,
issued in 1930, state that the group is not involved in politics. Article
2 states that "this group shall not become involved in political affairs,
whatever they may be." Article 15 emphasizes non-engagement in
political affairs during the group's meetings. Even more notable is the
fact that Article 42, which sets the mechanism for amending the by-
laws, completely forbids changing some of the articles, including the
aforementioned Article 2, which prohibits the group from engaging in
political work.[2]

With these regulations in mind, the goals of the organization are
limited to the social and moral sphere. This includes spreading Islamic

teachings, combating illiteracy, raising awareness on healthcare (especially in the villages), fighting the scourges of society such as drugs and prostitution, and remedying economic crises through preaching and guidance. Accordingly, the group's activities centered on opening schools, holding lectures, and establishing headquarters for the organization in the various provinces.

However, priorities changed. In the opening of the first issue of *al-Natheer* magazine in May 1938, Hassan al-Banna declared:

> Until now, brothers, you have not opposed any party or organization, nor have you joined them ... but today you will strongly oppose all of them, in power and outside of it, if they do not acquiesce and adopt the teachings of Islam as a model that they will abide by and work for.... There shall be either loyalty or animosity.[3]

Banna was not especially clear in defining his next steps, and, as a result, the reality of his vision—and the best ways to achieve it—remain contested. Banna mobilized the masses to build a strong social and religious base, and over the years, he began to mobilize this base politically. This manifested itself in a number of ways, such as forming groups within the military, judiciary, and police that were loyal to the Brotherhood. Another example includes creating the Special Military Apparatus in the 1940s, which was perceived as a possible threat to the regime.

In Banna's imagination, did the Brotherhood's ultimate goal necessitate political rule after gaining a broad societal mandate? In other words, was building a wide social base merely a means to the end of gaining political power? This may not be as far-fetched as one might think, especially given that Hassan al-Banna described the "stages of *da'wa* [religious education and preaching]" as first, defining the idea and spreading it; second, selecting supporters and members to form a strong base for the organization; and finally, "implementation," a nebulous term that has perplexed insiders and outsiders alike. Banna did not elaborate on what he meant by "implementation." Confusion abounds since he firmly rejected political party work and was not enthusiastic about class revolutions built on favoring one class over the other. However, he also did not reject the idea of revolting against governments that did not

respond to the aspirations of the people. He affirmed that if constructive criticism and advice to rulers did not lead to change, then other
viable options ranged from the active repudiation of the ruling authority
(*khal'*) to separating and disengaging from it (*ib'ad*).[4]

However, the group adopted Hassan al-Banna's discourse of social
change, rather than direct political change. This discourse stressed
that building a broad base that believed in Banna's ideas was the only
path to building a political regime that would (eventually) implement
them. The Brotherhood's rejection of revolutionary change was further entrenched after its painful experience under Nasser. The organization was always ready to offer political concessions in exchange for
greater freedom to practice its social and religious activities, believing
this to be the investment needed to achieve any true political change.
Hassan al-Banna himself reinforced this trend when he and 16 others
withdrew their candidacies for the 1942 parliamentary elections in
exchange for greater leeway in carrying out the group's religious and
social work.

In 2004, the then General Guide Mohammed Mahdi Akef
announced that the Brotherhood was embarking on a new phase under
the banner of "Openness to Society." Internally, this signaled a progression up the theoretical ladder of priorities set by Hassan al-Banna (the
individual—the family—the society—the state—"mentorship" [*ustad-
hiyya*] of the world). This new phase was characterized by widespread
competitive political participation and unprecedented engagement in
the public sphere.

The limited emphasis on political activity inside the organization
is reflected in the structure of its central technical committees. The
committees are divided into the following: the Political Committee,
the Professionals Committee, the Workers Committee, the Students
Committee, the Sisters Committee, the Charity Committee, the
Committee for Spreading the Islamic Dawa, and the Cubs Committee
(for students who have not yet reached university). All of these committees, with the exception of the Political Committee, are concerned
with directly communicating religious and moral messages to different
segments of society. These committees did not adopt political messages
except perhaps during the periods of electoral campaigning, which the
group went through only a few times during the 30 years that preceded

the January 2011 revolution. These periods were always viewed within the group as the exception rather than the rule.

Did this change after the revolution? Certainly. There is a growing feeling that it's futile to believe that broad societal change is necessary before the ruling regime can be changed. Social change is a continuous process that cannot be measured easily. In addition, the state's centralized ideological apparatus has the ability to manipulate mass public opinion.[5] In other words, the capability of any social organization to mobilize the masses remains limited in the face of a powerful state. The centralization of the modern state—particularly in authoritarian regimes—furthered its dominance of the public sphere, including in education, media, and religious institutions. The Brotherhood experienced this first-hand during President Morsi's rule. The group found it difficult to compete with the official bureaucratic organs of the government. For instance, Egypt's gargantuan state-owned media was able to influence the Brotherhood's own constituency, despite having been exposed to the group's political and religious messages for years.

Despite this, it's important to highlight that the revolution inspired a renewed confidence in the viability of civil and nonviolent approaches to confronting authoritarian systems of control. Historically, emergent social and political organizations aiming to mobilize public opinion against the regime would be easily squashed in their infancy.

But after the revolution, a growing number of Brotherhood members, particularly youth activists, became convinced that achieving "revolutionary" goals like regime change could not be achieved through the comparatively feeble means of "gradual reform" suggested by the movement's founder. Banna was inspired by previous calls for Islamic reform that predate the modern state, when state–society relations were based on completely different power dynamics.

Going forward, the Brotherhood is unlikely to set aside societal reform to focus on capturing the state through political campaigning. Rather, internal debates within the organization will lead to *limiting* the group's direct participation in political activity. The Brotherhood is more likely to restore its fundamental role as a social and religious reform movement, as I discuss in the following section.

THE "PRIMARY GROUP"

Hassan al-Banna worked to promote the model of the "primary group,"[6] a vanguard that would provide the emotional support needed to integrate people into social and public life. The term "primary group" was coined by the sociologist Charles Horton Cooley to refer to a group characterized by intimate, face-to-face association, and cooperation. This produces strong ties of loyalty and solidarity.[7] This group, in the context of the Muslim Brotherhood, was to become a mediator between the individual and society. To maintain the nascent Brotherhood's cohesiveness, Banna's model emphasized the building and fostering of emotional and spiritual ties between members as much as it emphasized the role of social and economic ties.

Discussing the importance of spiritual bonds in the Brotherhood is beyond the scope of this chapter. But it is important to highlight that Hassan al-Banna grew up among the ranks of the Sufi orders (specifically the Hasafi order). He gained insights on the importance of spiritual ties in strengthening the structure of a social organization. Later, Banna would develop this philosophy and place it within a more cohesive and holistic model. Through the system of *usras*, or "families" of 5 to 10 members, he was able to strengthen the internal ties between individuals in the organization. This is confirmed by Waheed Abdul Mageed, who argues that, while Banna's Sufi tendencies were not apparent later in his life, they found new expression in the consciously cultivated spiritual bonds built between members of the Brotherhood.[8]

The three pillars of the *usra* as outlined by Banna emphasize the fraternal connections between members: getting to know one other (*ta'aruf*), understanding one another (*tafahum*), and looking out for one another (*takaful*). For decades, and to this very day, the Brotherhood has featured teachings and practices concerned with deepening the spiritual connection between members (*rabita*), including through cultural programs that focus on Islamic concepts such as "brotherhood," "preferring others over the self," "the love of God," and so on. Another example is that of the daily "Bonding Litany" (*wird al-rabita*), a prayer recited daily by Brotherhood members. The word *wird* in Arabic, translated here as "litany," refers to a set combination of supplications, specific selections from the Quran, and other selected religious passages.

This litany is a fixed daily ritual in which the individual vows to pray for his fellow Brothers, and to remember them and the spiritual connection that binds them together, even if he doesn't know them by name.

Since its founding, the notion of "comprehensiveness" (*shumuliya*) has also been an essential feature of the Brotherhood. The group's adoption of a comprehensive approach is reflected in its religious, educational, social, developmental, economic, and political activities. Hassan al-Banna envisioned Islam as a holistic system dealing with all aspects of life, one that leaves little room for modern notions of the secular. According to Banna, Islam's comprehensive nature does not mean that every aspiring Islamic organization must cater to all spheres of life. Yet for his organization, Banna explicitly desired to structure it in a way that would reflect this comprehensiveness.

This particular aspiration of the Brotherhood has generated quite a lot of analysis and speculation. It is unlikely that the organization will abandon its conviction that Islam is a comprehensive system. The Brotherhood views Islam's rulings and teachings as relevant to both private and public life, as well as in the economic and political spheres. But does the Brotherhood *as an organization* have to be comprehensive? Modern life has become exceedingly complex. The increased specialization of knowledge has only accelerated with the advent of the modern state and its ability to mobilize unprecedented power and resources. In short, is it better to be a jack of all trades yet a master of none?

The Brotherhood's brief experience of being in power and its subsequent removal by military coup has served to strengthen the idea of separating the Brotherhood's role as a social institution from its role as a political force. The two functions now operate in tension and even opposition, and the Brotherhood's traditional practice of grouping them together has only served to weaken both. The notion of Islam as "comprehensive" can still be maintained as an ideal, while organizationally one may choose to focus on certain aspects of this comprehensiveness (such as social, religious, or cultural programming) and eschew others (such as forming a political party or directly participating in elections). In this way, the group would be able to effectively leverage a strong and principled constituency to influence the political arena. In hindsight, it appears that the Brotherhood's direct participation in competitive politics has done substantial damage to decades of social and religious institution building.

Despite its problematic aspects, focusing on Islam's "comprehensiveness" has made the Brotherhood's activities quite diverse, providing it a number of ways to connect with varied sectors of society and helping it to maintain an impressive membership base. It was these myriad factors acting in concert that carried the Brotherhood to power in the 2011 elections, and *not* its reputation as a trustworthy and experienced political party, as is normally the case. Despite criticisms within the Brotherhood of its political performance, the diversity of its areas of focus and its intertwining of social, religious, and spiritual activities have continued to motivate members to work toward the realization of Hassan al-Banna's vision.

THE STATE AND THE ORGANIZATION: THE STRUGGLE OVER THE BROTHERHOOD'S SOCIAL BASE

During the Muslim Brotherhood's second phase (from the mid-1970s until around 1987), the leadership introduced several core features, such as increased centralization (to which a greater atmosphere of secrecy was added, contrary to Hassan al-Banna's organization, which worked as an official, known group). They also ratcheted up the group's activities in the political and economic spheres. Moreover, they set to work on the construction of a broad network of social institutions, including schools, service projects, charitable groups, and hospitals.

These changes produced a complex institutional structure that prioritized more direct engagement with society and lent itself to a heightened focus on a more "comprehensive" organizational model as described earlier. This produced both a strong interconnected organizational structure and a wide social base that could be relied upon to support the group during its intermittent conflict with the state in the years of Mubarak's rule.

The 2013 coup sought to eliminate these two sources of the group's power and resilience. Events first kicked off with an aggressive anti-Brotherhood media campaign, designed to impair the performance of President Morsi and his government, isolate the Brotherhood from its social base, and remove any excuse the general populace may have had to maintain sympathies with the organization. By the end of June 2013, the state succeeded in "factionalizing the Brotherhood"—portraying them as fifth columnists separate from the rest of the population with self-serving goals. The message was clear, that the Brotherhood didn't have Egypt's best interests at heart, only its own. This was followed by a rapacious security campaign that continues to the present day. Many have fled or otherwise gone into hiding, including most of the members of the Guidance Bureau, around half of the Shura Council, those in charge of the Brotherhood's administrative offices in the provinces, and most leaders of the Brotherhood's Freedom and Justice Party.

The targeting of the Brotherhood's social base required eliminating the group's civil and economic organizations. The state officially announced that the assets of 1,370 individuals had been confiscated, along with the assets of 81 companies, including 19 currency-exchange companies. A total of 1,125 associations, 105 schools, and 43 hospitals were confiscated, in addition to the Brotherhood's medical association, which has 27 branches, as well as the two branches of the Rabaa Adawiya Association.[9]

A widespread campaign of arrests, resulting in the apprehension of over 40,000 people, occurred alongside a vengeful security crackdown, which included acts of torture, public killings, and sexual assault. All these actions have made violent action easier for Brotherhood members to countenance. Violence found easier justification in a regional context beset by instability, civil war, and the success of fanatical Islamist groups such as the Islamic State.

A CLIMATE OF VIOLENCE AND CHAOS

The armed Islamist group Ansar Bayt al-Maqdis (ABM) strengthened its influence in the Sinai after the military coup. In its calculus, the collapse of Islamists' gamble on democracy proved the impossibility of change through normal politics. In short, it was a victory for those advocating force as the only effective route to change. This small group in the Sinai exploited events to press the need for directly confronting the state, and was able to attract members from outside the Sinai. The rise of the Islamic State and the subsequent military campaign in the

Sinai against ABM led to additional popular support for the group, which would go on to formally affiliate itself with the Islamic State, rebranding itself as "Sinai Province." This compelled Hisham Ashmawy, a prominent ABM leader and former officer in the elite Egyptian Special Operations "Thunderbolt" Force, to break off and form the group Al-Murabiteen.[10] Ashmawy's actions opened a wider arena for attracting members from Cairo and the Nile Delta.[11]

At the same time that Sinai jihadists were escalating their activities and seeking to expand their reach into the heart of the country, Egypt's largest civic Islamic organization was being crushed. The Brotherhood was cast out from all the "pillars of democracy"—the parliament, the presidency, and the constitution. In this context—and after the worst instance of mass killings in Egypt's modern history—it is not a surprise that armed groups sought to capitalize on these events and use them as a pretext for violent action. Pointing to the Brotherhood's aborted reign as evidence, militant groups argued that democracy would never permit an Islamist victory, even if fairly earned. It became simple to paint the picture of a supposed "war on Islam" that could appeal to disillusioned individuals.

There are a number of cases where members of or those close to the Brotherhood and members of revolutionary Salafi groups chose to take up arms within the ranks of the Islamic State's Sinai Province. A small number traveled to fight in Syria for armed opposition groups. Their letters and other statements reveal the degree of hostility toward the Brotherhood's peaceful, gradualist program and its disgraceful "surrender" to the state during the Rabaa massacre, as well as in the cases of rape of female prisoners. Sinai Province's media arms churned out messages directly aimed at young Islamists, particularly members of the Brotherhood, lambasting the ineffectiveness of nonviolence and democracy, and advocating jihad and armed resistance against the state as the only viable path forward.[12]

IS VIOLENCE THE BROTHERHOOD'S INEVITABLE CHOICE?

The University of Louisville's Steven Brooke, one of the contributing authors to *Rethinking Political Islam*, argues that the restriction of the

Brotherhood's social activities and the shuttering of the group's service networks have left the organization with only one choice: holding demonstrations. He argues, moreover, that demonstrations on their own are unlikely to produce a resolution to the conflict. Stuck in an organizational holding pattern, the appeal of violence will likely grow. Additionally, the destruction of the group's social service infrastructure strengthens the attraction of other, more violent models, such as those of the Islamic State or al-Qaeda in Yemen. Despite the strength of this hypothesis (particularly its compelling claim that violent approaches may find supporters among broad segments of society), there are a number of factors that limit the applicability of Brooke's argument to today's Muslim Brotherhood.

First, one's motivation for joining the Brotherhood cannot be reduced to a desire to be involved in social activism. There are any number of complex motivations that drive an individual's desire to be a member of the Brotherhood. Eliminating one aspect of the group's activities does not necessarily mean that members will look for alternatives, whether a violent approach that rejects the state or one accepting of state authority. A field study that I conducted from October to December 2013 made clear that, for many members of the Brotherhood, the top priority was not social work. Rather, it involved providing support and care to the families of the victims of the coup and those imprisoned, as well continuing protests against the coup.[13]

In the current environment, it will be difficult to pursue social activities for a number of reasons. First, Brotherhood members are subject to far-reaching surveillance by state security, making it almost impossible to carry out any activities unnoticed. Second, the group's service networks and other social institutions have been almost entirely shuttered by the regime. Third, due to the large number of people who have been arrested, forcibly disappeared, or made to flee the country, it has become necessary to focus internal efforts on supporting those bearing the brunt of repression inside of Egypt, as well as on activities aimed at delegitimizing the coup. Though there has been no decision to suspend the group's religious or social activities, they are simply not the priority. They have instead been left to individuals and smaller, more local units to decide what headway can realistically be made in the current environment.

Second, there is no doubt that the line between peaceful revolutionary protest and the use of more violent means is sometimes "blurry," as described by Steven Brooke. However, more than three years have passed since the Rabaa massacre, and the predominant trend within the Brotherhood (and the anti-coup movement in general) remains committed to peaceful political action. All the groups that have tried to adopt some form of violence continue to be marginal with limited appeal. The adoption of violence clearly contradicts the reigning cultural and educational model within the Brotherhood. It is of course true that, theoretically, any dominant culture can undergo change, but this requires a conducive environment. For example, there were ample opportunities in the 1960s to adapt the group's culture in response to Nasserist oppression, but the Brotherhood leadership was able to successfully challenge those pressures and maintain the group's positions against violence and *takfir* (accusing a fellow Muslim of apostasy).[14] The current debate inside the group has provoked some similar responses. When rumors began circulating that some leaders were moving toward violent options in their opposition to the coup, this was met with broad rejection within the group, both inside and outside the country. Later, it became clear that the question of violence is not, in fact, the central dispute. Rather, disputes appear more related to a clash between a traditional leadership unwilling to give up their control of the Brotherhood and a new group of leaders that came to prominence after the coup that rejects the "old" administrative model and seeks to implement structural changes. Change in the organization's culture as a result of the military coup and its aftermath is possible, but, at the time of writing, the basic requirements for such a shift aren't present. One such requirement is the emergence of legitimate and charismatic leadership with a clear strategy and vision to manage internal conflicts within the organization.

A legitimate, charismatic leadership is necessary to effect radical change of this kind, not only on an intellectual level but also on a practical one. In a centralized, conservative organization like the Brotherhood, reshaping the organization's structure and hierarchy is difficult to say the least. Decentralization within the Brotherhood has been limited to organizational and administrative activities and the allocation of resources. Political decision making, or the crafting of a vision for handling internal conflict, remains extremely centralized. One reason for the recent exacerbation of internal divisions is the fact that most who remain from the old Guidance Bureau are insistent that major decisions must remain solely the purview of the acting General Guide Mahmoud Ezzat—a position accepted by all but one member of the Guidance Bureau (Dr. Mohamed Kamal, killed by Egyptian police on October 4, 2016) and a number of recently elected provincial leaders. Likewise, the Brotherhood's Shura Council still maintains a palpable level of administrative control, despite the majority being taken under arrest or otherwise prevented from engaging in organizational activity.

The Brotherhood has demonstrated a considerable level of flexibility in adopting different methods under difficult circumstances to achieve its priorities (protesting the coup and taking care of families of those killed or imprisoned). However, the most important political decisions, the setting of overarching organizational strategies, and the management of financial resources within the group remain highly centralized. It should be noted that many older leaders who have not been arrested have been willing to give substantial roles to younger members. However, these roles are confined to mid-level administrative positions and seats on technical committees. In effect, the Brotherhood's centralized character remains, making it extremely difficult to effect major changes to its intellectual trajectory.

Third, other models for social service provision do not necessarily represent alternatives to the Brotherhood, as the group adopts a very specific approach to social work. The Brotherhood in Egypt considers social activities to be one of its primary roles and has historically carried them out transparently and under the authority and laws of the government. On the one hand, the Brotherhood, from an Islamic perspective, sees social work as a necessity in and of itself. Social work builds solidarity with local communities and is connected to Islamic teachings on showing kindness to the poor and the downtrodden. Yet on the other hand, the Brotherhood is well aware that its social activities help it achieve a broader reach within the country and strengthen its social base. In contrast, armed Islamist groups are not motivated to carry out social activities in cooperation with the state, since their goal is to bring about the state's demise. As a result, these groups do not undertake social work to win over constituents. Rather, they enter into such projects as a "ruling authority" that seeks to present a model for "Islamic rule," which comes about after taking control of certain areas or when the state's hold on these areas weakens. This is the current situation in the Sinai, in parts of Yemen, and in the territory controlled by the Islamic State. However, where the state is clearly present, such groups have little interest in the provision of social services, as the elimination of the state through armed action takes priority.

The difference between these two models is fundamental. The Brotherhood, like other Islamic organizations such as al-Gam'iyya al-Shar'iyya and Ansar al-Sunna, provides social and charitable services for goals primarily related to Islamic values, which encourage caring for the poor, the weak, and the hungry. Additionally, the Brotherhood's social and charitable activities have elicited increased popular support for the group's political activities. As Steven Brooke discusses in his chapter, this model carries out social services through official institutions subject to the law and operates under the authority of the state. The other "model," meanwhile, carries out social services only to further the direct replacement of an absent or failed state with "Islamic rule."

Of course, one could argue that the Brotherhood is, in a similar but less confrontational way, trying to present an attractive picture of its own vision for Islamic rule. However, the alternative it seeks to establish is a new political regime with a different ruling elite, but still emerging from the extant structures of the current state. In contrast, armed groups do not recognize the legitimacy of the state at all, and therefore do not concern themselves with social service provision unless they are able to replace the state's authority with their own. Only then would these armed groups—acting as the ruling power—exert their authority in all areas of governance, including social welfare.

This does not rule out the possibility that the harshness of the political climate in Egypt may compel more individuals or unorganized groups to embrace violence. Armed groups may exploit the current environment to attract new members from beyond the Sinai, into the Nile Valley and Delta. However, as discussed earlier, this expansion would not be based around the goal of providing social services. Rather, these armed groups' top priorities are explicitly political and related to rejecting the current regime, and are powered by a belief in the impossibility of challenging it through peaceful means.

My argument leads me to an additional conclusion. Due to continued oppression from above without any serious prospects of political organization from below (what Shadi Hamid has called "a collective loss of faith in politics"[16]), as well as the built-in organizational red lines mentioned earlier, it is unlikely that the Brotherhood will make a turn to violence from within. However, all this pressure leaves space open for new groups to emerge that could polarize Brotherhood members— especially its youth—towards violence. This has been partially born out already with the rise of self-styled revolutionary resistance groups such as "Hasm" and "Lewaa al-Thawra."[16]

AN UNCERTAIN FUTURE

The number and size of Brotherhood-linked demonstrations have greatly decreased over the past two years for various reasons, including the violent security response to protests, widespread arrests, and mass prosecutions by kangaroo courts. This has led tens of thousands of people to become either prisoners or outlaws forced to flee their homes, or even Egypt altogether. Likewise, the long-term continuation of protests requires a clear political vision, especially since the cost of participating in a demonstration could be death or years of imprisonment. Generic slogans and platitudes, however enthusiastic, will not do the trick.

The Brotherhood has yet to offer an alternative strategy to protesting and mobilizing opinion against the regime. Many in the group wager that the revolutionary moment has not passed, as the factors that inspired the revolution have yet to be addressed (poverty, unemployment, a lack of social justice, oppression by the security forces, and so on). Therefore, the thinking is that continued Brotherhood demonstrations, despite smaller numbers, can still encourage others and help them maintain a mindset of protest until a new spark takes hold, snapping the spell of fear and frustration that has settled over the supporters of the 2011 revolution.

This theory is plausible, since the revolution's initial impetus did not come from the Brotherhood and was driven instead by years of built-up grievances in the population at large. However, reproducing such a mobilization in the face of the security force's unprecedented repression will prove difficult. First, it requires building alliances based around broad demands, slogans, and programs that go beyond the tired dichotomies of the Brotherhood versus the Egyptian military, or a legitimately elected government versus a regime that came to power though a coup. In other words, the animating premise of the Brotherhood's continuing protests and demonstrations is unlikely to appeal to wider audiences or recreate the conditions of the January 2011 revolution. As long as the Brotherhood's political imagination is unable to overcome the mind-set of "coup versus legitimacy" and develop an alternative political discourse that meets the demands of the disaffected social segments that ignited the revolution, then the Brotherhood itself may be an obstacle in efforts to build a new culture of protest. Such attitudes will hinder attempts to build broader political alliances between the various non-Brotherhood forces that also reject the military coup and Sissi's rule.

Likewise, the Muslim Brotherhood has not been able to adopt a clear vision, nor does it have clear answers when it comes to the possibility of coexisting with the current Egyptian state. The Sissi regime has taken a hostile position toward the Brotherhood through every means available to it, from the police to the judiciary and the bureaucracy. If coexistence is not possible, does the group have recourse to any alternative scenario? Does the group truly seek, through its anti-coup protest activities, to exert pressure with the end goal of reaching some sort of modus vivendi? What would be the contours and limits of such a settlement, and what are the concessions that the group can give without damaging its internal cohesion and morale?

The current internal conflict within the Brotherhood mainly revolves around phrases such as "leadership change," "institutionalization," "amending the bylaws," and "rejecting individualism," but more conceptual and foundational questions and discussions over the group's long-term vision are often absent from the debate. Some hypothesize that leadership change—if it occurs—is what will lead to a more substantive internal discussion on these issues, as a new leadership would be more keen on reversing the current state of intellectual stagnation.

In any case, attempting to categorize the different trends within the Brotherhood by age or generation will be of limited use. Though it may not seem immediately obvious, particular ideas do not remain the single purview of a specific age group. Different points of view find supporters among all age groups and at all organizational levels.

As always, there are those who adopt a radical vision of the current struggle with the Egyptian regime, considering it to be a zero-sum conflict in which there can be no compromise. There are also those who are more willing to offer concessions with the aim of coming to some sort of deal, which would redraw the relationship between the Brotherhood and the state. However, there is unanimous agreement within the Brotherhood that it is impossible to achieve any meaningful progress as long as Sissi remains in power. It is very unlikely—at least in my opinion—that this basic fact will change.

In my view, the coup and the unexpected repression that followed it produced a change in the nature of the conflict at hand and complicated opportunities for compromise with the regime. The conflict has shifted from a political conflict between the Brotherhood and the ruling regime into a conflict between the Brotherhood and the idea of the Egyptian state itself. This "transition" occurred after the active involvement of the state's various institutions—such as the police, the military, the judiciary, and the bureaucracy—which had not been directly engaged in the conflict with the Brotherhood since the group's re-establishment in the 1970s. Additionally, for the first time in its history, the Egyptian Coptic Church became directly involved in the state's war on the Brotherhood and the Islamists. This has made church leaders, in the view of many, abettors to the killings and ongoing repression perpetrated by the authorities after the coup.

These complications require a comprehensive settlement, and not a token one. Likewise, they necessitate painful concessions and defined commitments. At this point, however, there is no justification or capacity for either side to do these things.

CONCLUSION

Why hasn't the Muslim Brotherhood in Egypt resorted to violence? Examining this question can lead to a better understanding of the consequences of the ongoing unprecedented security crackdown. This chapter has used a sociocultural approach that acknowledges the complicated relationship between individual members of the Brotherhood and the character of the organization as a whole, which, on the whole, still does not lean towards violence. I have also relied on the definition of the Brotherhood and its various roles, as understood by its members. The group fulfills different roles and carries out diverse activities to meet the needs and interests of its members. This is what gives the group the ability to maintain a portion of its internal operations even if its external activities directed toward society are suspended for the time being.

This is not to say that the Brotherhood will be able to contain the anger of all of its supporters, or even that it represents the best available model for those Islamists who reject the military coup. Armed groups are still very much able to capitalize on this delicate political moment. The military coup affected the Brotherhood in ways that could substantially change the face of the organization in the years to come. This could open the door for a redefinition of the nature of its political, social, and religious roles.

Can the Brotherhood coexist with the current state, regardless of whether Sissi stays or goes? Answering this question is the Brotherhood's central challenge. Until now, the group has not formulated a clear political vision. Nor does it have the tools to remove the military from its political calculus. Therefore, the Brotherhood must work with other forces that reject the policies of the current regime. Such an alliance can form a broad national front whose goals and programs are based on the priorities of the revolution at large. This national front could also delineate pragmatic proposals and plans to coexist with the political and economic influence of the military for the foreseeable future.

Some Brotherhood members have grappled with these questions and presented various proposals, but the group is yet to hold an internal dialogue to develop and adopt a unified position. Likewise, military leaders have not shown any inclination to reach a settlement with the Brotherhood, the conclusion of which could end their reliance on continuing repression. This makes it likely that the status quo will persist, with all its tragic consequences.

16

The Islamist Experience in Pakistan

Asif Luqman Qazi, Jamaat-e-Islami

Editor's Note: Asif Luqman Qazi is a senior figure in Jamaat-e-Islami.

In his chapter, Matthew Nelson has attempted to cover a multitude of different organizations. To focus the discussion, I will elaborate my views on Jamaat-e-Islami Pakistan, from my perspective as a senior figure in the movement. Jamaat-e-Islami ("Jamaat," or the JI) is a mainstream political organization that represents a legalist approach to change. This was the original framework that one traditionally referred to when speaking about "political Islam." Though this chapter is focused on Jamaat, one may attempt to draw conclusions regarding political Islam more generally.

Jamaat-e-Islami Pakistan is distinct among contemporary Islamic movements in that it had strong democratic traditions right from its inception in 1941; has a written constitution to govern its organization; and has always operated within the framework of the country's constitution. It seeks to bring about societal transformation is through appealing to the intellect, organizing communities, and rallying masses around its program—just like any other political party in the East or West. It believes that Islam provides a universal and dynamic vision of life that is valid and relevant for human welfare in all times and places.

Jamaat adopted the four-point program presented by its founder, Abul Ala Maududi, soon after Pakistan came into existence in 1947. This program encompasses all its activities. They are: reforming the life

262

and mind at the individual level; organizing, motivating, and training virtuous individuals; reforming society more broadly; and reforming the government and political structure. From the beginning, Jamaat made clear that it would operate through legal means and would not resort to secret or underground activities to achieve its objectives. It was in this backdrop that Maududi, along with 33 other prominent Islamic scholars, took a keen interest in the development of Pakistan's first constitution. These leading scholars—belonging to all recognized schools of thought in Islam—unanimously adopted a 22-point char- ter to serve as an Islamic basis for the constitution of the country.[1] Maududi was subsequently invited by Pakistan's founding father, Muhammad Ali Jinnah, to deliver five lectures on the foundations of an Islamic system of life. These lectures were broadcast from offi- cial radio channels and elaborated the social, political, and economic underpinnings of a Muslim society that the newly established state was to adopt.

THE INFLUENCE OF ISLAM IN PAKISTAN'S FOUNDING

This invitation by Jinnah was in keeping with his vision to establish a system based on Islamic ideology. Although there are elements in Pakistan that would like to paint Jinnah with a secular brush, the fact of the matter is that he made numerous speeches between 1940 and 1947 where he assured the Muslim masses that the Pakistan he envisaged was an Islamic one. For example, in one of his speeches he says, "Pakistan does not mean just independence and sovereignty. It means [an] Islamic ideology that we have to safeguard; it has been conveyed to us as a valuable gift and a treasure."[2] On November 2, 1942, while addressing students at Muslim University in Aligarh, in reference to the proposal to partition the Indian subcontinent, he said: "Let me live according to my history in the light of Islam, my tradition, culture, and language, and you do the same in your zones [of activity]."[3] His unequivocal resolve reflected the aspirations of the Muslims of the subcontinent, who had offered sacrifices for a homeland where they could fashion their lives according to their faith. The first prime minister of Pakistan, Liaqat Ali Khan, spoke to the Constituent Assembly upon the adoption of the Objectives Resolution. Named for how it lays out the objectives for the future constitution of Pakistan, the Objectives Resolution was adopted in 1949. On the occasion, Khan said:

> I would like to remind the house that the Father of the Nation, Quaid-e-Azam [Muhammad Ali Jinnah], gave expression of his feelings on this matter on many an occasion, and his views were endorsed by the nation in unmistakable terms. Pakistan was founded because the Muslims of this subcontinent wanted to build up their lives in accordance with the teachings and traditions of Islam.[4]

Within this Islamic framework, the Objectives Resolution proclaims Pakistan a democracy with equal rights for all citizens. It pays special attention to safeguarding the rights of non-Muslim minorities. What this means in essence is that although all citizens have equal rights, the state's ideology will remain Islamic.

What proponents of secularism in Pakistan have presented from other speeches of Jinnah is in fact a negation of theocracy, not Islam. It is important to understand this difference.[5] There is no concept of a formalized clergy in Islam with the function of serving as an intermediary between God and man. Islamic principles are liberating and emancipatory, and uphold a form of government that is participatory, not autocratic. This was something that was very clear to both of Pakistan's founding fathers, Mohamed Iqbal and Jinnah. In fact, the Constituent Assembly of Pakistan presented a workable model for a modern Islamic nation-state under the influence of the narrative developed by Iqbal and Jinnah. At the 1930 Muslim League convention held in Allahabad, Iqbal said: "What, then, is the problem and its implications? Is religion a private affair? Would you like to see Islam as a moral and political ideal, meeting the same fate in the world of Islam as Christianity has already met in Europe?"[6] Additionally, Iqbal's poetry in Urdu and Persian is an elaborate testimony to his vision of Islam as a comprehensive way of life, one inclusive of politics and governance alike.

In his message to the American people, Jinnah said:

> The constitution of Pakistan has yet to be framed by [the] Pakistan Constituent Assembly. I do not know what the ultimate shape of this constitution is going to be, but I am sure that it will be of a democratic type, embodying the essential principles of Islam. Today, they

are as applicable in actual life as they were 1300 years ago. Islam and its idealism have taught us democracy. It has taught [the] equality of man, justice, and fair play to everybody. We are the inheritors of these glorious traditions and are fully alive to our responsibilities and obligations as framers of the future constitution of Pakistan.[7]

And in another speech to government functionaries on October 11, 1947, he stated:

The creation of a state of our own was a means to an end and not the end in itself. The idea was that we should have a state in which we could live and breathe as free men and which we could develop according to our own lights and culture, and where principles of Islamic social justice could find free play.[8]

The Muslims of the subcontinent remained masters of their own destiny for 800 years. They made up more than a quarter of its total population. With their large numbers, and owing to their distinct culture, civilizational heritage, patterns of social organization, and faith, they saw themselves not as a minority community, but as a nation in their own right. Accordingly, Jinnah supported the two-nation theory and the demand for a separate homeland for the Muslims of the subcontinent. The movement for Pakistan was preceded by several social movements spanning two centuries, searching for the soul of Muslim societal life within a broader community of faith and belonging. The educational movements of Deoband, Nadwatul Ulema, and Aligarh College were social expressions of this revivalist quest.

The separation of state and faith, or secularism, is a concept developed in the Western world by virtue of its own peculiar historical process. The West found renaissance and enlightenment by limiting what it considered an oppressive dogmatic theology that had become an obstacle to progress and development. Muslims, on the other hand, have a history contrary to this narrative. For them, faith itself was the source of enlightenment, renaissance, and progress. Their glory era—from the 7th century AD to the 18th century—was marked by a strict observance to their belief system. Enlightened by their faith, they expanded from the Prophet's city of Medina to three continents. They reached the zenith of knowledge, arts and sciences, warfare and statecraft, trade, industry, and agriculture, and produced a rich treasure of law and jurisprudence. As Israeli scholar Martin Kramer writes, "Had there been Nobel prizes in 1000, they would have gone almost exclusively to Moslems."[9]

Their civilizational progress has remained directly proportional to their observance of a dynamic faith, one that provided an enabling environment for advancement. Islam transformed their lives and introduced them to freedom, justice, equality, pluralism, tolerance, human dignity, ethics, and morality. They had a message that was not ethnic, divisive, or sectarian but appealed to all of humanity as one fraternity. Although the political form of this high moral ground was lost to hereditary dynasties 30 years after the death of the Prophet, these principles remained part of Muslim societies to various degrees for more than 1,000 years until their decay in the 19th century.

Today, the Islamic State is an expression of ignorance about, and not an observance of, those glorious traditions. The more Muslims deviated from their faith, the more socially primitive they became. The present-day decay of Muslims is a consequence of deviation from the political and social vision of human life offered up by Islam. Their conditions are further complicated by widespread poverty, illiteracy, ignorance, corruption, and the oppressive rule of an elite class often subservient to Western dominance. Despite these challenges, Islamist movements in particular, and Muslim societies in general, see a reversion to an Islamic ethos and worldview as a path to progress. In it they see not only a path for salvation in the hereafter but also remedies for their worldly woes. This sustained relevance of Islam to contemporary conditions, or "Islamic exceptionalism" as termed by Shadi Hamid, behooves observers of Muslim societies to cultivate deep insights not just into political Islam, but into Islam itself.[10]

ISLAM AND THE CONSTITUTION

Islamism in Pakistan has a history of harmony with constitutional and democratic processes. Jamaat, for one, does not demand any radical changes to the constitution of Pakistan. It is, in fact, the constitution's implementation in letter and spirit that Jamaat has always struggled for. Frequent military interventions have held the full force of the constitution in abeyance for about half of Pakistan's life as a country. Even those leaders who have been democratically elected have remained more focused on perpetuating their own rule than on functions of governance. Neglecting constitutional imperatives has fomented dissent and mistrust in the country. Had the government fulfilled its constitutional obligations toward the Islamic clauses of constitution, the narrative presented by militants might not have found an audience.

The constitution already has prescribed a framework for all state organs to function within the confines of principles of the Quran and Sunna. It approves of the advisory status of the Council of Islamic Ideology (CII) and the supremacy of parliament in enacting legislation. The CII is a constitutional body that advises the legislature on whether or not a particular piece of legislation is repugnant to Islam. It consists of Islamic scholars adhering to the major schools of thought, as well as technocrats. Over the past few decades, the CII has generated an enormous number of reports in response to parliamentary inquiries, but these reports failed to shape legislation due to government neglect. Jamaat is also more than content with the judiciary's final authority to interpret laws and the constitution. Despite the fact that Islamist parties have had very limited success in parliamentary elections in Pakistan, they have always accepted the results and conceded calmly. Their electoral failure has never wavered their commitment to legalist, constitutional, and gradualist approaches to bringing about political change. They have demonstrated pragmatism and flexibility, particularly during their forays into electoral alliances and coalition governments. Jamaat has remained a coalition partner with Nawaz Sharif's Pakistan Muslim League-Nawaz (PML-N) and was part of the Muttahida Majlis-e-Amal (MMA), an alliance of Islamic political parties that led regional governments in two provinces. It is currently a coalition partner with Imran Khan's Tehreek-e-Insaf Party (PTI) in Khyber Pakhtunkhwa province.

RELIGION AND "THE PURSUIT OF HAPPINESS"

It is essential to understand that Islam is referred to as a "faith" that encompasses the whole of life, and not as a "religion" that concerns itself with a limited set of rituals, ethics, and spirituality. In Pakistan, even non-Islamist or secular political parties acknowledge Islam as their *deen* (an all-encompassing way of life). Being a faith, Islam is very much concerned with both what is mundane and what is worldly. It is precisely through an engagement with worldly matters that it becomes practical and relevant, rather than an abstract theology. "Life, liberty, and the pursuit of happiness" is as much an Islamic phrase as it is an American one. But the pursuit of happiness has a different cast within an Islamic framework, far from the pursuit of worldly desires. A human being has spiritual and emotional needs apart from physical needs that contribute to his or her happiness. It should not, therefore, come as a surprise that Jamaat engages in politics and governance in addition to its social and religious activities.

Jamaat has been part of several administrations at the local and provincial levels and has contended with the challenges of governance, as well as issues of public welfare and accountability. For long stretches, Jamaat's mayors have led local bodies in Karachi, Pakistan's largest metropolitan city with a population of over 23 million, and have even earned appreciation from presidents hostile to the organization, such as Pervez Musharraf. The World Bank has acknowledged provincial ministers of Jamaat in Khyber Pakhtunkhwa province for their integrity and performance.[11] A whole host of issues make up its political agenda: education, health care, agriculture, youth employment, ensuring a continuous supply of electricity and other public utilities, and rooting out corruption.

There are divergent views among Jamaat members on the question of whether the organization should enter into coalitions with other parties. While some are of the view that remaining inside the corridors of power is useful to gain political influence, others think that we should enter into coalitions only when we are in a leading role to influence decisions. What distinguishes Jamaat's leadership at various levels is its religious zeal for public service and a track record of transparency and integrity that even political rivals like Imran Khan acknowledge. The success of the Turkish Justice and Development Party (AKP) has particularly inspired Jamaat members to adjust their agenda according to the needs of the masses. The dynamic personality of Turkish President Recep Tayyip Erdogan has had an impact on Pakistani society across political parties and has compelled Islamists to rethink their strategies and become more inclusive. The Turkish AKP has presented a model for Islamist parties with its modern outlook, broad-based organizational structure, and pragmatic bread-and-butter political agenda.

THE QUESTION OF VIOLENCE

It should be mentioned here that there is nothing intrinsic in Jamaat's program that sets it on a collision course with the West. Even if there are divergent views on policies with Western governments, Jamaat makes a distinction between a government, on one hand, and its people and values on the other. This is the reason Jamaat banned its members from burning the flags of any country when protesting against any one government's policies. It is, however, necessary to understand that we are situated in our own time and space. We cannot remain indifferent to events and incidents around us. The events in Afghanistan and Kashmir and the continuous "war on terror" over the last 15 years have directly affected the life of every Pakistani citizen. When you have more than 3 million refugees and another 1 million internally displaced persons in your country, you have to grapple with and respond to the situation. Jamaat has always been against foreign intervention in Afghanistan, be it by Soviet or NATO forces. During the Soviet intervention, Jamaat provided political support to the mujahideen and their struggle for the liberation of Afghanistan from foreign forces. Similarly, Jamaat organized mass rallies against the American invasion of Afghanistan. Its members have been engaged in relief activities for Afghan refugees on humanitarian grounds. However, contrary to negative propaganda, Jamaat never itself engaged in militant resistance. During the Soviet occupation, some Jamaat members, motivated to support Afghans in their resistance against foreign occupation, joined the mujahideen entirely on their own accord as volunteers, without any involvement from the organization. This occurred during a time in which the Pakistani government itself, as well as many other countries (including the United States), lent their support to the Afghan resistance. These Jamaat members were asked to return after the Soviet withdrawal.

Apart from Afghanistan, Matthew Nelson's chapter mentions two other contexts where Jamaat is alleged to have been involved in militancy: East Pakistan (now Bangladesh) and occupied Kashmir. Both of these cases are exceptional and extraordinary situations where the people of these regions found themselves the victims of foreign military invasion and occupation. The invading Indian army engaged in gross human rights violations in both places. On the Kashmir issue, there are United Nations resolutions that call for the right of the Kashmiri people to self-determination by plebiscite. Over 100,000 Kashmiris, mostly peaceful, have given their lives in their struggle for self-determination. Their resistance is indigenous, principled, and legal. Pakistan is committed to support this movement, as Kashmir is an unfinished story in the partition of the subcontinent. Jamaat, however, condemns attacks on innocent civilians, whether in India or in any other part of the world. That being said, such attacks by dubious elements should not be used as a pretext to malign the genuine resistance of Kashmiris against Indian occupation.

In East Pakistan, it was the Indian army that organized a separatist militia named Mukti Bahni. The current Indian prime minister, Narendra Modi, proudly admitted that India supported Bangladesh to attain its freedom from Pakistan. [12] Mukti Bahni started targeting and killing those who were against the secession of East Pakistan. Jamaat members were compelled to form the Al-Badar organization in defense, with the support of the Pakistan army. Over the past 45 years, Jamaat-e-Islami Bangladesh has actively participated in the electoral process in Bangladesh. The people of Bangladesh have shown their trust in Jamaat. There, the Jamaat was part of the coalition government.[13] The executions of Jamaat leaders in Bangladesh have been condemned by international human rights organizations, who have questioned the integrity and legality of the judicial process.[14] The Bangladeshi government is also heavily influenced by the Indian government and has tried to level false allegations against Jamaat's leadership as a way to appease India.

It would be unfair to ignore the more than seven decades of peaceful, political, and social activism of Jamaat-e-Islami Pakistan and instead focus on regional disputes to define Jamaat. In all three of the aforementioned cases, foreign military invasions and the failure of the state to provide security to all its citizens have been major factors contributing to violent conflict. This is akin to blaming the Muslim Brotherhood in Egypt for Palestinian resistance by linking the actions of Hamas to that of the Egyptian Muslim Brotherhood, as if it were a direct proxy.

On the topic of Jamaat's generally amicable relations with Pakistan's military, such engagement has been carried out in the national interest and in the framework of the Pakistani constitution. There have been moments of both convergence with and divergence from the military. On the latter, for example, Jamaat played a key role in the Lawyers Movement that brought an end to the unconstitutional regime of General Pervez Musharraf.

As far as militant organizations in Pakistan such as Tehreek-e-Taliban (TTP) are concerned, there are domestic root causes that have contributed to their emergence, but, at the same time, these factors have been exploited by foreign intelligence agencies to further their own regional objectives. In any case, Jamaat has always condemned these mindless attacks on innocent civilians that cannot be justified under any logic. Jamaat leaders have also paid the price for these condemnations. Several of its local leaders in areas like Peshawar, Darra Adam Khel, Hangu, and Swat have been and continue to be killed by these militants. Particularly notable was the targeting of Jamaat's former emir, Qazi Hussain Ahmad in November 2012.[15] Along with other political parties, Jamaat has also supported the government's National Action Plan that provides full moral, political, and legal support to Pakistan's armed forces operating against militant groups to rid the country of the scourge of terrorism.

CHANGING INTERNAL STRUCTURES AND FOCUSING ON ELECTIONS

While its ideological impact has been fairly broad, Jamaat has thus far had limited success in parliamentary elections. There are several reasons for this. Jamaat's distinctive organizational structure is frequently cited as a reason for its limited electoral victories. Some analysts note that our organizational structure is more suitable for a revolutionary struggle, and not necessarily parliamentary elections. Jamaat leaders like Qazi Hussain Ahmad, Khurram Murad, and Khurshid Ahmad have expressed the need to adopt a more open and broad-based organization suitable to political campaigning. This is despite the fact that Jamaat is considered the most internally democratic party in Pakistan, one that conducts regular elections at each level of the organization. A report published by a think tank, the Pakistan Institute of Legislative Development and Transparency (PILDAT), testifies to this fact.[16] At times, one feels a lethargic contentedness among some of Jamaat's leaders and members, despite its poor electoral performance. They are not particularly obsessed with winning elections as much as they are keen on participating in them. For us, mass communication of our message is an objective in its own right, and elections provide an occasion for this. This approach has been the subject of debate within Jamaat for quite some time now.

The electoral success of Islamically oriented political parties in Turkey, Egypt, and Tunisia has underlined the need for bringing about basic changes in political strategy and organizational structure. Jamaat certainly wishes to broaden its social base to achieve greater electoral success as well as to have a more pragmatic structure that encourages influential personalities to run for leadership positions, rather than treating them as equal to ordinary members. Jamaat experimented with the Pakistan Islamic Front and a youth organization named Pasban in the early 1990s, creating quite a stir in national politics, but elections came too early for them to properly prepare. These innovative structures created friction among the old guard and the new recruits within the organization, and consequently, they were rolled back after the 1993 elections to maintain organizational unity.

Another issue is a lack of real focus on winning elections as an objective. Jamaat's organization has a heavy ideological and social agenda that consumes considerable human and financial resources. Other political parties make elections their sole focus. One solution currently on the table is the creation of an independent political wing, although under the same central emir. It appears this debate will surface more strongly after the 2018 general elections. Before then, Jamaat's leadership will likely have to make some kind of decision on the issue. If and when this decision is made, it would allow room for the now-marginalized but more capable cadre of affiliates to get involved in the party. These people prefer to stay on the margins because of Jamaat's regimental structure and rigorous organizational activities, which they find difficult to keep up with. The new structure would also allow the political wing to remain focused on elections; provide an enabling environment, one that would have softer rhetoric with regard to ideology; and adopt a more credibly populist approach that would resonate with the masses. This, in turn, would allow the party to relax its generally strict culture to attract a broader base of women and youth. The party has already started taking some substantive measures in this direction. Women and youth have been designated as priority areas in the Shura Council's 2015 plan for the following three years. Eleven special seats have also been added for women in the 75-member Central Shura. The Women's Wing is now more active in international fora. A more popular culture for youth has been adopted with a focus on sports. In addition, Jamaat's social media operation is one of the most proactive among political parties in Pakistan.

"POLITICAL ISLAM" IS OFTEN used in a very broad sense, often lacking in nuance. The phrase is employed to include far more than just political groups or parties. Militant, terrorist, and social service relief organizations are also grouped under the term. Lumping them together can lead to serious misconceptions. It bothers us that Jamaat is being viewed through lenses of hostility and suspicion, in part because of an alleged association with extremist groups that are also considered "Islamists." It bothers us because we don't form our perception of America by looking at the likes of the alt-right or white nationalists, even though such groups and individuals may enjoy significant public support. We will not be able to develop mutual trust if we base our relations on stereotyping and assuming the worst. I firmly believe that cordial relations between mainstream Islamist movements and the West can and should be developed. I end here with a quote from the analyst and expert on Islamist movements Graham Fuller:

> Does Political Islam represent the last heroic stand of Muslim cultural resistance to galloping globalization with an American accent? Or does it represent the beginning of a new synthesis of Islam with contemporaneity, enabling Muslim society and culture to move into the new millennium more confident of its own cultural foundations?[17]

I certainly believe in the latter of the two prospects.

More than the Muslim Brotherhood: The Problem of Hamas and Jordan's Islamic Movement

Nael al-Masalha, of the Jordanian Muslim Brotherhood in Conversation with Shadi Hamid

THE LONGSTANDING STABILITY BETWEEN Jordan's Muslim Brotherhood and the Jordanian regime has often been interrupted by changes in strategy on both sides. We are in one of those fluid phases right now. In his chapter, Brandeis University's David Patel also addresses the effects of the Arab Spring—especially after Mohamed Morsi and the Muslim Brotherhood won in Egypt—which led to a series of internal revisions and changes within Jordan's Islamic movement. That said, I do agree with Patel that there hasn't been much *fundamental* change in how the movement and the regime perceive each other. In other words, the relationship will neither end completely nor change dramatically.

Speaking as a longtime figure in the Brotherhood, there are, in my opinion, several reasons for the recent divisions with the Jordanian Brotherhood's ranks. The first has to do with Hamas's complicated and controversial relationship with the Islamic movement in Jordan. Hamas changed its organizational structure and strategic vision to more effectively deal with both the Jordanian regime and the Jordanian Muslim Brotherhood, with which it has deep ties (*irtibat al-'adawi*). These changes began in earnest after Hamas moved its leadership from Jordan to Syria in 1999.

Hamas has now turned into an organic and independent organization. These developments started in early 2001 and ended in 2008, which is when Hamas became a regional organization directly affiliated with the Jordanian Muslim Brotherhood's Guidance Bureau rather than its own formal leadership in Jordan.

After this organizational independence solidified, Hamas found itself looking for a strong base of support for the movement, one deeply rooted in society that would allow it to operate in broad daylight rather than in an opaque manner. Thus, Hamas looked strategically at Jordan for its deeply rooted Palestinian presence and the growth potential of its population. According to some estimates, as many as 60 percent of Jordanians are of Palestinian origin. Also, the Muslim Brotherhood in Jordan and its affiliated institutions—including the Islamic Action Front—have traditionally enjoyed considerable financial and political resources. Therefore, it was both natural and easy to penetrate the Brotherhood's organization given Hamas's capabilities, namely, its overwhelming popularity as a result of its repeated victories in Gaza, its steadfastness in Palestine within and beyond the Green Line (pre-1967 borders), and the sympathy and support it enjoyed from Palestinians in the diaspora and by Arab Muslims across the globe.

There arose a change in the Jordanian Muslim Brotherhood's leadership in 2008, in conjunction with Hamas's breakaway from the Brotherhood's leadership in Jordan. This amounted to a coup within the Brotherhood, which came about as a result of the Brotherhood's leadership crossing all the red lines that had come to define relations between Islamists of Palestinian origin and those of Jordanian origin. Of particular significance was the appointment of a general overseer[1] for the Brotherhood and a secretary-general for the Islamic Action Front—both of Palestinian origin—who were well known for their loyalty to Hamas. More important, however, was how Hamas was able to penetrate and consequently exert control over all aspects of the Jordanian Brotherhood. In so doing, they were able to make it seem that if you weren't with Hamas, you were against the Islamic movement overall, or that if you weren't for the Palestinian cause, you were for the Jordanian regime and its various agencies.

Hamas worked in an organized fashion within the Jordanian Brotherhood and its affiliated institutions, injecting huge amounts of money to recruit members—some of Jordanian origin—who became increasingly active and engaged in the Brotherhood's projects. This resulted in Hamas consolidating control over the Brotherhood's organization in Jordan. Longtime Brotherhood members of Jordanian origin started to become nervous after sensing that the group's new leadership was adopting a non-Jordanian unpatriotic agenda. They felt that the leadership was using the membership as pawns to implement the policies of Hamas, which had begun to interfere in every detail.

This situation—which started worsening during the Arab Spring—led to the following splits: first, a group of first- and second-rank Brotherhood leaders put forward the Jordanian Building Initiative, known popularly as Zamzam. Zamzam concentrates on presenting a project of national reform based on citizenship; loyalty to Jordan (while retaining an Islamic identity in line with the Jordanian constitution); the acceptance of others regardless of religion and political orientation as long as they accept joint action within a national inclusive framework; and a desire to maintain a collegial and non-confrontational spirit when interacting with any party, including the Jordanian regime.

This approach was met with harsh rejection by the Brotherhood's leadership, which, as discussed earlier, had come to represent Hamas's interests. Consequently, the leadership instructed its affiliated writers—who enjoy financial and logistical support from Hamas—to attack the idea and link it to being a scheme of Jordanian intelligence, and subsequently claim that Zamzam was a means by which to bring the Islamic movement under state influence.

Second, because of adverse reactions to the Zamzam initiative within the broader Islamic movement, another group of Brotherhood members tried to put forward a reform project of their own, leading to the formation of the "Group of Elders" (*Majmu'a al-Hukama*). Comprised of first-generation former Brotherhood and Islamic Action Front leaders, this new body could also claim a significant membership of Palestinian origin. The Group of Elders warned against the Brotherhood leadership's behavior, stating that it was putting the group and its future in Jordan at risk and calling for its dismissal and restructuring. This resulted in the Group of Elders coalescing around a centrist position. They proclaimed that they had lost hope in the leadership of the Brotherhood and mobilized supporters to announce the establishment of a new party. This group has been revitalizing its internal procedures and engaging in discussions with many parties—including those behind the Zamzam Initiative. However, Zamzam's leadership rejected in principle the idea of a merger with the Group of Elders. Zamzam ultimately put the issue to rest by registering a new party of their own called the National Congress Party (*Hizb al-Mu'tamar al-Watani*). As of the time of writing, the party is still in its early stages, with roughly 20 percent of its members coming over from the Jordanian Brotherhood, and 80 percent from elsewhere.

Third, the establishment of a new organization called the Muslim Brotherhood Society (*Jam'iyyah al-Ikhwan al-Muslimeen*)—with the installation of Abdul Majeed Thneibat as the society's general overseer—was a significant development. The society was established following conferences discussing the Brotherhood's reform efforts. A chorus of voices then emerged calling for the dismissal of then-General Overseer Hammam Said, a revision of the Brotherhood's organizational statutes, and a restructuring of its leadership.

During these developments (which were being watched closely by the Jordanian government), a discreet meeting was held in January 2015 between Abdul Majeed Thneibat and His Majesty King Abdullah II at the Royal Palace. According to Abdul Majeed Thneibat, His Majesty the King expressed concern that Arab leaders would bring up the case of the Muslim Brotherhood in member states, including Jordan, during their next meeting—which was scheduled to be held in early March. He added that many wanted designate the Muslim Brotherhood as an illegal terrorist group within Arab League member states. In this meeting, a request was made to help the Jordanian state avoid any embarrassment, especially since the Brotherhood had a long history of legal participation in Jordan, to the point where it had its own Jordan-specific slogans. The request was clear: the Jordanian Muslim Brotherhood had to rectify its legal status in terms of its registration permit to continue operating according to the current Jordanian laws in force. It also had to change its founding statutes, which asserted the group's organizational ties with the Brotherhood in Egypt. Abdul Majeed Thneibat then invited a group of Brotherhood members and explained the situation. They then discussed possible ways forward, arriving at a decision to register the group under the name "Muslim

Brotherhood Society," and to appoint an interim leadership for six months until elections were held to choose a new leadership. They would then be in compliance with Jordanian law.

All in all, there are now four organizations or groups that have emerged from the Jordanian Muslim Brotherhood thus far:

1. The old or parent group led by Hammam Said
2. The Muslim Brotherhood Society led by Abdul Majeed Thneibat
3. The group functioning under the auspices of Zamzam and its attendant National Congress Party
4. The Group of Elders, which has recently announced the formation of a new political party under the name of the Partnership and Rescue Party (*Hizb al-Shiraka w'al-Inqadh*).

THE CURRENT REALITY

When Zaki Bani Irsheid—then the Brotherhood's deputy general overseer—was released from prison in 2016, he put forward an initiative based on the principles of Zamzam to contain the ongoing division, but it was shrouded in uncertainty and mistrust and was thus met with extreme caution.[2] The proposal promoted cooperation across the range of views within the organization, as well as dialogue between the various factions.

To the ever-watchful Jordanian government, the Islamist scene today is in a state of disarray and division. The government is attempting to perpetuate this weakness in any way possible to keep the Islamic movement weak, rather than risk the likely costlier option of attempting to eliminate it.

Consequently, this weakness and division is reflected in the Islamic movement's other social, political, advocacy, and union initiatives. It has also lowered public confidence in its ability to serve the nation, rectify the culture of corruption, or address the general weakness of civil society.

THE VISION

The overall situation in and around Jordan—especially given the presence of Daesh (the Islamic State) at its borders, the failure to reach a fair solution to the Palestinian conflict, and the region's preoccupation with different and sometimes conflicting agendas—keep each party within Jordan and within the Islamic movement in a near-constant state of suspense. The state, taking advantage of the situation, is trying to weaken the Islamic movement's presence and activity. In response, the movement is trying to endure, while sometimes overlooking the gravity of the situation, waiting for things to pass like a summer cloud. This paves the way for other groups—such as Zamzam—to fill political vacuum and address blind spots. This gives them a better chance, especially given that Zamzam's ideology is a departure from the path of *da'wa* (religious education and advocacy), which the parent Muslim Brotherhood group, the Muslim Brotherhood Society, and the Group of Elders have all retained.

SHADI HAMID RESPONDS

I have two quick comments and questions. First, would it be possible for you to address David Patel's thesis that "what is almost always described as an ideological divide is better understood as an 'ethnic' or 'communal' one"? It sounds like you would agree with this to an extent, but I would be curious to hear a bit more, including on the question of whether ideology and religious and moral issues are important in understanding tensions between "hawks" and "doves" within the Muslim Brotherhood. Also, you focus on the question of Hamas, which is obviously very important, but what about divides over how confrontational the Jordanian Brotherhood should be toward the government? There's the perception among some in the old Hammam Said–led Brotherhood that the new (breakaway) Muslim Brotherhood Society has been too deferential toward the monarchy and hasn't pushed hard enough for political change. To what extent is this a legitimate concern?

Second, could you say a bit more about the effects of the military coup in Egypt on Jordan's Islamic movement? How much did what was going on in Egypt and the fear of a repeat scenario drive the new strategy of those like Zamzam, the Muslim Brotherhood Society, and the Group of Elders?

NAEL AL-MASALHA RESPONDS

On your first question, I think that the ideological and religious dimensions of the orientation of the group's doves and hawks are completely different from the regional dimension.

Brotherhood members of Palestinian origin do not differ on the need to support Hamas's project in Jordan and Palestine; rather, they only differ at times on the details. The Brotherhood members of Jordanian origin and the hawks who support Hamas's project and work for its support apparatuses do so because they are attracted to its religious and ideological framing. They are also sometimes drawn in as a result of their personal and religious interests converging.

On the other hand, doves of Jordanian origin who are either involved in the Zamzam project, the Group of Elders, or the new Muslim Brotherhood Society engage in religious activity to serve the interests of a national project. They are thus closer to the regime in approach and are more likely to avoid confrontation, preferring to stick to "soft" opposition in pursuit of political reform within the framework of their ideological convictions.

Regarding the coup in Egypt, it has become evident that the coup has failed to provide for the needs of the Egyptian people. The gradual decline in enthusiasm among the Egyptian public toward the coup and the resulting regime has provided an impetus for Islamic movements to once again embark upon a project of reform and proffer political Islam as society's next alternative.

Furthermore, in addition to the Egyptian experience, both the Libyan experience (with General Khalifa Haftar) and the Yemeni experience (with former president Ali Abdullah Saleh) have failed to provide a viable alternative to political Islam.

The societal consciousness of the Arab people is gradually moving toward a greater level of mistrust in the military. This reality will surely be exploited in the future by Islamic movements running on platforms of peaceful and gradual reform and will aid their being accepted by the people. This is precisely what is encouraging a few trends in Jordan at the moment, such as:

1. Zamzam's establishment of an affiliated political party, The National Congress Party, and the establishment of the Elders' party, the Partnership and Rescue Party, as I mentioned earlier.

2 A change within even the parent Muslim Brotherhood movement toward greater openness, coalition-building with a more national orientation, and a focus on "soft" opposition.

3. A decline in support for the Muslim Brotherhood Society, due to its inability to formulate a new and inspiring political project. It is currently lost, having failed to distinguish itself from various other emerging ideas and political parties.

Religion, Ideology, and Organization

18

How Much Do Organizational Structures Matter?

Jacob Olidort in Conversation with Raphaël Lefèvre

JACOB OLIDORT

Given the changes in identities, doctrines, and actions of Islamist groups vying in the tumultuous past six years, *Rethinking Political Islam* is a critical opening for a new conversation on how we—in academic, policy, and public debates—think about those Islamist groups we consider to be politically relevant. The 20 chapters all underscore the common tension between the ideological principles of these organizations and the alliances they have made, some of which go against these very principles. To those who consider the long view of modern Middle East history, these tensions come as no surprise, given that these are all movements whose founding doctrines and early development during the 20th century were just as much determined by political pressures and personal interests.

While personality and generational differences have historically been factors in how and whether groups survive in shifting political environments, the pressures and stakes changed dramatically after the 2011 uprisings, when many Islamists were able to test their principles in positions of power and when the significance of their actions was amplified across the region through social media channels. As the chapters of Monica Marks and Raphaël Lefèvre show, the missteps of the region's oldest Islamist group, the Egyptian Muslim Brotherhood, had the effect of alienating it from other Islamist groups in the region.

The impact of the Egyptian Muslim Brotherhood's actions on the self-perceptions and maneuvers of Islamists elsewhere are one example of the ways in which local actions can have new kinds of transregional impact. However, even where this impact is felt, these chapters remind us of the need to tread carefully when describing how these groups relate to and influence one another in their ambitions and priorities. Here Joseph Liow provides a helpful reminder in the case of Southeast Asia and the connections between local groups and their counterparts in the Middle East. He argues that Islamists were able to build transnational connections through both the organizational efforts of student groups, such as the Himpunan Mahasiswa Islam in Indonesia and Angkatan Belia Islam Malaysia, and through coordinated humanitarian efforts on behalf of regional political causes.

Liow's discussion of the role of humanitarian campaigns and student organizations in forging transnational bonds raises some of the key questions we face when trying to understand the formation of new "imagined communities" of Islamists both across and beyond the Middle East, as well as within particular countries. Namely, do the members of local Islamist groups build transregional links because they identify with a common Islamist ideology; or because of shared communal experiences of living under authoritarian states (as, for example, Marks shows with Tunisian nahdawis recalling their treatment under Ben Ali when looking at Sissi); or perhaps it is because of the sectarian nature of certain conflicts; or still professional and personal ties?

Ironically, the nature of these connections has become more confused with the greater visibility we now have with social media platforms. Likewise, changes at home can be caused by foreign policy decisions, and the reverse. Here Toby Matthiesen, in his chapter, shows how local Saudi support for the king ebbed and flowed not because of domestic issues but rather because of perceptions of the king in relation to major foreign policy developments, especially the country's backing of Sissi's government in Egypt and its response to heightened Iranian influence in the region. Similarly, David Patel reminds us concerning Islamists in

Jordan that "the difference between so-called 'hawks' and 'doves' has more to do with disagreements about how accommodationist the Islamic movement should be with the Jordanian government than it does with ideological differences." In other words, the local and the regional environment can be equally, if not more, determinative of Islamist politics than ideological principles. Indeed, with the increased sectarian dimension of many Middle East conflicts, it is these external factors that help define the narratives and ideological priorities of Islamist groups and influence their political alignments.

This raises another important issue of locating the influence and impact of these groups. Much like the caution with which we describe relationships between Islamist movements, so too is it especially important to rethink the assumptions of where their political influence actually comes from. Here Matthew Nelson's chapter on Islamist parties that wield considerable influence in Pakistan despite their poor electoral performance is a trend increasingly on display in the Middle East, particularly given voters' low confidence (and interest) in formal political processes. This general political apathy may mean that, in contrast to the early days of the Arab uprisings when Islamists found opportunity within formal political institutions, perhaps Islamists today don't feel they need to rely on these spaces to claim influence. And it is perhaps for this reason that ultraconservative Salafi groups, who for decades explicitly eschewed formal politics, are today more capable of maneuvering within political spaces that are either fluid or failed. Thus, much like Nelson's argument concerning Pakistan's Islamist groups, the poor performance of the Salafi Nour party, which won only 12 seats in the 2015 Egyptian elections, should in no way be misconstrued as a commentary on the weak influence of Islamic politics in Egypt. Rather, to locate the dynamics of Islamic politics in Egypt, as in other countries, we now need to look elsewhere—in particular to social media platforms, publications, mosques, and the various public spaces throughout Egypt—to witness where real political influence is being negotiated.

Curiously, the chapters generally don't highlight the most important change that took place—that all of these movements were products of a late 20th-century political space characterized by a stable, or at the very least predictable, political infrastructure and culture. By the time these groups had politically matured, they found themselves operating within semi-authoritarian states whose accommodation (or, more often, lack thereof) of Islamist participation was relatively easy to assess. And it was in response to such predictable and stable political spaces that these Islamist groups formed their identities. Today, by contrast, in nearly every country surveyed, the local government has a mere façade of stability, at best, and rather little about its policies that can be described as predictable. This adds a measure of uncertainty for the Islamists operating within those borders—indeed, just as we are trying to rethink political Islam, so too are Islamists rethinking their Islamism in relation to uncertain local and regional settings.

Aside from the stability of local governments, the other major difference from the pre-2011 political situation is that political culture is increasingly being defined and arbitrated in sectarian terms—a point that, interestingly, only one chapter discusses in any significant way. Even though the main theater of sectarian tensions is in Iraq, Syria, and Yemen, and while at the state level only Saudi Arabia and Iran have officially embraced the themes that would make it relevant, it is the sectarian significance of these conflicts that reverberates across borders and could determine, for example, the "mouvance" (to use Monica Marks's term) of Salafi-jihadists in places like Tunisia. More discussion of this new sectarian flavor in regional politics would provide added insight into the regional rise of voices, such as those of the Salafis, precisely because it is they who have created the political language for reading significance into sectarian tensions.

Third is the question of social media, which earned no significant treatment in these studies. While it is certainly easy to overstate the importance of social media, there are significant analytical risks of understating it. After all, it is through social media that the sectarian portrayal of regional conflict is promoted, and it is through social media that new transregional links are created in ways that hadn't existed prior to 2011. Therefore, not considering the role, if not the responsibility, of social media in some of these large-scale shifts risks mischaracterizing the dynamics of Islamist groups as merely local phenomena (and they may, in some cases, be just that).

Finally, in terms of categories and terms, we too often remain married to pre-2011 typologies. Here Marks's observation regarding "the tendency, in both local and Western press, to label religiously oriented actors as diverse as Salafi-jihadists, Boko Haram, the Egyptian Brotherhood, and Ennahda as 'Islamists' [having] generated additional confusion regarding Ennahda's identity" is just as relevant beyond the case of Ennahda, and for which my own work tries to provide some granularity.[1] When looking at the Kuwaiti case, for example, even the line between "Muslim Brotherhood" and "activist Salafi" has been blurred. It is precisely when these groups are rethinking their founding doctrines within fluid political settings that the academic and policy communities would do well to revisit the fundamental differences between these groups (e.g., the legal-theological Salafi orientation vs. the modern political ideology of the Brotherhood) as entry points for understanding them. Specifically, it is the very distinctions between the priorities of Salafis and Brotherhood-inspired organizations—the former aiming to ensure that only *their* understanding of Islamic ritual and creed dominates, the latter that Islam in general be in a position of social and political influence—that provide the key to understanding the different approaches to popular mobilization each uses and why the former may resonate more today.

Indeed, given the scale of all of these political shifts and the blurring of lines between groups, how precisely can we tell "extremists" from "nonextremists," and what does it mean to be "radical" (i.e., radical in relation to what?) versus "moderate"? Certainly, the Islamic State is unique in its grotesque brutality, which has alienated the organization from even other jihadist groups, and can therefore be treated as an isolated phenomenon. But when comparing the objectives and nature of the many other groups, from the al-Qaeda-affiliated jihadists to the Syrian militants to the nonviolent Salafis, might we as scholars not do well to provide to readers some deeper and more descriptive vocabulary for distinguishing these myriad groups at a time when so much is at stake? Moreover, there is an added epistemological risk of using terms like "extremist" and "moderate" to distinguish, for example, between the various Syrian opposition groups; we need to remember that local voices (Assad, for example) use these same terms to push their own very different, and often destructive, interests and agendas.

Here it is surprising to see some of the chapters promote the "inclusion-moderation hypothesis" as applied to the Muslim Brotherhood, especially given that we now know the opaque nature of the causes and contexts in which they have evolved over the last six years. Here Courtney Freer offers the helpful reminder that "Islamists do not necessarily moderate when included in a political system, nor do they always privilege ideological policies over systemic political change more broadly."

It seems that given the transformative nature of these large-scale political changes, these circumstances must be somehow integrated into our new thinking about political Islam, and specifically toward understanding various Islamic groups as *dynamic* and *relational* to their political environments. Here I disagree somewhat with Raphaël Lefèvre's argument that we need "a renewed focus on the kind of internal dynamics which take place within Islamist groups [that] may shed light on the factors accounting for their resilience." He argues for adopting resource mobilization theory, in which Islamist groups are studied according to their "organizational survival," and suggests looking at the internal bureaucracy that provides political and professional opportunities to those who commit to a group's cause. This may be the case, but I wonder about the relevance of using these bureaucratic relationships as an analytical prism at a time when Islamist groups' political context is not always bureaucratic, much less local, and when the increasing fragility of states does not always accommodate the functions of organized bureaucracies. Rather, with the globalization of the political sphere and the greater contact between various Islamist groups, it may be more productive to understand them in relation to those broader circumstances. Specifically, borrowing from a typology I used to describe the different kinds of sectarianisms in the Middle East, we could better understand Islamist groups today in functional terms as they carve out spaces for themselves within these new settings: institutional—whether and to what degree they directly engage with local political institutions; exploitative—whether they embrace violent mechanisms to exploit local instability; or accommodationist—in which they engage politically relevant themes without challenging existing institutions or directly becoming involved in formal politics.[2]

RAPHAËL LEFÈVRE RESPONDS

Rethinking Political Islam has offered welcome room for debate on the shifting dynamics shaping Muslim Brotherhood groups in a new Middle East. Jacob Olidort's contribution is particularly useful in two respects. First, he highlights some of the contemporary issues affecting the Brotherhood that scholars have not sufficiently examined, such as the role of social media and simmering sectarian tensions. Second, and most important, he steps into the theoretical debate about Islamic mobilization to argue that researchers must rethink certain assumptions in light of what we know now. In his view, today's Islamist movements are the "products" of their immediate political environment—in other words, to understand the decisions made by the Egyptian Muslim Brotherhood, one needs to look primarily at the "external circumstances" surrounding it, such as the Egyptian regime's crackdown on the movement since 2013. He worries that scholars, in formulating their analyses, have not sufficiently taken into account the sheer scale of political change the region has witnessed since the Arab Spring.

That context deeply matters and impacts political—and, in our case, Islamist—mobilization is actually a central theme of the chapters included in *Rethinking Political Islam* and is, more broadly, a well-established argument in the theoretical literature. But there are major issues with viewing this approach as the primary factor explaining the "ideological priorities" and "political alignment" of Islamist groups. Indeed, it implicitly denies them agency and autonomy from their immediate political environment while effectively sidelining complementary theoretical perspectives. What instead appears timely, in a Middle Eastern context marked by repression, civil war, and state collapse, is to look at how national and regional politics impact internal dynamics within these groups. Movements affiliated with the Muslim Brotherhood are characterized by a complex decision-making process, thus making their very strategies and ideological platforms the result of virulent debates and internal power struggles. These are sophisticated organizations and informal bureaucracies with an agency of their own.

The Brotherhood as a "Bureaucracy"

Considering Muslim Brotherhood movements as "bureaucracies" may at first glance seem out of tune with prevailing perceptions of the current state of the Middle East. Jacob Olidort thus wonders about the relevance of this approach "at a time when their political context is not always bureaucratic, much less local, and when the increasing fragility of states does not always accommodate the functions of organized bureaucracies." In reality, however, there is no necessary contradiction between these groups' organizational sophistication and the unstable political context around them. First, viewing the Muslim Brotherhood as an informal bureaucracy does not imply that it functions like a Weberian-style centralized and hierarchical public administration. It merely refers to the organization's seemingly unique capacity, in the Islamist field, to develop its own decision-making model and mobilize resources and staff to achieve its ends. This perspective on the Brotherhood is not in contradiction with others—in fact, it seeks to offer a more complete picture of the movement by going beyond discourse analysis to understand the complex web of factors that shape its decisions on crucial issues.

Second, the currently dire situation faced by Muslim Brotherhood branches in Syria and Egypt, both in exile due to the considerable repression they face at home, does not diminish the relevance of such an approach—if anything, it heightens it. This may seem counterintuitive. Yet my research into the evolution of the Syrian Muslim Brotherhood's networks since 1982 (when it was forced out of the country) suggests that as Islamist groups go into exile, their priority shifts to organizational survival—and bureaucracy is the only tool they are left with. They use it to continue thriving abroad by developing a professional cadre of members, socializing sympathizers into party loyalty, mobilizing resources to create social and political opportunities for members, and protecting themselves against major splits. In fact, the Brotherhood's ability to use its bureaucratic structures and networks is what has allowed it, in the Syrian case and, I suspect, in the Tunisian and Libyan cases too, to survive against the odds for decades in exile before making surprisingly successful comebacks. They may have lost ground since 2012 but their resilience owes much to their organization.

Setting a New Research Agenda

While this institutionalist approach points to the Muslim Brotherhood's strengths, it also highlights some of the group's weaknesses. As a social movement grows older and gains in organizational sophistication, its structures are likely to become more "oligarchized." Members, who often depend on its bureaucracy for social and professional reasons, may become guided more by a desire to preserve the organization than to achieve its stated goals. This has two negative implications for the Muslim Brotherhood that may help explain the lack of popularity it sometimes faces even in the more pious subsections of society. First, the fact that the Brotherhood might be guided by an instinct for organizational maintenance might lead it to make decisions that contradict its ideological message. This heightens popular mistrust of the organization's "real" agenda and paves the way for the often more uncompromising Salafis to challenge its authenticity and religious legitimacy. Second, the Brotherhood's "oligarchization" means the emergence of clique structures within the organization that can lead to the concentration of power in the hands of just a select few. The group's branches from Syria to Egypt and Jordan are all directed by figures who have been in control for decades—they are "career Muslim Brothers" and their continued monopoly on power is harming the groups' outside image and leading to generational splits.

This institutionalist approach to the Muslim Brotherhood draws on the conceptual tools developed by sociologists Roberta Ash,[3] John Mc Carthy, and Mayer Zald[4] in relation to their work on "resource mobilization theory" in the context of "social movement organizations." Their theoretical insights are rich, and they offer avenues for the type of multidisciplinary research into the Brotherhood that the literature on Islamist groups is sometimes still lacking. They point to the need for studying these movements' extensive networks, organizational structures, decision-making arrangements, and internal politico-ideological debates. Yet they also demonstrate the importance in times of political uncertainty of focusing greater attention on the nature of tensions between the base and leadership and older and younger generations. These internal dynamics weigh more heavily than we might expect on Islamist groups' political and ideological choices and, thus, need to be examined more carefully. Being equipped with some of the conceptual tools mentioned above and with the theoretical insights of political science, sociology, and even anthropology and ethnography can help us address these understudied yet increasingly important themes at a critical point in time.

19

How "Religious" Are ISIS Fighters?

The Relationship Between Religious Literacy
and Religious Motivation

Andrew Lebovich

ONE ASPECT OF THE emergence of sharia, or Islamic law, into the fore-front of public debate is that those trying to understand radicalization have had to deal more seriously with the question of Islamic educa-tion and the role that specific belief structures—from Sufi to Salafi and everything in between—might play in somehow containing or shaping forms of Islamic practice.

This relates to the endless, and often frustrating, back and forth over whether or not fighters from the Islamic State are really "Islamic." One side of this debate has rightly noted that most of the group's foreign recruits are not religiously literate. Revelations in 2016 of Islamic State internal memoranda appear at first glance to support this assertion.

This mass disclosure of documents catalogs foreign recruits to the Islamic State, including in sometimes minute detail their personal information, past histories, and motivations for joining the fight. Thus far, it is largely journalists who have explored the documents, and they have done a good job of finding interesting information and aggregat-ing initial trends.[1] This is especially true when a journalist with deep experience and research skills like Yassin Musharbash goes in-depth with a collection of 3,000 of these documents.[2] One element that Musharbash noted in his initial distillation is that a large majority of Islamic State recruits rank their own knowledge of the sharia as "weak," and relatively few of these fighters seem to have advanced training in sharia.

Based on past debates about radicalization and the intersection between belief and jihadist recruitment, it seems likely that at least some observers will conclude from these documents that the Islamic State and its recruits are cynically using religion or that the phenomenon really has little to do with religion in the first place. However, such a conclusion would be unwarranted based on the evidence available and takes a far too simplistic approach to understanding the complexity of the sharia and Islamic knowledge in general.

The relative weakness of someone's knowledge of sharia does not necessarily say much about how religious he or she is or wants to be. For one thing, a depth of knowledge of sharia is not particularly common even for observant Muslims, and it is in many ways a construct of outsiders to think that it should be. The old Orientalist academic tradition was built around the close study of texts drafted by religious scholars (*ulama*) or well-educated and highly literate Muslims concerned with in-depth issues of exegesis and interpretation. Some of these academics like Joseph Schacht focused on the study of sharia and component legal issues (*fiqh*), and placed it in many ways at the center of Islamic meaning and life.[3] More recently, although scholars like Wael Hallaq have questioned these older understandings, they too have placed the sharia at the center of constructions of morality and practice in precolonial societies. Hallaq describes the death of the "sharia system" that accompanied colonialism as one of the reasons a certain Islamic past and concept of statehood is simply irretrievable today.[4]

What these descriptions can elide in popular discussion is that deep study of Islamic law was never particularly common among the masses in the Muslim world and was generally reserved for the ulama, or religious scholars, who devoted their lives to the study of these issues. Criticizing the depth of people's religious feeling or even knowledge on the basis of their lack of knowledge of sharia would be like questioning Americans' sense of civic association because they didn't make their career as a lawyer. They might not know anything about the law, but there is much more to a sense of being American than just that. Similarly, religious belief and practice—even in more rigorous forms—is about far more than just the law. Academic debates have sometimes been slow to understand this, particularly when it comes to lazy descriptions of Sufism based on its supposed "mysticism" and supposed (but often false) lack of religious orthodoxy—ignoring the rigorous educational and interpretative training and histories of many Sufi leaders over the centuries.

For Islamic State recruits, a weak knowledge of sharia could mean many things. It could and does sometimes mean genuine ignorance of even basic religious precepts, but not always. People join militant movements for a variety of intersecting reasons, including belief, politics, economics, and more. Limited knowledge of an area of Islam traditionally left to dedicated experts says little about the contours of individual religious belief; if anything, it reflects our own projections onto others about modernity and education. Someone can be an ardent and even (dare I say) informed believer in the cause and justness of the Islamic State without having much knowledge of the sharia. And the group is certainly happy to propagate its own interpretations through instruction and the dissemination of texts on sharia, but it is more than likely that the people joining the Islamic State were already inclined to support these interpretations.

Moreover, as the Muslim Brotherhood's Amr Darrag argues in this volume, one of the challenges for Western analysts in understanding Islamic movements is accepting the role of faith in shaping the actions of the movements' members. Faith is difficult to define and measure as an analytical category, and this is one reason the early Orientalist scholars sought refuge in sources they could touch and see.

However, Darrag may overstate his arguments about faith when differentiating between organizations like the Muslim Brotherhood and the Islamic State. He suggests that "the chasm between the Muslim Brotherhood and these other groups is the Brotherhood's privileging of faith over utility while not discounting the latter, where other groups, such as the Islamic State, privilege utility over morality and faith while occasionally discounting the latter in the name of the former." Whether or not this is true from an institutional perspective, we should not discount the role that faith plays in motivating the decisions of Islamic State recruits—a faith that may not be dependent on specific religious knowledge or that may actively discount certain interpretations over others, even if these recruits do not think highly of their own learning in sharia. Additionally, in discounting faith as a possible motivation for the Islamic State, Darrag makes the same mistake for which he critiques those writing about the Brotherhood and assumes an instrumentalization of Islam for political ends while ignoring the possibility that the reverse might be true.

This point brings us to the question of countering recruitment to the Islamic State and similar organizations. Because of the perception that jihadist recruits were deficient in their knowledge of the "true" religion, a number of figures over the years, ranging from the king of Morocco to the Metropolitan Police's first head of the Muslim Contact Unit Robert Lambert to imams and lay Muslims, have argued that a major corrective must come from better Islamic education from ostensibly moderate principles.[5] There is nothing wrong with this argument per se, but it ignores several issues. For instance, recruits to jihadist groups may have thought about and rejected these "moderate" principles and systems of belief before joining, rather than joining because they were simply not aware of other interpretations. Additionally, American, European, and even Muslim governments have to varying degrees sought to promote so-called moderates, potentially discrediting these Muslim leaders through their association with government programs.

Finally, these questions about Islamic education and regulating authority structures are far from apolitical. Even though leaders of Muslim countries and communities want to (understandably) inhibit radicalism and violence, exerting control over religious structures also means exerting control over believers. Countries like Turkey, Algeria, and Morocco, for instance, have made efforts to take closer control of mosques and appoint pro-government imams partially under the guise of countering radicalization. Morocco has also increasingly framed itself as a counter-radicalization partner not just in Morocco and Europe, but in Sub-Saharan Africa as well. Whether or not these programs and initiatives are effective is a subject for another essay. But these initiatives not only further politicize Islamic education and training but also serve as foreign policy tools for governments to reinforce their legitimacy abroad—further tempting Western governments to ignore issues like corruption and judicial abuses in favor of having strong partners against extremism.[6]

20

Do Islamists Have an Intellectual Deficit?

Ovamir Anjum

ALTHOUGH MY PRIMARY AREA of research has been premodern Islamic tradition, my interest in "political Islam" in general and in *reformists* in particular goes back further than that, and has been the subject of my more recent thinking. When interviewing leaders of the Egyptian "revolution"—as it was then being called—during the summer of 2011 in Tahrir Square, I developed a suspicion that has since developed into something stronger, though not quite a coherent thesis just yet. It is that the reformists—by which I mean "moderate Islamists" who are, almost by definition, committed to working within the modern nation-state system—have been devoid of a well-grounded vision of Islamic politics, by which I mean a vision backed by a densely elaborated discursive tradition.[1] Notwithstanding the debate over the extent to which social movements' success depends on a coherent ideology (as opposed to just effective framing), I note that in the context of fierce competition from militant, quietist, and pro-establishment Islamic groups, this deficiency appears to be taxing Islamists' ability to deliver the goods they promise and prevent radicalization.[2]

The impressive array of chapters on Islamists included in this volume, enhanced by the authors' productive engagement with each other's contributions, sheds unprecedented light on Islamists' predicaments, transformations, strategies of survival, and future prospects, and gives much food for thought for future scholarship. I will direct my comments here to the question of "framing" and "ideology," or what I shall refer to as discursive tradition.[3] The distinction between the two concepts, pointed out in a number studies, turns on notions of durability, coherence, and manipulation: framing being "innovative amplifications and extensions of, or antidotes to, existing ideologies," whereas ideology is a "fairly broad, coherent, and relatively durable" set of beliefs and values that are "pervasive and integrated" and concern not just politics but life in general.[4] Since Islamism sees itself as primarily about contesting ideology (rather than alleviating a limited kind of injustice), such a distinction may not be justified. However, a modified form of this distinction may still be useful, since Islamic activists' framing of discourses designed for the political arena may differ from, even as they draw on, theorists' and clerics' participation in Islam as a discursive tradition. I explore the notion of discursive success in terms of the *density* and *coherence* of a discourse and, taking my cue from the contributions in the previous chapters, ask how the Islamic movements' "success" is related to their discursive success. I suggest that mainstream Islamists (who are the focus of most of the contributions here) suffer from an intellectual deficit, and that this deficit is observable both at the level of movement framing and the deeper ideological discourse.

This deficit can be discerned in the set of challenges facing Islamists that most contributors have pointed out, such as intergenerational tensions; perceptions by youth activists that their leaders lack principles and compromise endlessly; defection to more radical or militant groups; and the growing frustration with the democratic experiment. All these suggest an intellectual deficit on the part of the Islamists in question, who have yet to produce a better, more coherent defense of their politics. Compare the sleek media production of the Islamic State, due in part to its framing success in attracting young, Westernized, and tech-savvy youth, or even to the impressive scholarly resources offered by the Saudi sheikhs of the Gulf, to the soporific websites of the Brotherhood or the South Asian Jamaat groups. Nonetheless, the discourse of Muslim Brotherhood-inspired groups has shown notable success in some respects. For instance, despite all of the current developments, a number of chapters have noted the ideological or discursive distance of "the Islamist ideological corpus" from *takfiri* ideologies, as well as from the notion of violence as the primary mechanism for change. In this respect, and others, the role of ideas is crucial, although not determinative. Yet on the whole, if ideas that are ensconced in a dynamic and deeply grounded discursive tradition constitute an important factor in the success of movements, the relative weakening of such a discourse has been one of the Islamists' weaknesses in recent decades.

Without reiterating the well-worn debate on whether ideas matter, I would like to suggest a couple of specific ways in which the ideology-phobia of some important social scientific trends should be qualified, and I do so as a foil to open up space for my argument. Materialist explanations tend to push back against the claim that ideas have an independent role, however variable and small, in the explanatory apparatus. They do so in at least two ways: first, even when ideas do seem to matter, their operationalization is decisively determined by their material context; and second, ideologies are little more than frozen expressions of commitments and interests whose material contexts have been lost to us. The latter objection is non-falsifiable and hence itself ideological. The former claim, in my view, is overstated. Mental constructs and systems of ideas are not determined by context in any simple sense. Such systems not only influence the weighing of moral options or how scriptural interpretations are to be operationalized but also, just as important, shape the very mental construction of the material context. In other words, although context matters, the very perception and parsing of context depends on pre-existing ideas and frames.

Pushing this line of argument a bit, the materialist claim could be turned on its head; no institutions and material factors in fact exist except as mental constructs, at the mercy of the discursive traditions of which the subject is a part.[5] Both idealists and materialists have learned to restrain their claims; one can commend Stacey Philbrick Yadav's formulation in chapter 5 that emphasizes the "iterative relationship between discourse and institutions." To the extent that discourse matters, Islamic reformist discourse (by which I mean not only framing but also what has been called "ideology") deserves social scientists' attention.

The gap between thinkers and the organizational leadership is often minimal in movements in their early years, as in the lifetime of Hassan al-Banna, Abul Ala Mawdudi, and, more recently, the Moroccan Al Adl Wal Ihsan under the charismatic leader and scholar-intellectual Abdesslam Yassine.[6] The difference between Morocco's Al Adl and the Justice and Development Party (PJD), as profiled by Avi Spiegel in his chapter, suggests to me that the Al Adl members who draw on the more confident and deeper writings of their late leader enjoy a great deal of success *without* electoral participation. Yassine's insistence, for instance, that democracy is not quite the same as Islamic *shura*—exploring the associations and corollaries of both while also rejecting the subservience to the king—sits more harmoniously with the desire for an authentic Islamic existence in modern times, as it recalls the prophetic critique of the rulers by the ulama in the Islamic imagination.[7] The Egypt-centered Islamists' ambivalent embrace of democracy, in contrast, draws nearly universal criticisms of inauthenticity.[8] I agree with Spiegel that we need to think of success in terms broader than electoral gains, and I would suggest that discursive depth and the personal and political transformation of individuals ought to count for more. The success of Egypt's Salafis in 2012 shows that such transformative religious influence may be turned into electoral gains relatively easily. Pakistan's Islamists also offer an instructive example where Mawdudi's powerful writings once shaped the larger national discourse without earning the Jamaat any electoral victories. In contrast, when such grassroots religious influence is lacking, even political access is of limited use as the leaders are reduced to making deals with other powers. In the Yemeni context, for example, Yadav details such compromise in her discussion of "the limits of [partisan] politics without a strong grassroots movement."

Other Islamic trends, in contrast, fare somewhat better in their discursive density. The accretist-traditionalists (my neologism for the generally pro-establishment Sunni ulama defined by commitment to the established schools of law, *kalam* theology, and moderate Sufism) can boast a dense tradition, even if it loses in terms of sociopolitical relevance and popularity to the Islamists. The Salafis, whom I categorize as originalist-traditionalists, draw on long-standing traditions of *ahl al-hadith*, the Hanbali legal school, and premodern sharia elaborated most powerfully by late medieval traditionalists like Ibn Taymiyya, Ibn al-Qayyim, and others. South Asian traditionalists have long looked to the expansive Hanafi-Maturidi tradition, reinvigorated by authorities like Shah Wali Ullah, who can be seen as lying in some respects between the Arab accretists and the Salafis. The Twelver Shi'a, similarly, boast a comprehensive and dense legal and philosophical tradition stretching without serious rupture back to the beginning of the Safavid period in the 16th century. The Islamists of the Brotherhood "school," in contrast, while open to drawing selectively on most of these traditions—and most alive to issues of social and political justice precisely because of their receptivity to modernity—exhibit an ambivalent relationship to the historical Islamic tradition. They relate to it to reform and transform it, rather than be deeply transformed *by* it. However, despite their modernism, their relationship to modernity remains somewhat skeptical and tenuous. At an intellectual level, this could plausibly result in a lack of interest in sustained investigation of either tradition, the classical and the modernist. Alternatively, it could generate exceptional interest in juxtaposing and investigating both. The institutional conditions for the latter being nearly nonexistent in the region, it is the former of the two options that is often taken.

For most Islamist activists, the original vision and style of Hassan al-Banna—a charismatic leader and master of synthesis and compromise—continue to set the tone. Mawdudi, a more theoretical, systematic, and polemical mind, can be credited for being the first to furnish the Islamists with a model of Islamic history, society, and state. In Egypt, Qutb was the next influential figure after Banna, albeit one on the margins of the organization, who possessed the literary force, intellectual passion, and charisma to create a self-confident vision, one that may have been derailed by his immoderation (or perhaps attractive precisely due to that), attributable in part to his prolonged imprisonment. Otherwise, the Muslim Brotherhood's leaders have been technocrats and bureaucrats, not inspiring thinkers and visionaries. The Pakistani Jamaat has done no better after Mawdudi. Perhaps the closest thing mainstream Islamists have had to a powerful visionary since Qutb is the Al Adl Wal Ihsan's Abdesslam Yassine, whose luster has been dulled due to Morocco's marginality in the broader region. Despite these important influences, the mother organization in Egypt, and to varying degrees elsewhere, seem to have Banna's indelible mark of pragmatism, compromise, as well as a measure of anti-intellectualism.

The draining of intellectual resources may be one of the causes of organizational insularity. Anti-intellectualism, aggravated under repressive conditions, seems to preclude any path to the top of the organizational ladder other than loyalty and seniority, perpetuating the old-timers' hold on authority. There are no Bannas, Mawdudis, or Qutbs anymore, only aging avuncular figures best at surviving, not inspiring. This *seems* to me to be the case with the two movements I am most familiar with, the Egyptian Brotherhood and the Pakistani Jamaat. Whether it is in fact so, and to what extent, is an interesting problem for investigation.

My hypothesis of intellectual deficit could be challenged by at least three kinds of reformist contributions to Islamic discursive tradition. First, starting in the 1980s if not earlier, a newer generation of reformist Azhari ulama such as Mohamed al-Ghazali and Yusuf al-Qaradawi, and intellectuals such as Salim al-'Awa, Mohamed Imara, and Fahmy Huwaydi, whom Raymond Baker has labeled "the new Islamists," have laid a framework for a more tolerant (read: less anti-Western, which may have something to do with Egypt's liberalization under Sadat), although not necessarily more coherent or cogent, sociopolitical vision of Islam.[9] Second, a powerful trend of the "economization of Islamism" has grown since the 1970s.[10] As the international focus shifted from an ethos of developmentalism that had encouraged Islamist thought in the direction of state-centered ideologies, the focus partly shifted from capturing states to the creation of "Islamic" economy and banking. This latter trend has produced in its wake not only a new global economic sector but also an ever-growing literature on the subject. A third focus of Islamic reformists has been on the "fiqh of minorities" with a view to the growing minorities of Muslims in the West and the increasing globalization of reformist communities and concerns.[11] All three types of projects, underway at a few reformist institutions in Pakistan, Malaysia, and the West, are straddled by a concern to adjust Islam to modernity.

Even if some mainstream Islamists and their reformist ilk are producing political, economic, and social scholarship in response to modern challenges, in what respects might they still be considered deficient? Although the debate is far from over, much recent scholarship, by both Western academics and Islamic traditionalists, has called into question the cogency of each of these reformist discourses. The Islamists seek to justify, it has been argued, an Islamic state without exploring the full implications of the modern nation-state and asking whether an "Islamic state" is desirable or even possible; they call for social justice but ignore or neglect the destructive aspects of neoliberalism vis-à-vis family, community, and the environment; they make the case for a modern Islamic economy, without sufficient reflection on how "modernity" is to be attained without the uniquely materialist motivations at its heart furnished by capitalism and secularism; and they offer a *fiqh* of minorities without a well-formed understanding of the host societies in the West.[12] Furthermore, they are accused of impatience vis-à-vis the meticulous, erudite scholasticism of medieval Islamic tradition and take refuge in generalistic, result-oriented instruments such as the notion of public benefit (*maslaha*) and objectives (*maqasid*) of Islamic law—instruments that are similarly available for abuse by their equally result-oriented militant counterparts.[13]

To be sure, the Islamists have not failed in disseminating their message. To the contrary, unlike the militant fringe, the reformist influence of Brotherhood-style Islamism is in varying degrees nearly ubiquitous among literate religious Muslims. But precisely because of this, at least some responsibility for the widespread intellectual malaise in the Muslim world could be blamed on the Islamists, on their tendency to paper over serious conflicts, such as between Islamic tradition and the secular and liberal commitments of modern democracy; and their failure to provide meaningful ways to address threats posed by modernity, such as economic inequality and environmental challenges, leaving the large swaths of Muslims under their sway unprepared to take meaningful action.

On the activist side, loyalty to the organization seems to be the first principle of Islamist activism, and the large gap between learned and potentially creative reformist thinkers and the organizations' leaders chosen on the basis of seniority and loyalty seems largely impenetrable. It is a legitimate question, then, to ask whether such an intellectual deficit contributed to the Islamists' lackluster performance in the events of the Arab uprisings, particularly to what many scholars have viewed as the Egyptian Brotherhood's governance failures in the admittedly all-too-brief opportunity granted them.

Simple intellectual incompetence or failure need not be construed as a cause unto itself, and several explanations may be offered for this deficit. One might argue that it is the very activist structure of social movement organizations like the Brotherhood that precludes intellectual or theoretical depth. Perhaps it is just the burden of having to survive under brutal repression for generations that has led to conservatism and engendered fear of critical scholarship that might call into question the group's foundational principles. In other cases, as in Pakistan, perhaps it is participation in the messiness of electoral politics that dilutes the impulse to dig in and ask tough questions. Alternatively, perhaps it is just that all religions in the age of globalization are fated to inhabit a world of "holy ignorance," as the French scholar Olivier Roy has poignantly argued.[14] These arguments may all be correct. In any case, they highlight a set of fascinating problems for Islamists and scholars of Islamism alike.

NOTES

━━◆◈◆━━

Introduction

1. This book defines "mainstream" Islamist groups as those that operate within the confines of institutional politics and are willing to work within existing state structures, even ostensibly secular ones. They have, with few exceptions, embraced parliamentary politics, electoral competition, and mass politics more broadly. They are generally, though not always, "gradualist" in orientation, favoring a slow, bottom-up approach to social and political change. We are not making a normative judgment about the content of their beliefs and whether any of these characteristics are good or bad. Most mainstream Islamist groups are either Brotherhood or Brotherhood-inspired movements, drawing in some fashion on the Brotherhood's frame of reference and "school of thought."

2. For more on Ennahda's evolving relationship with Salafis in Tunisia, see Shadi Hamid, *Islamic Exceptionalism: How the Struggle Over Islam is Reshaping the World* (New York: St. Martin's Press, 2016): 208–211.

3. Mareike Transfeld, "Houthis on the Rise in Yemen," *Carnegie Endowment for International Peace,* October 31, 2014, http://carnegieendowment.org/sada/?fa=57087.

4. Avi Spiegel, Reaction essay, (The Brookings Institution, Rethinking Political Islam project, December 2015), https://www.brookings.edu/wp-content/uploads/2016/07/Morocco_Spiegel-2.pdf.

Chapter 1

1. While the Brotherhood–regime conflict is particularly prominent, it is important to contextualize it within other episodes of regime violence: targeting non-Islamist activists with a draconian protest law; delegating control of restive universities to the security services; targeting prominent NGOs and rights activists, and stirring up moral panics in an attempt to co-opt religious discourse for itself. See Josh Stacher, "Fragmenting States, New Regimes: Militarized State Violence in the Middle East," *Democratization* 22, no. 2 (2015): 259–275.

2. On the Brotherhood's electoral strategy in less-than-democratic systems, see Nathan Brown, *When Victory Is Not an Option: Islamist Movements in Arab Politics* (Ithaca, NY: Cornell University Press, 2012). See also Vicki Langohr, "Of Islamists and Ballot Boxes: Rethinking the Relationship Between Islamisms and Electoral Politics," *International Journal of Middle East Politics* 33, no. 4 (November 2001): 591–610.

3. David D. Kirkpatrick, "Egyptian Court Bans the Muslim Brotherhood," *New York Times,* September 23, 2013, http://www.nytimes.com/2013/09/24/world/middleeast/egyptian-court-bans-muslim-brotherhood.html?_r=0.

4. As discussed later in this chapter, the campaign encompassed two types of institutions: educational facilities and community associations. Mohammed Sa'adni, "al-Masry al-Youm Tanshir Qa'ima bi-Isma' Jama'iyat 'al-Ikhwan' al-Mujammida (1) [al-Masry al-Youm Publishes the List with Names of the Brotherhood Community Associations Whose Funds Are Frozen]," *al-Masry al-Youm,* December 24, 2014, http://www.almasryalyoum.com/news/details/363611.

5. Al-Gam'iyya al-Shar'iyya has apparently been able to sufficiently distance its branches from the Brotherhood, and thus it has been allowed to resume operations. Aaron T. Rose, "Administrative Court Lifts al-Gameya al-Shareya," *Daily News Egypt,* June 25, 2014, http://www.dailynewsegypt.com/2014/06/25/administrative-court-lifts-al-gameya-al-shareya/.

6. Sarah Jamil, "*al-Masry al-Youm* Tanshir Qa'imat Wazirat al-'Adl bi-Isma 87 Madrassa Taba'a lil-'Ikhwan' [*al-Masry al-Youm* Publishes the Ministry of Justice's List of Names of 87 Schools Affiliated to the Muslim Brotherhood]," *al-Masry al-Youm,* December 30, 2013, http://www.almasryalyoum.com/news/details/369022.

7. Sayyid Abdel Rahim, "Misr: Al-tahafuth 'ala 16 jama'iya ahliyya lil-Ikhwan [Egypt: Seizure of 16 Associations Belonging to the Muslim Brotherhood]," *al-Arabiyya al-Jadid,* May 6, 2016, https://goo.gl/K4prdU; Hani Fathi, "'Hasr Amwal al-Ikhwan' Tatahafuz 'Ala Mumtalakat Mistashfa al-Zahra' wa al-Lu'Lu'a bi Beni Suef [Seizure of the Brotherhood's Assets Including the Zahra' (Flower) and Lu'Lu'a (Pearl) Hospitals in Beni Suef]," *al-Youm al-Sabea',* December 13, 2015, http://goo.gl/EbUzNF.

8. "Seized Properties of Egypt's Banned Muslim Brotherhood Worth $1.1 Bln," *al-Ahram,* January 24, 2016, http://english.ahram.org.eg/News/185791.aspx.

9. Todd Ruffner, "Under Threat: Egypt's Systematic Campaign Against NGOs," *Project on Middle East Democracy*, March 2015, http://pomed.org/wp-content/uploads/2015/03/Under-Threat-Egypts-Systematic-Campaign-against-NGOs.pdf.

10. Ibid., 5.

11. "Egypt: Planned Asset Freezes Are Government's Latest Tool to Eradicate Civil Society," Amnesty International, March 18, 2016, http://www.amnestyusa.org/news/press-releases/egypt-planned-asset-freezes-are-government-s-latest-tool-to-eradicate-civil-society; Shahira Amin, "Egypt's NGOs Face 'Orchestrated, Escalating' Assault from Authorities," *Al-Monitor*, March 23, 2016, http://www.al-monitor.com/pulse/originals/2016/03/egypt-rights-crackdown-bahgat-arrests-ngos-sisi-travel-bans.html#.

12. Mohammed Taha, "Dirasa: al-Jama'iyya al-Tibiyya' tu'alij nahu 7 milyon marid khilal 4 sanawat [Study: '(Islamic) Medical Association' Treats Approximately Seven Million Sick over Four Years]," *al-Jam'iyya al-Tibiyya al-Islamiyya*, January 2, 2015, http://www.ima-egy.net/2013-09-24-14-31-06/607-7-4.

13. "Mudeer Mistashfa al-Rahma 'aqab al-istila' 'aleyha: al-inqilab faqada 'aqlahu [The Director of the Rahma (Mercy) Hospital Following Its Seizure: The Coup Regime Has Lost Its Mind]," *Rassd*, January 14, 2015, http://rassd.com/15-128042.htm.

14. Baheyya Mekki, "bil-Sawr . . . Amin al-Qaloubiyya yatahafiz 'ala Mishtashfiyyat al-Ikhwan bil-Khanka [In Pictures . . . Security Forces in Qaloubiyya Seize the Brotherhood's Hospitals in Khanka]," *Bawabat al-Qahira*, January 14, 2015, http://goo.gl/V3aoYQ; Islam Abu Wafaa, "Tafasil al-tahafuz 'ala mistashfa Dar al-Salam al-taba'a lil-Ikhwan bil-Beheira [Details of the Seizure of the Brotherhood's Dar al-Salam Hospital in Beheira]," *Roz al-Yusuf*, January 14, 2015, http://goo.gl/nG2WZQ; Karim al-Bakri, "al-Saha: La niya lidayna liighlaq mistashfiyyat al-Ikhwan [Ministry of Health: We Have No Intention to Close the Brotherhood's Hospitals]," *al-Shorouk*, January 14, 2015, http://www.shorouknews.com/mobile/news/view.aspx?cdate=14012015&id=3f8b4507-8ef4-40ba-8ac1-bc6674e59c3d.

15. Hossam Rabea, "al-Quwwat al-Musallaha al-Misriyya tuhawil al-Ta'weed 'an dawr jam'iyaat al-Ikhwan al-khayriyya [The Egyptian Armed Forces Are Attempting to Substitute for the Role of the Brotherhood's Charity Associations]," *Raseef 22*, July 22, 2015, http://raseef22.com/politics/2015/07/22/egyptian-armed-forces-are-trying-to-make-up-for-the-charitable-role-of-the-brotherhood-associations/.

16. Maha Salem, "al-Quwwat al-Musallaha tawzea' milyoniyyan wa nusf al-milyon kartona aghdhiya bil-manatiq al-akthar ihtiyajiyan [The Armed Forces Distribute 1.5 Million Boxes of Food in Areas with the Greatest Need]," *al-Ahram*, July 15, 2015, http://gate.ahram.org.eg/News/698177.aspx; "Qafela tibiyya min al-Quwwat al-Musallaha Lil-ahali bi'r al-a'bd

fi Shamal Sina' [Medical Caravan from the Armed Forces for the People of al-Bir al-Abed in North Sinai]," *Dot Misr,* February 7, 2016, http://goo.gl/QDH7ks; "al-Quwwat al-Musallaha tarasil qafela tibiyya ila al-Wadi al-Jedid [The Armed Forces Send a Medical Caravan to Wadi Jedid (Province)]," *Dot Misr,* March 1, 2016, http://goo.gl/xc7a72; "Al-jaish yuwaza' milyon wa nisf hassa ghathai'yya 'ala al-muwatineen bi al-munasiba Ramadan [Egyptian Army Distributes 1.5 Million Boxes of Food to the Citizens on the Occasion of Ramadan]," *al-Masry al-Youm,* June 4, 2016, http://www.almasryalyoum.com/news/details/959443; "General Intelligence Service Hands Out Subsidized Food in Beni Suef," *Egypt Independent,* June 4, 2016, http://www.egyptindependent.com//news/general-intelligence-service-hands-out-subsidized-food-bani-swaif.

17. Steven Brooke, interview with IMA Manager, January 2014. Regarding Wael Talib, see the photos from the campaign protesting his arrest at: https://goo.gl/VsjKy7.

18. *Al-Ahram,* December 28, 2013, 1.

19. Steven Brooke, interview with IMA manager, January 2014; Saeed Abdel Rahim, "Misr 'tatahafuz' 'ala al-mistashfiyyat al-islamiyya [Egypt "Seizes" Islamic Hospitals]," *al-Arabi al-Jadid,* January 19, 2015, http://goo.gl/20dzY8.

20. Mohammed Taha, "Dr. Ali Abu Saif: Basoos wa al-Khalil wa Beni Suef mistashfiyyat jadida tadakhil al-khidmat qariban [Dr. Ali Abu Saif: New Hospitals in Basoos, al-Khalil, and Beni Suef are Entering Service Soon]," *al-Jam'iyya al-Tibiyya al-Islamiyya,* August 15, 2014, http://www.ima-egy.net/2013-09-24-14-31-06/497-2014-08-15-00-57-03.

21. "Hasr amwal al-Ikhwan: mistashfiyyat al-Jama'iyya al-Islamiyya mustamirra fi 'amalha [Seizure of the Brotherhood's Funds: The Islamic Association's Hospitals Continue Their Work]," *Ru'yah,* January 15, 2015, http://goo.gl/Lu25uB; "State Confiscates Medical Charity Associations for Brotherhood Affiliation," *Aswat Masriyya,* January 14, 2015, http://en.aswatmasriya.com/news/view.aspx?id=2951c14e-b994-4101-ac16-e28f29532889.

22. Baheyya Mekki, "bil-Sawr . . . Amin al-Qaloubiyya yatahafiz 'ala mishtashfiyyat al-Ikhwan bil-Khanka [In Pictures . . . Security Forces in Qaloubiyya Seize the Brotherhood's Hospitals in Khanka]," *Bawabat al-Qahira,* January 14, 2015, http://goo.gl/V3a0YQ; Islam Abu Wafaa, "Tafasil al-tahafuz 'ala mistashfa Dar al-Salam al-taba'a lil-Ikhwan bil-Beheira [Details of the Seizure of the Brotherhood's Dar al-Salam Hospital in Beheira]," *Roz al-Yusuf,* January 14, 2015, http://goo.gl/nG2WZQ; Karim al-Bakri, "al-Saha: La niya lidayna liighlaq mistashfiyyat al-Ikhwan [Ministry of Health: We Have No Intention to Close the Brotherhood's Hospitals]," *al-Shorouk,* January 14, 2015, http://www.shorouknews.com/mobile/news/view.aspx?cdate=14012015&id=3 f8b4507-8ef4-40ba-8ac1-bc6674e59c3d.

23. "Al-tahafuz 'ala amwal al-Jama'iyya al-Tibiyya al-Islamiyya [Seizure of
the Islamic Medical Association's Funds]," *Hizb al-Hurriya wa al-'Adala*,
January 14, 2015, http://www.fj-p.com/Our_news_Details.aspx?News_
ID=61304; A. Sh. A., " 'Lajnat idarat amwal al-Ikhwan' tatahafiz 'ala al-
Jama'iyya al-Tibiyya al-Islamiyya [Committee Managing the Brotherhood's
Funds Seizes the Islamic Medical Association]," *al-Masry al-Youm*,
January 14, 2015, http://www.almasryalyoum.com/news/details/629557;
Ali Ghanem, "Al-inqilab yasriq al-Jama'iyya al-Tibiyya al-Islamiyya . . .
al-harb 'ala milayeen al-marda [The Coup Regime Steals the Islamic Medical
Association . . . War on Millions of Patients]," *Ikhwanonline*, January 14,
2015, http://ikhwanonline.com/Article.aspx?ArtID=218310&SecID=230.

24. Amr Osman, "Religion and Politics in Post-Coup Egypt," *Open
Democracy*, November 28, 2013, https://www.opendemocracy.net/arab-
awakening/amr-osman/religion-and-politics-in-post-coup-egypt; David
D. Kirkpatrick and Mayy El-Sheikh, "Military Enlists Religion to Quell
Ranks," *New York Times*, August 25, 2013, http://www.nytimes.com/2013/
08/26/world/middleeast/egypt.html?_r=0.

25. "Mudeer mistashfa al-Rahma 'aqab al-istila' 'aleyha: al-inqilab faqid 'aqilu
[The Director of the Rahma (Mercy) Hospital Following Its Seizure: The
Coup Regime Has Lost Its Mind]," *Rassd*, January 14, 2015, http://rassd.
com/15-128042.htm.

26. The "Vetogate" website reported on a number of violations based on a
series of reports obtained from the Egyptian Ministry of Education. These
reports are compiled at http://www.vetogate.com/list/783.

27. Rishwa al-Tahtawi, "Mudaris '30 Yunio:' Amwal taht al-tahafuz . . . wa
Mudarisoon fawq al-riqaba [June 30th Schools: The Money Is Seized, but
the Instructors Are Above the Monitoring]," *al-Masry al-Youm*, January 10,
2015, http://www.almasryalyoum.com/news/details/626211.

28. Mahmoud Taha Hussein, "Al-Ta'leem: Lajnatan li-bahath wadia' madrasat
al-Medina al-Menawara al-Ikhwaniyya bi al-Iskanderiyya [Ministry
of Education: Two Committees to Investigate the Situation of the
Brotherhood's Medina Schools in Alexandria]," *al-Youm al-Sabea'*, October
18, 2014, http://goo.gl/4VidzL.

29. "Ba'd al-tahafuz 'ala mudaris al-Ikhwan . . . Khibraa': 'al-qarar siyasi wa
laysa ta'leemi' [After Seizure of the Brotherhood's Schools . . . Experts: This
Is a Political Decision, Not an Educational One]," *Rassd*, April 21, 2014,
http://goo.gl/g2wHL1.

30. "Revolution of all the Brotherhood schools," *Facebook*, http://goo.gl/
MSzbPm.

31. Ibrahim Qasim and Mohammed al-'Alim, " 'Hasr amwal al-Ikhwan' . . .
Tahel mudeer mudiriyya al-Ta'leem bil-Giza lil-niyaba idariyya [Seizure
of the Brotherhood's Funds . . . The Referral of the Director of the Giza
Directorate of the Education Ministry to the Administrative Prosecutor],"
al-Youm al-Sabea', September 24, 2014, http://goo.gl/3uJC9n; "Al-niyaba

al-idariyya tua'qib maso'uli al-Ta'leem bi al-Giza bisabab mudaris al-Ikhwan [The Administrative Prosecutor Punishes the Responsible Officials in the Giza Ministry of Education Because of the Brotherhood's Schools]," *al-Mogaz*, March 3, 2015, http://almogaz.com/news/crime/2015/03/03/1895331.

32.   Risha al-Tahtawi, "'Mudaris al-Ikhwan' kharij saytirat al-Ta'leem [The Brotherhood's Schools Are Outside the Control of the Ministry of Education]," *al-Masry al-Youm,* January 4, 2015, http://www.almasryalyoum.com/news/details/620528.

33.   Hazem 'Adel, "20 Yanayir . . . Al-hukm fi da'wa bi talaan qararat lajnat al-tahafuz 'ala amwal al-Ikhwan (Translation)," *al-Youm al-Sabea'*, January 6, 2015, http://goo.gl/J8Vt5b. Hazem 'Adel, "25 November . . . Al-hukm fi 9 da'awi li waqf al-tahafuz 'ala amwal mudaris al-Ikhwan [November 25 . . . Judgment in 9 Cases to Stop the Seizure of the Funds of the Brotherhood's Schools]," *al-Youm al-Sabea'*, October 21, 2014, http://goo.gl/bzWXKw; Hazem 'Adel, "Ta'jeel da'awi bi talaan qarar al-tahafuz 'ala 9 mudaris taba'a li al-Ikhwan li21 Uktubir (Translation)," *al-Youm al-Sabea'*, September 2, 2014, http://goo.gl/dQMJ4s.

34.   Risha al-Tahtawi, "Ba'd riqabat 'al-Ta'leem: Mudaris al-Ikhwan . . .' Aam min 'al-ishraf 'ala al-waraq' (Tahqiq) [After Ministry of Education Monitoring . . . A Year of 'Supervision on Paper' (Report)]," *al-Masry al-Youm*, January 10, 2015, http://www.almasryalyoum.com/news/details/626218.

35.   Shaima al-Qarnashawi, "al-Masry al-Youm tanshir haythiyat waqaf al-tahafuz 'ala amwal 9 mudaris Ikhwaniyya [*al-Masry al-Youm* Publishes the Rationale (Behind) Halting the Sequestration of the Money of 9 Brotherhood Schools]," *al-Masry al-Youm*, November 25, 2014, http://www.almasryalyoum.com/news/details/584773; Wissam Abdel 'Alim, "Nunshir hukm waqf tanfiz qarar al-tahafuz 'ala amwal mudaris al-Ikhwan [We Publish the Details of the Judgement Halting the Implementation of the Decision to Seize the Funds of the Brotherhood's Schools]," *Bawabat al-Ahram*, January 25, 2014, http://goo.gl/BulmFl.

36.   Rishwa al-Tahtawi, "'Al-Ta'leem:' Al-Khorouj 'an al-nas mahdoud . . . Wa ijra'at jadida lil-saytara [Ministry of Education: Departure from the Text Is Limited, and There Are New Procedures for Control]," *al-Masry al-Youm*, January 10, 2015, http://www.almasryalyoum.com/news/details/626212.

37.   *Egypt Independent*, January 10, 2015, http://www.almasryalyoum.com/news/details/626218; Risha al-Tahtawi, "'Mudaris al-Ikhwan' kharij saytirat al-Ta'leem [The Brotherhood's Schools Are Outside the Control of the Ministry of Education]," *al-Masry al-Youm*, January 4, 2015, http://www.almasryalyoum.com/news/details/620528.

38.   Mahmoud Taha Hussein, "Musdar bi al-Ta'leem: 'Al-Wazir yajtama' ghadan bi al Ra'is majmua'at 30 Yunio li wadaa' ijra'at li al-saytara 'ala mudaris al-Ikhwan . . . Wa qariban tughayyir ba'd mudeeri al-mudaris . . . Wa 'ard al-qararat 'ala lajnat idarat al-Amwal bi Wazirat al-'Adl [Ministry of

Education Source: The Minister Will Tomorrow Meet with the Head of the
June 30th Schools to Clarify the Procedures for Control over the
Brotherhood's Schools . . . And Soon Will Change Some of Their Directors . . .
And Publicize the Decisions of the Committee Managing the Funds at the
Ministry of Justice]," *al-Youm al-Sabea',* October 26, 2014, http://goo.gl/
gWkxMb.

39. Mahmoud Taha Hussein, "'Al-Ta'leem' tentahi min mujalis mudaris
al-Ikhwan . . . Wa irsal al-isma' li al-lajnat al-aminiyya [The Ministry of
Education Is Ending the Boards of the Brotherhood Schools . . . and
Sending the Names to the Security Committees]," *al-Youm al-Sabea',*
January 10, 2015, http://goo.gl/ZDFzHa.

40. Alaa Hassanein, "Nunshir shurut al-Tarbiyya wa al-Ta'leem li al-musalaha
ma'a mudaris al-Ikhwan [We Publish the Ministry of Education's Terms for
Reconciliation with the Brotherhood's Schools]," *al-Wady,* January 1, 2015,
http://elwadynews.com/news/2015/01/01/62708.

41. "Al-Hayah al-Youm liqa' wazir al-Tarbiyya wa al-Ta'leem Doctor
Mahmoud Abu al-Nasir wa istarad al-tabilat al-ta'leemi al-jadid [*Al-
Hayah al-Youm* Speaks with the Minister of Education Doctor Mahmud
Abu al-Nasr and Reviews the New Educational Tablet]," *al-Hayah al-
Youm* (TV Program), February 17, 2014, https://www.youtube.com/
watch?v=IVt-ORfAgrk.

42. "President Approves New Anti-Terrorism Law," *Daily News Egypt,*
February 24, 2015, http://www.dailynewsegypt.com/2015/02/24/president-
approves-terrorist-entities-law/.

43. "Egypt Prosecutor Names Brotherhood Leaders as Terrorists,"
Associated Press, March 29, 2015, http://abcnews.go.com/International/
wireStory/egyptian-militant-group-claims-cairo-university-bombing-
29985042; "State Confiscates Assets of Sentenced Defendants,
Charity Organization for Brotherhood Affiliation," *Aswat
Masriyya,* March 26, 2015, http://en.aswatmasriya.com/news/view.
aspx?id=0517282d-bfbe-4247-8d43-4dce184bd6db.

44. Rasha Tahtawi, "Wazir al-Ta'leem: Ihkam al-Riqaba 'ala al-Mudaris al-
Ikhwaniyya Durura [Minister of Education: Tightening Oversight of the
Brotherhood's Schools is a Necessity]," *al-Masry al-Youm,* April 16, 2015,
http://www.almasryalyoum.com/news/details/708508.

45. Ayman Ali, "Qidayat Mudaris al-Ikhwan Taht al-Qubba [The Issue of the
Muslim Brotherhood's Schools in Parliament]," *al-Masry al-Youm,* June
1, 2016, https://goo.gl/YsQWJJ; Reem Mahmoud, "al-Ta'leem Tabhath
Malafat Mu'allemi Mudaris al-Ikhwan Qabl al-Aa'm al-Dirasi al-Jadid [The
Ministry of Education Investigates Files of Teachers of the Brotherhood
Schools Prior to the New School Year]," *al-Fagr,* September 5, 2016,
http://www.elfagr.org/2263470.

46. Hussam Tammam, *The Salafism of the Muslim Brothers,* Marased Paper No. 1
(Alexandria, Egypt: Biblioteca Alexandria, 2011), 9.

47. Ishaq Musa al-Husaini, *The Muslim Brethren* (Beirut: Khayat, 1956), 52.

48. Maha M. Abdelrahman, *Civil Society Exposed: The Politics of NGOs in Egypt* (London: I.B. Tauris, 2004).

49. Steven Brooke, interview with IMA manager, January 2014.

50. Saeed Abdel Rahim, "Misr 'tatahafuz' 'ala al-mistashfiyyat al-islamiyya [Egypt "Seizes" Islamic Hospitals]," *al-Arabi al-Jadid,* January 19, 2015, http://goo.gl/20dzY8.

51. Quintan Wiktorowicz, "Civil Society as Social Control: State Power in Jordan," *Comparative Politics* 33, no. 1 (October 2000): 43–61.

52. Specifically, before proceeding outside the Ministry of Social Solidarity, any dispute must first go before a three-person board, consisting of two Ministry of Social Solidarity representatives and a representative of the concerned organization. A majority vote by that body determines whether or not the claim advances to the courts (article 7). See also Kristina Kausch, *Defenders in Retreat: Freedom of Association and Civil Society in Egypt* (Madrid: FRIDE, April 2009), 7, http://fride.org/download/WP82_Egypt_Defenders_Retreat_ENG_may09.pdf.

53. Marina Makary, "More Muslim Brotherhood-Affiliated NGOs Dissolved in Egypt," *Daily News Egypt,* March 1, 2015, http://www.dailynewsegypt.com/2015/03/01/more-muslim-brotherhood-affiliated-ngos-dissolved-in-egypt/; Nourhan Fahmy, "Egypt Dissolves 169 Muslim Brotherhood-Affiliated NGOs," *Daily News Egypt,* February 23, 3015, http://www.dailynewsegypt.com/2015/02/23/egypt-dissolves-169-muslim-brotherhood-affiliated-ngos/.

54. "Ministry Dissolves 99 NGOs for Brotherhood Ties," *Aswat Masriyya,* March 18, 2015, http://en.aswatmasriya.com/news/view.aspx?id=d6d9c3ea-127d-40ff-8724-5d1fe36389ca.

55. Eli Berman and David D. Laitin, "Religion, Terrorism and Public Goods: Testing the Club Model," *Journal of Public Economics* 92, no. 10 (2008); Melani Cammett, *Compassionate Communalism: Welfare and Sectarianism in Lebanon* (Ithaca, NY: Cornell University Press, 2014).

56. The Brotherhood runs a parallel internal system of goods provision whereby the organization furnishes aid (mostly in cash) to the families of detained members. The previously described shift would essentially convert the entire enterprise to this system, in which members and sympathizers are privileged over outsiders.

57. Eva Wegner, *Islamist Opposition in Authoritarian Regimes: The Party of Justice and Development in Morocco* (Syracuse, NY: Syracuse University Press, 2011), 68. See also Avi Spiegel, *Young Islam* (Princeton, NJ: Princeton University Press, 2015).

58. See for instance, "Muslim Brotherhood: Services for Egyptian Public Regular, Unrelated to Any Election," *Ikhwanweb,* January 20, 2013, http://www.ikhwanweb.com/article.php?id=30582; "Ikhwan: la 'alaqa lihamlat 'ma'an nabni Misr' bi mo'ad al-intikhabat [Brotherhood: There Is No Relation Between the 'Together We Build Egypt Campaign' and the Date

of the Elections]," *Akhbar al-Youm*, January 22, 2013, http://akhbarelyom.com/news/newdetails/121766/1/0.html#.U5C5L5RdVSr.

59.   Abdelrahman Youssef, "Egyptian Brotherhood Leader Reflects on Group's Fate, Future," *al-Monitor*, May 22, 2016, http://www.al-monitor.com/pulse/originals/2016/05/egypt-brotherhood-leader-interview-sisi-mistakes-future.html#.

60.   See chapter 13 for Amr Darrag's conversation with Steven Brooke.

61.   Talaat Fahmy, "Muslim Brotherhood Press Statement," *Ikhwanweb*, May 25, 2016, http://www.ikhwanweb.com/article.php?id=32544.

62.   Osama al-Sharif, "Will Jordan Ban the Muslim Brotherhood," *al-Monitor*, April 6, 2016, http://www.al-monitor.com/pulse/originals/2016/04/muslim-brotherhood-group-jordan-government-tension.html#.

63.   Amal al-Hilali, "La wa'dth wa la irshad ba'd al-youm [No Preaching and No Guiding After Today]," *Huffpost Arabi*, May 8, 2016, http://www.huffpostarabi.com/2016/05/08/story_n_9862998.html.

64.   Monica Marks, "How Big Were the Changes Tunisia's Ennahda Just Made at Its National Congress?" *Washington Post*, May 25, 2016, https://www.washingtonpost.com/news/monkey-cage/wp/2016/05/25/how-big-were-the-changes-made-at-tunisias-ennahda-just-made-at-its-national-congress/.

Chapter 2

1.   For a discussion of democratic loyalty, semiloyalty, and disloyalty, see Juan Linz and Alfred Stepan, *The Breakdown of Democratic Regimes* (Baltimore: Johns Hopkins University Press, 1979).

2.   On Gulf actors see Marc Lynch, *The New Arab Wars* (New York: Public Affairs, 2016).

3.   Tunisia's revolution began in December 2010 with protests in the interior and eventually spread to the capital, ousting dictator Zine el-Abidine Ben Ali on January 14, 2011. For more on factors that sparked Tunisia's revolution, see Laryssa Chomiak, "The Making of a Revolution in Tunisia," *Middle East Law and Governance* 3, no. 1–2 (2011): 67–83.

4.   See Vincent Geisser and Michel Camau, *Le Syndrome Autoritaire. Politique en Tunisie de Bourguiba à Ben Ali* (Paris: Presses de Sciences Po, 2003); Joshua Rogers, "'There Is No Room for a Religious Party': Negotiating the Islamist Challenge to State Legitimacy in Tunisia 1987-1991" (MPhil Thesis, Oxford University, Oxford, 2007).

5.   For more on Salafi jihadism in Tunisia, see Fabio Merone and Francesco Cavatorta, "The Emergence of Salafism in Tunisia," *Jadaliyya*, August 17, 2012, http://www.jadaliyya.com/pages/index/6934/the-emergence-of-salafism-in-tunisia; Monica Marks, "Youth Politics and Tunisian Salafism: Understanding the Jihadi Current," *Mediterranean Politics* 18, no. 1 (2013); Francesco Cavatorta, "Salafism, Liberalism, and Democratic Learning in Tunisia," *Journal of North African Studies* 20, no. 5 (2015).

6.   For more on Ennahda's founding and evolution, see Francois Burgat and William Dowell, *The Islamic Movement in North Africa* (Austin: University

of Texas, 1993); John Entelis, *Islam, Democracy and the State in North Africa* (Bloomington: Indiana University Press, 1997); Kenneth Perkins, *A History of Modern Tunisia* (New York: Cambridge University Press, 2004).

7. Author interviews, 2011–2016. Also see Susan Waltz, "Islamist Appeal in Tunisia," *Middle East Journal* 40, no. 4 (1986); Henry Munson, "Islamic Revivalism in Morocco and Tunisia," *The Muslim World* 76, no. 3–4 (1986).

8. See Larbi Sadiki, "Political Liberalization in Bin Ali's Tunisia: Façade Democracy," *Democratization* 9, no. 4 (2002): 122–141; Emma Murphy, *Economic and Political Change in Tunisia: From Bourguiba to Ben Ali* (London: MacMillan Press, 1999).

9. Author interviews, 2011–2016. See also Doris Gray, "Islamist & Secular Quests for Women's Rights," *Mediterranean Politics* 17, no. 3 (2012); Tunisia reports from Amnesty International, Human Rights Watch, and the International Center for Transitional Justice (ICTJ).

10. Ennahda leaders had promised the party would not run a presidential candidate and that it would seek a coalition government months before the 2011 elections. See Monica Marks, "Purists vs. Pluralists: Cross-Ideological Coalition Building in Tunisia," in *Tunisia's Democratic Transition in Comparative Perspective*, ed. Alfred Stepan (forthcoming 2017).

11. Monica Marks, interview with Said Ferjani, July 5, 2011.

12. Monica Marks, interview with Yesmin Masmoudi, August 7, 2011.

13. Nahdawis grew more reticent to cite the AKP as a model to outsiders after it came under increasing international criticism since the Gezi Park protests of summer 2013. For more on Ennahda's perception of the AKP, see Monica Marks, "Erdogan Comes to Tunisia," *Foreign Policy*, June 6, 2013, https://foreignpolicy.com/2013/06/06/erdogan-comes-to-tunisia/; Oguzhan Goksel, "Perceptions of the Turkish Model in Post-Revolutionary Tunisia," *Turkish Studies* 15, no. 3 (2014).

14. Monica Marks, interview with Rached Ghannouchi, August 22, 2011.

15. The 150-member Shura Council is the highest regularly sitting body in Ennahda. It is intended to be a representative institution in which the party debates and decides positions on important issues via a one-person, one-vote system.

16. Monica Marks, interview with Osama Essaghir, March 20, 2013.

17. See Monica Marks, "How Egypt's Coup Really Affected Tunisia's Islamists," *Washington Post*, March 16, 2015.

18. Marc Lynch, "Rached Ghannouchi: The FP Interview," *Foreign Policy*, December 5, 2011, https://foreignpolicy.com/2011/12/05/rached-ghannouchi-the-fp-interview/.

19. Monica Marks, interview with Rached Ghannouchi and other party leaders, 2011.

20. Monica Marks, interview with Rached Ghannouchi, August 22, 2013.

21. Monica Marks, interview with Ennahda Executive Committee member, December 18, 2012.

22. Monica Marks, interview with members of Ennahda's Executive and Shura Councils, 2013 and 2014.

23. See Nadeen Shaker, "In Cairo, Ghannouchi Warns Against 'Democracy of the Majority'," *Ahram Online*, June 4, 2013, http://english.ahram.org.eg/NewsContent/2/8/73167/World/Region/In-Cairo,-AlGhannouchi-warns-against-democracy-of-.aspx.

24. See Human Rights Watch, "All According to Plan: The Rab'a Massacre and Mass Killings of Protesters in Egypt," August 12, 2013, https://www.hrw.org/report/2014/08/12/all-according-plan/raba-massacre-and-mass-killings-protesters-egypt.

25. See "Remarks by the President on the Middle East and North Africa," White House Office of the Press Secretary, May 19, 2011, https://www.whitehouse.gov/the-press-office/2011/05/19/remarks-president-middle-east-and-north-africa.

26. Lee Jae-Won, "Saudi Arabia and UAE to Lend Egypt up to 8 Billion," *Reuters*, July 9, 2013, http://www.reuters.com/article/us-egypt-protests-loan-idUSBRE9680H020130709.

27. See chapter 14 for Ennahda parliamentarian Sayida Ounissi's perspectives on the effects of the Egyptian coup and Ennahda's relationship with the Muslim Brotherhood.

28. Author interviews, 2011–2015.

29. For more on Tunisian Salafi-jihadism, see the work of Fabio Merone, particularly Fabio Merone and Francesco Cavatorta, "Salafist Mouvance and Sheikh-ism in the Tunisian Democratic Transition" (Working Papers in International Studies, Dublin City University, 2012).

30. Monica Marks, "Youth Politics and Tunisian Salafism: Understanding the Jihadi Current," *Mediterranean Politics* 18, no. 1 (2013).

31. Fabio Merone and Francesco Cavatorta, "Salafist Mouvance and Sheikh-ism in the Tunisian Democratic Transition," Working Papers in International Studies, Dublin City University, 2012.

32. On the Islamic State's "start-up" appeal, see Quinn Mecham, "How Much of a State is the Islamic State?" in *Islamism in the IS Age*, Project on Middle East Political Science, POMEPS Studies 12, March 17, 2015, http://pomeps.org/wp-content/uploads/2015/03/POMEPS_Studies_12_ISAge_Web.pdf.

33. The Soufan Group, *Foreign Fighters: An Updated Assessment of the Flow of Foreign Fighters to Syria and Iraq*, December 2015, http://soufangroup.com/wp-content/uploads/2015/12/TSG_ForeignFightersUpdate3.pdf. The Soufan Group's estimates are as of November 2015.

34. See Francesco Cavatorta, "The Rise and Fall of Uncivil Society? Salafism in Tunisia after the Fall of Ben Ali," Middle East Institute, October 6, 2015, http://www.mei.edu/content/map/rise-and-fall-uncivil-society-salafism-tunisia-after-fall-ben-ali-0; Monica Marks, "Who Are Tunisia's Salafis?" *Foreign Policy*, September 28, 2012, http://foreignpolicy.com/2012/09/28/who-are-tunisias-salafis/.

35. Author interviews with nahdawis, 2011–2013. See also Monica Marks, "Ennahda's Rule of Engagement," in Sada. Carnegie Endowment for International Peace, September 2012, http://carnegieendowment.org/sada/?fa=49728.

36. See also Monica Marks, "Ennahda's Rule of Engagement," September 2012.

37. Many Tunisian Ansar al-Sharia members switched allegiances to the Islamic State when the group rose to prominence in 2014.

38. Monica Marks, interview with Houda (a pseudonym), a female Salafi student, August 10, 2012.

39. Monica Marks, interview with Houda's mother, August 2012.

40. Leftist politician Chokri Belaid was assassinated on February 6, 2013, and Arab nationalist politician Mohamed Brahmi was assassinated on July 25, 2013. See Francesco Cavatorta, "Salafism, Liberalism, and Democratic Learning in Tunisia," *Journal of North African Studies*, 20, no. 5 (2015): 770–783.

41. John Thorne, "Tunisia Shuts Down Medieval City to Prevent Salafi Demonstrations," *Christian Science Monitor*, May 20, 2013, http://www.csmonitor.com/World/Middle-East/2013/0520/Tunisia-shuts-down-medieval-city-to-prevent-Salafi-demonstrations.

42. Rory McCarthy, "Protecting the Sacred: Tunisia's Islamist Movement Ennahda and the Challenge of Free Speech," *British Journal of Middle Eastern Studies* 42, no. 4 (2015): 447–464.

43. Human Rights Watch, "Tunisia: Flaws in Anti-terrorism Draft Bill," April 8, 2015, https://www.hrw.org/news/2015/04/08/tunisia-flaws-revised-counterterrorism-bill.

44. Monica Marks, interview with Ennahda Shura Council member, November 4, 2015.

45. Approximately a dozen leading parties had signed a pre-election pledge promising to complete these tasks within one year of election—that is, by October 23, 2012. See Monica Marks, "Convince, Coerce, or Compromise? Ennahda's Approach to Tunisia's Constitution," The Brookings Institution, February 10, 2014.

46. That is, a coup driven by soft political power rather than hard, violent power such as the use of the military force or the threat of it.

47. Amal Boubekeur, "The Politics of Protest in Tunisia," SWP Comments 13, March 2015.

48. Monica Marks, "What Did Tunisia's Nobel Laureates Actually Achieve?," *Washington Post*, October 27, 2015, https://www.washingtonpost.com/news/monkey-cage/wp/2015/10/27/what-did-tunisias-nobel-laureates-actually-achieve/.

49. Monica Marks, "Convince, Coerce, or Compromise? Ennahda's Approach to Tunisia's Constitution," The Brookings Institution, February 10, 2014, https://www.brookings.edu/research/convince-coerce-or-compromise-ennahdas-approach-to-tunisias-constitution/; Rory McCarthy, "Protecting the Sacred: Tunisia's Islamist Movement Ennahda and the Challenge of Free Speech," *British Journal of Middle Eastern Studies* 42, no. 4 (2015): 447–464.

50. Author interviews, 2012–2013.

51. Essebsi had held positions under both the Bourguiba and Ben Ali administrations.

52. Monica Marks, interview with Rached Ghannouchi, November 3, 2015.

53. Mounia al-Arfaoui, "Sanusejjil hudurana bi-tariqa ghair mu'tada," *Correspondents.org*, December 5, 2014, http://www.correspondents.org/ar/node/5282.

54. Monica Marks, interview, June 4, 2014.

55. Monica Marks, interview, November 10, 2014.

56. For more on Ennahda's 10th Congress, see Monica Marks, "How Big Were the Changes Ennahda Just Made at Its National Congress?" *Washington Post*, May 25, 2016, https://www.washingtonpost.com/news/monkey-cage/wp/2016/05/25/how-big-were-the-changes-made-at-tunisias-ennahda-just-made-at-its-national-congress/.

Chapter 3

1. For more information on the meeting, see Avi Spiegel, *Young Islam: The New Politics of Religion in Morocco and the Arab World* (Princeton, NJ: Princeton University Press, 2015).

2. For more on Islamist participation in elections, see the work of Shadi Hamid, Nathan Brown, Jillian Schwedler, and Carrie Wickham, among many others.

3. On "familial resemblances" between Morocco's PJD and the Egyptian Muslim Brotherhood, see Carrie Wickham, *The Muslim Brotherhood: Evolution of an Islamist Movement* (Princeton, NJ: Princeton University Press, 2013).

4. Adding to this effect is that much of the recent scholarly material written on Morocco's Islamists appears in Arabic and French. See for example the work by leading scholars Mohamed Darif and Mohamed Tozy. The exceptions are Malika Zeghal, *Morocco: Religion, Authoritarianism and Electoral Politics* (Princeton, NJ: Marcus Wiener, 2008); and Emad Eldin Shahin, *Political Ascent: Contemporary Islamic Movements in North Africa* (Boulder, CO: Westview, 1997).

5. On Morocco as a model, see Avi Spiegel, "Just Another King's Speech?" *Foreign Policy*, March 18, 2011, http://foreignpolicy.com/2011/03/18/just-another-kings-speech/.

6. Tariq Ramadan, professor of contemporary Islamic Studies at Oxford University and grandson of the founder of the Muslim Brotherhood, also noted the shifting sources and influences of new Islamist thought: "It's not coming just from the Middle East anymore," Ramadan noted. "It's coming from North African countries and from the West. There are new visions and there are new ways of understanding. Now they are bringing these thoughts back to the Middle East." (Anthony Shadid, "Islamists' Ideas on Democracy and Faith Face Test in Tunisia," *New York Times*, February 17,

2012, http://www.nytimes.com/2012/02/18/world/africa/tunisia-islamists-test-ideas-decades-in-the-making.html).

7. For more on the PJD's path to party formation, see Michael Willis, "Between Alternance and the Makhzen: At-Tawhid wa al-Islah's Entry into Moroccan Politics," *Journal of North African Studies* 4, no. 3 (1999): 45–80.

8. For more on alternance, see Susan Miller, *A History of Modern Morocco* (Cambridge: Cambridge University Press, 2013).

9. Myriam Francois-Cerrah, in her ongoing doctoral research at Oxford University, makes the compelling argument that certain senior leaders did, in fact, believe that Morocco was an "Islamic state."

10. Quoted in Emad Shahin, *Political Ascent: Contemporary Islamic Movements in North Africa* (Boulder, CO: Westview Press, 1998).

11. "We are not Algerian Islamists," Abdelilah Benkirane would say, to avoid scaring supporters or the state.

12. The PJD was mindful of what happened after the Shabiba Islamiyya challenged the monarchy, which immediately prompted the regime to suppress the group. The Shabiba soon splintered and was driven underground.

13. In this case, the Democratic and Constitutional Popular Movement party (MPDC).

14. One plea, for example, proceeds roughly as follows: "The main discussion today is targeted at Moroccan youth. The Moroccan youth that we have our hope invested in. We believe that they will respond to the needs of the country, on the path towards ending corruption and tyranny.... We must stand against corruption and stand with those that fight for our rights. Every Moroccan, whether living in the mountains or valley or desert, must give your vote to he/she who deserves your vote, who truly deserves it. Hence, the PJD invites you, and all citizens, to vote for it, so that our voice may be a voice and opportunity strong against all tyranny and corruption." From "PJD2011 CHABAB," YouTube video, posted by Pjd Communication, 3:24, November 21, 2011, https://www.youtube.com/watch?v=fUoZGv-trAs.

15. "Video: Benkirane Walks Out of Event After Being Booed," *Morocco World News,* August 25, 2015, https://www.moroccoworldnews.com/2015/08/166376/video-benkirane-walks-out-of-event-after-being-booed/.

16. For a humorous take on Benkirane's favorite metaphors, see Hamdan Design, "Benkirane vs Crocodiles & Ghosts |Photomanipulation Progress|," Facebook video, 1:06, July 16, 2013, https://www.facebook.com/video.php?v=10201006535184485&theater.

17. Intissar Fakir and Maati Monjib, "Rabat's Undoing: Why the Moroccan Monarchy Should Be Worried," *Foreign Affairs*, October 23, 2014, https://www.foreignaffairs.com/articles/morocco/2014-10-23/rabats-undoing.

18. For more on PJD party discipline, see Spiegel, *Young Islam.*

19. For a quote on Benkirane needing the king, see Youssef Roudaby, "Benkirane: «Il n'y a pas d'avenir pour le Maroc si nous entrons en conflit

avec le roi»," *Telquel,* March 16, 2015, http://telquel.ma/2015/03/16/
benkirane-il-ny-pas-davenir-maroc-rentrons-en-conflit-roi_1438474.

20. "Kalima ra'ees al-hukuma fi mu'tamir jam'iyya khareeij Harvard," Youtube
video, posted by Pjd Communication, 20:22, March 14, 2015, https://www.
youtube.com/watch?v=4_qJ9ZRhpKQ.

21. For more on PJD recruitment and structure, see Spiegel, *Young Islam.*

22. "Morocco Women Protest Islamist PM's Stay at Home Speech," *Yahoo,*
June 24, 2014, http://news.yahoo.com/morocco-women-protest-islamist-
pms-stay-home-speech-183358711.html; and "Moroccan PM Furious
with Jennifer Lopez for Revealing Act," *Yahoo,* June 8, 2014, https://
news.yahoo.com/video/moroccan-pm-furious-jennifer-lopez-061416576
.html.

23. See campaign videos and statements in run-up to September 2015 local
elections.

24. For more on the feuding of Istiqlal and PJD, see Benjamin Roger, "Maroc:
crise gouvernementale, quelle solution pour le PJD?" *Jeune Afrique,* July 12,
2013, http://www.jeuneafrique.com/169708/politique/maroc-crise-
gouvernementale-quelle-solution-pour-le-pjd/; "L'éternel combat Istiqlal-
PJD. . . ," *La Vie éco,* March 16, 2015, http://www.lavieeco.com/news/
actualites/l-eternel-combat-istiqlal-pjd...-33244.html.

25. For more on this, see Avi Spiegel, "The Fate of Morocco's Islamists,"
Foreign Policy, July 9, 2013, http://foreignpolicy.com/2013/07/09/the-fate-
of-moroccos-islamists/.

26. "Le Maroc souligne la nécessité de préserver l'unité nationale de l'Egypte,"
Map Express, July 3, 2013, http://www.mapexpress.ma/actualite/activite-
gouvernementale/le-maroc-souligne-la-necessite-de-preserver-lunite-
nationale-de-legypte/.

27. For a quote on the king's support of the government, see Mohamed
Etayea, "Abdelilah Benkirane, menacé, se voit attribuer des gardes du
corps," *Telquel,* March 16, 2015, http://telquel.ma/2015/03/16/benkirane-
menace-se-voit-attribuer-gardes-du-corps_1438496.

28. For more on Yassine and the early Al Adl, see the work of Mohamed Darif,
Malika Zeghal, and Avi Spiegel. Yassine's personal website is also a great
source: http://yassine.net/ar/index/index.shtml.

29. For insightful analysis of the Yassine letter, see Henry Munson, *Religion
and Power in Morocco* (New Haven, CT: Yale University Press, 1993).

30. For more analysis of the February 20 Movement, see Ahmed Benchemsi,
"Morocco's Makhzen and the Haphazard Activists," in *Taking to the
Streets: Activism, Arab Uprisings, and Democratization,* ed. Lina Khatib and
Ellen Lust (Baltimore: Johns Hopkins University Press, 2014).

31. For a report of one such debate on cross-ideological cooperation, see
"Hiwar al-furaqa' al-siyasiyeen awwal al-ghayth qatra," *Jama'ah al-'Adl wal-
Ihsan,* April 16, 2014, http://www.aljamaa.net/ar/document/79700.shtml.

32. See Al Adl communiqué at http://www.aljamaa.net/ar/index/index.
shtml.

33. For a different take, see *Taking to the Streets: Activism, Arab Uprisings, and Democratization,* chap. 7.

34. "World Report 2014: Morocco/Western Sahara," *Human Rights Watch,* 2013, https://www.hrw.org/world-report/2014/country-chapters/morocco/western-sahara.

35. See Spiegel, *Young Islam,* for a more thorough analysis.

36. Abdelwahed El Moutawakkil, "Le Président du Cercle Politique félicite Erdogan pour la victoire de son parti aux communales," *Al Adl wal Ihsane,* March 31, 2014, http://www.aljamaa.net/fr/document/5404.shtml.

37. See Al Adl 2013 statement at http://www.aljamaa.net.

38. This body of work is voluminous. A good place to start is the diverse writings of Jason Brownlee, Eva Bellin, Ellen Lust-Okar, Lisa Anderson, and Gregory Gause.

39. Perhaps for the opposite reason, Al Adl's Yassine readily looked elsewhere for insights, even as far as Iran.

40. Second quote relayed to author by Michael Willis, from a 2014 address by a PJD official in England.

41. For a fascinating analysis of PJD youth and varied responses to Sissi meetings, see Idriss Benarafa, "Morocco Divided over Relationship with Egypt's Sisi," *Your Middle East,* April 8, 2015, http://www.yourmiddleeast.com/culture/morocco-divided-over-relationship-with-egypts-sisi_31255.

Chapter 4

1. John McCarthy and Mayer Zaid, "Resource Mobilization and Social Movements: A Partial Theory," *American Journal of Sociology* 82, no. 6 (1977): 1212–1213.

2. Mayer Zaid and Roberta Ash, "Social Movement Organizations: Growth, Decay and Change," *Social Forces* 44, no. 3 (1966): 329–330.

3. See for instance Ayman Sharrouf, "The Destructive Ascendancy of Syria's Muslim Brotherhood," *Now,* December 3, 2014.

4. See for instance "From Dallas to Damascus: The Texas 'Straight Shooter' Who Could Replace Syria's Assad," *NBC World News,* March 30, 2013, http://worldnews.nbcnews.com/_news/2013/03/30/17500980-from-dallas-to-damascus-the-texas-straight-shooter-who-could-replace-syrias-assad.

5. For a detailed and balanced account of the Muslim Brotherhood's role in the Syrian opposition, see Aron Lund, "Struggling to Adapt: The Muslim Brotherhood in a New Syria," in *Carnegie Papers* (Washington, DC: Carnegie Endowment for International Peace, May 7, 2013).

6. Raphaël Lefèvre, "Saudi Arabia and the Syrian Brotherhood," Middle East Institute, September 27, 2013, http://www.mei.edu/content/saudi-arabia-and-syrian-brotherhood.

7. Unless stated otherwise, this chapter draws from a series of interviews conducted by the author from December 2012 until March 2015.

8. Raphaël Lefèvre, "New Leaders for the Syrian Muslim Brotherhood," Carnegie Endowment for International Peace,

December 11, 2014, http://carnegieendowment.org/2014/12/11/
new-leaders-for-syrian-muslim-brotherhood-pub-57453.

9.   Mohammed Hikmat Walid, "Interview: Muslim Brotherhood Leader
     Walid," *Zaman al-Wasl*, February 17, 2015.

10. "Syria's Muslim Brotherhood Leader Highlights Reforms, Future
     Plans," Yusra Ahmed, trans., *Zaman al-Wasl*, March 20, 2015, https://
     en.zamanalwsl.net/news/9402.html.

11. Zuheir Salem, "The Brotherhood's Man in London," interview by Tam
     Hussein, *Al Majalla Magazine*, April 23, 2013.

12. The Muslim Brotherhood in Syria, "Statement of the Muslim Brotherhood
     in Syria on Current Developments," *The Syrian Observer*, May 7, 2013,
     http://syrianobserver.com/EN/Resources/24756.

13. Ali Sadreddine al-Bayanouni, "A Brotherhood Vision for Syria: In
     Conversation with the Former Leader of the Syrian Muslim Brotherhood,"
     interview by Tam Hussein, *Al Majalla Magazine*, November 29, 2013.

14. Zaman al-Wasl, "Interview: Muslim Brotherhood Leader Walid," *The
     Syrian Observer*, February 17, 2015.

15. Zaman al-Wasl, "Waad Party Is Not Muslim Brotherhood Affiliate:
     Deputy," *The Syrian Observer*, March 19, 2014.

16. Zaman al-Wasl, "Interview: Muslim Brotherhood Leader Walid," *The
     Syrian Observer*, March 19, 2014.

17. For more on the Syrian Muslim Brotherhood's internal dynamics, see
     Raphaël Lefèvre, "The Muslim Brotherhood Prepares for a Comeback
     in Syria," *Carnegie Papers* (Washington, DC: Carnegie Endowment for
     International Peace, May 7, 2013).

18. "Syria's Muslim Brotherhood Leader Highlights Reforms, Future Plans,"
     Zaman Al-Wasl, March 20, 2015.

19. These generational dynamics are covered in further detail in Raphaël Lefèvre,
     "The Muslim Brotherhood Prepares for a Comeback in Syria," *Carnegie Papers*
     (Washington, DC: Carnegie Endowment for International Peace, May 7, 2013).

20. Quoted in Raphaël Lefèvre, "A Revolution in Syria's Muslim Brotherhood?"
     Carnegie Endowment for International Peace, January 23, 2014.

21. Raphaël Lefèvre, "New Leaders for the Syrian Muslim Brotherhood,"
     Carnegie Endowment for International Peace, December 11, 2014,
     http://carnegieendowment.org/2014/12/11/
     new-leaders-for-syrian-muslim-brotherhood-pub-57453.

22. "Syria's Muslim Brotherhood Leader Highlights Reforms, Future Plans,"
     Zaman Al-Wasl, March 20, 2015.

23. Ruth Sherlock, "Muslim Brotherhood Establishes Militia Inside Syria,"
     Daily Telegraph, August 3, 2012.

24. Riyadh al-Shuqfa quoted in Raphaël Lefèvre, "The Brotherhood Starts
     Anew in Syria," *Al Majalla Magazine*, March 19, 2013. For a more
     comprehensive account of the relationship between the Shields of the
     Revolution Commission and the Syrian Muslim Brotherhood, see Ali el-
     Yessir and Raphaël Lefèvre, "Militias for the Syrian Muslim Brotherhood?"
     Carnegie Endowment for International Peace, October 29, 2013.

25. This is an excerpt from the political platform of the Shields of the Revolution Commission quoted in Raphaël Lefèvre, "The Muslim Brotherhood in Syria: A 'Centrist' Jihad?" *Turkish Review* 4, no. 2 (March 2014).

26. "Syria's Muslim Brotherhood Leader Highlights Reforms, Future Plans," *Zaman Al-Wasl*, March 20, 2015.

27. Raphaël Lefèvre, "The Sham Legion: Syria's Moderate Islamists," Carnegie Endowment for International Peace, April 15, 2014.

28. Elad Benari, "Syria's Muslim Brotherhood: There's No Extremism in Syria," *Arutz Sheva*, April 16, 2013.

29. "Syrian Muslim Brotherhood Leader: We Disagree with ISIS in Principle, Approach," *Ikhwan Web*, October 4, 2014.

30. Zaman al-Wasl, "Interview: Muslim Brotherhood Leader Walid," *The Syrian Observer*, March 19, 2014.

31. Ibid.

32. For more on the thought of Said Hawwa, see Itzchak Weismann, "Sa'id Hawwa: The Making of a Radical Muslim Thinker in Modern Syria," *Middle Eastern Studies* 29, no. 4 (1993): 601–623.

33. The complete video of the speech of Sheikh Abu Hafez is available at "Kalima liShaykh al-Da'iya Abu Hafez hawl al-tadakhkhul al-amriki wa istihdaf Da'ish [Speech of Preacher Sheikh Abu Hafez about US Intervention and Targeting Daesh]," YouTube video, posted by "durue alththawra," September 21, 2014, https://www.youtube.com/watch?v=qfKol6YwTsI.

34. Zaman al-Wasl, "Interview: Muslim Brotherhood Leader Walid," *The Syrian Observer*, March 19, 2014.

35. "Syria's Muslim Brotherhood Leader Highlights Reforms, Future Plans," *Zaman Al-Wasl*, March 20, 2015.

Chapter 5

1. Nathan Brown, *When Victory Is Not an Option: Islamist Movements in Arab Politics* (Ithaca, NY: Cornell University Press, 2012), 60.

2. Susanne Dahlgren, *Contesting Realities: The Public Sphere and Morality in Yemen* (Syracuse, NY: Syracuse University Press, 2010).

3. J. Leigh Douglas, *The Free Yemeni Movement, 1935–1962* (Beirut: American University in Beirut Press, 1987), 124. For an elaboration of this point, see Sheila Carapico's discussion of Free Yemeni and Muslim Brotherhood convergence around publication of the Sacred National Charter in 1948 (Carapico, *Civil Society in Yemen: The Political Economy of Activism in Southern Arabia*, Cambridge: Cambridge University Press, 2007, 98).

4. According to Dresch, Brotherhood leader Yassīn 'Abd al-'Aziz al-Qubātī was among those expelled from Cairo following the Nasser regime's execution of Sayyid Qutb. See Paul Dresch, *A History of Modern Yemen* (Cambridge: Cambridge University Press, 2001), 246n58.

5. As an indication of the limits of arguments about sectarianism, the Aḥmars are traditionally Zaydi, yet Shaykh 'Abd Allah was one of the founding

members of the presumptively Sunni Islah party and his son Hamīd is one of its leaders—and leading financiers—today.

6. Michaelle Browers, *Political Ideology in the Arab World: Accommodation and Transformation* (Cambridge: Cambridge University Press, 2007), 141–142.

7. Dresch, *A History of Modern Yemen*, 175–176.

8. Dresch, *A History of Modern Yemen*, 176.

9. Literally partisanship, but connoting a form of division among Muslims likely to provoke *fitna*, or disorder, within the umma. The decision to participate in an imperfect system was a wedge issue, as it has been among Islamists elsewhere, and many Salafis opted not to participate in partisan politics they decried as a form of *hizbīyya*.

10. Brown, *When Victory Is Not an Option*, 69.

11. Oral history interviews with midlevel Islahi leaders in the mid- to late 2000s consistently indicated the role of university politics and campus organizing in the development of political skills and ideological coherence, as well as to the building of postpartisan networks. See Stacey Philbrick Yadav, "Antecedents of the Revolution: Intersectoral Networks and Post-Partisanship in Yemen," *Studies in Ethnicity and Nationalism* 11, no. 3 (2011): 550–563.

12. Stacey Philbrick Yadav, *Islamists and the State: Legitimacy and Institutions in Yemen and Lebanon* (London: I.B. Taurus, 2013), 42–43.

13. Sarah Phillips, *Yemen and the Politics of Permanent Crisis* (New York, NY: Routledge for the International Institute for Strategic Studies, 2011).

14. Lengthy extracts from a number of interviews with leading JMP figures at the time of the postponement are included in Stacey Philbrick Yadav and Janine Clark, "Disappointments and New Directions: Women, Partisanship, and the Regime in Yemen," *HAWWA* 8 (2010): 83–88.

15. As Muhammed Qaḥtān explained to Egypt's *Al-Ahram*, "There can be no compromising on this principle and the republican theory. At the very least, the Houthis have to say that they accept this. We need a nation state that offers partnership to all and in which every person is free in his beliefs. We are for democracy and the principle that the people are the source of power." (Ahmed Eleiba, "Interview: Mohammed Qahtan, Senior Member of Yemen's al-Islah," *Al-Ahram*, November 27, 2014, http://english. ahram.org.eg/WriterArticles/NewsContentP/2/116588/World/Interview-Mohammed-Qahtan,-senior-member-of-Yemens.aspx).

16. Stacey Philbrick Yadav, interview with Raufa Hassan, January 7, 2009. In individual (but significant and publicly discussed) cases, there was demonstrable movement toward the political center by Brotherhood figures. A prominent feminist figure, for example, recalled that a well-known Islahi leader from the Brotherhood faction once participated in physically barring a bus of female students from reaching a research center devoted to gender studies at Sana'a University, and then less than a decade later threatened to resign from the party unless the Brotherhood faction's more gender-progressive positions were adopted by the whole.

17. Like Yemen's other major political parties, no internal elections have been held within Islah since the 2011 uprising. This makes it difficult to assess the distribution of views within the party today, though a poll of partisan youth ahead of the National Dialogue Conference suggested that senior Brotherhood figures welcome youth mobilization more than youth voice. (Ala Qassem, "Five Barriers to Youth Engagement, Decision-Making, and Leadership in Yemen's Political Parties," *Saferworld Briefing*, December 2013, http://www.saferworld.org.uk/resources/view-resource/785-five-barriers-to-youth-engagement-decision-making-and-leadership-in-yemens-political-parties).

18. For a good discussion of the consequences of the Dammaj conflict and the dispersion of defeated Salafi students and militants, see Peter Salisbury, "Yemen: Stemming the Rise of Chaos State," Chatham House Middle East and North Africa Program (London: Royal Institute for International Affairs, May 25, 2016), https://www.chathamhouse.org/publication/yemen-stemming-rise-chaos-state.

19. Anthony Shadid, Nada Bakri, and Kareem Fahim, "Waves of Unrest Spread to Yemen, Shaking a Region," *New York Times*, January 28, 2011, http://www.nytimes.com/2011/01/28/world/middleeast/28unrest.html?_r=1. According to my own discussions with members of the JMP at the time, the color-coding of the early protests in January 2011 was deliberately chosen to signal the "color of love" and to indicate that the JMP, unlike opposition activists in Tunisia, was calling for reform, not revolution.

20. Erik Stier, "Saleh, Yemen Opposition Agree on Plan to Transfer Power," *Christian Science Monitor*, April 26, 2011, http://www.csmonitor.com/World/Middle-East/2011/0426/Saleh-Yemen-opposition-agree-on-plan-to-transfer-power.

21. For an excellent account of the transformations that unfolded among partisan and independent youth during 11 months of protest, see Laurent Bonnefoy, Marine Poirer, and Jasper Cooper, trans., "The Structuration of the Yemeni Revolution: Exploring a Process in Motion," *Revue Française de Science Politique* 62, no. 5–6: 131–150.

22. The JMP has always operated on a formal power-sharing model internally, but Islahi and non-Islahi members have also long recognized Islah's disproportionate weight within the alliance. Under Saleh, members of the smaller parties in the JMP suggested that they viewed their relationship with Islah pragmatically, ceding some agenda-setting power to the larger party in exchange for its protection.

23. While Islah's grassroots standing declined significantly over the 2000s, no other member of the JMP saw great grassroots gains, meaning that Islah's claim to popular leverage over the other JMP member parties was largely intact at the beginning of its shift into government in 2011.

24. United Nations Department of Political Affairs, "Agreement on the Implementation Mechanism for the Transition Process in

Yemen in Accordance with the Initiative of the Gulf Cooperation Council (GCC)," December 5, 2011, http://peacemaker.un.org/yemen- transition-mechanism2011.

25. Ibid.

26. Abubakr Al-Shamahi, "New 'Parallel Revolution' Against Corruption," *Al-Jazeera*, January 2, 2012, http://www.aljazeera.com/indepth/opinion/2012/01/201211114410857143.html.

27. Media coverage of the Life March, in which tens of thousands of Yemenis walked 264 kilometers over the course of four days, was muted, but Yemeni activists and journalists at the #SupportYemen media collective and Global Voices, among others, made ample use of social media and citizen journalism to document the events. See http://lifemarch.supportyemen.org/ and "Yemen: The Amazing Life March Arrives in Sanaa," *Global Voices*, December 24, 2011, http://globalvoicesonline.org/2011/12/24/yemen-the-amazing-march-of-life-arrives-in-sanaa/ for examples. Yemeni analyst Atiaf al-Wazir covered the event for *Muftah*. See Atiaf al-Wazir, "In Yemen, the Life March Revives the Debate on Immunity for Saleh," *Muftah*, December 22, 2011, http://muftah.org/in-yemen-the-life-march-revives-the-debate-on-immunity-for-saleh/#.VaAvgPPD_5q.

28. Farea al-Muslimi, "Yemen's Brotherhood: Early Losses and an Unknown Future," *Al-Monitor*, September 25, 2013, http://www.al-monitor.com/pulse/originals/2013/09/yemen-brotherhood-losses-unknown-future.html#.

29. "Protests Continue Over 'Life March' Killings," *Yemen Times*, December 26, 2011, http://www.yementimes.com/en/1532/news/146/Protests-continue-over-%E2%80%98Life-March%E2%80%99-killings.htm.

30. Farea al-Muslimi, "Deadlocked Yemen," Sada. Carnegie Endowment for International Peace, June 20, 2013, http://carnegieendowment.org/sada/2013/06/20/surmounting-southern-stalemate/gb6g.

31. Arab Center for Research and Policy Studies, "Outcomes of Yemen's National Dialogue Conference: A Step Toward Conflict Resolution and State-Building?" February 2014, http://english.dohainstitute.org/file/get/a6de2897-5e7e-417d-953a-90f10a527da9.pdf.

32. Nasser Arrabaye, "National Dimensions of the Saada Conflict," Sada. Carnegie Endowment for International Peace, November 26, 2013, http://carnegieendowment.org/sada/2013/11/26/national-dimensions-of-saada-conflict/guol.

33. Khalid al-Karimi, "Islah Appoints Arrested Members as Dialogue Representatives," *Yemen Times*, March 16, 2015, http://www.yementimes.com/en/1868/news/4970/Islah-appoints-arrested-members-as-dialogue-representatives.htm.

34. See Toby Matthiesen's chapter in this volume, p. 126.

35. Some analysts (like Salisbury, earlier) conflate the power of General Ali Muhsin with the power of Islah and thus argue that his rising fortunes are coequal to the rising fortunes of Islah. While the general certainly has ties to the

organization and has played a coordinating role among Islah-aligned militias, he reflects neither the ideological nor the institutional foundations of the Muslim Brotherhood cohort.

36. Laurent Bonnefoy, "The Islah Party in Yemen: Game Over?" *Muftah*, February 27, 2015, http://muftah.org/Islah-party-yemen-game/ #.VQLcOvnF8VA.

Chapter 6

1. Omar Ashour, interview with Belhaj Al-Amin, Tripoli, March 1, 2012.
2. Ahmad Mansour, interview with Soliman Abd al-Qadr (former general observer of the Muslim Brotherhood in Libya), "'Ilaqat al-Ikwan ma' al-nizam al-Libi [The Relationship Between the Brothers and the Libyan Regime]," *Bila Hudud*, al-Jazeera Arabic, August 7, 2005; Mahmoud Al-Naku', "Al-Harakat al-islamiyya al-haditha fi Libya [Modern Islamist Movements in Libya]," *Libya Forum for Human Development* (2010): 23.
3. Ahmad Mansour, interview with Fawzi Abu Kitef [Muslim Brotherhood leader and head of the Revolutionary Brigades Coalition], *Shahid 'Ala al-Asr*, al-Jazeera Arabic, February 8, 2012.
4. Sami Kleib, interview with Soliman Abdel Qadir, Liqa' Khas, *Al-Jazeera*, May 30, 2009.
5. Mansour, *Shahid 'Ala al-Asr*, February 8, 2012.
6. Abu Selim is a maximum-security prison in Tripoli, Libya. It was notorious during the rule of Muammar Qaddafi for human rights abuses, including a 1996 massacre in which Human Rights Watch estimated that more than 1,270 prisoners were killed by regime forces in two days.
7. Soliman Abdel Qadir, *Al-Jazeera*, May 30, 2009.
8. Khaled al-Mahreer, interview with Bashir al-Kubty, *Al-Jazeera*, November 21, 2011.
9. Ali al-Zafiri, interview with Jum'a Al-Gumati (former NTC representative in London), *Fi al-'Umq*, al-Jazeera Arabic, February 16, 2011.
10. Omar Ashour, interview with Ali al-Sallabi, February 1, 2012.
11. Bashir al-Kubty, *Al-Jazeera*, November 21, 2011.
12. Omar Ashour, interview with Abdel Nasser Shamata, June 15, 2011.
13. Omar Ashour, interview with Noman Benotman (former Shura Council member of the LIFG), April 27, 2010.
14. Omar Ashour, interview with Salem Mohamed (head of Salafi Forum in Libya), June 17, 2011; Omar Ashour, interview with Noman Benotman, April 12, 2011.
15. Al-Sadiq Al-Ruqay'i, "Al-Islamiyun fi Libya: tarikh wa jihad—Juz' 3 [The Islamists in Libya: History and Jihad—Part 3]," *Al-Manara*, January 12, 2012; Omar Ashour, interview with Noman Benotman, April 12, 2011.
16. Omar Ashour, interview with Salem Mohamed, June 17, 2011.
17. Omar Ashour, interview with Sami al-Saadi, Cairo, August 2012.
18. Omar Ashour, interview with Mohamed Abdul Hakim, Benghazi, June 2012.

19. Omar Ashour, interview with Jamila Marzouki, Benghazi, June 2012.

20. Omar Ashour, "The Sisi Leaks and Intra-Regime Power Dynamics," *Al-Araby*, February 17, 2015, http://www.alaraby.co.uk/english/comment/82beaa66-eeb4-4725-8dfa-d6e4f905958c.

21. https://www.youtube.com/watch?v=WssBlKvUbq4. This video has since been deleted from YouTube.

22. David D. Kirkpatrick and Eric Schmitt, "Arab Nations Strike in Libya, Surprising U.S.," *New York Times*, August 25, 2014, http://www.nytimes.com/2014/08/26/world/africa/egypt-and-united-arab-emirates-said-to-have-secretly-carried-out-libya-airstrikes.html?_r=0.

23. "Ma wara' al-khabr—Imkaniyya al-hall al-diplomasi fi Libya," YouTube video, 26:01, posted by Al Jazeera Arabic, February 18, 2015, http://youtu.be/WWEd6V2LPyQ.

24. David D. Kirkpatrick and Eric Schmitt, "Arab Nations Strike in Libya, Surprising U.S.," *New York Times*, August 25, 2014.

25. Composed primarily of Misratan military units.

26. Omar Ashour, interview with Mohamed Abdullah (General National Congress [Tripoli Parliament] member and the leader of the National Front Party), Istanbul, March 2015.

27. Missy Ryan, "US Strikes Islamic State Strongholds in Libya," *Washington Post*, August 1, 2016, https://www.washingtonpost.com/news/checkpoint/wp/2016/08/01/united-states-strikes-islamic-state-stronghold-in-libya-expands-campaign-against-militant-group/.

28. Mohamed al-Herbawy, "Majlis Shura Shabab al-Islam yumahid li iqamit al-khilafa fi Derna [Consultative Council of Islamic Youth Prepares for Establishing a Caliphate in Derna]," *Al-Wasat*, October 6, 2014.

29. Ibrahim Darwish, " 'Adat muqatili al-Battar [The Return of al-Battar Fighters]," *Al-Quds al-Arabi*, December 7, 2015.

30. "Libya a Massive Safe Haven for ISIS Now, U.N. Warns," *CBS News*, December 1, 2015, http://www.cbsnews.com/news/libya-safe-haven-isis-3000-fighters-un-warns/.

31. Andrew Tilghman, "Size of ISIS Force Declining in Iraq and Syria, According to New Intel," *Military Times*, February 4, 2016.

Chapter 7

1. Faysal sought to employ Islam as a counternarrative in his rivalry with President Nasser and the latter's form of Arab nationalism. In what was termed the "Arab Cold War," Saudi Arabia sought to reposition itself as the central country of the "Islamic world" and established institutions such as the Muslim World League and the Organisation of Islamic Cooperation (OIC). See, among others, Jesse Ferris, *Nasser's Gamble: How Intervention in Yemen Caused the Six-Day War and the Decline of Egyptian Power* (Princeton, NJ: Princeton University Press, 2013), and for the original argument, Malcolm Kerr, *The Arab Cold War: Gamal 'Abd al-Nasir and His Rivals, 1958-1970*, 3rd ed. (Oxford: Oxford University Press, 1971).

2. James P. Piscatori, "Islamic Values and National Interest: The Foreign Policy of Saudi Arabia," in *Islam and Foreign Policy*, ed. Adeed Dawisha (Cambridge: Cambridge University Press, 1983); Menno Preuschaft, "Islam and Identity in Foreign Policy," in *Saudi Arabian Foreign Policy: Conflict and Cooperation*, ed. Neil Partrick (London: I.B. Tauris, 2016).

3. See for example Mary Atkins, "Saudi Arabia Has 'No Problem' with Muslim Brotherhood: Foreign Minister," *Middle East Eye*, February 11, 2011; Ibrahim al-Hatlani, "Next Saudi Royal Generation Takes Lead," *Al-Monitor*, June 24, 2015, http://www.al-monitor.com/pulse/originals/2015/06/saudi-arabia-future-challenges-king-salman.html.

4. Of course, these Arab nationalist states also cooperated with Islamists and had a much more nuanced approach than is generally assumed. For an account of the Syrian case, see Thomas Pierret, *Religion and State in Syria: The Sunni Ulama from Coup to Revolution* (Cambridge: Cambridge University Press, 2013).

5. For background on the relationship between religion and politics in Saudi Arabia, see David Commins, *The Wahhabi Mission and Saudi Arabia* (London: I.B. Tauris, 2006); Natana J. DeLong-Bas, *Wahhabi Islam: From Revival and Reform to Global Jihad* (London: I.B. Tauris, 2007); Nabil Mouline, *Les clercs de l'Islam: autorité religieuse et pouvoir politique en Arabie Saoudite, XVIIIe–XXIe siècle* (Paris: Presses Universitaires de France, 2011); Guido Steinberg, *Religion und Staat in Saudi-Arabien: Die wahhabitischen Gelehrten 1902–1953* (Würzburg: Ergon Verlag, 2002).

6. "Saudi Grand Mufti Slams Popular Protests as Anti-Islamic," *Now*, November 28, 2012; " 'ISIS Is Enemy No. 1 of Islam,' says Saudi Grand Mufti," *Al Arabiya*, August 19, 2014, http://english.alarabiya.net/en/News/middle-east/2014/08/19/Saudi-mufti-ISIS-is-enemy-No-1-of-Islam-.html; "KSA Stalled Safavid March," *Arab News*, February 10, 2016, http://www.arabnews.com/featured/news/878246.

7. For an analysis of how they reacted to the regional events in early 2011, see Stéphane Lacroix, "Is Saudi Arabia Immune?" *Journal of Democracy* 22, no. 4 (October 2011): 48–59.

8. Nora Abdulkarim, "Trial of Saudi Civil Rights Activists Mohammad al-Qahtani and Abdullah al-Hamid," *Jadaliyya*, September 3, 2012, http://www.jadaliyya.com/pages/index/7174/trial-of-saudi-civil-rights-activists-mohammad-al-.

9. Over the past decades, and in particular since 9/11 and the start of the jihadist insurgency in Saudi Arabia in 2003, thousands of Saudis have been imprisoned and in some cases held for years without public trial. Estimates of the numbers of prisoners vary, but there are likely thousands. Small, flash-mob-like protests calling for the release of political prisoners have erupted in many places across the country, including in Riyadh and Qasim, from 2011 onwards. Stéphane Lacroix, *Saudi Islamists and the Arab Spring*, Kuwait Programme on

Development, Governance and Globalisation in the Gulf States, 2014, http://eprints.lse.ac.uk/56725/1/Lacroix_Saudi-Islamists-and-theArab-Spring_2014.pdf, 15–18. See also the main Twitter account of the movement for the release of political prisoners, https://twitter.com/e3teqal.

10. For more on Al-Awda see Madawi Al-Rasheed, "Salman Al-Awdah: In the Shadow of Revolutions," *Jadaliyya*, April 27, 2013.

11. The letter was released on his Twitter account, @salman_ alodah. See also Toby Matthiesen, *Sectarian Gulf: Bahrain, Saudi Arabia, and the Arab Spring That Wasn't* (Stanford, CA: Stanford University Press, 2013), 85f.

12. Lacroix, *Saudi Islamists and the Arab Spring*.

13. See for example Stéphane Lacroix, "Osama bin Laden and the Saudi Muslim Brotherhood," *Foreign Policy*, October 3, 2012.

14. Toby Matthiesen, "Sectarianism After the Saudi Mosque Bombings," *Washington Post*, May 29, 2015.

15. Stéphane Lacroix, *Awakening Islam: The Politics of Religious Dissent in Contemporary Saudi Arabia* (Cambridge, MA: Harvard University Press, 2011).

16. Ibid.

17. Kuwait, the United Arab Emirates, and Saudi Arabia pledged funds to Egypt immediately after the coup that brought Abdel Fattah al-Sissi to power. They again pledged $4 billion each at the start of the Egypt Economic Development Conference held in March 2015 in Sharm El-Sheikh. See "Gulf States Again Prove to Be Egypt's Bulwark," *Gulf News*, March 21, 2015, http://gulfnews.com/business/economy/gulf-states-again-prove-to-be-egypt-s-bulwark-1.1475506. See also David D. Kirkpatrick, "Recordings Suggest Emirates and Egyptian Military Pushed Ousting of Morsi," *New York Times*, March 1, 2015, http://www.nytimes.com/2015/03/02/world/middleeast/recordings-suggest-emirates-and-egyptian-military-pushed-ousting-of-morsi.html?_r=0, and David D. Kirkpatrick, Peter Baker, and Michael R. Gordon, "How American Hopes for a Deal in Egypt Were Undercut," *New York Times*, August 17, 2013, http://www.nytimes.com/2013/08/18/world/middleeast/pressure-by-us-failed-to-sway-egypts-leaders.html.

18. Khaled Abou El-Fadl, "Failure of a Revolution," in *Routledge Handbook of the Arab Spring: Rethinking Democratization,* ed. Larbi Sadiki (New York: Routledge, 2015), 265f. Other Egyptian Salafi groups and parties, however, did not endorse the coup and in fact denounced it. For more on the Salafis in Egypt see Stéphane Lacroix, "Sheikhs and Politicians: Inside the New Egyptian Salafism," Brookings Policy Brief, June 11, 2012, http://www.brookings.edu/research/papers/2012/06/07-egyptian-salafism-lacroix.

19. The Saudi cleric Nasir al-Umar, seen as the leader of the Sururis, was particularly vocal. See Jon B. Alterman and William McCants, "Saudi Arabia: Islamists Rising and Falling," in *Religious Radicalism After the*

Arab Uprisings, ed. Jon B. Alterman (Washington, DC: Center for Strategic & International Studies, 2015), 166f, http://csis.org/publication/ saudi-arabia-islamists-rising-and-falling.

20. See, for example, "Saudi Religious Scholars Accuse Egyptian Salafist Al-Nour Party of Obstructing Sharia," *Middle East Monitor*, January 13, 2014, https://www.middleeastmonitor.com/news/africa/9200-saudi-religious-scholars-accuse-egyptian-salafist-al-nour-party-of-obstructing-sharia.

21. Marc Lynch, "Gulf Islamist Dissent over Egypt," *Foreign Policy*, August 18, 2013; Lacroix, *Saudi Islamists and the Arab Spring*, 25–27.

22. "Saudi Arabia Declares Muslim Brotherhood 'Terrorist Group'," *BBC News*, March 7, 2014, http://www.bbc.co.uk/news/world-middle-east-26487092; Stéphane Lacroix, "Saudi Arabia's Muslim Brotherhood Predicament," *Project on Middle East Political Science*, March 20, 2014, http://pomeps.org/2014/03/20/ saudi-arabias-muslim-brotherhood-predicament.

23. Madawi Al-Rasheed, "Saudi Officials Shut Down Display at Book Fair," *Al-Monitor*, March 13, 2014, http://www.al-monitor.com/pulse/originals/ 2014/03/saudi-book-display-shut-down.html.

24. For the statements made at the summit see "Qimma Sharm al-Sheikh 28–29 Mars 2015," *League of Arab States*, March 28, 2015, http://www.lasportal. org/ar/summits/Pages/default.aspx?Stype=1&imgLib=ArabicSummit& year=2015#tab6; Hamza Hendawi, "Arab League Unveils Joint Military Force amid Yemen Crisis," *Associated Press*, March 29, 2015, https:// www.yahoo.com/news/pakistan-sending-plane-evacuate-those-stranded-yemen-052519007.html?ref=gs.

25. "Islamische Kritik an der saudischen Regierung: Gespräch mit dem Kleriker Salman al-Audah," *Neue Zürcher Zeitung*, April 17, 2012, http://www.nzz.ch/aktuell/international/ islamische-kritik-an-der-saudischen-regierung-1.16481903.

26. "UN Says '25,000 Foreign Fighters' Joined Islamist Militants," *BBC News*, April 2, 2015, http://www.bbc.com/news/world-middle-east-32156541.

27. Lacroix, *Saudi Islamists and the Arab Spring*, 4f.

28. Control over Mecca and Medina was crucial for the legitimacy of caliphs throughout much of Islamic history.

29. Toby Matthiesen, "Sectarianism Comes Back to Bite Saudi Arabia," *Washington Post*, November 18, 2014, cage/wp/2014/11/18/ sectarianism-comes-back-to-bite-saudi-arabia.

30. Toby Matthiesen, "Sectarianism After the Saudi Mosque Bombings," *Washington Post*, May 29, 2015, http://www.washingtonpost.com/blogs/ monkey-cage/wp/2015/05/29/sectarianism-after-the-saudi-mosque-bombings. For a detailed analysis see Cole Bunzel, *The Kingdom and the Caliphate: Duel of the Islamic States*, Carnegie Endowment for International Peace, February 2016,

http://carnegieendowment.org/2016/02/18/kingdom-and-caliphate-duel-of-islamic-states/iu4w. Al-Rafida is commonly used as a term by Saudi Islamists to describe the Shi'a and signifies their rejection of the caliphs Abu Bakr, 'Umar, and 'Uthman as rightful successors of Muhammad. See Raihan Ismail, *Saudi Clerics and Shi'a Islam* (New York: Oxford University Press, 2016).

31. "Nineteen People Arrested over Saudi Arabia Attacks," *Al-Jazeera*, July 8, 2016, 160707214101387.html.

32. For this argument, see Toby Matthiesen, *Sectarian Gulf.*

33. Thomas Hegghammer, *Jihad in Saudi Arabia: Violence and Pan-Islamism Since 1979* (Cambridge: Cambridge University Press, 2010).

34. Yaroslav Trofimov, "New Saudi King Brings Major Change at Home and Abroad," *Wall Street Journal*, April 29, 2015.

35. "Liqa' al-Yawm - Salman al-'Awda," Youtube video, posted by Al Jazeera Arabic, March 30, 2015, https://www.youtube.com/watch?v=1R5K4eNV_ww#t=38.

36. "'Asifat al-Hazm," *Islam Online*, 2015, http://www.islamtoday.net/files/DecisiveStorm.

37. "Al-Safawiyyin wa-'asifat al-hazm [The Safavids and Operation Decisive Storm]," YouTube video, posted by Al-Qanat al-Rasmiyya li Shaykh Dr. Muhammad al-'Arifi, March 28, 2015, https://youtube/RHCgeukHkss.

38. "'Labayk ya Salman': Jadeed al-Shaykh Dr. 'A'id al-Qarni," *Sabq Online,* March 31, 2015, https://sabq.org/yE2gde.

39. Awad al-Qarni, Twitter, https://twitter.com/awadalqarni.

40. Toby Matthiesen and Sebastian Sons, "The Yemen War in Saudi Media," *Muftah*, July 20, 2016, http://muftah.org/yemen-war-saudi-media.

41. There was a controversy on Twitter when one Saudi Shiite writer, Tawfiq al-Sayf, expressed his regret for the victims of a suicide bombing during a Houthi gathering in March 2015. Sayf was attacked on Twitter for saying this, which some Saudis saw as an endorsement by a Saudi Shiite for the Houthis for sectarian reasons. As soon as the war started, however, Sayf sided with the Saudi government, saying on Twitter that he would support any effort to protect the nation that would bring Saudis together. He argued that some wars could lead to more wars, but that he thought the idea of an Arab military force as a stabilizing factor was a good idea and could lead to a resolving of the region's issues. Sayf's views are important, because he was in the early 1990s the secretary general of the Reformist Movement, as the main Saudi Shiite Islamist organization, the Shirazi Movement, was known at the time. He has since served as an interlocutor between the Shiites and the government. See Tawfiq al-Sayf, Twitter post, March 25, 2015, 10:27 PM, https://twitter.com/t_saif/status/580964238153273344; "Hashtag «al-Houthi yuhaddid al-Sa'udiyya» didd «Librali Shi'i» a'lana t'atufahu ma'a

al-Houthiyeen," *Al-Khabr*, March 22, 2015, http://www.alkhabarnow. net/news/182783/2015/03/22; "War Gives Birth to a Solution," *Aawsat*, April 1, 2015, http://aawsat.com/home/article/326156/%D8%AA%D9% 88%D9%81%D9%8A%D9%82-%D8%A7%D9%84%D8%B3%D9%8A %D9%81/%D8%AD%D8%B1%D8%A8-%D8%AA%D9%84%D8%AF- %D8%AD%D9%84%D8%A7%D9%8B.

42. He also called on people in the south of Saudi Arabia to be on high alert and defend themselves against any Houthi attack without relying on the government. See for example the following speech: "Halaqa al-bath al-mubashir li-yawm al-khamis," YouTube video, posted by Qanat al-Islah, April 10, 2015, https://www.youtube.com/watch?v=D3fkTD57D0A.

43. See for example the tweets by Hamza al-Hasan and Fouad Ibrahim.

44. See Claudia Ghrawi, "Structural and Physical Violence in Saudi Arabian Oil Towns, 1953-1956," in *Urban Violence in the Middle East: Changing Cityscapes in the Transition from Empire to Nation State,* ed. Ulrike Freitag et al. (New York: Berghahn, 2015), 243–264; Claudia Ghrawi, "A Tamed Urban Revolution: Saudi Arabia's Oil Conurbation and the 1967 Riots," in *Violence and the City in the Modern Middle East,* ed. Nelida Fuccaro (Stanford, CA: Stanford University Press, 2016), 109–126; Toby Matthiesen, "Migration, Minorities and Radical Networks: Labour Movements and Opposition Groups in Saudi Arabia, 1950-1975," *International Review of Social History* 59, no. 3 (Autumn 2014), 473–504.

45. For background on political movements among the Saudi Shi'a, including the Shirazi movement, see Fouad Ibrahim, *The Shi'is of Saudi Arabia* (London: Saqi Books, 2006), and Toby Matthiesen, *The Other Saudis: Shiism, Dissent and Sectarianism* (Cambridge: Cambridge University Press, 2015).

46. For background on this political trend see Toby Matthiesen, "Hizbullah al-Hijaz: A History of the Most Radical Saudi Shi'a Opposition Group," *Middle East Journal* 64, no. 2 (Spring 2010), 179–197.

47. For more on the protest movement in the Eastern Province see Toby Matthiesen, "A 'Saudi Spring'? The Shi'a Protest Movement in the Eastern Province 2011–2012," *Middle East Journal* 66, no. 4 (Autumn 2012), 628–659; Toby Matthiesen, "The Local and the Transnational in the Arab Uprisings: The Protests in Saudi Arabia's Eastern Province," in *The Silent Revolution: The Arab Spring and the Gulf States,* ed. May Seikaly and Khawla Matar (Berlin: Gerlach Press, 2014), 105–143.

48. Rori Donaghy, "Police Officer Killed in Security Raids on Saudi Arabia's Eastern Province," *Middle East Eye*, April 5, 2015, http://www. middleeasteye.net/news/security-forces-raid-saudi-arabias-eastern-province-stop-anti-yemen-war-protests-451186533.

49. Toby Matthiesen, "The Shi'a of Saudi Arabia at a Crossroads," *Middle East Report Online,* May 6, 2009.

50. Brian Murphy, "Saudi Shiites Worry About Backlash from Yemen War," *Washington Post,* April, 8, 2015, https://www.washingtonpost.com/world/

middle_east/saudi-shiites-worry-about-backlash-from-yemen-war/
2015/04/07/10b01be2-dc7e-11e4-b6d7-b9bc8acf16f7_story.html?utm_
term=.91ee91385241.

51. For more on this group of people see Madawi Al-Rasheed, *Muted
Modernists: The Struggle over Divine Politics in Saudi Arabia*
(London: Hurst, 2015).

Chapter 8

1. Courtney Freer, interview with Sami al-Farraj, Kuwait, November 13, 2013.
2. Courtney Freer, interview with British diplomat stationed in Kuwait, Kuwait, November 14, 2014.
3. Nathan J. Brown and Scott Williamson, "Kuwait's Muslim Brotherhood Under Pressure," *Foreign Policy*, November 20, 2013, http://foreignpolicy.com/2013/11/20/kuwaits-muslim-brotherhood-under-pressure/.
4. Sylvia Westall, "Egypt Says Two Muslim Brotherhood Members Arrested in the Gulf," *Reuters*, March 12, 2014, http://www.reuters.com/article/2014/03/12/us-egypt-brotherhood-gulf-idUSBREA2B23V20140312.
5. Habib Toumi, "Kuwait Former MP Sentenced for Insulting UAE," *Gulf News*, April 13, 2016, http://gulfnews.com/news/gulf/kuwait/kuwait-former-mp-sentenced-for-insulting-uae-1.1710578.
6. Courtney Freer, interview with Sami al-Farraj, Kuwait, November 13, 2013.
7. Nathan J. Brown, "Kuwait's 2008 Parliamentary Elections: A Setback for Democratic Islamism?" Carnegie Endowment for International Peace, May 2008, http://carnegieendowment.org/files/brown_kuwait2.pdf, 9.
8. Courtney Freer, interview with Usama al-Shahim, Kuwait, November 24, 2013.
9. Courtney Freer, interview with Abd al-Aziz al-Shayeji, Kuwait, November 27, 2013.
10. Nathan J. Brown, "Pushing Toward Party Politics? Kuwait's Islamic Constitutional Movement," *Carnegie Papers* 79 (January 2007): 15, http://carnegieendowment.org/files/cp79_brown_kuwait_final.pdf.
11. David Commins, *The Gulf State: A Modern History* (London: I.B. Tauris, 2012), 236.
12. Sami Nasir al-Khalidi, *Al-Ahzab al-Islamia fial-Kuwait: al-Shi'a, al-Ikhwan, al-Salaf* (Kuwait: Dār al-Nabā' Lil-Nashar wa-l-Tawzī', 1999), 175.
13. Ibid.
14. Ibid.
15. Sami Awadh, "Islamic Political Groups in Kuwait: Roots and Influence" (PhD diss., University of Portsmouth, 1999), 185.
16. Al-Khalidi, *Al-Ahzab*, 176.
17. Jill Crystal and Abdullah al-Shayeji, "The Pro-Democratic Agenda in Kuwait: Structures and Context," in *Political Liberalization and Democratization in the Arab World: Arab Experiences,* ed. Baghat Korany, Paul Noble, and Rex Brynen (Boulder, CO: Lynne Rienner Publishers, 1998), 105.

18. Mustafa Muhammad al-Tahan, ʿAbdullah al-ʿAli al-Mutawa wa Qadaya al-Muslimin fial-ʾAlam (Kuwait: Mustafa Muhammad al-Tahan, 2010), 94–95.
19. Awadh, "Islamic Political Groups in Kuwait," 192.
20. Ibid.
21. Ibid., 193.
22. Abdallah al-Nafisi, quoted in al-Khalidi, Al-Ahzab, 180.
23. Joseph Kostiner, "Kuwait and Bahrain," in The Politics of Islamic Revivalism: Diversity and Unity, ed. Shireen Hunter (Bloomington: Indiana University Press, 1988), 126.
24. Ibid.
25. Al-Khalidi, Al-Ahzab, 181.
26. Falah Abdallah al-Mudairis, Jamaʿat al-Ikhwan al-Muslimin fi-l-Kuwait (Kuwait: Huqūq al-Tabaʿ wa-l-Nashar Maḥfūẓa, 1994), 40–41.
27. Ibid.
28. In Arabic, the bloc's name is al-Haraka al-Dusturiyya al-Islamiyya, or the Islamic Constitutional Movement.
29. Courtney Freer, interview with former ICM member of parliament, Kuwait, November 21, 2013.
30. Courtney Freer, interview with former ICM member of parliament, Kuwait, November 24, 2013.
31. Al-Khalidi, Al-Ahzab, 188.
32. Al-Tahan, ʿAbdullah al-ʿAli al-Mutawa wa Qadaya al-Muslimin fial-ʾAlam, 111.
33. Al-Khalidi, Al-Ahzab, 189.
34. Awadh, "Islamic Political Groups in Kuwait," 210.
35. "ICM Vision, Mission and Objectives," Islamic Constitutional Movement, 3rd ed., January 2007, 3–4.
36. Brown, "Pushing Toward Party Politics?" 11.
37. Courtney Freer, interview with Shamlan al-Isa, Kuwait, November 17, 2013.
38. Brown, "Kuwait's 2008 Parliamentary Elections," 7.
39. Courtney Freer, interview with Ibrahim Hadhban, Kuwait, November 14, 2013.
40. Ismail al-Shatti, quoted in Shafeeq Ghabra, "Balancing State and Society: The Islamic Movement in Kuwait," Middle East Policy 5, no. 2 (May 1997): 69.
41. Nathan J. Brown, "When Victory Becomes an Option: Egypt's Muslim Brotherhood Confronts Success," Carnegie Endowment for International Peace, January 2012, http://carnegieendowment.org/files/brotherhood_success.pdf, 17.
42. There is no official membership list, though some 100 people are in leadership positions, suggesting a broad following. Furthermore, regardless of official membership, nonmembers often vote for the ICM due to its involvement in broader political coalitions.
43. Shadi Hamid, Temptations of Power: Islamists and Illiberal Democracy in a New Middle East (Oxford: Oxford University Press, 2014), 51.
44. Zoltan Pall, "Kuwaiti Salafism and Its Growing Influence in the Levant," Carnegie Endowment for International Peace, May 2014, http://carnegieendowment.org/files/kuwaiti_salafists.pdf, 3.
45. Ibid., 1.

46. Ibid.
47. Awadh, "Islamic Political Groups in Kuwait," 232.
48. Ibid., 238.
49. Shaykh 'Abdullah al-Sabt, quoted in Awadh, "Islamic Political Groups in Kuwait," 233.
50. Pall, "Kuwaiti Salafism," 5.
51. Ibid.
52. Bjorn Olav Utvik, "The Ikhwanization of the Salafis: Piety in the Politics of Egypt and Kuwait," *Middle East Critique* 23, no. 1 (April 2014): 19.
53. Pall, "Kuwaiti Salafism," 6.
54. Ibid.
55. Steve L. Monroe, "Salafis in Parliament: Democratic Attitudes and Party Politics in the Gulf," *Middle East Journal* 66, no. 3 (Summer 2012): 421–422.
56. William McCants, "Joining the Fray: Salafi Politics after the Arab Spring," *World Politics Review*, January 22, 2013, http://www.worldpoliticsreview. com/articles/12655/joining-the-fray-salafi-politics-after-the-arab-spring.
57. Pall, "Kuwaiti Salafism," 6.
58. Awadh, "Islamic Political Groups in Kuwait," 241.
59. Ibid., 250.
60. Pall, "Kuwaiti Salafism," 7.
61. Ibid.
62. Ibid.
63. Ibid.
64. Ibid.
65. Ibid., 8.
66. Ibid., 9.
67. Utvik, "The Ikhwanization of the Salafis," 20.
68. Ibid.
69. Ibid., 9–10.
70. Ibid.
71. Ibid., 11.
72. Utvik, "The Ikhwanization of the Salafis," 19–20.
73. Pall, "Kuwaiti Salafism," 11.
74. Ibid., 11.
75. Ibid., 22.
76. Ibid., 23.
77. Pall, "Kuwaiti Salafism," 11–12.
78. Ibid., 11–12.
79. Ibid., 12.
80. David S. Cohen, quoted in Karen DeYoung, "Kuwait, Ally on Syria, Is Also the Leading Funder of Extremist Rebels," *Washington Post*, April 25, 2014, http://www.washingtonpost.com/world/national-security/kuwait-top-ally-on-syria-is-also-the-leading-funder-of-extremist-rebels/2014/04/25/10142b9a-ca48-11e3-a75e-463587891b57_story.html.

81. Ibid., 17.

82. Ibid., 21.

83. Ibid., 17.

84. Brown, "Pushing Toward Party Politics?" 17.

85. Ibid.

86. Al-Tahan, '*Abdullah al-'Ali al- Mutawa wa Qadaya al-Muslimin fi al-'Alam*, 125.

87. Monroe, "Salafis in Parliament," 412–413.

88. Brown, "Pushing Toward Party Politics?" 9.

89. Monroe, "Salafis in Parliament," 416.

90. Ibid.

91. Kjetil Selvik, "Elite Rivalry in a Semi-Democracy: The Kuwaiti Press Scene," *Middle Eastern Studies* 47, no. 3 (2011): 479.

92. Utvik, "The Ikhwanization of the Salafis," 20.

93. Ibid.

94. Ibid.

95. Sylvia Westall, "The Quiet Influence of Kuwait's Salafis," *Reuters*, June 27, 2012, http://www.reuters.com/article/2012/06/27/us-kuwait-salafi-idUSBRE85Q0Y220120627.

96. Sharmaake Sabrie and Pekka Hakala, "Policy Briefing: Kuwait's Political Crisis Deepens," *European Union*, January 2013, http://www.europarl.europa.eu/RegData/etudes/briefing_note/join/2013/491461/EXPO-AFET_SP%282013%29491461_EN.pdf, 10.

97. Mohamed Badri 'Aid, "Al-tayar al-Salafi fi al-Kuwait: Al-waqa' wa al-mustaqbal," *Al Jazeera Center for Studies*, May 29, 2012, http://studies.aljazeera.net/reports/2012/05/201252912302826133.htm.

98. Kristin Smith Diwan, "Kuwait's Balancing Act," *Foreign Policy, The Middle East Channel*, October 13, 2012, http://mideast.foreignpolicy.com/posts/2012/10/23/kuwait_s_balancing_act.

99. Ibid.

100. Sabrie and Hakala, "Policy Briefing: Kuwait's Political Crisis Deepens," 11.

101. "Kuwait Election: Opposition Hails Boycott as Turnout Falls," *BBC News*, December 2, 2012, http://www.bbc.co.uk/news/world-middle-east-20571958.

102. Ibid.

103. Courtney Freer, interview with Nasir al-Sani.

104. Ibid.

105. "Freed Kuwait Opposition Leader Vows Protests Will Continue," *Gulf News*, July 8, 2014, http://gulfnews.com/news/gulf/kuwait/freed-kuwait-opposition-leader-vows-protests-will-continue-1.1357223.

106. E.A.D., "Kuwait's Opposition: A Reawakening," *The Economist*, April 17, 2014, http://www.economist.com/blogs/pomegranate/2014/04/kuwaits-opposition.

107. Ibid.

108. Ibid.

109. "Kuwait Arrests Opposition Figure After Saudi Embassy Complaint," *Middle East Eye*, March 18, 2015, http://www.middleeasteye.net/news/kuwait-arrests-opposition-figure-after-saudi-embassy-complaint-1329348434.

110. Brown and Williamson, "Kuwait's Muslim Brotherhood Under Pressure."

111. Ibid.

112. Toumi, "Kuwait Former MP Sentenced for Insulting UAE."

113. "UAE to Try Kuwaiti Ex-MP over Remarks on Abu Dhabi Crown Prince," *Middle East Eye*, March 9, 2015, http://www.middleeasteye.net/news/uae-try-kuwaiti-ex-mp-over-remarks-abu-dhabi-crown-prince-1546132555.

114. Shadi Hamid, *Temptations of Power*, 54–55.

115. "Al-Duwaila: 'Ala al-quwa al-siyasia an tafham hasasiat al-marhala tatalab 'an al-khalafat al-taqlidia [Al-Duwaila: The Political Forces Must Understand That the Sensitivity of the Stage Requires the Transcendence of Traditional Differences]," *ICM*, January 11, 2015, http://www.icmkw.org/site/pages/topics/alduilx_-yl649-alqu649-alsiasi629-623n-tfx_m-623n-xhsasi629-almrxhl629-ttt_lb-altyali-yn-alxlafat-altqlidi629.php?p=60#.VTOHgxfndKo.

116. Ahmed al-Baghdadi, quoted in Carrie Rosefsky Wickham, *The Muslim Brotherhood: Evolution of an Islamist Movement* (Princeton, NJ: Princeton University Press, 2013), 230.

117. Courtney Freer, interview with Abdallah al-Nibari, Kuwait, February 2, 2014.

118. Rosefsky Wickham, *The Muslim Brotherhood*, 220.

119. Nathan J. Brown, *When Victory Is Not an Option: Islamist Movements in Arab Politics* (Ithaca, NY: Cornell University Press, 2012), 239.

120. Westall, "The Quiet Influence of Kuwait's Salafis."

121. Ali al-Omair, quoted in Monroe, 413.

122. Pall, "Kuwaiti Salafism," 11–12.

123. Michael Herb, "Emirs and Parliaments in the Gulf," *Journal of Democracy* 13, no. 4 (October 2002): 47.

Chapter 9

1. Bassam al-Emoush, *Mahatat fi tarikh Jama'at al-Ikhwan al-Muslimin fi al-Urdun* [Stations in the History of the Society of the Muslim Brothers in Jordan] (Amman: Academics for Publishing and Distribution, 2008); Marion Boulby, *The Muslim Brotherhood and the Kings of Jordan, 1945-1993* (Atlanta, GA: Scholars Press, 1999).

2. Carrie Rosefsky Wickham, *The Muslim Brotherhood: Evolution of an Islamist Movement* (Princeton, NJ: Princeton University Press, 2013).

3. The Islamic Movement in Jordan, "The Islamic Movement's Vision for Reform in Jordan" (Public document, Amman, Jordan, 2005).

4. The Muslim Brotherhood and its political party boycotted in 1997 and 2010 and participated in 2003 and 2007.

5. For one explanation why, see David Siddhartha Patel, "Roundabouts and Revolutions: Public Squares, Coordination, and the Diffusion of the Arab Uprisings" (Unpublished manuscript, 2013).

6. Tareq Al Naimat, "The Jordanian Regime and the Muslim Brotherhood: A Tug of War," *Viewpoints* no. 58 (2014).

7. Their number two priority for reform is to bring legislation and official policy in harmony with the constitutional statement that Islam is the source of legislation. See Islamic Movement, "The Islamic Movement's Vision for Reform in Jordan," 12.

8. The committee proposed 41 amendments to the constitution in mid-August, none of which addressed Articles 34 through 36, which relate to the powers the Brotherhood had challenged.

9. Abdullah II ibn Al Hussein, "Discussion Papers," Official Website - King of the Hashemite Kingdom of Jordan, http://www.kingabdullah.jo/index.php/en_US/pages/view/id/244.html.

10. Jillian Schwedler and Ryan King, "Political Geography," in *The Arab Uprisings Explained: New Contentious Politics in the Middle East,* ed. Marc Lynch (New York: Columbia University Press, 2014).

11. Curtis R. Ryan, "The Implications of Jordan's New Electoral Law," *Foreign Policy*, April 13, 2012, http://foreignpolicy.com/2012/04/13/the-implications-of-jordans-new-electoral-law/.

12. National Democratic Institute, "Jordanian Elections Show Marked Improvement from Past Polls but Shortcomings Remain, NDI Delegation Finds," National Democratic Institute, January 24, 2013, https://www.ndi.org/2013-jordan-elections; "The Carter Center Releases Study Mission Report on Jordan's 2013 Parliamentary Elections," *Carter Center,* February 14, 2013, http://www.cartercenter.org/news/pr/jordan-021413.html.

13. On the Jordanian regime's tactic of deliberately dividing opposition, see Quintan Wiktorowicz, *The Management of Islamic Activism: Salafis, the Muslim Brotherhood, and State Power in Jordan* (Albany, NY: SUNY Press, 2000); Ellen Lust-Okar, *Structuring Conflict in the Arab World: Incumbents, Opponents, and Institutions* (New York: Cambridge University Press, 2007).

14. Many Islamists in Jordan are sensitive to the label "Salafi"; I have been told by several interviewees that "I am salafiyya in *aqida* [creed], but not in movement." It is not clear if Salafi participation in electoral politics in Egypt has changed how Jordanian Islamists use the term.

15. Wiktorowicz, *The Management of Islamic Activism*; Jacob Olidort, "The Politics of 'Quietist' Salafism," The Brookings Institution, Analysis Paper no. 18, February 2015.

16. For more on Mohamed Abu Faris' ideas in the context of Jordanian politics, see Shadi Hamid, *Temptations of Power: Islamists and Illiberal Democracy in a New Middle East* (New York: Oxford University Press, 2014), 161–162.

17. Mohammad Abu Rumman and Hassan Abu Hanieh, *The Jihadi Salafist Movement in Jordan After Zarqawi: Identity, Leadership Crisis and Obscured Vision* (Amman: Friedrich Ebert Stiftung, 2009).

18. Mona Alami, "The New Generation of Jordanian Jihadi Fighters," Carnegie Endowment for International Peace, February 18, 2014, http://carnegieendowment.org/sada/?fa=54553.

19. Ibrahim Gharaibeh, *Jama'at al-Ikhwan al-Muslimin fi al-Urdun, 1946-1996* [The Society of the Muslim Brothers in Jordan, 1946-1996] (Amman: Sindabad Publishing House, 1997); Nathan Brown, "Jordan and Its Islamic Movement: The Limits of Inclusion?" *Carnegie Papers*, no. 74 (2006); Mohammad Abu Rumman, *The Muslim Brotherhood in the 2007 Jordanian Parliamentary Elections: A Passing "Political Setback" or Diminished Popularity* (Amman: Friedrich Ebert Stiftung, 2007); Hamid, *Temptations of Power*.

20. David Siddhartha Patel, "From Islamic to Ethnic Politics in Jordan" (Unpublished manuscript, 2011).

21. In several respects, the Zamzam platform echoes the goals and language of both the Egyptian Wasat Party and the Jordanian government's "Islamic outreach" efforts. See Wickham, *The Muslim Brotherhood*; Lawrence Rubin and Michael Robbins, "The Rise of Official Islam in Jordan," *Politics, Religion, and Ideology* 14, no. 1 (2013).

22. I do not have the full list of 10, but all the names I know are Transjordanian.

23. Khaled Neimat, "Brotherhood Moving Against Members Involved in Zamzam," *Jordan Times*, November 28, 2013, http://jordantimes.com/news/local/brotherhood-moving-against-members-involved-zamzam%E2%80%99.

24. Khetam Malkawi, "Brotherhood Picks Moderate Leader to Manage New Stage," *Jordan Times*, June 13, 2016, http://jordantimes.com/news/local/brotherhood-picks-moderate-leader-manage-new-stage.

25. Alami, Aida, "Rift Deepens Within Jordan's Muslim Brotherhood," *Al Jazeera*, August 17, 2015, http://www.aljazeera.com/news/2015/08/rift-deepens-jordan-muslim-brotherhood-150810121308733.html.

26. Jeffrey Goldberg, "The Modern King in the Arab Spring," *The Atlantic*, April 2013, 45–55.

27. Ibid., 54.

28. The most notable exception is when a prominent Muslim Brotherhood leader, Zaki Bani Ersheid, was sentenced to 18 months in prison for criticizing the United Arab Emirates in a Facebook post. Months after

being arrested, however, the post was still publicly available; Bani Ersheid courted arrest and punishment.

Chapter 10

1. Deobandi Sunni clerics trace their roots to the Dar-ul-Uloom madrasa in Deoband, India. They are characterized by a "reformist" critique of the shrine-based religiosity associated with some forms of South Asian Sufism.

2. Further differences are worth noting. Whereas Hassan al-Banna sought to reform Muslim society from *within*, JI leaders like Maududi sought to establish a revolutionary vanguard party set *apart* from the *jahil* (ignorant) Muslim masses and poised to lead from above. This was not an extension of Banna's ideas; it was a response to early 20th-century Muslim political fragmentation in South Asia—fragmentation extending from the Khilafat Movement and Muslim leaders within both the Indian National Congress and the Muslim League to the clerical leadership of the Dar-ul-Uloom madrasa at Deoband and many others. Maududi's ideas were rooted in South Asia. However, they influenced ideologues within the Brotherhood as well—above all, Sayyid Qutb. See Abdelwahab El-Affendi, "The Long March from Lahore to Khartoum: Beyond the 'Muslim Reformation'," *Bulletin* 17, no. 2 (1990): 137–151; Eran Lerman, "Mawdudi's Concept of Islam," *Middle Eastern Studies* 17, no. 4 (1981): 492–509.

3. See Matthew J. Nelson, "Islamic Law in an Islamic State: What Role for Parliament?" in *Constitution Writing, Religion, and Democracy*, ed. Asli Bali and Hanna Lerner (New York: Cambridge University Press, 2017).

4. See Vali Nasr, "Students, Islam, and Politics: Islami Jamiat-e-Tuleba in Pakistan," *Middle East Journal* 46, no. 1 (1992): 59–76.

5. See Vali Nasr, *Vanguard of the Islamic Revolution: The Jama'at-i Islami of Pakistan* (London: I.B. Taurus, 1994), 28–43.

6. It is worth pointing out that, compared to the modest electoral success of the JI and the JUI, the electoral success of shrine-oriented "Barelwi" parties—Barelwis constitute Pakistan's largest denominational group—has been negligible. And to date, Pakistan's "Salafis" have not sought to establish their own political party at all.

7. See Sayyid A. S. Pirzada, *The Politics of the Jamiat Ulema-i-Islam Pakistan: 1971-1977* (Karachi: Oxford University Press, 2000); Joshua T. White, *Pakistan's Islamist Frontier* (Arlington, VA: Center on Faith in International Affairs, 2008), 29.

8. See Matthew J. Nelson, "Embracing the Ummah: Student Politics Beyond State Power in Pakistan," *Modern Asian Studies* 45, no. 3 (2011): 565–596.

9. Nasr, "Students, Islam, and Politics."

10. Nasr, *Vanguard of the Islamic Revolution*, 153–154.

11. The JUI's efforts to form coalition governments with "regional" (as opposed to purely religious) parties in Balochistan and the NWFP split the party— once again, between religious ideologues and political pragmatists. This split was reinforced in 1988 when Fazlur Rahman took over from his father Mufti Mahmud. Sami-ul-Haq (JUI-S) led a group of ideologues working closely with General Zia-ul-Haq and the JI; Fazlur Rahman (JUI-F) led a group of "regional" populists who sought to distance themselves from the JI. See Nasr, *Vanguard of the Islamic Revolution*, 164–168; Pirzada, *The Politics of the Jamiat Ulema-i-Islam Pakistan*, 67; White, *Pakistan's Islamist Frontier*, 29.

12. When Prime Minister Bhutto dismissed the JUI-affiliated provincial government of Balochistan in 1973, the NWFP government (led by JUI Chief Minister Mufti Mahmud) resigned in protest. See Pirzada, *The Politics of the Jamiat Ulema-i-Islam Pakistan*, 73.

13. See Vali Nasr, "Islamic Opposition to the Islamic State: The Jama'at-e-Islami, 1977-1988," *International Journal of Middle East Studies* 25, no. 2 (1993): 261–283.

14. Of the 68 candidates supported by the JI during the nonparty elections of 1985, only 10 were successful. In effect, the JI was punished for collaborating with the dictatorship of General Zia-ul-Haq between 1977 and 1985. See Nasr, *Vanguard of the Islamic Revolution*, 196–197.

15. "Salafi" partners like Lashkar-e-Taiba also figure prominently.

16. See Humeira Iqtidar, *Secularizing Islamists? Jama'at-e-Islami and Jama'at-ud-Dawa in Urban Pakistan* (Chicago: University of Chicago Press, 2011), 93–95.

17. White notes that the JI also signaled its dissatisfaction with various IJI (and PPP) governments by criticizing their foreign policies, including the IJI's decision to accept a negotiated settlement to the civil war in Afghanistan— a decision that, according to White, eventually led the Jama'at to quit the IJI in 1992. See White, *Pakistan's Islamist Frontier*, 33–34.

18. The JI fielded 26 candidates. The JUI-F, contesting separately, won 7 seats.

19. The JI fielded 18 candidates. The JUI-F, contesting separately, won 6 seats.

20. Together, the "Deobandi" JUI-F and the "Barelwi" JUP (Jamiat-e-Ulema-e-Pakistan) won four seats.

21. See *The First 10 General Elections of Pakistan* (Islamabad: PILDAT, 2013), 57.

22. The JI and the JUI also benefited from General Musharraf's efforts to marginalize Pakistan's political "old guard" by requiring candidates to hold a university or high-level madrasa degree. (The former helped the lay leadership of the JI; the latter helped the ulema-based leadership of the JUI.)

23. See *The First 10 General Elections of Pakistan*, 62.

24. For a detailed account of MMA policymaking in the NWFP, see White, *Pakistan's Islamist Frontier*, 47–83.

25. Many of Imran Khan's election rallies featured religious leaders from a Far Right amalgamation known as the "Defense of Pakistan" (Difa-e-Pakistan) Council—a group that, in addition to the JI, included the JUI-S and pro-army Salafis like Hafiz Saeed and his militant group Lashkar-e-Taiba (LeT).

26. My own research suggests that material demands rooted in tribal "customs" often clash with the terms of sharia, leading many families to pursue forms of political patronage grounded in an appeal for protection *from* the enforcement of Islamic law. (This is particularly true with respect to Islamic laws of inheritance governing family property—Islamic laws that fly in the face of patrilineal customs insofar as they guarantee specific "Quranic shares" to Muslim women.) See Matthew J. Nelson, *In the Shadow of Shari'ah: Islam, Islamic Law, and Democracy in Pakistan* (New York: Columbia University Press, 2011).

27. The space occupied by religious social welfare organizations has expanded alongside the conditionalities imposed by international financial institutions like the International Monetary Fund—institutions seeking to reduce the fiscal footprint of the Pakistani state in a context still defined by very low levels of tax collection; see Chris Candland and Raza Khan Qazi, "Pakistan: Civil Conflict, Natural Disaster, and Partisan Welfare," *International Policy Digest*, July 14, 2015, http://intpolicydigest.org/2015/07/14/pakistan-civil-conflict-natural-disaster-and-partisan-welfare/.

28. See Masooda Bano, "Contesting Ideologies and Struggle for Authority: State-Madrasa Engagement in Pakistan" (Working paper no. 14, Religions and Development Research Programme, University of Birmingham, Birmingham, England, 2007), http://www.birmingham.ac.uk/Documents/college-social-sciences/government-society/rad/working-papers/wp-14.pdf. In Pakistan, JI-affiliated private schools include both the Hira and the Dar-e-Arqam networks; those affiliated with "Barelwis" include the Minhaj-ul-Qur'an network and AIMS (the Academy for Islamic and Modern Studies).

29. See Mumtaz Ahmad, "Media-Based Preachers and the Formation of New Muslim Publics in Pakistan," in *Who Speaks for Islam? Muslim Grassroots Leaders and Popular Preachers in South Asia* (Seattle: National Bureau of Asian Research, 2010), 1–28, and also Khalid Masud, *Travellers in Faith: Studies of the Tablighi Jama'at as a Transnational Islamic Movement for Faith Renewal* (Leiden: Brill, 2000).

30. In 1991, Tanzim-e-Islami was joined by Tehreek-e-Khilafat to "bring about an Islamic revolution by a 'disciplined force' that will culminate in the establishment of [a] global caliphate"; see Ahmad, "Media-Based Preachers," 14. More than any other figure in South Asia, Israr Ahmed's ideas reflect the millenarian views of the Islamic State.

31. Ahmad, "Media-Based Preachers," 18.

32. See Husnul Amin, "Post-Islamist Intellectual Trends in Pakistan: Javed Ahmad Ghamidi and His Discourse on Islam and Democracy," *Islamic Studies* 51, no. 2 (2012): 169–192.

33. For an extension of Robert Michels's inclusion-moderation theory to Muslim contexts, see Mona El-Ghobashy, "The Metamorphosis of the Egyptian Muslim Brothers," *International Journal of Middle East Studies* 37, no. 3 (2005): 373–395; and Jillian Schwedler, *Faith in Moderation: Islamist Parties in Jordan and Yemen* (New York: Cambridge University Press, 2006).

34. One of the last holdouts was an Afghan Taliban commander by the name of "Mullah Rasool."

35. Afghan Taliban commanders like Abdul Qayyum Zakir opposed formal negotiations with the Afghan government until all of the international forces supporting that government had left. (Zakir withheld his allegiance to Mullah Mansour until March 2016—just a few weeks before his death.)

36. See Michael Semple, "The Pakistan Taliban Movement: An Appraisal," *Barcelona Centre for International Affairs,* November 2011, http://www.cidob.org/en/content/download/56611/1455664/version/3/file/MICHAEL%20SEMPLE_NOVEMBRE%202014%20%281%29.pdf, 5.

37. High-profile attacks orchestrated by Baitullah and Hakimullah Mehsud signaled the antistate politics of the TTP, with Baitullah suspected in the 2008 assassination of Pakistan's prime minister Benazir Bhutto and the appearance of Hakimullah in a 2011 video recording the murder of a Pakistan intelligence officer known as "Colonel Imam." (Colonel Imam played a key role in grooming Afghan Taliban figures like Mullah Omar. His murder drew a sharp line between the loyalties of the Afghan Taliban and those of the TTP.)

38. During the 1990s, Swat was home to a rebel movement known as the Tehreek-e-Nifaz-e-Shariat-e-Mohammadi (TNSM), which pressed for a special corps of qazis to "oversee" the government's district courts. The TNSM was founded by Fazlullah's father-in law, a former member of the JI named Sufi Mohammad.

39. Unusually, the first leader of AQIS (Asim Umar) was known for his "Deobandi" connections. A former deputy leader (Ustadh Ahmad Farooq), known for his IJT connections, was killed in a U.S. drone strike in April 2015. See Sajid Iqbal, "Is Al-Qaeda Seeking a New Constituency in Pakistan?," *BBC News,* July 20, 2015, http://www.bbc.co.uk/monitoring/is-alqaeda-seeking-a-new-constituency-in-pakistan, and also Hasan Abdullah, "Pakistan's Top Militant Commanders," *Dawn,* July 10, 2015, http://www.dawn.com/news/1170164.

40. Building on the ideological spadework of earlier JI defectors like Israr Ahmed, the views articulated by Baghdadi are not unfamiliar in Pakistan;

see Ali Akbar, "From TTP to IS: Pakistan's Terror Landscape Evolves," *Dawn*, March 16, 2015, http://www.dawn.com/news/ 1169542/.

Omar Khalid Khorasani (Jama'at-ul-Ahrar) orchestrated the April 2014 killing of 23 Pakistani soldiers who had been held captive for several years, spurring an anti-TTP operation in FATA known as Zarb-e-Azb. Fazlullah responded to this operation with an attack on the Army Public School in Peshawar (December 2014), killing 141 people, including 132 children. See also Bill Roggio, "Taliban Splinter Group Jama'at-ul-Ahrar Forms in Northwestern Pakistan," *Long War Journal*, August 26, 2014, http://www.longwarjournal.org/archives/2014/08/taliban_splinter_ gro.php.

41. See Nasir Jamal, "Analysis: Why Jama'at Discarded Munawar Hasan," *Dawn*, April 1, 2014, http://www.dawn.com/news/1096947. After Munawar Hasan described Hakimullah Mehsud as a Muslim martyr, the Pakistan Army demanded an apology; the JI reported that Hasan was expressing his personal views.

Chapter 11

1. Even by the end of Suharto's New Order era, greater space was created for Islamic activism as Muslim leaders, hitherto marginalized from positions of power, were brought into government. Suharto also formed Ikatan Cendekiawan Muslim Indonesia (ICMI, or the All-Indonesian Association of Muslim Professionals), which would serve as the primary vehicle for the New Order's re-engagement with Islamic social and political activism. During this time, Islamist influence was also gradually emerging within Golkar, the primary organizational vehicle of the New Order.

2. In addition, there were a number of Islamic (as opposed to "Islamist") parties aligned with Indonesia's two main Muslim organizations, Muhammadiyah and Nahdlatul Ulama. These were Partai Amanat Nasional (PAN, or National Mandate Party) and Partai Kebangkitan Bangsa (PKB, or National Awakening Party).

3. In 2004 and 2009, the PKS managed to score in the region of 7 percent of popular votes. A regional exception was Aceh, where the Acehnese provincial government was permitted to introduce various aspects of Islamic law as part of the resolution of the longstanding separatist struggle between the Gerakan Aceh Merdeka (GAM, or Free Aceh Movement) and the Indonesian state.

4. Sunny Tanuwidjaja, "Political Islam and Islamic Parties in Indonesia: Critically Assessing the Evidence of Islam's Political Decline," *Southeast Asia: A Journal of International and Strategic Affairs* 32, no. 1 (2010): 29–49.

5. Greg Fealy, "Islam in Southeast Asia: Domestic Pietism, Diplomacy and Security," in *Contemporary Southeast Asia: Regional Dynamics, National Differences*, ed. Mark Beeson (New York: Palgrave Macmillan, 2004), 137. He highlighted the international media's inclination to refer to Southeast

Asia as a "second front" in the war on terror, as exemplified in Anthony Spaeth, "Rumbles in the Jungle," *Time*, February 25, 2002, http://www.time.com/time/world/article/0,8599,212723,00.html.

6. Dean Yates, "Indonesia's Moderate Islamic Image Under Threat," *Reuters*, September 16, 2005, http://www.redorbit.com/news/health/245577/indonesias_moderate_islamic_image_under_threat/index.html.

7. Having said that, it is important to place the electoral fortunes of Islamist parties in Malaysia and Indonesia in context. Not unlike Pakistan, where the visibility and activism of Jamaat-e-Islami (JI) and the Jamiat-e-Ulema-e-Islam (JUI) have only resulted in modest electoral gains, the performance of the PKS and PAS at their peaks has not translated into significant numbers of seats in the respective parliaments—certainly not enough to press an Islamist agenda in any meaningful way in parliament. But at least in the case of Malaysia, there has been a discernible convergence of outlook on Islamic governance between PAS and UMNO, as the chapter will show.

8. Vincent J. H. Houben, "Southeast Asia and Islam," *Annals of the American Academy of Political and Social Science* 588 (2003): 163. There are a number of factors that have given rise to this greater Islamic consciousness, not least the fact that people have increasingly studied in state religious schools, which provide a curriculum endorsed by Islamic scholars rather than the more syncretic or idiosyncratic and "localized" variant of the faith taught by local preachers. See for instance Greg Fealy, "Understanding Political Islam in Southeast Asia," *Asia Society: A Summary*, May 21, 2003, http://www.asiasociety.org/understanding-political-islam-southeast-asia.

9. The PAS Supporter's Club was created in 2010 in response to the perceived growing interest and appeal of PAS to non-Muslims. However, although the club has since been "upgraded" into a wing, its members are still not allowed to vote in party elections or have representation in the party's central working committee. The PAS Supporters' Wing claims a membership of 40,000. In the case of the PKS, the number of non-Muslims who are associated with the party is negligible given that the Indonesian population as a whole is up to 87 percent Muslim. See Shazwan Mustafa Kamal, "Branded Toothless, PAS Non-Muslim Wing Wants Votes, Posts in Party Polls," *Malay Mail*, May 18, 2015.

10. Muhammad Ayoob, *The Many Faces of Political Islam: Religion and Politics in the Muslim World* (Ann Arbor: University of Michigan Press, 2008), 94.

11. Michael Buehler, "The Rise of Shari'a By-Laws in Indonesian Districts," *South East Asia Research* 16, no. 2, (2008): 255–285.

12. Greg Fealy, "Resurgent Political Islam or astute Islamic parties?" *New Mandala*, April 14, 2014, http://asiapacific.anu.edu.au/newmandala/2014/04/14/resurgent-political-islam-or-astute-islamic-parties/.

13. Joseph Chinyong Liow, interview with Dr. Zulkifliemansyah.

14. Tiffatul Sembiring, "Shari'a a Reality and Asset of National Law," *Jakarta Post*, March 27, 2006.

15. "PKS tidak akan paksakan syariat Islam," April 19, 2006, http://zulkifliemansyah.com/in/pks-tidak-akan-paksakan-syariat-islam.html.

16. Heffernan Van Zorge, "Creeping Sharia?" *Van Zorge Report on Indonesia* VIII, no. 8, May 9, 2006.

17. Nadirsyah Hosen, "Religion and the Indonesian Constitution: A Recent Debate," *Journal of Southeast Asian Studies* 36, no. 3, (2006): 419–440.

18. Consider, for instance, the following anecdote from PKS member of parliament Zulkieflimansyah: "For us (PKS), the issue of sharia puts us between a rock and a hard place. For example, when I ran as a gubernatorial candidate in Banten last year, if you went to a traditional community and didn't support sharia then you were in trouble. They don't really care what sharia means, because for them sharia is an obligation because they are Muslim. But the problem now is how do we define sharia; that is the challenge." See Dr. Zulkieflimansyah, "Special Interview with Van Zorge Report," *Zulkieflimansyah, PhD*, http://zulkieflimansyah.com/en/special-interview-with-van-zorge-report.html.

19. See Buehler, "The Rise of Shari'a By-Laws in Indonesian Districts"; Robin Bush, "Regional Syari'ah Regulations: Anomaly or Symptom?" in *Expressing Islam: Religious Life and Politics in Indonesia,* ed. Greg Fealy and Sally White (Singapore: Institute of Southeast Asian Studies, 2008).

20. Yenn Kwok, "Gang Rape Then Caning: Welcome to Aceh's Bizarre Moral Crusade," *Time*, May 8, 2014, http://time.com/91873/aceh-sharia-law-islam-rape-kelantan-brunei/.

21. Pew Research Center, "The World's Muslims: Religion, Politics and Society," *Religion & Public Life Project*, April 30, 2013, http://www.pewforum.org/2013/04/30/the-worlds-muslims-religion-politics-society-overview/.

22. On June 1, 1945, President Sukarno enumerated five principles of the postindependence state in a speech to the preparatory committee for Indonesian independence. Collectively known as Pancasila, the five principles referred to (1) belief in a supreme God, (2) humanitarianism, (3) the unity of Indonesia, (4) consultative democracy, and (5) social justice. Significantly, the principles of Pancasila, and in particular the first principle, was an attempt to accommodate the aspirations of activist Muslim and Islamist nationalist counterparts who sought to define the postindependence Indonesian nation with specific reference to sharia, yet without compromising the imperative of national unity. These principles continue to govern Indonesian society today.

23. Anthony Bubalo, Greg Fealy, and Whit Mason, "Zealous Democrats: Islamism in Egypt, Indonesia, and Turkey," *Lowy Institute Papers 25* (South Wales: Longueville Media, 2008), 68.

24. Fauzan Zidni, "Shariah Law in Indonesia," *Bukit Timah School*, February 2, 2008, http://bukittimahschool.blogspot.com/2008/02/sharia-law-in-indonesia.html.

25. Joseph Chinyong Liow, *Piety and Politics: Islamism in Contemporary Malaysia* (Oxford: Oxford University Press, 2009), 129.

26. Dewan Ulama PAS, "Negara Islam: Antara Realiti Dan Cabaran," *Mimbar Ulama* 7 (2004): 25–27.

27. Mohammad Hashim Kamali, *Punishment in Islamic Law: An Enquiry into the Hudud Bill of Kelantan* (Kuala Lumpur: Ilmiah Publishers, 1995), see appendix for the full text of the bill.

28. Ahmad Ibrahim, "Implementation of *Hudud* Laws in Malaysia," in *Hudud in Malaysia: The Issues at Stake*, ed. Rose Ismail (Kuala Lumpur: SIS Forum Berhad, 1995).

29. Joseph Chinyong Liow, interviews with Nik Aziz, Hadi Awang, and Harun Taib, July 2004.

30. Wan Zahidi Wan Teh, "Ciri-Ciri Sebuah Negara Islam," in *Seminar Perlaksanaan Hukun Syarak Di Malaysia*, February 9–10, 2001, 2.

31. Nakhaie Ahmad, "*Hudud* Dalam Konteks Perlaksanaan Syariat Islam Yang Menyeluruh," in *Seminar Kebangsaan Cabaran Perlaksanaan Islam Dalam Konteks Masyarakat Malaysia*, June 28, 1992, 10. Those who opposed the bill had argued that the bill was not comprehensive enough and must cover more aspects of the *hudud*. See Abdul Halim Muhammady, "Undang-Undang Jenayah Syariah Dan Perlaksanaannya Di Malaysia," in *Seminar Perlaksanaan Hukun Syarak Di Malaysia*, February 9–10, 2001. There are, however, many government ulama who support the bill, such as the Mufti of Perak and Selangor; See Sayuti Omar, *Talqin Untuk Mahathir* (Kuala Lumpur: Tinta Merah, 1994).

32. Ibid., 13–19. See speeches of UMNO leaders that criticize the *hudud*, in Institut Polisi Studi dan Lajnah Penerangan Dewan Pemuda PAS Pusat, *Mahathir Serta Beberapa Pemimpin UMNO dan Penyokongnya Anti-Islam* (Gombak: Dewan Pemuda PAS Pusat, 2002), 17–24.

33. Md Izwan, "Umno sokong PAS laksana Hudud di Kelantan," *Malaysian Insider*, November 16, 2013, http://www.themalaysianinsider.com/bahasa/article/umno-sokong-pas-laksana-*hudud*-di-kelantan.

34. Joseph Chinyong Liow, interview with Ong Kian Ming (DAP strategist and member of parliament for Serdang), February 24, 2014.

35. For a detailed discussion about these impediments, see Chinyong Liow, *Piety and Politics*, 58–72.

36. "Dewan Ulama Sokong Penuh Kenyataan Presiden PAS," *Harakah*, December 29, 2009.

37. Party reformists have also maintained that Islamic law is not on the agenda of the opposition coalition of which PAS is a part. See "Negara Islam bukan agenda Pakatan—Husam Musa," April 9, 2008, http://ganulening.wordpress.com/2008/04/09/negara-islam-bukan-agenda-pakatan-husam-musa/.

38. Joseph Chinyong Liow, interview with Dzulkefly Ahmad.

39.   Briefly, PAS has performed better in national elections when it has downplayed the goal of an Islamic state and focused on the pressing issues of the day. For more on this, see Joseph Chinyong Liow, "Exigency or Expediency? Contextualising Political Islam and the PAS Challenge in Malaysian Politics," *Third World Quarterly* 25, no. 2 (2004): 359–372.

40.   PAS Youth Annual Report (1976–1977), 36.

41.   Joseph Chinyong Liow, interview with Hassan Shukri.

42.   Joseph Chinyong Liow, interview with Azzam Tamimi (director of the Institute of Islamic Political Thought and an Islamist figure associated with the Muslim Brotherhood).

43.   See program booklet of the International Gathering for the Solidarity of Muslims, September 9–10, 1998, Masjid Rusila, Terengganu, as cited in Mohamed Nawab Bin Mohamed Osman, "Transnational Islamism and Its Impact in Malaysia and Indonesia," Rubin Center, August 29, 2011, http://www.rubincenter.org/2011/08/transnational-islamism-and-its-impact-in-malaysia-and-indonesia/#_ednref42.

44.   Joseph Chinyong Liow, interview with Nasharuddin Mat Isa (deputy president of PAS).

45.   "Justice Party Chairman Condemns Attacks on America," *Antara*, September 14, 2001; "PAS Describes Attacks as 'Heinous Crime'," *New Straits Times*, September 13, 2001.

46.   Nik Aziz, "US Threat to Attack America Unreasonable," *Bernama*, September 23, 2001.

47.   Patvinder Singh and Zubaidah Abu Bakar, "PM Exposes Militant Links," *New Straits Times*, August 5, 2001.

48.   "What the World Thinks in 2002," Pew Research Center, December 2002, 5–10.

49.   Joseph Chinyong Liow, interview with Nasharuddin Mat Isa.

50.   Mohamed Nawab Mohamed Osman, "Israel, Lebanon and the Rise of the Islamists," *RSIS Commentaries* 88, no. 6, August 24, 2006, https://www.rsis.edu.sg/rsis-publication/rsis/843-israel-lebanon-and-the-rise-o/.

51.   Ambassador Yeop Adlan Rose, speech, Conference of ASEAN and Asian Islamic NGOs, Century Paradise Club, Kuala Lumpur, August 12, 2006.

52.   Ibid., 3.

53.   Institute for Policy Analysis of Conflict, "The Evolution of ISIS in Indonesia," *IPAC Report* no. 13, September 2014, http://www.understandingconflict.org/conflict/read/30/The-Evolution-of-ISIS-in-Indonesia.

54.   "Lotfi a 'Martyr' for Sacrificing His Life for ISIS, Says Nik Abduh," *Malaysian Insider*, September 15, 2014, http://www.themalaysianinsider.com/malaysia/article/lotfi-a-matyr-for-sacrificing-his-life-for-isis-says-nik-abduh.

55.   A comprehensive discussion of the eschatological dimensions of the Islamic State's popularity in Indonesia can be found in IPAC, "The Evolution of ISIS in Indonesia."

56. Shiite Islam has been banned as a consequence of two factors. First, since the mid-1980s, the Malaysian state has taken the initiative to define "correct" Islam and to dictate the manner in which it can be practiced. This has meant that any deviation from Sunni orthodoxy was deemed a threat to "mainstream" Malaysian Islam and hence subject to circumscription. By this logic, not only have Shiite Muslims been targeted but also other Muslim sects like the Ahmadiyyah and the Al-Arqam as well. Second, the ban on Shiite Islam has been the result of the Malaysian state's interpretation of the centuries-old Sunni–Shiite doctrinal divide. Not only is Shiite Islam banned, but also the Department of Islamic Development of Malaysia (otherwise known as JAKIM), which provides Friday sermons for all mosques in the country, has frequently launched vitriolic attacks against Shiite Islam through these sermons. See "Shia Are Not Muslims, Claims JAKIM," *Malaysian Insider*, December 13, 2013, http://www.themalaysianinsider. com/malaysia/article/all-branches-of-syiah-teachings-in-malaysia-are-un-islamic-claim-jakim-bern. A similar dynamic is evident in Indonesia. See Azis Anwar Fachrudin, "Endless Sunni-Shia Sectarianism in Indonesia," *Jakarta Post*, March 11, 2015.

57. Yang Razali Kassim, "Post-Mubarak Egypt: Is Indonesia the Right Model?" *East Asia Forum*, March 3, 2011, http://www.eastasiaforum.org/2011/03/ 03/post-mubarak-egypt-is-indonesia-the-right-model/. See also Tom Pepinsky, "There Is No Indonesian Model for the Arab Spring," *Foreign Policy*, February 27, 2013, http://foreignpolicy.com/2013/02/27/there-is-no-indonesia-model-for-the-arab-spring/; Yenni Kwok, "What Indonesia Can Teach Thailand and Egypt About Democracy," *Time*, May 29, 2014.

58. Tim Dakwatuna, "Arab Spring Bakar Semangat PKS," *Dakwatuna*, September 23, 2012, http://www.dakwatuna.com/2012/09/23/23078/arab-spring-bakar-semangat-pks/#axzz3acdmXXpU.

59. In fact, several Malaysian politicians I spoke with regarding this pointed out that Qaradawi's leading of Friday prayers on Tahrir Square on February 18, 2011, rallied bipartisan Malaysian support for the Arab Spring in Egypt.

60. "Huge Protest in Malaysia Against the Coup in Egypt - Friday 28/3/2014," YouTube video, 1:39, posted by Omar Aldeeb, March 28, 2014, https:// www.youtube.com/watch?v=jeogRrKyjmI.

61. "Top PAS Leader Lashes Out at Saudi Regime," *Harakah Daily*, August 21, 2013.

62. Muhammad Akbar, Mutia Ramadhani, and Yeyen Rostiyani, "MPs: Egyptian Coup Is Bad Example for Democracy," *Republika Online*, July 21, 2013, http://www.republika.co.id/berita/en/national-politics/13/07/20/ mq8qyt-mps-egyptian-coup-is-bad-example-for-democracy.

63. Several videos of these protests have been uploaded on YouTube.

Chapter 12

1. Steven Brooke, "U.S. Policy and the Muslim Brotherhood," in *The West and the Muslim Brotherhood After the Arab Spring* (Dubai: Al-Mesbar Studies & Research Centre in Collaboration with The Foreign Policy Research Institute, February 2013), http://www.fpri.org/docs/201303.west_ and_the_muslim_brotherhood_after_the_arab_spring.pdf.

2. Robert Satloff, *U.S. Policy Towards Islamism: A Theoretical and Operational Overview* (New York: Council on Foreign Relations, 2000), http://www. cfr.org/content/publications/attachments/Satloff2.pdf.

3. See Maria de Ceu Pinto, *Political Islam and the United States* (Reading, UK: Ithaca Press, 1999), and Fawad Gerges, *American and Political Islam: Clash of Cultures or Clash of Interests?* (New York: Cambridge University Press, 1999).

4. James Traub, "Islamic Democrats?" *New York Times*, April 29, 2007.

5. Pew Research Center, "One Year After Morsi's Ouster, Divides Persist on El-Sisi, Muslim Brotherhood," May 22, 2014, http://www.pewglobal. org/2014/05/22/one-year-after-morsis-ouster-divides-persist-on-el-sisi-muslim-brotherhood/.

6. Sayida Ounissi, "Ennahda from Within: Islamists or 'Muslim Democrats'," The Brookings Institution, Rethinking Political Islam project, February 2016, https://www.brookings.edu/wp-content/uploads/2016/07/Ounissi-RPI-Response-FINAL_v2.pdf.

Chapter 13

1. Steven Brooke, "The Muslim Brotherhood's Social Outreach after the Egyptian Coup," The Brookings Institution, Working paper, Rethinking Political Islam project, August 2015, https://www.brookings.edu/wp-content/uploads/2016/07/Egypt_Brooke-FINALE-2.pdf.

2. Abdullah Saeed, "Rethinking Citizenship Rights of Non-Muslims in an Islamic State: Rashid al-Ghannushi's Contribution to the Evolving Debate," *Islam and Christian-Muslim Relations* 10, no. 3 (1999), http:// www.abdullahsaeed.org/sites/abdullahsaeed.org/files/Rethinking_ citizenship_rights.pdf.

3. Essam Talema, "Huquq Al-Muwatanah fe al-Mujtama' al-Islami [Citizenship Rights in a Muslim Society]," Ikhwan Wiki, last modified January 2011, http://goo.gl/1woZCf.

4. Samir Shalabi, "Why Do Egypt's Rulers Fear the Working Class?" *Egyptian Streets*, November 1, 2015, http://egyptianstreets.com/2015/11/01/why-do-egypts-rulers-fear-the-working-class/.

5. Amr Darrag, "Muslim Brotherhood Currently Undertaking Comprehensive Political Reviews," *Middle East Observer*, March 13, 2016, http://www.middleeastobserver.org/muslim-brotherhood-currently-undertaking-comprehensive-political-reviews.

6. Steven Brooke, "The Muslim Brotherhood's Social Outreach after the Egyptian Coup," The Brookings Institution, Working paper, Rethinking

Political Islam project, August 2015, https://www.brookings.edu/wp-content/uploads/2016/07/Egypt_Brooke-FINALE-2.pdf.

7. Shadi Hamid and William McCants, "Rethinking Political Islam," The Brookings Institution, May 6, 2016, https://www.brookings.edu/research/rethinking-political-islam/.

8. Marc Lynch, "Is the Muslim Brotherhood a Terrorist Organization or a Firewall Against Violent Extremism?," in *Evolving Methodologies in the Study of Islamism*, POMEP Studies 17 (Washington, DC: Project on Middle East Political Science, March 5, 2016), http://pomeps.org/wp-content/uploads/2016/03/POMEPS_Studies_17_Methods_Web.pdf.

9. *All According to Plan: The Rab'a Massacre and Mass Killings of Protestors in Egypt* (New York: Human Rights Watch, August 12, 2014), https://www.hrw.org/report/2014/08/12/all-according-plan/raba-massacre-and-mass-killings-protesters-egypt; Neil Ketchley, "The Muslim Brothers Take to the Streets," *Middle East Research and Information Project*, Spring 2016, http://www.merip.org/mer/mer269/muslim-brothers-take-streets.

10. Steven Brooke, "Old Questions and New Methods in the Study of Islamism," *Project on Middle East Political Science*, January 26, 2016, http://pomeps.org/2016/02/09/old-questions-and-new-methods-in-the-study-of-islamism/.

Chapter 14

1. "The Arab Uprisings and the Next Generation of Islamists," The Brookings Institution, May 26, 2015, http://www.brookings.edu/research/opinions/2015/06/next-generation-islamists.

2. "Tunisie: quels sont les défis qui attendent le nouveau pouvoir? - #DébatF24 (partie 2) [Tunisia: What Are the Challenges Facing the New Government? - #DebateF24 (part 2)]," YouTube video, posted by France 24, October 28, 2014, https://www.youtube.com/watch?v=MoCYOnO34LU.

3. "Notre voie vers la démocratie [Our Path to Democracy]," Collectif 18 octobre pour les droits et des libertés en Tunisie (The 18 October Coalition for Rights and Freedoms in Tunisia), June 15, 2010, https://goo.gl/nPTn8s.

4. From a recording of Ghannouchi's speech taken by author. See also the transcript of Ghannouchi's speech in Ennahda's newspaper, *Al-Fajr*, printed May 22, 2016.

5. See Henry Munson, "Islamic Revivalism in Morocco and Tunisia," *Muslim World* 76, no. 3–4 (1986): 203–218. Also see Emma Murphy, *Economic and Political Change in Tunisia: From Bourguiba to Ben Ali* (New York: St. Martin's Press in association with University of Durham, 1999).

6. Francesco Cavatorta and Fabio Merone, "Post-Islamism, Ideological Evolution, and 'la tunisianité' of the Tunisian Islamist Party al-Nahda," *Journal of Political Ideologies* 20, no. 1 (2015): 37.

7. Ibid., 38.

8. Monica Marks, "Convince, Coerce, or Compromise? Ennahda's Approach to Tunisia's Constitution," *Brookings Doha Center Analysis Paper 10*, The Brookings Institution, February 2014, http://www.brookings.edu/research/papers/2014/02/10-ennahda-tunisia-constitution-marks.

9. For more on the importance of these cross-ideological opposition talks, see Monica Marks, "Purists vs. Pluralists: Cross-Ideological Coalition Building in Tunisia," in *Tunisia's Democratic Transition in Comparative Perspective*, ed. Alfred Stepan (forthcoming 2017).

10. Monica Marks, "How Big Were the Changes Tunisia's Ennahda Party Just Made at Its National Congress?" *Washington Post*, May 25, 2016, https://www.washingtonpost.com/news/monkey-cage/wp/2016/05/25/how-big-were-the-changes-made-at-tunisias-ennahda-just-made-at-its-national-congress/. For a flavor of this coverage see Rached Ghannouchi, interviewed by Christiane Amanpour, *Amanpour*, CNN, May 23, 2015, http://edition.cnn.com/videos/tv/2016/05/23/intv-amanpour-rached-ghannouchi-tunisia-ennahda-islam.cnn.

11. "Taqiyya" refers to the legality of denying one's Islamic faith in dangerous situations. Some critics of Ennahda whom I have interviewed accuse the party of playing down its Islamism as a form of tactical "taqiyya," that is, a means to negotiate through a tricky political situation rather than a genuine philosophical progression.

Chapter 15

1. Rafiq Habib, "A Vision for the Political Future of the Muslim Brotherhood," in *The Crisis of the Muslim Brotherhood*, ed. Amr El-Shobaki (Cairo: Al-Ahram Center for Political and Strategic Studies, 2009), 27–28.

2. "The First Law of the Muslim Brotherhood in Ismailia," in *Ikhwan Wiki: The Official Encyclopedia for the History of the Muslim Brotherhood*, http://goo.gl/DlaoOj.

3. Hassan al-Banna, *Al-Natheer*, no. 1, May 30, 1938, http://www.ikhwanwiki.com/index.php?title=%D8%A7%D9%84%D8%B9%D8%AF%D8%AF_1_%D9%85%D9%86_%D9%85%D8%AC%D9%84%D8%A9_%D8%A7%D9%84%D9%86%D8%B0%D9%8A%D8%B1.

4. Hassan al-Banna, "Letter of Teachings," from *The Compiled Letters of Imam Hassan al-Banna*.

5. For more information, see Louis Althusser, "Ideology and Ideological State Apparatuses," in *Lenin and Philosophy and Other Essays*, trans. Ben Brewster (New York: Monthly Review Press, 1971).

6. Henri Thery, *Les Groupes Sociaux, Forces Vives?*, trans. Rushdi Kamel Saleh (Cairo: General Authority for Cultural Palaces, 2013), 46–52.

7. Henry L. Tischler, *Introduction to Sociology* (Belmont, CA: Wadsworth Publishing, 2007).

8. Waheed Abdul Mageed, *The Muslim Brotherhood Between History and Future: How Was It and How Is It Now?* (Cairo: Al-Ahram for Publishing, Translation, and Distribution, 2010).

9. The committee formed by the government announced the confiscation of the Muslim Brotherhood's assets. These are the final numbers, as of January 24, 2016. See Tarek Najim al-Din, "Fardanaan Hasilat Almutahaffiz Ealaa 'amwalahum min Al'iikhwan Bimisr," *al-Jadeed al-Arabi*, January 24, 2016, http://goo.gl/pndDW5.

10. "A Former Officer in the Egyptian Army Calls for Jihad Against Sissi," *New Khalij*, July 22, 2015, http://www.thenewkhalij.net/node/17534.

11. Mokhtar Awad and Samuel Tadros, "Baya Remorse: Wilayat-Sinai and the Nile Valley," *CTC Sentinel* 8, no. 8, August 2015, https://www.ctc.usma.edu/posts/baya-remorse-wilayat-sinai-and-the-nile-valley.

12. "Egypt's Executions: A Green Light for ISIS Recruitment of the Muslim Brotherhood's Young Men," *Al-Monitor*, June 24, 2015, http://www.al-monitor.com/pulse/ar/originals/2015/06/egypt-sinai-muslim-brotherhood-terrorism-death-sentences.html#. See also "Wilayat Sinai Sends the Second Round of 'Sawlat Al-Ansar' and Promises to 'Butcher' Sissi," *New Khalij*, March 3, 2015, http://www.thenewkhalij.net/node/14135.

13. I conducted this study in coordination with the Egyptian researcher Ahmed Zaghloul. The primary conclusion I reached during the interviews is that members are convinced that the organization's main responsibility is, first, working to reject and confront the military coup and continuing activities that express this rejection, and, second, providing the necessary support to the families of those arrested and killed. In light of events, the majority felt that this is what demanded the Brotherhood's attention, rather than that the group should return to the religious and social realm. Likewise, there wasn't a great fear of getting swept into the perpetration of violence. Many members expected that some individuals would turn to violence but that the Brotherhood in general, given its structure and its political and religious choices over the decades, would not alter its main strategy built on peaceful civil activities and political opposition.

14. See Hassan al-Hudaybi, "Preachers, Not Judges," *Ikhwan Wiki*, http://www.ikhwanwiki.com/index.php?title=%D8%AF%D8%B9%D8%A7%D8%A9_%D9%84%D8%A7_%D9%82%D8%B6%D8%A7%D8%A9.

15. Shadi Hamid, *Islamic Exceptionalism: How the Struggle Over Islam is Reshaping the World* (New York: St. Martin's Press, 2016).

16. Mohamed Saied, "What's Behind Uptick of Attacks in Cairo?" *Al-Monitor*, November 13, 2016, http://www.al-monitor.com/pulse/originals/2016/11/egypt-terrorist-attacks-cairo-groups-sinai-meaning.html.

Chapter 16

1. Ali Tariq, "Ulama's 22 Points," *History Pak*, http://historypak.com/ulamas-22-points/.

2. Jamiluddin Ahmad, ed., *Speeches and Writings of Mr. Jinnah*, 7th ed. (Lahore: Shaikh Muhammad Ashraf, 1960), 175.

3. Ibid., 458–459.
4. Abdu Sattar Ghazali, *Islamic Pakistan: Illusions & Reality* (Islamabad: National Book Club, 1996), chap. 3.
5. For a detailed discussion, see Tarik Jan et al., *Pakistan Between Secularism and Islam* (Islamabad: Institute of Policy Studies, 1998), 121–130.
6. Latif Ahmad Sherwani, *Speeches, Writings and Statements of Iqbal,* 4th rev. ed. (Lahore: Iqbal Academy, 2005), 302.
7. Ibid., 463.
8. Rizwan Ahmad, *Sayings of Quaid-I-Azam*, 4th ed. (Karachi: Elite Publishers, 1980), 463.
9. Graham Fuller, *The Future of Political Islam* (New York: Palgrave, 2003), 12.
10. Shadi Hamid, *Islamic Exceptionalism: How the Struggle over Islam is Reshaping the World* (New York: St. Martin's Press, 2016).
11. Report presented by Marc-Andre Franche, UNDP Country Director for Pakistan on August 29, 2016.
12. Prime Minister Narendra Modi's speech in Dhaka, Bangladesh on June 7, 2015.
13. Jamaat e Islami Bangladesh was coalition partner in Bangladesh Nationalist Party-led regimes twice, in 1991-1996 and in 2001-2006.
14. See "Bangladesh: Halt Imminent War Crimes Executions," Human Rights Watch, September 1, 2016, https://www.hrw.org/news/2016/09/01/bangladesh-halt-imminent-war-crimes-executions.
15. Qazi Hussain Ahmad was the target of a suicide attack in Mehmand Agency region in tribal areas of Pakistan on November 19, 2012.
16. See the Pakistan Institute of Legislative Development and Transparency's (PILDAT) Annual Report on Internal Democracy of major Pakistani political parties for the years 2015 and 2016.
17. Fuller, *The Future of Political Islam*, xv.

Chapter 17
1. General Overseer is highest-ranking position in the Jordanian Muslim Brotherhood as well as other Brotherhood affiliates outside Egypt.
2. Zaki Bani Irsheid was convicted and sentenced in February 2015 under a provision in Jordan's anti-terrorism law criminalizing "disturbing [Jordan's] relations with a foreign state."

Chapter 18
1. Jacob Olidort, "Fall of the Brotherhood, Rise of the Salafis," *Omphalos: Middle East Conflict in Perspective*, Lawfare Institute, October 11, 2015, https://www.lawfareblog.com/fall-brotherhood-rise-salafis.
2. Jacob Olidort, "The Truth About Sectarianism: Behind the Various Strands of Shiite-Sunni Discord," *Foreign Affairs*, January 25, 2016,

https://www.foreignaffairs.com/articles/middle-east/2016-01-25/truth-about-sectarianism.

3. Mayer N. Zald and Roberta Ash, "Social Movement Organizations: Growth, Decay and Change," *Social Forces* 44, no. 3 (1966): 327–341.

4. John D. McCarthy and Mayer N. Zald, "Resource Mobilization and Social Movements: A Partial Theory," *American Journal of Sociology* 82, no. 6 (1977): 1212–1241.

Chapter 19

1. Mike Giglio, Munzer al-Awad and Mitch Prothero, "Leaked ISIS Documents Tell the Stories of Hundreds of Foreign Jihadis," *Buzzfeed*, March 19, 2016, https://www.buzzfeed.com/mikegiglio/leaked-isis-documents-tell-the-stories-of-hundreds-of-foreig?utm_term=.cgQ2VEkxO#.rlJlXozn8.

2. Yassin Musharbash, "An Analysis of 3000 Islamic State Entry Documents," *Abu Susu's Blog*, April 7, 2016, https://abususu.blogspot.com/2016/04/an-analysis-of-3000-islamic-state-entry.html.

3. Joseph Schacht, *The Origins of Muhammedan Jurisprudence* (Oxford: Clarendon Press, 1967), 1.

4. On the sharia system and its demise, see Wael Hallaq, *Shari'a: Theory, Practice, Transformations* (New York: Cambridge University Press, 2009), 360–366, 500.

5. Raffaello Pantucci, "British Government Debates Engagement with Radical Islam in New Counterterrorism Strategy," *The Jamestown Foundation*, April 24, 2009, http://www.jamestown.org/single/?no_cache=1&tx_ttnews%5Btt_news%5D=34898#.VwaoIbTm9RE.

6. Antony Drugeon, "Comment le Maroc vend «l'islam du milieu» à l'international [How Morocco sells "moderate Islam" internationally]," *Telquel*, February 21, 2015, http://telquel.ma/2015/02/21/comment-maroc-vend-lislam-du-milieu-linternational_1435442.

Chapter 20

1. By discursive depth, I mean that a set of ideas is deeply explored in such a way that the implications of and tensions among the various key commitments of a given family of ideas has been explored sufficiently. Marxism, for instance, is a dense modern tradition; Islamic *kalam* theology and law are dense premodern traditions spread across centuries and continents; so far, mainstream Islamism is not.

2. David Snow, E. Burke Rochford Jr., Steven K. Worden, and Robert D. Benford, "Frame Alignment Processes, Micromobilization, and Movement Participation," *American Sociological Review* (1986): 464–481; Colin J. Beck, *Radicals, Revolutionaries, and Terrorists* (Cambridge, UK: Polity Press, 2015), 163.

3. Ovamir Anjum, "Islam as a Discursive Tradition: Talal Asad and His Interlocutors," *Comparative Studies of South Asia, Africa, and the Middle East* 27, no. 3 (2007): 656–672.

4. Robert D. Benford and David Snow, "Framing Processes and Social Movements: An Overview and Assessment," *Annual Review of Sociology* 26 (2000): 611–639, 613.

5. A discussion of the various approaches to ideology among social movement scholars can be found in Beck, "Is Radicalism About Ideas and Ideology?" in *Radicals, Revolutionaries, and Terrorists*, chap. 5.

6. Stacy Philbrick Yadav, "Yemen's Muslim Brotherhood and the Perils of Powersharing" (Working paper, The Brookings Institution, August 2015), http://www.brookings.edu/~/media/Research/Files/Reports/2015/07/rethinking-political-islam/Yemen_Yadav-FINALE.pdf?la=en.

7. Hoffner differentiates between the initial phase of a movement that often needs a "man of words," succeeded later by "fanatic" believers who convert the ideas into practice. See Eric Hoffner, *The True Believer: Thoughts on the Nature of Mass Movements* (New York: Harper and Row, 1951). A more recent and nuanced scheme suggests that "effective leadership will have the characteristics of each of these roles—the ability to creatively start a radical movement, the Machiavellian ruthlessness to see it through, and the pragmatism to know when to choose different strategies." See Beck, *Radicals, Revolutionaries, and Terrorists*, 67. Weber describes this process in terms of charisma and its routinization. See Max Weber, "The Nature of Charismatic Authority and Its Routinization," in *Theory of Social and Economic Organization*, trans. A. M. Henderson and Talcott Parsons (New York: Oxford University Press, 1947).

8. Avi Spiegel, "Succeeding by Surviving: Examining the Durability of Political Islam in Morocco" (Working paper, The Brookings Institution, August 2015), http://www.brookings.edu/research/reports2/2015/08/~/media/A02C6E64675D44E3BAF9BA97E3D19DF7.ashx.

9. 'Abdesslam Yassine, *al-Shūra wa'l-Dimuqraṭiyya*, 1995, http://www.yassine.net/ar/document/835.shtml.

10. Ovamir Anjum, "Salafism and Democracy: Doctrine and Context," *Muslim World* 106, no. 3 (2016): 448–473.

11. Raymond W. Baker, *Islam Without Fear: Egypt and the New Islamists* (Cambridge, MA: Harvard University Press, 2003).

12. Charles Tripp, *Islam and the Moral Economy: The Challenge of Capitalism* (New York: Cambridge University Press, 2006).

13. Tariq Ramadan, *Radical Reform: Islamic Ethics and Liberation* (New York: Oxford University Press, 2008).

14. Wael Hallaq, *The Impossible State* (New York: Columbia University Press, 2013); Mahmoud A. El-Gamal, "Contemporary Islamic Law and Finance: The Trade-Off Between Brand Name Distinctiveness and Convergence," *Berkeley Journal of Middle Eastern and Islamic Law* 1, no. 1 (Spring 2008): 193–201.

15. See Wael Hallaq, *Shari'a: Theory, Practice, Transformations* (New York: Cambridge University Press, 2009), 511, for his account of the Syrian accretist jurist Said Ramadan al-Buti's critique of the modern *maqasid* discourse.

16. Olivier Roy, *Holy Ignorance: When Religion and Culture Part Ways* (New York: Oxford University Press, 2006).

INDEX